German Quickly

American University Studies

Series VI
Foreign Language Instruction

Vol. 5

PETER LANG
New York • Washington, D.C./Baltimo

April Wilson

German Quickly

A Grammar for
Reading German

Revised Edition

PETER LANG
New York • Washington, D.C./Baltimore
Bern • Frankfurt am Main • Berlin • Vienna • Paris

Library of Congress Cataloging-in-Publication Data

Wilson, April.
German quickly: a grammar for reading German/ April Wilson—Rev. ed.
p. cm. — (American University Studies. Series VI,
Foreign language instruction; vol. 5)
Includes index.
1. German language—Grammar—1950–. 2. German language—Textbooks for
foreign speakers—English. I. Title. II. Series.
PF3112.W55   438.2'421—dc20   93-30325
ISBN 0-8204-2324-6 (pbk)
ISSN 0739-6406

Die Deutsche Bibliothek–CIP–Einheitsaufnahme

Wilson, April.
German quickly: a grammar for reading German/ April Wilson—Rev. ed..
- New York; Washington, D.C./ Baltimore; Bern; Frankfurt am Main;
Berlin; Vienna; Paris: Lang.
(American University Studies: Ser. 6, Foreign language instruction; Vol. 5)
ISBN 0-8204-2324-6 (pbk)
NE: American University Studies/06

The paper in this book meets the guidelines for permanence and durability
of the Committee on Production Guidelines for Book Longevity
of the Council of Library Resources.

© 1993, 1996, 2002, 2003 Peter Lang Publishing, Inc., New York

Printed in the United States of America

Foreword

German Quickly: A Grammar for Reading German evolved from the German reading course I have taught to more than 1,000 University of Chicago graduate students over the past several years. It has the following features which make it a valuable text for students who need to learn German quickly:

(1) Explanations have been revised several times in response to student questions and comments, so that the book provides important grammatical information simply not provided by other German textbooks.

(2) It carefully describes key grammatical points in detail without overwhelming students with superfluous information. Consequently, students have been able to translate passages from authors as complex as Freud, Kafka, and Mann after only 100 hours of study.

(3) Proverbs are used as translation exercises, even in the early pages of the text. These help sustain students' enthusiasm for German when their ability to read is at an elementary level.

(4) Rather than containing selections which are supposed to interest students, the text takes a more pragmatic approach and includes materials that students actually enjoy. It avoids the traditional information about Germany found in most texts and instead includes material which appeals to students of diverse backgrounds.

(5) In the appendix, there is a summary of German grammar which is a handy reference for students once they have completed the course. In the appendix, there is also a Humanities Vocabulary which is especially valuable for students beginning to read scholarly articles in specialized fields. Moreover, there is also a partial answer key (pp. 267-284) which should prove helpful to students studying German independently.

The Structure of *German Quickly*, and How to Use it

This text consists primarily of grammar explanations with sample exercises and an accompanying vocabulary. There is also a vocabulary aid consisting mostly of sentences which provide important vocabulary words of each section and which help students review the grammar of that chapter.

Most of the exercise sentences consist either of proverbs or of a running saga of two major characters—Fräulein Meier and a mailman. Some of the proverbs included are unfamiliar to most Germans and are not representative of German culture. However, I have included them because they are intriguing. They contain a wide variety of ideas about life and human nature—some insightful, some bizarre, and some even whimsical—which tend to add to the interest of learning a foreign language. Fräulein Meier and the mailman are intended for fun.

In addition to reading passages from Bichsel, Kleist, Buber, and Nietzsche, I have included some Biblical passages because they are familiar and repetitive, and because people enjoy reading something "real" even when their grasp of German is not quite solid.

German Quickly is best suited for a semester reading course; it can be covered in a quarter, however. In a five week (highly) intensive course, I have been able to go through it in four weeks. In a fifteen week course, I generally cover it in from ten to eleven weeks. In any class, this text should be supplemented with outside readings. I have deliberately kept the number of reading passages to a minimum so that, with additional readings, *German Quickly* could be adapted to any German reading course in the general humanities, philosophy, theology, art history, history, sociology, or the like. A teacher also could have the freedom to update reading materials whenever he or she wished. Some useful German readers might be: Wilson: *Es geht weiter*; Goedsche and Spann: *Deutsche Denker und Forscher*; Vail and Sparks: *Der Weg zum Lesen*; Gewehr and Von Schmitt: *Reading German in the Humanities*; Muehsam: *German Readings Two: A Brief Survey of Art from the Middle Ages to the Twentieth Century*.

I have discussed the advantages and disadvantages of various German dictionaries on page 254-260, and I would strongly recommend reading this section before purchasing a dictionary.

I hope that *German Quickly* will live up to its title, and that people will enjoy this introduction to German as well as any subsequent readings. After all, *Frisch begonnen ist halb gewonnen!*—A fresh start is half the victory!

Acknowledgements

Thanks are due to the publishers for permission to reproduce the following copyright texts:

"November" from *Eigentlich möchte Frau Blum den Milchmann kennenlernen* by Peter Bichsel, copyright 1964. Walter-Verlag, Olten. Reprinted by permission of the publisher.

Selections from *Die Erzählungen der Chassidim* by Martin Buber, copyright 1949. Manesse Verlag, Zürich. Reprinted by permission of the publisher.

Selections from *Die Verwandlung*, copyright renewed 1976 and *Parables and Paradoxes*, copyright renewed 1975. By Franz Kafka. Schocken Books of New York. Reprinted by permission of the publisher.

Selections from *Die Erzählungen* by Thomas Mann, copyright 1966. S. Fischer Verlag, Frankfurt am Main. Reprinted by permission of the publisher.

Selections from *Deutsche Literaturgeschichte* by Fritz Martini, copyright 1965. Alfred Kröner Verlag, Stuttgart. Reprinted by permission of the publisher.

"Der Schwan" (translated by Ludwig Zimmerer) and "Der Elefant" from *Der Elefant* by Slawomir Mrozek, copyright 1967. Gustav Kiepenheuer, Berlin. Reprinted by permission of the publisher.

Selections from *Zettel* by Ludwig Wittgenstein, copyright 1967. Basil Blackwell, Oxford. Reprinted by permission of G. E. M. Anscombe.

Table of Contents

APPENDIX

English Grammar Necessary for Learning German

Nouns

A noun is a word which names a person, place, thing, or abstraction. Nouns have cases. German has four cases: nominative (English subjective), accusative (English objective), genitive (usually, but not always, English possessive), and dative (usually, but not always, English indirect object).

Nominative is the subject; all sentences have subjects:

The man is friendly.
The bear dances.

A predicate nominative is a noun after the verbs "to be," "to become," "to remain," and similar verbs. The predicate nominative indicates that the subject and the object are one and the same:

The poet is *a great man.*
The woman becomes *a professor.*

A direct object answers the question *what* or *whom* after the verb:

The man kills *the wolf.*
The woman writes *a poem.*

A possessive noun is in an inextricable relationship with another noun:

The *man's* friend is nice.
He loves the *woman's* sister.

An indirect object is an object for which the prepositions "to" or "for" are understood:

The man writes *his fiancée* a love letter.
The woman sends *her mother* a Mother's Day card.

Note: Even when a sentence begins with prepositional phrases, the verb will appear directly after the subject and before the object:
During the dark and stormy night, in the middle of the woods, the storyteller *frightened* the campers.

Pronouns

Pronouns take the place of nouns. They also have cases.
Nominative (subjective): *He* is rich.
Accusative (objective): The wolf devours *him*.
Dative (indirect object): The woman gives *him* a big smile.

Pronouns in front of nouns are **possessive adjectives:**
His friends are nice.
Her cat seems playful.
Our goals are difficult to attain.

Pronouns are:

Personal (I, you, he, she, it, we, you, they): *I* am happy.
Interrogative (who, whom, which, what, or whose): *Who* loves him?
Indefinite (such as: one, someone, many, everyone, some, nobody, everything, nothing, something): *Everyone* likes her; *Something* is missing.
Demonstrative (this, that, these, those): *This* is wonderful.
Relative (who, whom, whose, what, which, that): Everyone *who* knows her likes her; Everyone *whom* she knows is brilliant.
Reflexive: He looked at *himself* in the mirror. Note: German uses reflexive pronouns much more than English does, and often verbs will have reflexive definitions, which then mean that the *self* pronoun should *not* be translated (cf. chapter 26).

Adjectives

Adjectives describe nouns or pronouns: A *nice* man; a *certain* someone
Adjectives usually appear *before* the noun they modify: An *interesting* concept; a *useless* animal; an *engaging* woman

Articles and numbers are also kinds of adjectives:
A kind woman; *the* interesting book; *three* blind mice; *ten* partridges

Adjectives after the verbs "to be," "to become," "to remain," and verbs involving the senses are **predicate adjectives:**

She is *funny*.
He became *rich*.
They remained *angry* for a long time.
She seems *sad*.
He looks *happy*.

Adjectives can also appear in **comparative** and **superlative** forms: A *better* idea; a *nicer* cat; a *more beautiful* child (comparative)
The *best* idea; the *nicest* cat; the *most beautiful* child (superlative)

Two verb forms (**present participles** — sing*ing*, climb*ing* — and **past participles** — stolen, admired) can be used as adjectives *if* they appear directly before a noun (usually after an article):

They gazed at the *dancing* bear.
The *frightened* elephant hid behind a tree.

Adverbs

Adverbs modify verbs, adjectives, or other adverbs:
He runs *quickly*; The *beautifully* singing woman is homely; He speaks German *quite fluently*.

Typical adverbs are; mostly, usually, perhaps, moreover, especially, thus, therefore, still, yet, certainly, consequently, very, however, quite, really, also, now, only, soon, then, just, even, rather, indeed, probably, immediately, yesterday, too, here, there, tomorrow, often, rarely, nearly, always, never, not

A noun and an adjective, or a prepositional phrase can also have an adverbial function in a sentence: to be sure; last week; some day; for years; to the right; first of all

Like adjectives, adverbs can also have comparative and superlative forms:
She runs *more quickly* than he does.
He is the *least likely* to succeed.

Prepositions

Prepositions indicate the relation of a noun or pronoun to another word in the sentence. A prepositional phrase consists of the preposition, the noun that follows it, and any modifiers of the noun:

She walks *through* the park.
She walks *around* the beautiful park *with* the red geraniums.
She walks *across* the park which is *in* the center *of* the city.

Compound prepositions, those consisting of more than one word, also exist:
because of; instead of; with regard to
She walks *outside of* the park.

Verbs

A verb is a word or group of words stating something about the subject of the
sentence. This statement can describe an action, or an identity, or a state of
being:

The mouse *roared* (action).
The elephant *is* enormous (state of being).

Verbs can be either *transitive* or *intransitive*. They are transitive when they are
followed by a direct object:

He loves the woman.
The obese man ate the entire pizza.

They are intransitive when they cannot be followed by a direct object:

He *sleeps* restlessly.
The child *dives* into the swimming pool.
The wicked witch *died*.

Verbs are *conjugated*, their conjugation depending on the subject:

The wolf *kills* the sheep.
The bears *dance* in a circle.
I *am* confused.

Verbs have the following **tenses**: present, past, present perfect, past perfect,
and future.

He *stares* at the spectacle. (present)
He *stared* at the spectacle. (past, also called preterite)
He *has stared* at the spectacle. (present perfect)
He *had stared* at the spectacle. (past perfect)
He *will stare* at the spectacle. (future)

When the three main forms of the verb are given, they are listed as the **infinitive**, the **past**, and the **perfect** form. Verbs in English, as well as in German, can be either "**strong**" or "**weak**."

They are weak when -ed is added to their past and perfect forms:

look, look*ed*; look*ed*; ask, ask*ed*, ask*ed*; hope, hop*ed*, hop*ed*

They are strong when their past and perfect forms do not end in -ed; often a vowel change is involved. Many strong participles will end in -n, -en, -d, or -t:

write, wrote, written; bring, brought, brought; cut, cut, cut; lose, lost, lost; find, found, found; fall, fell, fallen; do, did, done; sing, sang, sung

Verbs will sometimes require *auxiliary* (i.e. *helping*) verbs. Here are examples:

Present perfect: They *have* gone to the zoo.
Past perfect: They *had* gone to the zoo.
Future: They *will* go to the zoo.
Future perfect: They *will have* gone to the zoo.

Modals, words which change the *aspect* of the verb, are also auxiliaries:
He *must* learn German
He *wants to* learn German
He *should* learn German
He *can* learn German

The **passive** is formed by using the verb "to be" as an auxiliary along with the main verb in its participial form:

The man *is eaten* by the wolf. (Cf. active: The wolf *eats* the man.)
The apple *was stolen* by a child.
The song *has been sung* by millions of people.
The window *had been opened* by a visitor.
The film *will be seen* by millions.
The dancing bear *must be fed* often.

The **subjunctive** is used with conditions contrary to the fact, and with conjectures or desires. Here are some examples:

If he *were* wise, he *would save* his money.
If he *had been* wise, he *would have saved* his money.

If he *had saved* his money, he *would have been* rich.
The dancing bear looks as if it *were* hungry.
Long *live* the King!
God *protect* me from my friends!

Conjunctions

Conjunctions can be either **co-ordinating** or **subordinating**.

Co-ordinating conjunctions join words, phrases, and clauses of equal importance in the same sentence. Common co-ordinating conjunctions are: and, or, either...or, neither...nor, but, however:

She studies philosophy, *and* she enjoys it.
She is beautiful, *but* she doesn't know it.
Neither the student *nor* the teacher wants to read the boring book.

Subordinating conjunctions change clauses into *dependent* clauses, which means they are unable to exist without the help of independent clauses. They *still* need to have a subject and a verb, however. They generally begin the clause:

Because he was happy, he sang joyously.
If he has any sense, he will marry her.
When she was in Switzerland, she saw thousands of cows.
He was not happy *until* he saw her again.
Although she had many friends she was still sometimes lonely.
He suffered a great deal *when* he was young.
After she had learned German she felt as if she could do anything.

Relative pronouns are forms of subordinating conjunctions. When the relative pronoun is the subject of the clause, the verb follows it immediately:

I know the man *who* loves her.

When the relative pronoun is the object of the clause, the verb follows the subject:

The man *whom* she loves is quite intense.

Pronunciation Guide

When you are pronouncing these words, try to guess their definitions as well. All German nouns are capitalized (examples are: *Garten, Lampe*, and *Gras*) and all German infinitives end in *-n* or *-en* (examples are: *bringen, finden*, and *kommen*).

Vowels

Vowels are either long or short.
They are long . . .
when they are doubled: *Paar, Haar, Schnee*;
when they are followed by h: *sehen, Jahr, Ohrring*;
or when they are followed by a single consonant: *gut, rot*
Vowels are short . . .
when they are followed by a double consonant: *Bett, Mann, hoffen*;
or when followed by two or more consonants: *sitzen, ernst*

a   long (as the a in father): *Vater, haben, sagen*
a   short (as the o in hot): *Wasser, Hand, alt*
e   long (as in may): *See, geben*
e   short (as in let): *Ende, Henne*
i   long (as in greet): *Tiger, Universität*
i   short (as in sit): *ist, dick, Mitte, Mittag, Mittwoch*
ie   is like the long i: *Bier, hier, fliegen, liegen*
o   long (as open): *Sohn, Brot, Segelboot*
o   short (as in song): *Sonne, Sommer*
u   long (as in dune): *Blume, Pudel (a dog!), Handschuh*
u   short (as in bush): *Mutter, und, unter*

Umlauted vowels (modified vowels)

ä   long (as in hair): *Mädchen, Väter, Waschbär (literally: washing-bear)*
ä   short (is the same as the short e): *Männer, Länder, Rotkäppchen*
ö   long (there is no equivalent in English. Pronounce the German long e with rounded lips): *Söhne, schön (beautiful)*
ö   short (there is no equivalent in English. Pronounce the German short e with rounded lips): *öffnen, östlich*
ü   long (there is no equivalent in English. Pronounce the German long i with rounded lips): *kühl, grün, Bücherwurm*

ü   short (there is no equivalent in English. Pronounce the German short i with
     rounded lips): *Hütte, küssen*

ä, ö, and ü are occasionally written **ae, oe**, and **ue**. Examples are: *spaet* rather
than *spät*; *Oel* rather than *Öl*; and *Bueffel* rather than *Büffel* (*an animal*).

The diphthongs

ei, ai, ey, and **ay** (are like the i in wine): *Wein, Mai*

au (like the ou in mouse): *Maus, Haus, Augenblick*

äu and **eu** (are like the oy in joy): *Feuer, neu, Fräulein, Nachteule*

Consonants

The following consonants and combinations of consonants are pronounced as
they are in English: **f, h, k, m, n, p, t, ck, nk, ph**

b   (is like the English b when it begins a word): *beißen, Baumwolle*
     (*literally: tree-wool*);
     but when ending a word, it is like the English p: *halb, Grab*

c   is seldom seen at the beginning of a German word; in German, it is always
     either a proper name or a "foreign" (Latin, French) word.

c   before ä, e, i is like the ts in bats: *Cäsar, Cicero*

c   before a, o, u is like the English k: *Café*

ch   There are four different ch sounds . . .

ch   is pronounced in the front part of the mouth, and it approximates the h in
     hew. It follows e, i, umlauts, consonants, and in a few words it precedes e
     or i: *ich, mich, Licht, China*

ch   is pronounced in the back part of the mouth as in the Scotch Loch, and it
     follows a, o, u, and au: *Nacht, Macht*

ch   is pronounced like the English k when beginning words of Greek origin or
     preceding the vowels a and u or consonants: *Christus, Charakter*

ch   is pronounced like the sh in chef when beginning words of French origin:
     Chauvinist

chs is pronounced like the x in six: *sechs, Lachs* (*goes well with bagels!*)

d   when beginning a word is like the English d: *Donnerstag, Dingsbums*
     (*thing-a-ma-jig*)
     when ending a word, it is like the English t: *Hund, Gesundheit*

g   when beginning a word is like the English g in good: *Goldfisch*; or when it
     begins a syllable, it also takes a hard g: *Regen*
     but when it ends a word or syllable, it is like the English k: *Tag, weg*
     (*away*)

-ig as an ending is pronounced like the German ich: *König, hungrig, durstig*
     but when an ending is added, g becomes a hard g again: *Königin,*
     hungriger, durstiger

h   when beginning a word or syllable is like the English h: *hören, helfen,*
     harmlos, aha

j   is like the English y in young: *jung, ja, Jahrhundert*

l   is like the English l in land: *laut, Lippe*

ng is pronounced like the English ng in singer (and **never** as in finger): *England, länger, Fingerhut* (*literally: finger-hat*)

pf both letters are pronounced: *Apfel, Pfund, pfui*

qu is pronounced like the English kv: *Quecksilber, Qualität*

r   has no equivalent in English. It is somewhat like the French r: *studieren, reparieren, klar*

s   when it begins a word or syllable is like the English z in zest: *senden, Suppe, Sanduhr* (*literally: sand-clock*);

otherwise, it is like the English s in sun: *Fledermaus, Gast*

ß and **ss** are pronounced like the English ss in mass. ss is often used between two short vowels: *Klasse, besser*; ß often is used at the end of a word or syllable: *Maß, Erdnuß, barfuß*

Note: the letter **ß** **never** begins a word.

sp and **st** are both pronounced like the English sh in she: *spanisch, Spinne* (*an insect*), *Staat, Stinktier* (*an animal*)

th is like the English t: *Luther, Goethe, Theologie*

v   is pronounced like the English f in words of German origin: *Volk, Vorwort, vier, Vergißmeinnicht* (*a flower*);

but in words of "foreign" origin, v is pronounced like the English v: *November*

w is like the English v: *Wald, Wörterbuch, Wassermelone*

x   is like the English ks: *Axt, Vexierbild* (*literally: vexing-picture*)

z   is pronounced like the English ts in bats: *Zoo, Zigarre, Zickzack*

Chapter One

A General Introduction: Cognates, Genders, Compounds, and Plurals

1.1. Cognates

A cognate is a word which is derived from the same original form; *kühl* and cool are cognates, as are **Maus** and mouse; **Vater** and father; and *frei* and free. Here are some consonant relationships which exist between German and English and which will help you figure out German-English cognates more easily.

German		*English*
f, ff (medial or final)	usually corresponds to	*p*
Affe		*ape*
hoffen		*to hope*
scharf		*sharp*
pf (initial, medial, or final)	usually corresponds to	*p, pp*
Pfeife		*pipe*
Pflaster		*plaster*
Apfel		*apple*
b (medial or final)	usually corresponds to	*v* or *f*
geben		*to give*
Grab		*grave*
halb		*half*
d	usually corresponds to	*th*
Pfad		*path*
Feder		*feather*
Dorn		*thorn*
ch	usually corresponds to	*k*
Buch		*book*

German		**English**
Koch		*cook*
suchen		*to seek*
cht	usually corresponds to	*ght*
Macht		*might*
Sicht		*sight*
Recht		*right*
g	usually corresponds to	*y* or *i*
sagen		*to say*
legen		*to lay*
Nagel		*nail*
Segel		*sail*
k	usually corresponds to	*ch* or *c*
Kalb		*calf*
Kapelle		*chapel*
s, ss, ß (medial or final)	usually corresponds to	*t*
hassen		*to hate*
grüßen		*to greet*
Fuß		*foot*
tz, z	usually corresponds to	*t*
Zunge		*tongue*
Pflanze		*plant*
Katze		*cat*
t	usually corresponds to	*d*
trinken		*to drink*
Tochter		*daughter*
Karte		*card*
kalt		*cold*

1.2. Figure out the following

(a) Wörter: Pfefferminze, Kirchenmaus, Nachtigall (*a bird*), tanzen
(b) Sprichwörter: Blut ist dicker als Wasser.
Die Ratten verlassen das sinkende Schiff.
Reiche (*rich*) Leute (*people*) haben fette Katzen.

(c)   Buchtitel: Dante: *Die göttliche Komödie*
                   Shakespeare: *Hamlet, Prinz von Dänemark; Ende gut,
                                  alles gut; König Lear*
                   Beckett: *Warten auf Godot*
                   Albee: *Wer hat Angst vor Virginia Woolf?*
                   Simon: *Barfuß im Park*

1.3. Genders

German nouns can be one of three genders: masculine, neuter, or feminine. If
an article precedes a noun, it will indicate the gender of the noun. Examples
are:

masculine	**feminine**	**neuter**
der Mann (*the man*)	*die* Frau (*the woman*)	*das* Kind (*the child*)
der Wind (*the wind*)	*die* Lampe (*the lamp*)	*das* Tier (*the animal*)
der Apfel (*the apple*)	*die* Sonne (*the sun*)	*das* Buch (*the book*)
der Löffel (*the spoon*)	*die* Gabel (*the fork*)	*das* Messer (*the knife*)

Although you do not need to memorize the genders of nouns in order to read
German, it will later be important for you to identify these genders in context.
Therefore, you may eventually wish to use the following basic rules to
determine the gender of a noun as a reference section:

Masculine

(a)   nouns which denote male beings: der Vater (*father*), der Onkel (*uncle*),
      der Stier (*steer*), der König (*king*)

(b)   nouns which end in -*er* which have been formed from verbs:
      der Fahrer (*the driver*)   cf. fahren (*to drive*)
      der Erfinder (*the inventor*)   cf. erfinden (*to invent*)

Feminine

(a)   nouns which denote female beings: die Mutter (*mother*), die Tante (*aunt*),
      die Henne (*hen*)

(b)   nouns ending in -*ei*, -*ie*, -*heit*, -*keit*, -*ik*, -*schaft*, -*tät*, -*tion*, -*ung*:
      die Geologie, die Gesundheit (*health*), die Freundlichkeit (*friendliness*),
      die Musik, die Freundschaft (*friendship*), die Universität, die Rotation, die
      Übung (*practice*)

(c)   nouns which end in **-in** (a suffix added to nouns which are usually masculine):

die Nachbarin (*the neighbor lady*)   cf. der Nachbar (*the neighbor*)
die Freundin (*the girl friend*)   cf. der Freund (*the friend*)
die Königin (*the queen*)   cf. der König (*the king*)

(d)   moreover, many (but not all) nouns which end in *-e* are also feminine:
die Erde (*earth*), die Rose (*rose*), die Hölle (*hell*)

Neuter

(a)   nouns which end in **-chen** or **-lein** (which are diminutives):

das Fräulein (*the little woman*)   cf. die Frau (*the woman*)
das Häuschen (*the little house*)   cf. das Haus (*the house*)
das Brüderlein (*the little brother*)   cf. der Bruder (*the brother*)

(b)   nouns which have been formed directly from verbs

das Singen (*the singing*)   cf. singen (*to sing*)
das Leben (*the life*)   cf. leben (*to live*)
das Streben (*the striving*)   cf. streben (*to strive*)

(c)   nouns which end in **-ium, -tum, -ment**, and **-sel**:
das Studium (*study*), das Christentum (*Christianity*), das Abonnement (*subscription*), das Rätsel (*riddle*)

1.4. Compounds

New words in German sometimes can be formed by combining simpler words. Some of these words can be particularly graphic. Here are examples:

Abend (*evening*) + Land (*country*) – Abendland (*occident*)
Morgen (*morning*) + Land (*country*) – Morgenland (*orient*)
Eier (*eggs*) + Auflauf (*riot, running amuck*) – Eierauflauf (*soufflé*)
sauer (*sour*) + Stoff (*material*) – Sauerstoff (*oxygen*)

The gender of the noun is determined by its final component. Thus, even in a word as long as Unfallversicherungsgesellschaft (*accident-insurance-society*), the article will be *die* because the suffix *-schaft* is feminine.

1.5. Plurals

Because it is very important for you to be able to recognize plural forms, I have discussed them in more detail in Chapter Sixteen (16.1 - 16.3). However, here is a general introduction to them. Plurals of German nouns are indicated by the use of the definite article *die* (*the*) plus one of the following endings:

(a) the ending *-e* (sometimes with, sometimes without an umlaut):

singular:	der Gast (*guest*);	das Jahr (*year*)	
plural:	die Gäste (*guests*);	die Jahre (*years*)	

singular:	der Sohn (*son*);	der Freund (*friend*)	
plural:	die Söhne (*sons*);	die Freunde (*friends*)	

(b) the ending *-er* (with an umlaut, providing the vowel is a, o, u):

singular:	das Land (*country*);	das Licht (*light*)	
plural:	die Länder (*countries*);	die Lichter (*lights*)	

singular:	das Haus (*house*);	das Kind (*child*)	
plural:	die Häuser (*houses*);	die Kinder (*children*)	

(c) the ending *-(e)n* (never with an umlaut):

singular:	der Student (*student*);	die Frau (*woman*)	
plural:	die Studenten (*students*);	die Frauen (*women*)	

singular:	die Nummer (*number*);	die Lampe (*lamp*)	
plural:	die Nummern (*numbers*);	die Lampen (*lamps*)	

(d) a few nouns of "foreign" origin form their plurals by adding an -s ending:

singular:	das Auto (*the car*);	der Chef (*boss*)	
plural:	die Autos (*cars*);	die Chefs (*bosses*)	

(e) there are also some nouns which have *no* plural ending. Some of them have an umlaut added to the medial vowel:

singular:	der Vater (*father*);	der Apfel (*apple*)	
plural:	die Väter (*fathers*);	die Äpfel (*apples*)	

However, many of these nouns have neither an ending nor an umlaut:

singular:	*der* Titel (*title*);	*der* Leser (*reader*);	*das* Mädchen (*girl*)
plural:	*die* Titel (*titles*);	*die* Leser (*readers*);	*die* Mädchen (*girls*)

The plural of these nouns is shown *only* by the definite article *die*; therefore, watch the article carefully. Nouns ending in *-chen* are always neuter, and nouns that end in either *-er* or *-en* are generally either neuter or masculine, so watch for plurals whenever nouns with these endings have *die* as their definite article. Moreover, be careful whenever a noun ends in *-l*, *-e*, *-r* or

-n, for it could be either singular or plural. A noun ending with any other letter (except, occasionally, *-s*) will *always* be singular.

1.6. Indicate which word in the following pairs is plural. Since all the words are cognates, guess their definitions as well:

Die Katze, die Katzen; die Damen, die Dame; die Tochter, die Töchter; die Mädchen, das Mädchen; der Tiger, die Tiger; das Wörterbuch, die Wörterbücher; die Großväter, der Großvater; die Nadeln, die Nadel; der Schreiber, die Schreiber; die Woche, die Wochen.

1.7. Now indicate which of the following words is plural. How do you know? (Hint: anything that does not end in *-l, -e, -r, -n*, or, occasionally *-s*, can *not* be plural.)

Der Singer; die Söhne; die Universität; der Junge; die Männer; der Apfel; das Schreiben; die Fledermaus; der Affe; die Bücher; die Nacht; die Musik; der Muskel; die Studenten; das Auge; die Freundschaft; die Übung; die Hühner, die Freundlichkeit.

Chapter Two

The Present Tense of Verbs and the Personal Pronouns

2.1. All verbs in their infinitival form end in *-en*, or sometimes in *-n*.

Examples are: *singen* (*to sing*), *finden* (*to find*), *tanzen* (*to dance*), *bringen* (*to bring*); and *wandern* (*to wander*), *tun* (*to do*), and *handeln* (*to act*).

These verbs are conjugated in the following way:

	singen	*bringen*	*wandern*
ich (*I*)	singe	bringe	wandere
du (*you*)*	singst	bringst	wanderst
er (*he*), es (*it*), sie (*she*)	singt	bringt	wandert
wir (*we*)	singen	bringen	wandern
ihr (*you*)*	singt	bringt	wandert
sie (*they*)	singen	bringen	wandern
Sie (*you*)	singen	bringen	wandern

*du (one person) and *ihr* (two or more people) are informal forms of *you*, and they are to be used only with close friends, family, children, animals, and God. Because these forms seldom appear in scholarly writings, you need not be too concerned about memorizing them.

2.2. The pronoun *Sie* (which can refer either to one person or to several people) **is formal,** and it is the only German pronoun to be capitalized regularly.

The pronoun *ich (I)* is never capitalized.

Note that all plural pronouns – *wir* (*we*), *sie* (*they*), and *Sie* (*you*) – with the exception of *ihr* (*informal you*) have the same form as the infinitive (gehen, sagen, hören, etc.).

Note also the similarity among *sie* (*she*), *sie* (*they*) and *Sie* (*you*). Because the same word is used for both she and they, you must pay careful attention to the verb in order to translate *sie* correctly. Compare sie geht – *she* goes with sie gehen – *they* go. When *Sie* is capitalized in mid-sentence, it will **always** be translated as "you."

2.3. When the subject is a singular noun, the third person singular verb form will be used, while when the subject is plural, the plural verb form will be used: Die Katze spielt – The cat plays. Die Katzen spielen – The cats play.

2.4. One German verb form expresses all three forms of the English present – the present (*I sing*), the progressive (*I am singing*), and the emphatic (*I do sing*). Here are examples:

Es *regnet* – It *is raining*.

Obwohl er nichts *sagt, weiß* er doch die Antwort – Although he *is saying* nothing, he *does know* the answer, nevertheless.

Er *grübelt* nicht, wenn er *tanzt* – He *does* not *brood* when he *is dancing*.

Therefore, it is best to translate the verb according to which form sounds smoothest to you in English.

2.5. The three most crucial verbs (which are all irregular) **are:** *sein* (*to be*), *haben* (*to have*) and *werden* (*to become, to grow*). Memorize their forms:

	sein (*to be*)	*haben* (*to have*)	**werden** (*to become*)
ich (*I*)	bin	habe	werde
du (*you, informal*)	bist	hast	wirst
er (*he*), es (*it*), sie (*she*)	ist	hat	wird
wir (*we*)	sind	haben	werden
ihr (*you, informal*)	seid	habt	werdet
sie (*they*)	sind	haben	werden
Sie (*you*)	sind	haben	werden

2.6. Translate the following pronouns and verbs; state the infinitive of each of the verbs:

sie denkt; er findet; ich vergesse; sie haben; Sie sind; wir brauchen; sie wird; sie lassen; ich gebe; sie sind; er hat; ich sage; es heilt; sie tut; Sie werden; sie helfen

2.7. Some verbs will have a vowel change in both second and third person singular. Here is an example, and here are the infinitival and third person singular forms of the most important of these verbs:

sprechen (*to speak*):

	ich spreche	(*I speak*)	wir sprechen	(*we speak*)
	du sprichst	(*you speak*)	ihr sprecht	(*you speak*)
*	er spricht	(*he speaks*)	sie sprechen	(*they speak*)
*	es spricht	(*it speaks*)	Sie sprechen	(*you speak*)
*	sie spricht	(*she speaks*)		

1) **Variation I:**

brechen (*to break*); er bricht;   essen (*to eat*); er ißt;
geben (*to give*); er gibt;   gelten (*to be valid*); er gilt;
helfen (*to help*); er hilft;   nehmen (*to take*); er nimmt;
treten (*to step*); er tritt;   vergessen (*to forget*); er vergißt;

2) **Variation II:**

geschehen (*to occur*); es geschieht;   lesen (*to read*); er liest;
sehen (*to see*); er sieht;   stehlen (*to steal*); er stiehlt;

3) **Variation III:**

fahren (*to travel*); er fährt;   fallen (*to fall*); er fällt;
lassen (*to let*); er läßt;   schlafen (*to sleep*); er schläft;
wachsen (*to grow*); er wächst;   waschen (*to wash*); er wäscht;

4) **Another important irregular verb is** *wissen* (*to know*), **which is conju**gated as follows:

ich weiß (*I know*)   wir wissen (*we know*)
du weißt (*you know*)   ihr wißt (*you know*)
sie weiß (*she knows*)   sie wissen (*they know*)
                                          Sie wissen (*you know*)

When not used as a verb, *weiß* means *white*.

2.8. Translate the following pronouns and verbs:

er nimmt; du liest; sie sieht; es geschieht; er weiß; es bricht; sie vergißt; du ißt; du wächst; sie wäscht

2.9. Translate these sentences. (Ignore the endings on the adjectives; they will be explained in Chapter Four: 4.1-4.3)

1. Hunger ist eine gute Stundenuhr (*clock*).
2. Klagen (*complaining*) füllt keinen Magen (*stomach*).
3. Keine Antwort ist auch eine Antwort.
4. Der Arzt hilft, die Natur heilt.
5. Das Herz lügt nicht.
6. Schöne (*beautiful*) Gesichter haben viele Richter (*judges*).
7. Ein neuer (*new*) Arzt braucht einen neuen Kirchhof (*graveyard*).
8. Ein gutes Wort findet einen guten Ort (*place*).
9. Der Mensch wird alt.
10. Ein gebranntes (*burned*) Kind scheut das Feuer.
11. Kinder und Narren (*fools*) sagen die Wahrheit.
12. Es regnet Bratwürste! (This is an odd description of a down-pour!)
13. Gutes Gespräch kürzet den Weg.
14. Ich bin ein Berliner.

Vocabulary (words marked * should be memorized eventually.)
Note: Plurals of nouns are listed in parentheses.

* **aber** — but, however
* **alt** — old
* die **Antwort (-en)** — answer
  der **Arzt (¨e)** — doctor
* **auch** — also
  der **Berliner (-)** — Berliner; doughnut
  die **Bratwurst (¨e)** — sausage
  brauchen — to need
  brechen (bricht) — to break
* **bringen** — to bring
* **denken** — to think
* **der, das, die** — the
* **du** — you (informal)
* **ein, eine** — a, one
* **er** — he

* **es** — it
* **essen (ißt)** — to eat
  das **Feuer (-)** — fire
* **finden** — to find
  die **Frau (-en)** — woman, wife
  füllen — to fill
* **geben (gibt)** — to give
  geschehen (geschieht) — to happen, occur
  das **Gesicht (-er)** — face
  das **Gespräch (-e)** — conversation
* **gut** – good
* **haben (hat)** — to have
  heilen — to heal
* **helfen (hilft)** — to help
* der **Herr (-en)** — Lord, Mr.

* das **Herz** (-en) — heart
der **Hunger**(-) — hunger
* **ich** — I
* **ihr** — you (informal, pl.)
* **kein** — no
* das **Kind** (-er) — child
der **Kirchhof** (-̈e) — graveyard
das **Klagen** (-) — complaining
kürzen — to shorten
* **lassen** (**läßt**) — to let, leave
* **lesen** (**liest**) — to read
lügen — to lie, fib
der **Magen** (-) — stomach
* der **Mann** (-̈er) — man, husband
der **Mensch** (-en) — person
der **Narr** (-en) — fool
die **Natur** (-en) — nature
nehmen (**nimmt**) — to take
* **neu** — new
* **nicht** — not
* **oft** — often
der **Ort** (-e) — place

regnen — to rain
der **Richter** (-) — judge
* **sagen** — to say, speak
scheuen — to avoid
* **schön** — beautiful
* **sehen** (**sieht**) — to see
* **sein** (**ist**) — to be
* **sie** — she, they
* **Sie** — you (formal)
* **sprechen** (**spricht**) — to speak
die **Stundenuhr** (-en) — clock
* **tun** — to do
* **vergessen** (**vergißt**) — to forget
viel — many, much
wachsen (**wächst**) — to grow
* die **Wahrheit** — truth
waschen — to wash
der **Weg** (-e) — way, path
* **werden** (**wird**) — to become
* **wir** — we
* **wissen** (**weiß**) — to know
* das **Wort** (-e or -̈er) — word

2.10. Vocabulary aid: memorize the words in the following sentences:

1. Fräulein Meier hat eine fette Katze.
2. Sie ist schön.
3. Das Feuer wird warm.
4. Die Kinder sind gut.
5. Ich weiß nicht.
6. Der Arzt hilft nicht.
7. Oft sagen sie die Wahrheit.
8. Er ißt die Bratwurst. (Is *Bratwurst* singular or plural?)

Chapter Three

The Case Endings: Nominative, Accusative, Genitive, Dative

There are four different cases of German articles, nouns, pronouns, and adjectives. These cases are the nominative, accusative, genitive, and dative.

3.1. The nominative is the subject of the sentence, and it can also be the predicate noun (any noun after the verbs "to be," "to become," or "to remain.") Examples are:

Der Dichter schreibt gut — *The writer* writes well.
Das Kind ist *ein guter Spielkamerad* — *The child* is *a good playmate.*
Die Katze schläft viel — *The cat* sleeps a lot.
Die Frauen werden gute *Freundinnen* — *The women* become *good friends.*

The definite article, which indicates both the gender and case of the noun, is *der* for masculine nouns ("der Dichter"), *das* for neuter nouns ("das Kind"), and *die* for both feminine and plural nouns ("die Katze", "die Frauen") whenever the noun is in the nominative case.

3.2. The accusative is like the English direct object; it is the object of most verbs (including the verb *haben* — to have), and of some prepositions (listed in 5.2). Examples are:

Der Briefträger tötet *den Wolf* (*masculine*) — The mailman kills *the wolf.*
Das Kind hält *das Stofftier* (*neuter*) — The child holds *the stuffed animal.*
Die Katze frißt *die Maus* (*feminine*) — The cat eats *the mouse.*
Die Studenten schreiben *die Aufsätze* (*plural*) — The students write *the essays.*

Note that in any sentence, the subject will always have a more "active" role than an object. **In English, the subject will nearly always precede the verb, while the object will usually follow it.**

The accusative article is *den* for masculine nouns, *das* for neuter nouns, and *die* for feminine and plural nouns. Note that the accusative article is the same as the nominative article with the exception of the masculine gender (*). Here is a chart:

	masculine	neuter	feminine	plural
nominative	der*	das	die	die
accusative	den*	das	die	die

The difference in articles is **extremely** important because sometimes in German, the object will appear **before** the verb:

Den Mann tötet *der* Wolf (nominative) — *The wolf* kills *the* man.
Die Frau liebt *der* Mann (nominative) — *The man* loves *the* woman.

If you see **den** in a sentence, it will never be the subject. If you see **der** in a sentence attached to an "obvious" masculine noun (*der Mann, der Professor, der Wolf*), it will always be the subject, which means **you will have to put the noun in front of the verb** when you are translating the sentence into English.

Note also that if the first noun in the German sentence is singular and the verb is plural, or if the first noun in the German sentence is plural and the verb is singular, the object is again appearing *before* the verb, and therfore, the word order will have to be switched in your English translation:

Die Frau **töten** die Männer — The men **kill the woman**.
Die Männer **tötet** die Frau — The woman **kills the men**.

3.3. Translate these sentences, noting the case and, if possible, the gender of each noun:

1. Übung (*practice*) macht den Meister.
2. Der hinkende (*limping*) Bote (*messenger*) bringt die Wahrheit.
3. Anfang ist kein Meisterstück (*masterpiece*). (In other words, you cannot be an expert when starting something new.)
4. Fleiß (*effort*) bricht Eis. (What is the verb infinitive of *bricht*? Be careful.)
5. Die Wahrheit hat ein schönes Angesicht (*face*), aber zerrissene (*torn*) Kleider.
6. Ein Zwerg (*dwarf*) bleibt immer ein Zwerg.

7. Ein schlafender (*sleeping*) Fuchs fängt keinen Hahn.
8. Hast (*haste*) bricht Beine.
9. Bauern lieben lange Bratwürste und kurze Predigten.
10. Unglück hat breite Füße. (This is a strange proverb!)
11. Arbeit überwindet (*overcomes*) alle Schwierigkeiten.
12. Den Wolf tötet der Bauer.

Vocabulary (words marked * should be memorized at some point)

* **all** — all, every
* der **Anfang** (⁻e) — beginning
  das **Angesicht** — face
* die **Arbeit** (-en) — work
  der **Bauer** (-n) — farmer
  das **Bein** (-e) — leg
* **bleiben** — to remain
  die **Bratwurst** (⁻e) — sausage
* **brechen** (**bricht**) — to break
  breit — wide, broad
* **bringen** — to bring
  das **Eis** (-) — ice
  fangen (**fängt**) — to capture
  der **Fleiß** — effort
  der **Fuchs** (⁻e) — fox
* der **Fuß** (⁻e) — foot
  der **Hahn** (⁻e) — rooster
  die **Hast** — haste

* **immer** — always
  das **Kleid** (-er) — dress, clothes
* **kurz** — short
* **lang** — long
* **lieben** — to love
* **machen** — to do, make
  der **Meister** (-) — master
  das **Meisterstück** (-e) — masterpiece
  die **Predigt** (-en) — sermon
* **schön** — beautiful
  die **Schwierigkeit** (-en) — difficulty
  töten — to kill
  die **Übung** (-en) — practice
* das **Unglück** (-e) — misfortune
* die **Wahrheit** — truth
  der **Wolf** (⁻e) — wolf
  der **Zwerg** (-e) — dwarf

3.4. The genitive is a form used to indicate possession. It is also used with some prepositions (see 5.8) and verbs.

When the genitive appears (and when it is not the object of a preposition or a verb), an "of" must be added in order to have a correct translation. Examples are:

Der Freund *des Vaters* (*masculine*) ist hier — The friend *of the father* is here.
Das Lieblingstier *des Kindes* (*neuter*) ist ein Panther — The favorite animal *of the child* is a panther.
Die Mutter *der Braut* (*feminine*) ist noch jung — The mother *of the bride* is still young.
Die Freunde *der Studenten* (*plural*) sind intelligent — The friends *of the students* are intelligent.

The genitive article is ***des*** for masculine and neuter nouns, and it is ***der*** for feminine and plural nouns. Whenever you see the article ***des***, the noun will **always** be in the genitive case, and it will **always** be singular. **It will never be plural!!!** When the genitive is used with masculine and neuter nouns, the nouns generally will have an *-s* or an *-es* ending:

Glück ist die Mutter ***des*** Unglücks — Fortune is the mother of misfortune.
Die Leidenschaften sind die Würzen ***des*** Lebens — The passions are the spices of life.

The genitive noun usually will follow the noun it possesses:

Sie ist die Mutter ***des Kindes*** — She is the mother *of the child*.
Vorsicht ist die Mutter ***der Weisheit*** — Caution is the mother *of wisdom*.
Reichtum ist die Stiefmutter ***der Tugend*** — Wealth is the stepmother *of virtue*.

However, a genitive noun occasionally will precede the noun it possesses:

Der Mund ist ***des Bauches*** Henker — The mouth is *the stomach's* hangman.
Armut ist ***der Künste*** Mutter — Poverty is *the arts'* mother.
Die Welt ist ***des Teufels*** Braut — The world is *the devil's* bride.

The genitive of proper nouns can be written in either of the following two ways:

Er ist Homers Student — He is Homer's student.
Er ist der Student Homers — He is the student *of* Homer.

Be careful when you see a proper noun with an *s* on it. There obviously is a big difference between "He is the student, Homers" and "He is the student *of* Homer."

3.5. Translate these sentences, noting the case and gender of each noun:

1. Die Ziege (*goat*) ist die Kuh (*cow*) des kleinen Mannes.
2. Der Wille ist die Seele des Werkes.
3. Selbsterkenntnis ist der Anfang der Besserung.
4. Eile (*haste*) ist die Mutter der Unvollkommenheit (*imperfection*).
5. Die Augen sind der Spiegel (*mirror*) der Seele.
6. Flüche sind des Teufels Sprüche.
7. Das unordentliche (*disorderly*) Leben der Leute ist das Wohlleben (*well-being*) der Ärzte.
8. Der Schatten der Tugend ist Ehre.

9. Ein Sprichwort ist das Pferd des Gesprächs. (Ein afrikanisches Sprichwort)
10. Den Freund des Arztes liebt die junge Frau.
11. Ruhe ist der Tagelohn (daily reward) der Arbeiter. (Question: Is *Arbeiter* singular or plural? How do you know?)

Vocabulary (genitive and plural endings of masculine and neuter nouns and plural endings of feminine nouns are listed in parentheses)

* der **Anfang** (-s, ⸚e) — beginning
* die **Arbeit** (-en) — work
  der **Arbeiter** (-s, -) — worker
* der **Arzt** (-es, ⸚e) — doctor
* das **Auge** (-s, -n) — eye
  die **Besserung** (-en) — improvement
  die **Ehre** (-n) — honor
  der **Fluch** (-es, ⸚e) — curse
  das **Gespräch** (-es, -e) — conversation
  die **Kuh** (⸚e) — cow
* das **Leben** (-s, -) — life
  die **Leute** (pl.) — people
* der **Mann** (-es, ⸚er) — man, husband
* die **Mutter** (⸚) — mother

das **Pferd** (-es, -e) — horse
die **Ruhe** —rest
der **Schatten** (-s, -) — shadow
die **Seele** (-n) — soul
die **Selbsterkenntnis** — self-knowledge
der **Spiegel** (-s, -) — mirror
das **Sprichwort** (-s, ⸚er) — proverb
der **Spruch** (-s, ⸚e) — maxim
der **Teufel** (-s, -) — devil
die **Tugend** (-en) — virtue
das **Werk** (-es, -e) — work
* der **Wille** (-ns, -n) — will
das **Wohlleben** (-s, -) — well-being
die **Ziege** (-n) — goat

3.6. **The dative** is used for indirect objects, and it is the object of some prepositions (see 5.4) and of some verbs such as *helfen* (to help), *folgen* (to follow), *antworten* (to answer), *glauben* (to believe), and *gehören* (to belong to). When the dative is used as the object of a verb or of a preposition, you can translate the sentence literally, as you would in English:

Der Student hilft *dem Professor* — The student helps *the professor.*
Das Kind spielt mit *der Katze* — The child plays with *the cat.*
Fräulein Meier antwortet *dem Briefträger* — Fräulein Meier answers *the mailman.*

At other times, however, a "to" or a "for" must be added so that the sentence will make sense:

Dem Fuchs sind die Trauben zu sauer — *For the fox*, the grapes are too sour.
Das Kind ist *der Mutter* eine Freude — The child is a joy *for the mother.*
Die Erklärung ist *dem Professor* nicht klar — The explanation is not clear *to the professor.*

Here are masculine, neuter, feminine, and plural examples of the dative:

Der Mann schreibt *dem Freund* (*masculine*) den Brief — The man writes *the friend* the letter (or: The man writes the letter *to the friend*).
Das Kind gibt *dem Tier* (*neuter*) das Essen — The child gives *the animal* the food (or: The child gives the food *to the animal*).
Die Mutter gibt *der Tochter* (*feminine*) die Blume — The mother gives *the daughter* the flower (or: The mother gives the flower *to the daughter*).
Die Eltern schreiben *den Kindern* (*plural*) Briefe — The parents write *the children* letters (or: The parents write letters *to the children*).

The dative article is *dem* for masculine and neuter nouns, it is *der* for feminine nouns, and it is *den* for plural nouns. Moreover,

the dative endings for all plural nouns will always be -n. Here are examples:

Die Männer helfen *den* Männern — The men help the men.
Die Kinder folgen *den* Kindern — The children follow the children.
Die Frauen antworten *den* Frauen — The women answer the women.

Whenever you see the article *dem*, the noun will *always* be in the dative case. **Also note that in a sentence which begins with the subject, the noun in the dative case will always precede the noun in the accusative case:** Die Mutter (*nominative*) singt dem Kind (*dative*) das Lied (*accusative*) — The mother sings (to) the child the song.

Because *der* can be either dative feminine or genitive feminine, its placement in the clause is crucial. Compare:

Die Reise ist *der Frau* (*dative*) unangenehm — The trip is unpleasant for the woman.
Die Reise *der Frau* (*genitive*) ist unangenehm — The trip of the woman is unpleasant. (Or: The woman's trip is unpleasant.)
Er beschreibt *der Frau* (*dative*) den Begriff — He describes the concept to the woman.
Er beschreibt den Begriff *der Frau* (*genitive*) — He describes the woman's concept.

3.7. Translate these sentences, being particularly aware of nouns in the dative case for which you must supply a "to" or a "for":

1. Der Winter schadet (*harms*) dem fleißigen Hamster nicht.
2. Geduld (*patience*) ist der Seele (*soul*) ein Schild (*shield*).
3. Kein Kleid ist der Frau besser als (*than*) Schweigen (*being quiet*). (A chauvinistic proverb!)
4. Der Frau ist die Arbeit unangenehm.
5. Das Gebet (*prayer*) ist der Witwe (*widow*) ein Wall und eine Hütte.
6. Alles (*everything*) schmeckt (*tastes*) dem hungrigen Bauch (*stomach*) wohl (*good, well*).
7. Keine Brille (*eyeglasses*) hilft dem blinden Mann.
8. Die Bedeutung (*meaning*) des Dramas bleibt den Zuschauern (*viewers*) ein Rätsel (*riddle, puzzle*).
9. Das Kind sagt der Mutter die Wahrheit.
10. Die Frau bäckt (*bakes*) dem Briefträger einen Apfelkuchen.
11. Der Professor erklärt den Studenten das Problem.
12. Die Arbeit der Frau ist schwer.

Vocabulary (verbs marked i are intransitive)

* **alles** — everything
  der **Apfelkuchen** (-s, -) — apple cake
  die **Arbeit** (-en) — work
  der **Bauch** (-es, ¨e) — belly, stomach
* **bleiben** (i) — to remain
  blind — blind
  das **Drama** (-s, -en) — drama
  erklären — to explain
  fleißig — industrious
  das **Gebet** (-es, -e) — prayer
  die **Geduld** — patience
  der **Hamster** (-s, -) — hamster
* **helfen** (i) — to help
  hungrig — hungry
  die **Hütte** (-n) — hut
* **kein** — no

das **Kleid** (-es, -er) — dress
* **nicht** — not
  das **Rätsel** (-s, -) — riddle, puzzle
* **sagen** — to say
  schaden (i) — to harm
  der **Schild** (-s, -e) — shield
  schmecken (i) — to taste
  das **Schweigen** (-s) — silence, being silent
  schwer — difficult
  die **Seele** (-n) — soul
  unangenehm — unpleasant
* die **Wahrheit** — truth
  der **Wall** (-es, ¨e) — rampart, wall
  die **Witwe** (-n) — widow
* **wohl** — well, good
  der **Zuschauer** (-s, -) — viewer, audience

3.8. Here is a chart for all forms for both the definite (*der*) and indefinite (*ein*) articles. Both the definite and indefinite articles have the same endings except for the masculine and neuter nominative and the neuter accusative (note the asterisks on the chart).

	masculine	neuter	feminine	plural
nominative	der	das	die	die
	*ein	*ein	eine	—
accusative	den	das	die	die
	einen	*ein	eine	—
genitive	des	des	der	der
	eines	eines	einer	—
dative	dem	dem	der	den
	einem	einem	einer	—

3.9. **Here is another table** to help you become more familiar with these endings:

der can be:	masculine nominative	*Der Mann* ist hier.
		The man is here.
	feminine genitive	Der Freund *der Frau* ist alt.
		The friend *of the woman* is old.
	plural genitive	Der Freund *der Frauen* ist alt.
		The friend *of the women* is old.
	feminine dative	Der Freund schreibt *der Frau* etwas.
		The friend writes something *to the woman*.
das can be:	neuter nominative	*Das Buch* ist interessant.
		The book is interesting.
	neuter accusative	Der Student liest *das Buch*.
		The student reads *the book*.
die can be:	feminine nominative	*Die Frau* ist hier.
		The woman is here.
	plural nominative	*Die Frauen* sind hier.
		The women are here.
	feminine accusative	Der Mann sieht *die Frau*.
		The man sees *the woman*.
	plural accusative	Der Mann sieht *die Frauen*.
		The man sees *the women*.
des can be:	masculine genitive	Der Sohn *des Mannes* ist hier.
		The son *of the man* is here.
	neuter genitive	Die Katze *des Kindes* ist klein.
		The cat *of the child* is small.

dem can be: masculine dative	Wer gibt *dem Mann* den Brief?
	Who gives the letter *to the man*?
neuter dative	Wer singt *dem Kind* das Lied?
	Who sings the song *to the child*?

den can be: masculine accusative	Der Mann tötet *den Wolf*.
	The man kills *the wolf*.
plural dative	Die Frau schreibt *den Männern*.
	The woman writes *(to) the men*.

3.10. Translate the following sentences; state the gender and case of each noun (the vocabulary list is on p. 31):

1. Der Freund der Frau gibt der Mutter der Kinder die Bücher.
2. Die Mutter und die Kinder sehen die Kuh und die Stiere.
3. Das Kind ißt das Brot.
4. Die Frau des Arztes bezweifelt (*doubts*) die Wahrheit des Sprichwortes.
5. Die Frau schreibt dem Vater und dem Kind.
6. Der Professor zeigt den Studenten den Film.
7. Fräulein Meier schenkt der Briefträger eine rote Rose.

3.11. There are also some other words which have the same case endings as the definite articles, *der, das,* and *die*. They are: *dieser* (*this one*), *jener* (*that, that one*), *jeder* (*each, every*), *mancher* (*some, many a*), *solcher* (*such*), and *welcher* (*what, which*).

	masculine	neuter	feminine	plural
nominative	dieser	dieses	diese	diese
accusative	diesen	dieses	diese	diese
genitive	dieses	dieses	dieser	dieser
dative	diesem	diesem	dieser	diesen

Note that *dieser* means *this* when it is singular and *these* **only** when it is plural. Compare:
Dieser Mann kennt diese Frau — *This* man knows *this* woman.
Diese Männer kennen diese Frauen — *These* men know *these* women.

3.12. *Kein* (no) follows the same pattern as *ein* (a) (see 3.8). But the plural of *kein* follows the same paradigm as that of the *der* words:

nominative plural	keine (Kinder)
accusative plural	keine (Kinder)
genitive plural	kein**er** (Kinder)
dative plural	kein**en** (Kinder**n**)

3.13. The case endings must be memorized! Although you probably can read most sentences at this point without knowing case endings, you will run into trouble later when sentences become more complicated. In fact, if you do not understand cases and if you cannot identify case endings, you simply will not be able to read German. Make certain that you understand this chapter and review it often if you need to.

When I discuss word order in Chapter Six, I will indicate in detail the way that the subject can appear on either side of the verb. When the subject appears on the "other" side of the verb, recognition of case endings is crucial even in short sentences. Here are examples:

Ein vorwitziges Schäflein (*accusative*) frißt der Wolf (*nominative*) — The wolf eats an impertinent little sheep.
Der Tugend (*dative*) ist kein Ziel (*nominative*) zu hoch — No goal is too high for virtue.

3.14. Translate these sentences, indicating the gender and case of each noun. (If you are unaccustomed to recognizing case endings, it is a good idea to continue identifying the cases of nouns in future lessons until the process becomes automatic. Do not be surprised if memorizing the case endings takes you a long time.)

1. Wiederholung ist die Mutter der Weisheit.
2. Die Erde bedeckt die Fehler der Ärzte. (Doctors tend not to fare very well in German proverbs!)
3. Die Sonne leuchtet der ganzen Welt.
4. Fleiß ist der Vater des Glückes.
5. Der Segen der Eltern baut den Kindern Häuser. (This is difficult — it contains all four cases.)
6. Gesundheit ist die Tochter der Arbeit.
7. Ein böses (*guilty*) Gewissen (*conscience*) ist der Vorgeschmack (*pretaste*) der Hölle.
8. Man entgeht (*avoids*) vielleicht der Strafe, aber man entgeht nicht dem Gewissen.
9. Zeit ist die Arznei des Zorns.
10. Jedes Ding hat zwei Seiten.
11. Der Tochter schreibt der Vater.

12. Das gestohlene Brot schmeckt dem Mann gut; aber *am Ende* (*finally*) hat er den Mund voller (*full of*) Kieselsteine. (Proverbs)
13. Jeder Mutter Kind ist schön.
14. Wir sind die Kinder Gottes.
15. Was Fliegen (*flies — the insect*) sind den müßigen (*idle*) Knaben, das sind wir den Göttern. (*König Lear*) (Note that *Knaben* and *Göttern* are in the dative case. Are they singular or plural?)

Vocabulary (please memorize words marked *)

* **aber** — but, however,
* die **Arbeit (-en)** — work
* der **Arzt (-es, ⁻e)** — doctor
  die **Arznei (-en)** — medicine
  bauen — to build
  bedecken — to cover
* **böse** — bad, guilty
  das **Brot (-es, -e)** — bread
  das **Buch (-es, ⁻er)** — book
* **dies** — this, these
* das **Ding (-es, -e)** — thing
  die **Eltern** (pl.) — parents
  entgehen (i) — to escape
* die **Erde (-n)** — earth
* **essen (ißt)** — to eat
* der **Fehler (-s, -)** — error
  der **Film (-s, -e)** — film
  der **Fleiß (-es)** — effort
  die **Fliege (-n)** — fly
  der **Freund (-es, -e)** — friend
  ganz — entire
  gestohlen — stolen
  das **Gewissen (-s, -)** — conscience
  das **Glück (-es)** — happiness, luck
* der **Gott (-es, ⁻er)** — God, god
  das **Haus (-es, ⁻er)** — house
  die **Hölle (-n)** — hell
* **jeder (jedes, jede ...)** — each, every
  der **Kieselstein (-es, -e)** — pebble

der **Knabe (-n, -n)** — boy, knave
die **Kuh (⁻e)** — cow
leuchten (i) — illuminate
* **man** — one
der **Mund (-es, ⁻er)** — mouth
nicht — not
schenken — to give as a present
schmecken (i) — to taste
* **schön** — beautiful
* **schreiben** — to write
* **schwer** — difficult
die **Seele (-n)** — soul
der **Segen (-s, -)** — blessing
die **Seite (-n)** — side
die **Sonne** — sun
das **Sprichwort (-s, ⁻er)** — proverb
der **Stier (-s, -e)** — bull
die **Strafe (-n)** — punishment
die **Tochter (⁻)** — daughter
* **tun** — to do
* der **Vater (-s, ⁻)** — father
* **vielleicht** — perhaps
die **Weisheit** — wisdom
die **Welt (-en)** — world, universe
die **Wiederholung (-en)** — repetition
* **zeigen** — to show
* die **Zeit (-en)** — time
der **Zorn (-s, -)** — wrath
* **zwei** — two

3.15. Vocabulary aid

1. Die Arbeit dieses guten Arztes ist schwer.
2. Die Leute sagen die Wahrheit.
3. Fräulein Meier hilft jedem Freund des Briefträgers.
4. Alles schmeckt dem hungrigen Mann gut.
5. Man macht diesen Fehler oft.
6. Das Glück ist allzu (*all too*) kurz.
7. Der Briefträger tut viel.
8. Die Lösung (*solution*) dieses Problems ist den Studenten unklar.

Chapter Four

Adjectives and Adverbs

4.1. Adjectives

An adjective is a word which is used to modify a noun. Common adjectives are: *alt* (*old*), *jung* (*young*), *groß* (*large*), *klein* (*small*), and *gut* (*good*).

When adjectives appear directly before a noun with no article in front of them, they will have "strong" case endings which are similar to the endings of the definite article (*der, das, die*). A "strong" ending is simply one which reveals the gender and case of the noun. Here is a chart comparing definite article endings and strong adjective endings:

	masculine	neuter	feminine	plural
nominative	der Wein	das Essen	die Lampe	die Freunde
	guter Wein	gutes Essen	rote Lampe	neue Freunde
accusative	den Wein	das Essen	die Lampe	die Freunde
	guten Wein	gutes Essen	rote Lampe	neue Freunde
genitive	* des Weins	* des Essens	der Lampe	der Freunde
	guten Weins	guten Essens	roter Lampe	neuer Freunde
dative	dem Wein	dem Essen	der Lampe	den Freunden
	gutem Wein	gutem Essen	roter Lampe	neuen Freunden

* Note that the definite article endings and strong adjective endings are **identical** in all instances except for masculine and neuter genitive.

Here are examples:
Nominative: *Guter* Wein ist teuer — Good wine is expensive.
Accusative: Fräulein Meier trinkt *guten* Wein gern — Fräulein Meier likes to drink *good wine*.
Genitive: Die Farbe *guten* Weins ist manchmal rot — The color *of good wine* is sometimes red.
Dative: Der Student ist mit *gutem* Wein zufrieden — The student is satisfied with *good wine*.

Adjectives are most frequently strong when they appear in genitive plural case:

Die Eltern *kleiner* Kinder sind oft müde — The parents *of small* children are often tired.

4.2. Adjectives also will have strong endings when they succeed the indefinite article (*ein*) in masculine and neuter nominative cases and in the neuter accusative case. Here are examples:

Ein guter Mann (*masculine nominative*) ist hier — A good man is here.
Ein gutes Kind (*neuter nominative*) ist hier — A good child is here.
Der Mann kennt ein gutes Kind (*neuter accusative*) — The man knows a good child.

Since in these cases the indefinite article *ein* does not reveal the gender of the noun, the adjective following *ein* (guter, gutes) will tell you the gender instead.

All definite and indefinite articles are strong (since they are *always* the first adjectives to modify the noun; i.e., one always says: "*the* good cat" rather than "good *the* cat"). Other adjectives which are always strong are the possessive adjectives (**mein** — *my*; **dein** — *your*; **sein** — *his, its*; **ihr** — *her, their*; **unser** — *our*; **euer** — *your*; and **Ihr** — *your* [see 7.8]); **kein** — *no*; and the *der* words (**dieser** — *this, this one*; **jener** — *that, that one*; **jeder** — *each, every*; **solcher** — *such*; and **welcher** — *which, what*).

Any adjective (such as old, new, happy, etc.) can be strong when it is the only adjective modifying a noun. Examples are:

Alte Freunde sind *gute* Freunde — Old friends are good friends.
Gutes Gespräch kürzt den Weg — Good conversation shortens the way.

4.3. However, most adjectives follow an article or some other adjective which is always strong. Here are examples:

Das *gute* Beispiel ist nützlich — The good example is helpful.
Die Katze des *alten* Mannes ist dick — The cat of the old man is fat.
Jede *neue* Aufgabe ist schwer — Each new task is difficult.

Whenever an adjective follows an article or a *der* word, it will end in either -e or -en. The endings for these adjectives are called "weak" endings because, unlike the endings of articles or other strong adjectives, they do not reveal the gender or case of the noun. Here is a chart:

	masculine	neuter	feminine
nominative	der gute Wein	das neue Auto	die rote Lampe
accusative	den guten Wein	das neue Auto	die rote Lampe
genitive	des guten Weins	des neuen Autos	der roten Lampe
dative	dem guten Wein	dem neuen Auto	der roten Lampe

The weak adjective endings for all plural nouns will end in **-en**:

nominative	die langen Bücher
accusative	die langen Bücher
genitive	der langen Bücher
dative	den langen Büchern

Whenever adjectives appear before nouns they **always** will have endings; the endings will be: **-e, -en, -es**, or **-er**.

4.4. If two or more adjectives (other than articles or *der* words, etc.) **stand together, they generally will have the same endings.** They both will have strong endings if they are not preceded by an article, and they will have weak endings if they are preceded by an article. Here are examples:

Schwarze dicke Nashörner sind im Zoo — Fat black rhinoceri are in the zoo. (*strong endings*)
Die schwarzen dicken Nashörner sind im Zoo — The fat black rhinoceri are in the zoo. (*weak endings*)

4.5. When an adjective normally ends in *-el* **or** *-er*, **the** *e* **will be omitted whenever the adjective has an ending.** Here are examples of such adjectives: teuer, ungeheuer, übel, and dunkel. Compare:

Der Wein ist teuer; Der teure Wein schmeckt gut — The expensive wine tastes good.
Das Tier ist ungeheuer; Das ungeheure Tier ist dumm — The monstrous animal is dumm.
Die Hexe ist übel; Die üble Hexe ist häßlich — The evil witch is ugly.

4.6. An adjective with either a strong or a weak ending will always appear immediately before the noun it modifies, never afterwards. In this respect, German is **not** like French or Spanish.

4.7. Adjectives which do not appear before the noun they modify will take no ending. However, such adjectives will **always** be predicate adjectives (adjectives following verbs such as *to be, to become, to look, taste, feel, smell, seem, appear,* etc.) Here are examples:

Die Kerze ist *rot* — The candle is *red.*
Das Essen schmeckt *gut* — The food tastes *good.*
Es wird *dunkel* — It is growing *dark.*

4.8. Adverbs

Adverbs modify verbs, adjectives, or other adverbs.   Common adverbs are: *heute* (*today*), *bald* (*soon*), *hier* (*here*), *dort* (*there*), *beinah* (*almost*), *auch* (*also*), *noch* (*still*), *sehr* (*very*), *ganz* (*very, entirely*), *vielleicht* (*perhaps*), *meistens* (*for the most part, mostly*), *darum* (*therefore*), *aber* (*but, though*), and *nicht* (*not*).

Adverbs will usually be found close to the words they modify.   Here are examples of adverbs:

Das Kind geht *oft* in den Zoo — The child *often* goes to the zoo.
Der *sehr* fleißige Briefträger ist *immer hier* — The *very* industrious mailman is *always here.*
Vielleicht ist Fräulein Meier *deshalb meistens morgens* zu Hause — *Perhaps* Fräulein Meier is *therefore mostly* (or usually) at home *mornings* (or in the morning).

4.9.   Noncomparative adverbs will never have a special ending, as adjectives do. In fact, adverbs often can be differentiated from adjectives only by whether or not they have endings.   For example, Sie hat ein *schönes* gemaltes Bild — She has a *beautiful,* painted picture (a painted picture, which also happens to be beautiful) is different from: Sie hat ein *schön* gemaltes Bild — She has a *beautifully* painted picture (a picture which may have an ugly scene, but is still painted beautifully).

It is extremely important to remember that any descriptive words which do not have endings and which are not predicate adjectives will **always** be adverbs! Here are more examples:

Der Zug fährt *langsam* nach Kalifornien — The train goes *slowly* to California.
Der Kolibri summt *leise* in der Finsternis — The hummingbird hums *softly* in the darkness.
Die Katze fängt den Vogel *leicht* — The cat *easily* captures the bird.
Ein Reh steht *still* und *verklärt* wie im Traum — A deer stands *quietly* and *radiantly* as if in a dream.

However, German adverbs and predicate adjectives will have the same form:

Fräulein Meier schreibt *gut* — Fräulein Meier writes *well*. (adverb)
Fräulein Meier ist *gut* — Fräulein Meier is *good*. (predicate adjective)

4.10. Here are the most common types of adverbs. Since all of the following adverbs occur often, it may be useful for you to memorize them eventually. (For a complete list of adverbs, see: Robin Hammond, *A German Reference Grammar* [Oxford: Oxford University Press, 1981], pp. 180-82.)

A. Adverbs indicating time (cf. Appendix D, p. 251)

morgens (*mornings*), *abends* (*evenings*), *nachts* (*nights*), *damals* (*at that time*), *bald* (*soon*), *dann* (*then*), *jedesmal* (*each time*), *oft* (*often*), *schon* (*already*), *immer* (*always*), *nun* (*now*), *lange* (*for a long time*), *endlich* (*finally*).

B. Adverbs indicating place

hier (*here*), *dort* (*there*), *überall* (*everywhere*).

C. Adverbs indicating "manner"

1. *Limitation:* *beinah* (*almost*), *fast* (*almost*), *ungefähr* (*approximately*).
2. *Extension:* *außerdem* (*moreover*), *übrigens* (*by the way*), *sonst* (*otherwise*), *auch* (*also*), *sogar* (*even*), *ziemlich* (*rather*), *noch* (*still*), *eigentlich* (*actually*), *vielmehr* (*rather*).
3. *Exaggeration:* *sehr* (*very*), *recht* (*really*), *besonders* (*especially*), *ganz* (*quite, very, entirely*).
4. *Caution:* *vielleicht* (*perhaps*), *möglich* (*possibly*), *wahrscheinlich* (*probably*).
5. *Extent:* *meistens* (*mostly, for the most part*), *wenigstens* (*at least*), *zu* (*too*), *bloß* (*merely*), *genug* (*enough*).
6. *Cause or reason:* *daher* (*therefore*), *darum* (*therefore*), *deshalb* (*on that account*), *dabei* (*thereby*).

4.11. Note that many words have different meanings depending on whether they are adjectives or adverbs. *Gleich, gerade, eben, lauter* (see your **Troublesome Word** list, 35.1) are examples.

The word *gar* used as an adjective will mean *cooked, tender, well-done* while the adverb (which appears more often) will mean *entirely, fully, absolutely, very, quite.* The adjectival meaning usually will be listed first in your dictionary. If an adjective and an adverb have essentially the same meaning, only the adjective may be listed. For example, *leicht* will be listed as an adjective with the definitions *light, easy,* but it can also be translated as an adverb — *lightly, easily.*

4.12. Translate these sentences, noting which words are adjectives and which are adverbs. Try to guess the gender of the noun by looking at the adjectives:

1. Ein hungriger Bär tanzt schlecht.
2. Ein guter Hahn (*rooster*) wird selten fett.
3. Alte Kirchen haben dunkle Fenster.
4. Magre Mücken stechen (*sting*) übel. (They are mean because they are hungry!)
5. Gestrenge (*strict*) Herren regieren nicht lange.
6. Verbotenes Obst (*fruit*) ist süß.
7. Armut ist die Erfinderin aller Dinge. (**Erfinderin** is feminine because **Armut** is feminine.)
8. Stumme Hunde und stille Wasser sind gefährlich (*dangerous*). (Is **Wasser** singular or plural? How do you know?)
9. Eine alte Wunde blutet leicht.
10. Finstere Gedanken sind die Kinder eines melancholischen Kopfes.
11. Ein gutes Gewissen (*conscience*) ist ein sanftes (*soft*) Ruhekissen (*pillow*).
12. Kinder sind der Reichtum armer Leute.
13. Eine Hand wäscht die andere.
14. Arbeit hat bittere Wurzeln, aber süße Frucht.
15. Tod ist der Arzt des armen Mannes.
16. Der Teufel hindert und verdirbt das tägliche Brot und alle Gaben Gottes. (Luther)
17. Der Historiker sieht rückwärts (*backwards*); endlich glaubt er auch rückwärts. (Nietzsche)
18. Wind mit dunklen Wolken (*clouds*) bringt Regen, und heimliches (*secret*) Geschwätz (*gossip*) schafft saure Gesichter. (Proverbs)

19. Ein törichter (*foolish*) Sohn ist seines Vaters Herzeleid (*suffering*), und ein zänkisches (*cranky*) Weib ist wie (*like*) ein ständig triefendes (*dripping*) Dach (*roof*). (Proverbs)
20. Die üblen Mücken tötet Fräulein Meier.

* **all** — all, every
* **alt** — old
* **ander** (adj.) — other
* die **Arbeit** (-en) — work
* **arm** (adj.) — poor
  die **Armut** — poverty
* **auch** — also
  der **Bär** (-en, -en) — bear
  bitter (adj.) — bitter
  bluten (i) — to bleed
  das **Brot** (-es, -e) — bread
  das **Dach** (-es, ̈er) — roof
  das **Ding** (-s, -e) — thing
* **dunkel** (adj.) — dark
* **endlich** (adv.) — finally
  der **Erfinder** (-s, -) — inventor
  das **Fenster** (-s, -) — window
  fett — fat
  finster (adj.) — dark
* die **Frucht** (̈e) — fruit
  die **Gabe** (-n) — gift
  der **Gedanke** (-ns, -n) — thought
  gefährlich (adj.) — dangerous
* **gern** (adv.) — gladly;
  er tut das gern — he likes to do that
  das **Geschwätz** (-es) — gossip
  das **Gesicht** (-es, -er) — face
  das **Gewissen** (-s, -) — conscience
* **glauben** (i) — to believe
* **gut** (adj.) — good;
  (adv.) — well
  der **Hahn** (-es, ̈e) — rooster
* der **Herr** (-n, -en) — Lord, Master, Mr.
  das **Herzeleid** — suffering
  hindern — to hinder
  der **Historiker** (-s, -) — historian

* der **Hund** (-es, -e) — dog
* **hungrig** (adj.) — hungry
  die **Kirche** (-n) — church
* **klein** (adj.) — small
* der **Kopf** (-es, ̈e) — head
  der **Kritiker** (-s, -) — critic
* **lange** (adv.) — for a long time
* **leicht** (adj. & adv.) — easy, easily
* die **Leute** (pl.) — people
* **machen** — to make, do
  mager (adj.) — thin
  melancholisch — melancholy
* der **Mensch** (-en, -en) — person
  die **Mücke** (-n) — gnat
  das **Obst** (-es, -arten) — fruit
  der **Regen** (-s, -) — rain
  regieren — to rule
  der **Reichtum** (-s,) — wealth
  rückwärts (adv.) — backwards
  sanft (adj.) — soft
  sauer (adj.) — sour
  schaffen — to create
* **schlecht** (adj. & adv.) — bad, guilty
* **sehen** (sieht) — to see
* **sein** (poss. pron.) — his
* **selten** (adv.) — seldom
  der **Sohn** (-es, ̈e) — son
  ständig (adj. & adv.) — constant, constantly
* **still** (adj. & adv.) — quiet, quietly
  stumm (adj.) — mute
  süß (adj.) — sweet
* **täglich** (adj. & adv.) — daily
  tanzen — to dance
  der **Teufel** (-s, -) — devil
  der **Tod** (-es, -e) — death
  töten — to kill

* **viel** (adj.) — many;
  (adv.) — much, a lot
  vielleicht (adv.) — perhaps
  waschen (wäscht) — to wash
  das **Wasser (-s, -)** — water
  das **Weib (-s, -er)** — wife
  der **Wein (-s, -e)** — wine
* **werden** (i) — to become

das **Werk (-es, -e)** — work
die **Wolke (-n)** — cloud
die **Wunde (-n)** — wound
die **Wurzel (-n)** — root
übel (adj. & adv.) — evil, bad, wicked
verboten (adj.) — forbidden
verderben (verdirbt) — to spoil

4.13. Vocabulary aid

1. Der Weintrinker hat oft ein schlechtes Gewissen (*conscience*).
2. Der kleine Hund des Briefträgers ist vielleicht hungrig.
3. Die Kinder alter Leute werden auch alt.
4. Es wird dunkel.
5. Viele Leute trinken gern Wein.
6. Was (*what*) ist den Kindern verboten?
7. Die Arbeit des Historikers interessiert den Professor.
8. Die gesammelten (*collected*) Werke der amerikanischen Historiker gefallen (*please*) dem deutschen Kritiker.

Chapter Five

Prepositions

5.1. German prepositions are often quite difficult to translate because there is no simple one-to-one correspondence between them and English prepositions. Often they will have to be translated according to what seems intuitively right. Most so-called German idioms are merely German nouns or verbs used in conjunction with various prepositions.

German prepositions fall into four categories:

(1) those taking the **accusative** case: *bis* (*until*), ***durch*** (*through, by*), ***für*** (*for*), ***gegen*** (*against*), ***ohne*** (*without*), ***um*** (*around, at*), ***entlang*** (*along*), ***wider*** (*against*);

(2) those taking the **dative** case: ***aus*** (*out of, of, from*), ***außer*** (*except*), ***bei*** (*by, near, with*), ***mit*** (*with*), ***nach*** (*after, according to*), ***seit*** (*since*), ***von*** (*of, from*), ***zu*** (*to, at*), ***gegenüber*** (*opposite, vis-à-vis*);

(3) those taking either the **dative or** the **accusative** case according to the verb use: ***an*** (*on, at, to*), ***auf*** (*on, upon, on top of*), ***hinter*** (*behind*), ***in*** (*in, into*), ***neben*** (*next to*), ***über*** (*over, about*), ***unter*** (*under, among*), ***vor*** (*before, ago*), ***zwischen*** (*between*);

(4) those taking the **genitive**: ***trotz*** (*in spite of*), ***statt*** (*instead of*), ***während*** (*during*), ***wegen*** (*because of*), ***um ... willen*** (*for the sake of*).

In this chapter I have listed the most common definitions of each preposition, along with the most common idioms. At this point, you should memorize only the initial definitions of the prepositions and the idioms which I have asterisked. Note that the prepositions and the most common idioms are also listed on pp. 239-240 of the Appendix for a convenient reference.

5.2. Prepositions taking the accusative

bis — until (with reference to time), as far as (with reference to space)
Bis heute hat Fräulein Meier den Witz nicht gehört — *Until* today, Fräulein Meier had not heard the joke.

Der Student fährt nur *bis* Chicago — The student travels only *as far as* Chicago.

This preposition is often also used in conjunction with other prepositions such as:

Er fährt *bis um* neun Uhr — He travels *until* nine o'clock.
Er tut das *bis zum* bitteren Ende — He does that *to* the bitter end.

durch — *through, by means of, across*

Der Wanderer geht *durch* den Wald — The hiker goes *through* the woods.
Viele steigen *durch* Sünde, manche fallen *durch* Tugend — Many rise *through* (by means of) sin, some fail *through* (by means of) virtue.

für — *for, instead of*

Fräulein Meier bäckt *für* den Basar — Fräulein Meier bakes *for* the (charity) bazaar.

Here are some idioms:

* Der Briefträger *hält* es *für* gut — The mailman *considers* it (*to be*) good.
* *Was für* ein Mann ist er? — *What kind of* man is he?
  Tag *für* Tag — Day *by* day

gegen — *against, towards*

* Der Ritter kämpft *gegen* den Drachen — The knight fights *against* the dragon.
* Es wird *gegen* Abend kühler — It grows cooler *towards* evening.
* *Gegen* zehn Uhr kommt er — *Around* ten o'clock he is coming.
  Sie ist *gegen* 30 — She is *about* 30 years old.

ohne — *without*

Ohne seine Katze ist das Kind traurig — The child is unhappy *without* his cat.

Here are some idioms:

ohne Frage — doubtless
ohne weiteres — without more ado.

um — *at, around*

* *Um* sechs Uhr ist sie gewöhnlich hier — *At* six she is usually here.

Um with regard to time will *always* be translated as *at*.

* Der Briefträger läuft *um* die Rennbahn — The mailman runs *around* the track.

Fräulein Meier *bittet* den Briefträger *um* Hilfe — Fräulein Meier *asks* the mailman *for* help.

Manchmal schleicht Fräulein Meier wie die Katze *um* den heißen Brei — Sometimes Fräulein Meier beats *around* the bush. (Literally: creeps like a cat around the hot porridge).

wider — *against, contrary to*

Das ist *wider* meinen Willen — That is *against* my will.

There is also an accusative preposition which generally follows its object:

entlang — *along*

Der Wanderer läuft den Fluß *entlang* — The hiker walks *along* the river.

5.3. Translate these sentences:

1. Ein Glaube ohne Tat ist wie (*like*) ein Feld ohne Saat (*seed*).
2. Unglück, Nägel und Haar wachsen durch das ganze Jahr.
3. Liebe ohne Gegenliebe ist wie (*like*) eine Frage ohne Antwort.
4. Furcht (*fear*) hält alle Speisen (*food*) für Gift (*poison*).
5. Fünf Jahre lang kämpfte (*fought*) der Professor gegen die Windmühlen.
6. Fräulein Meier wickelt (*wraps*) den Briefträger um den kleinen Finger.
7. Was für ein Mann ist der Briefträger?
8. Der Gesundheitsfanatiker (*health fanatic*) schwimmt jeden Morgen um sechs Uhr wider den Strom.

Vocabulary

* die **Antwort** (-en) — answer
* **bis** — until
* **durch** — through
  das **Feld** (-es, -er) — field
* die **Frage** (-n) — question
* **fünf** — five
* **für** — for
  die **Furcht** — fear
* **ganz** — whole, entire

* **gegen** — against, towards, around
  die **Gegenliebe** (-n) — reciprocal love
  der **Glaube** (-ns, -n) — faith, belief
* das **Haar** (-s, -e) — hair
* **halten für** — to consider
* das **Jahr** (-s, -e) — year
* **jeder** — every, each

* **klein** — small, little
* **lang** — for
* die **Liebe** (-n) — love
* der **Morgen** (-s, -) — morning
  der **Nagel** (-s, ⸚) — nail
* **ohne** — without
  die **Saat** (-en) — seed
* **sechs** — six
  der **Strom** (-s, ⸚e) — stream

die **Tat** (-en) — deed
* die **Uhr** (-en) — clock
* **um** — at, around
  das **Unglück** (-s, -e) — misfortune
  wachsen (wächst) (i) — to grow
* **was für** — what kind of
* **wider** — against
  die **Windmühle** (-n) — windmill

5.4. Prepositions taking the dative

aus — out of, of, from (cities or countries)

* Sie geht *aus* dem Haus — She goes *out of* the house.
* Sie kommt *aus* Zürich — She is *from* Zurich.

Here are some idioms:

aus verschiedenen Gründen — *for* many reasons
Das Haus *besteht aus* Stroh — The house *consists of* straw.
aus Erfahrung — *from* experience

außer — out of, outside, without, except

* Alle *außer* dem Kind verstehen den Witz — *Except for* the child, everyone understands the joke.
  Außer Zweifel ist das wahr — *Without a doubt* that is true.

bei — by, near, with, among, at the house of, at
beim is a contraction of *bei* and *dem*.

* Die Kneipe liegt *bei* der Universität — The pub is *near* the university.
  Das Kind wohnt *bei* seinen Eltern — The child lives *with* his parents.

Here are some idioms:

Bei einer Firma sein — to be **with** a company.
bei Nacht — *at night*

Moreover, *beim* succeeded by any verb turned into a neuter noun means *while doing something*:

Beim Kaffeetrinken besprechen die Studenten die Philosophie Hegels — *While* drinking coffee, the students discuss the philosophy of Hegel.

Beim Studieren lernt man oft viele Kleinigkeiten — *While* studying, one often learns many trivial things.

mit — *with, by, at*

* Das Kind spielt *mit* seinen Freunden — The child plays with his friends.

Here are some idioms:

Er fährt *mit* dem Bus — He goes *by* bus.
Sie tut das *mit* Absicht — She does that *intentionally*.
Mit zehn Jahren begann der Briefträger zu arbeiten — *At the age of ten*, the mailman began to work.

nach — *after, according to, to (with regard to direction)*

*   *Nach* der Vorlesung geht der Student in die Kneipe — *After* the class, the student goes to the pub.
*   *Nach* meiner Uhr ist es halb elf — *According to* my watch it is 10:30.
*   Sie fliegt *nach* Europa — She is flying to Europe.

Here are some idioms:

Sie geht *nach* Hause — She goes home.
*   Die Studentin *fragt nach* der Bedeutung des Übels — The coed *asks about* the meaning of evil.
Diese Kneipe *riecht nach* Tabak — This pub *smells of* tobacco.
Der Kuchen *schmeckt nach* Äpfeln — The cake *tastes of* apples.
*   Moreover, this preposition often follows the noun when it means *according to*: *Meiner Meinung nach* ist das wahr — *In my opinion* that is true.

seit — *since, for*

*   *Seit* vielen Tagen warten Vladimir und Estragon auf Godot — *For* many days Vladimir and Estragon *have waited for* Godot.

Generally, although *seit* will be used with a present verb, it should be translated into English as a present perfect or a present perfect progressive to make the translation sound smoother. Germans use the present tense with *seit* in order to indicate an on-going activity: *Seit* acht Jahren wohnt die Studentin in Chicago — *For* eight years, the coed has been living in Chicago (and she is living there even now). Only the following sentence would signify a completed action: Acht Jahre *lang* hat die Studentin in Chicago gewohnt — *For* eight years the coed lived in Chicago (but now she is happily living elsewhere).

von — from, of, by, about
vom is a contraction of *von* and *dem*.

*   Schiller war ein Freund *von* Goethe — Schiller was a friend *of* Goethe's.
   Zwei *von* uns — Two *of* us
   Sie spricht *von* dem Dichter — She speaks *of* the poet.
   Ein Gedicht *von* Brecht — A poem *by* Brecht.

Here are some idioms:

Von jetzt an — **From** now on
Der Garten ist *von* Rosen umgeben — The garden is surrounded *by* roses.

zu — to, at, in addition to
zum is a contraction of *zu* and *dem*; *zur* is a contraction of *zu* and *der*.

Sie ist nett *zu* dem alten Mann — She is nice *to* the old man.

Here are some idioms:

*   *zum* Beispiel (often abbreviated z.B.) — *for* example.
*   *zu* Hause — *at* home
*   *zu* Fuß — *on* foot
   zum letzten Male — *for* the last time
   zu Weihnachten — *at* Christmas
   zum Glück — fortunately

gegenüber — vis-à-vis, opposite

This preposition will always follow the noun:

Sie sitzt dem Wahrsager *gegenüber* — She sits *opposite* the fortune teller.

5.5. Translate these sentences:

1. Hunger treibt (*drives*) den Wolf aus dem Busch.
2. Faulheit ist der Schlüssel (*key*) zur Armut.
3. Die Leidenschaft (*passion*) ist ein reißendes (*grasping*) Tier mit scharfen Zähnen (*teeth*).
4. Fräulein Meier macht oft einen Elefanten aus einer Mücke (*gnat*). (cf. *to make a mountain out of a molehill.*)
5. Der Mensch lebt nicht vom Brot allein.
6. Seit drei Jahren liest der Student die Philosophie Kants.
7. Nach Regen folgt Sonnenschein.
8. Der Stolz (*pride*) frühstückt mit dem Überfluß (*abundance*), speist (*eats*) zu Mittag mit der Armut und ißt zu Abend mit der Schande (*shame*). (Note that *Stolz* is personified.)

9. Krankheit kommt mit Extrapost und schleicht (*creeps*) wieder weg wie (*like*) Schnecken (*snails*).
10. Von Sparenberg (*thrift-mountain*) kommt man leicht nach Reichenberg (*fat city*).
11. Ich rede von Enten (*ducks*), und du sprichst von Gänsen (*geese*). (In other words, we are speaking at cross-purposes.)
12. Kinder sind eine Brücke (*bridge*) zum Himmel.
13. Hoffnung (*hope*) ist ein Schiff mit einem Mast von Stroh. (*Hoffnung* tends to be very unreliable in proverbs.)
14. Gott gegenüber hat der Christ (*Christian*) das Herz eines Kindes; dem Nächsten (*neighbor*) gegenüber hat er das Herz einer Mutter; und sich (*himself*) gegenüber hat er das Herz eines Richters (*judge*). (Note: **Gott** is **not** the subject of the first clause. What is?)

Vocabulary

* der **Abend** (-s, -e) — evening
* **allein** — alone
  die **Armut** — poverty
* **aus** — out of, of, from
* **außer** — except for, out of
* **bei** — near, by, with, at the house of
  das **Brot** (-s, -e) — bread
  die **Brücke** (-n) — bridge
  der **Busch** (-es, ̈-e) — bush
* der **Christ** (-en, -en) — Christian
  die **Ente** (-n) — duck
* **essen** (**ißt**) — to eat
  das **Europa** (-s) — Europe
  die **Extrapost** — special delivery
  die **Faulheit** — laziness
  folgen (i) — to follow
  frühstücken — to breakfast
  die **Gans** (̈-e) — goose
* **gegenüber** — opposite, vis-à-vis
* das **Herz** (-ens, -en) — heart
* der **Himmel** (-s, -) — heaven, sky
  die **Hoffnung** — hope
  die **Krankheit** (-en) — sickness
* **leben** — to live
* **leicht** — easily
  die **Leidenschaft** (-en) — passion

* **lesen** (**liest**) — to read
* **machen** — to do, make
  der **Mast** (-s, -en) — mast
* **mit** — with
  der **Mittag** (-es, -e) — noon
  die **Mücke** (-n) — gnat
* **nach** — after, according to, towards
* **oft** — often
  reden — to speak
  der **Regen** (-s) — rain
  reißend — grasping
  der **Richter** (-s, -) — judge
  die **Schande** — shame, scandal
  scharf — sharp
  das **Schiff** (-es, -e) — ship
  schleichen (i) — to creep
  der **Schlüssel** (-s, -) — key
* **seit** — since, for
  der **Sonnenschein** (-s) — sunshine
  der **Stolz** (-es) — pride
  das **Stroh** (-es) — straw
  das **Tier** (-es, -e) — animal
  treiben — to drive
  der **Überfluß** (-sses) — abundance
* **von** — of, from

* **weg** — away   der **Zahn** (-es, ⁻e) — tooth
* **wieder** — again   * **zu** — to, towards, at
  der **Wolf** (-es, ⁻e) — wolf

5.6. Prepositions taking either the dative or the accusative

These prepositions take the dative or the accusative, according to whether or not, in the course of the verbal action, a borderline is crossed by either the subject or the object. If a border is crossed, the preposition will take the accusative; if no border is crossed, the preposition will take the dative. Here are examples:

In the sentence, Der Mann *geht in das Haus* (*The man goes into the house*), the object of the preposition *in* will be accusative. In the sentence, Der Mann *ist in dem Haus* (*The man is in the house*), the object of the preposition *in* is dative because no border is being crossed.

In some instances, a sentence can have a slightly different meaning, depending on whether the object of the preposition is accusative or dative. For example, Das Flugzeug fliegt *über die* Berge (*accusative*) — The airplane flies over the mountains means that the plane has had to increase its altitude in order to fly over the mountains; Das Flugzeug fliegt *über den* Bergen (*dative*) — The airplane flies over the mountains, on the other hand, means that the airplane is flying over the mountains at a steady altitude; the airplane is parallel to the mountains.

When these prepositions follow verbs of "mental activity" such as *antworten* (*answer*), *denken* (*think*), *erinnern* (*remind*), *hoffen* (*hope*), *lachen* (*laugh*), *sprechen* (*speak*), and *warten* (*wait*), the object generally will be accusative. Examples are:

Fräulein Meier *hofft auf* einen schönen Tag — Fräulein Meier *hopes for* a beautiful day.
Der Student *wartet auf* den Professor — The student *waits for* the professor.
Sie *lacht über* den Witz — She *laughs at* the joke.

Whenever verbs such as *sein, bleiben,* and *sitzen* are used, the object of the preposition will always be dative, because these verbs simply cannot imply motion or direction. Here are examples:

Die Katze *ist in der* Küche (*dative*) — The cat *is* in the kitchen.
Der Student *sitzt an dem* Schreibtisch (*dative*) — The student *sits* at the desk.

For each of the following prepositions I have listed both a dative and an accusative example, as well as idioms:

an — *at, on, to, in, near to*
am is a contraction of *an* plus *dem*.

Ich hänge das Bild *an die* Wand (*acc.*) — I hang the picture on the wall.
Das Bild hängt *an der* Wand (*dat.*) — The picture hangs on the wall.

Here are some idioms:

* Sie *denkt an* eine Sache (*acc.*) — She thinks *of* a thing.
  Er *glaubt an* eine Sache (*acc.*) — He believes *in* a thing.
* Der Dichter *schreibt an* sie (*acc.*) — The poet writes *to* her.
* Der Professor *sitzt an* dem Schreibtisch (*dat.*) — The professor sits *at* his desk.
* *Am* Morgen (*dat.*) — *In* the morning
  Der Verkäufer steht *an* der Tür (*dat.*) — The salesman stands *at* the door.
  an sich — *in itself* (*dat.*)
  Der Professor unterrichtet *an* der Universität (*dat.*) — The professor teaches *at* the university.

auf — *on, upon, on top of, in, at, to*

Er stellt den Brief *auf den* Tisch (*acc.*) — He puts the letter *on* the table.
Der Brief liegt *auf dem* Tisch (*dat.*) — The letter is lying *on* the table.

Here are some idioms:

* *auf jeden* Fall (*acc.*) — *in* any case; *auf keinen* Fall (*acc.*) — *in* no case.
* warten *auf* (*acc.*) — to wait *for*. Sie *wartet auf den* Briefträger — She is *waiting for* the mailman.
  antworten *auf* (*acc.*) — to answer (no preposition in English).
  achten *auf* (*acc.*) — to pay attention *to*. Wir achten *auf die* folgenden Schwierigkeiten — We are paying attention *to* the following problems.
  hoffen *auf* (*acc.*) — to hope *for*
  auf Deutsch — *in German* (*acc.*)
  einen Eindruck machen *auf* (*acc.*) — to make an impression *on*
  Liebe *auf den* ersten Blick (*acc.*) — Love *at* first sight.

hinter — *behind*

Der Wolf läuft *hinter den* Busch (*acc.*) — The wolf goes *behind* the bush.
Der Wolf lauert *hinter dem* Busch (*dat.*) — The wolf lurks *behind* the bush.

in — *in, into*
im is a contraction for *in* plus *dem*; *ins* is *in* plus *das*

Ehrgeiz und Flöhe springen gern *in die* Höhe (*acc.*) — Ambition and fleas like to jump up *in*to the air.
Der Funke glimmt auch *in der* toten Asche (*dat.*) — The spark glimmers even *in* the dead ash.

Here are some idioms:

Der Agnostiker geht nicht sehr oft *in die Kirche* (*acc.*) — The agnostic does not go *to* church very often.
Man sieht den Agnostiker selten *in der Kirche* (*dat.*) — One seldom sees the agnostic *at* the church.
in den Ferien (*dat.*) — *during the holidays*

neben — *beside, near, next to*

Der Milchman stellt die Milch *neben die* (*acc.*) Tür — The milkman puts the milk *next to* the door.
Das Kind sitzt *neben dem* Vater (*dat.*) — The child sits *next to* the father.

über — *above, over, about, across*

Der Briefträger geht *über die* Straße (*acc.*) — The mailman goes *across* the street.
Die Sonne scheint *über den* Bergen (*dat.*) — The sun shines *over* the mountains.

Here are some idioms:

   Das Kind *lacht über den* Witz (*acc.*) — The child *laughs at* the joke.
*   *sprechen über* (*acc.*) — *to talk about*
   erstaunt sein *über* (*acc.*) — to be astonished *by*
   über 100 Elefanten — *more than* 100 elephants

unter — *under, beneath, among, below*

   Das Buch fällt *unter den* Tisch (*acc.*) — The book falls *under* the table.
   Unter dem Tisch liegt das Buch (*dat.*) — The book is lying *under* the table.
*   *Unter den* Blinden ist der Einäugige König (*dat.*) — *Among* the blind, the one-eyed person is king.
   Unter diesen Menschen hat der Philosoph nur einen Schüler (*dat.*) — *Among* these people, the philosopher has only one follower.

Here are some idioms:

Was verstehen Sie *unter diesem* Ausdruck (*dat.*)? — What do you understand *by* this expression?

unter vier Augen (*dat.*) — face-to-face. (Literally: under four eyes)

vor — *before, in front of, ago, with, of*

> Der Student geht ***vor die*** Kneipe (*acc.*) — The student goes *in front of* the pub.
>
> * Jetzt steht der Student ***vor der*** Kneipe (*dat.*) — Now the student stands *in front of* the pub.
>
> * ***Vor*** sechs Minuten stand der Student ***vor der*** Kneipe (*dat.*) — Six minutes *ago*, the student stood *in front of* the pub.

Vor used in conjunction with time will *always* mean "ago!"

Here are some idioms:

> * ***vor allem*** — above all. Fräulein Meier ist ***vor allem*** kein Dummkopf — Fräulein Meier is *above all* no dolt.
>
> * ***vor*** Freude (*dat.*) — *with* joy
>
> * Angst haben ***vor*** (*dat.*) — to be afraid *of*. Wer hat Angst ***vor*** Virginia Woolf? — Who is afraid *of* Virginia Woolf?
>
> ***vor*** Kälte zittern (*dat.*) — to shiver *with* cold.
>
> warnen ***vor*** (*dat.*) — to warn *about*

zwischen — *between*

Das Buch fällt ***zwischen den*** Tisch und ***den*** Stuhl (*acc.*) — The book falls *between* the table and the chair.
Der unglückliche Mann sitzt ***zwischen einem*** Felsen und ***einer*** harten Stelle (*dat.*) — The unlucky man sits *between* a rock and a hard place.

5.7. Translate these sentences, note the cases of all the nouns: (Hint: 95% of the time, **der** after a preposition will be feminine and dative.)

1. Zeit, Ebbe und Flut warten auf niemanden.
2. Ein alter Fuchs (*fox*) geht nie in die Falle.
3. Tugend (*virtue*) sitzt nicht an großer Herren Tische.
4. Neid (envy) gönnt (grants) dem Teufel nicht einmal die Hitze in der Hölle.
5. Vor vielen Jahren studierte (*studied*) der Briefträger die Philosophie Schopenhauers.
6. Des Menschen Leben hängt an einem Faden (*thread*).
7. Das Kräutlein (*little herb*) Geduld (*patience* — this is the name of the ***Kräutlein***) wächst nicht in allen Gärten.
8. Jammer (*sorrow*) steht vor der Tür, und Elend (*misery*) schlägt (*beats*) die Trommel (*drum*).

9. Schlafen bringt kein Geld ins Haus.
10. Zwischen Freude und Leid ist die Brücke nicht weit.
11. Im Wein ist die Wahrheit.
12. Der Briefträger trifft den Nagel (*nail*) auf den Kopf mit seinen (*his*) Beobachtungen (*observations*) über Fräulein Meier.
13. Alte Freunde, alter Wein und altes Geld haben Wert in aller Welt.
14. Fräulein Meier lebt *wie Gott in Frankreich*. (The English expression for this is: *leads the life of Riley* — i.e., leads a wonderful life. What does the German expression mean literally?)

Vocabulary

* **alle** — all, everyone
* **alt** — old
* **an** — on, at
* **auf** — on, on top of
  die **Beobachtung (-en)** — observation
  die **Brücke (-en)** — bridge
  die **Ebbe (-n)** — ebb
  einmal — once; **nicht einmal** — not even
  das **Elend (-s)** — misery
  der **Faden (-s, -̈)** — thread
  die **Falle (-n)** — trap
  die **Flut (-en)** — flow
* das **Frankreich (-s)** — France
* die **Freude (-n)** — joy
* der **Freund (-es, -e)** — friend
  der **Fuchs (-es, -̈e)** — fox
  der **Garten (-s, -̈)** — garden
  die **Geduld** — patience
* das **Geld (-es)** — money
* **groß** — large, great
  hängen — to hang
* der **Herr (-n, -en)** — lord, master
  hinter — behind
  die **Hitze** — heat
  die **Hölle** — hell
* **in** — in, into
  der **Jammer (-s)** — sorrow
* der **Kopf (-es, -̈e)** — head
* das **Leben (-s, -)** — life

  leben — to live
  das **Leid (-s, -en)** — sorrow
* der **Mensch (-en, -en)** — person
  der **Nagel (-s, -̈)** — nail
* **neben** — next to
* **nicht** — not
* **nie** — never
* **niemand** — no one
  das **Öl (-es, -e)** — oil
  der **Preis (-es, -e)** — price, praise, value
  das **Schlafen** — sleeping
  schlagen (schlägt) — to hit, to beat
* **sitzen (i)** — to sit
* **stehen (i)** — to stand
  der **Tisch (-es, -e)** — table
  treffen (trifft) — to hit
  die **Tugend (-en)** — virtue
  die **Tür (-en)** — door
* **über** — over, about
* **unter** — under, among
* **vor** — before, ago
  die **Wahrheit (-en)** — truth
* **warten auf** — to wait for
  weit — far
  der **Wein (-s, -e)** — wine
* die **Welt (-en)** — world
  der **Wert (-es, -e)** — value
* **zwischen** — between

5.8. Prepositions taking the genitive

These prepositions are used rarely. Here are the most common of them. Note that many of them include the English preposition *of* in their translation.

trotz — in spite of
Trotz des Einwandes seines Vaters besucht der Briefträger Fräulein Meier — *In spite of* the objection of his father, the mailman visits Fräulein Meier.

statt — instead of
Statt eines Hundes hat der Philosoph eine Katze — *Instead of* a dog, the philosopher has a cat.

während — during
Während des Tages denkt Fräulein Meier an den Briefträger — *During* the day, Fräulein Meier thinks about the mailman.

wegen — because of. (This is another preposition which occasionally follows the noun.)

    Wegen des schlechten Wetters bleibt Fräulein Meier zu Hause — *Because of* the bad weather, Fräulein Meier stays at home.
*   Des schlechten Wetters **wegen** bleibt der Briefträger auch zu Hause — *Because of* the bad weather, the mailman also stays at home.

Other prepositions taking the genitive which are encountered even more rarely, and which need not be memorized are: **außerhalb** (*outside of*), **innerhalb** (*inside of*), **diesseits** (*on this side of*), **jenseits** (*on that side of*), **oberhalb** (*above*), **unterhalb** (*below*).

**   **A final preposition consisting of two words is** *um . . . willen* **— for the sake of**
*   *Um* seiner Mutter *willen* geht er auf die Universität — *For* his mother's *sake*, he attends the university.
    Um ihrer Freundschaft *willen* bäckt Fräulein Meier oft für den Briefträger — *For the sake of* their friendship, Fräulein Meier often bakes for the mailman.

5.9. Translate these sentences:

1. Man leidet den Rauch des Feuers wegen.
2. Der Vater des Briefträgers wohnt außerhalb der Stadt.

3. Des schönen Wetters wegen ist Fräulein Meier bei guter Laune (*mood*).
4. Statt eines Briefes bekommt Fräulein Meier ein Geschenk von dem Briefträger.
5. Ein Fluch: um Gottes willen!
6. Trotz des Geschenkes des Briefträgers ist Fräulein Meier etwas traurig.
7. Während des Dramas *Warten auf Godot* lacht Fräulein Meier über die Rede Luckys.
8. Man küßt das Kind oft um der Mutter willen.

Vocabulary

* **anstatt** — instead of
außerhalb — outside of
* **bekommen** — to receive
das **Drama (-s, -men)** — drama
etwas (as an adverb) — somewhat
fast — almost
das **Feuer (-s, -)** — fire
der **Fluch (-es, ⸚e)** — curse
* **gern** — likes to, gladly
das **Geschenk (-s, -e)** — present
* **küssen** — to kiss
* **lachen** — to laugh
die **Laune (-n)** — mood
leiden — to suffer

* **man** — one
der **Rauch (-es)** — smoke
die **Rede (-n)** — speech
* **schön** — beautiful
die **Stadt (⸚e)** — city
* **statt** — instead of
* **traurig** — sad
* **trotz** — in spite of
* **um . . . willen** — for the sake of
* **vor** (with time) — ago
* **während** — during
* **wegen** — because of
das **Wetter (-s, -)** — weather
wohnen (i.) — to live

5.10. Vocabulary aid

1. Ein junger Student ißt jeden Morgen um seiner (*his*) Gesundheit willen zwei Äpfel.
2. Sein (*his*) ganzes Leben lang wohnte (*lived*) der Briefträger in Deutschland.
3. Alle Leute außer den amerikanischen Professoren halten den Autor für ein Genie (*genius*).
4. Die Liebe ist dem Briefträger vor allem sehr wichtig (*important*).
5. Der Student studiert jeden Nachmittag ohne Unterbrechung (*interruption*).
6. Vor vier Jahren blieb (*stayed*) Fräulein Meier oft allein zu Hause.
7. Niemand unter diesen Studenten versteht die Philosophie Heideggers.
8. Seit einem Jahr arbeitet Fräulein Meier halbtags (*part-time*).
9. Trotz seiner (*his*) unglücklichen Kindheit hat der Briefträger viel Hoffnung auf die Zukunft (*future*).

10. Fräulein Meier sitzt einem geilen (*lecherous*) Mann nie gegenüber.
11. Des schönen Wetters wegen spielt das Kind draußen (*outside*).
12. Fast jeden Abend um halb acht bekommt Fräulein Meier einen Brief mit Extrapost.

Reading Selection: *Fräulein Meier*

Fräulein Meier wohnt irgendwo in Deutschland, aber sie ist kein typisches deutsches Fräulein. Denn die Deutschen sind meistens fleißig, aber Fräulein Meier ist ein wenig faul. Sie bleibt mit ihrer (*her*) Katze zu Hause, und sie arbeitet halbtags (*part-time*) als Herausgeberin (*editor*) einer kleinen Zeitung für Unverheiratete (*singles*). Wegen ihres Berufes bekommt sie viele interessante Briefe, und der Briefträger besucht sie und spricht mit ihr (*her*) jeden Tag. Fräulein Meier und der Briefträger haben verschiedene (*different*) Weltanschauungen, und ihre (*their*) Gespräche sind deshalb sehr lebendig.

Fräulein Meier liest gern Sprichwörter, aber die Absichten dieser Sprichwörter sind diesem Fräulein unklar. Die Sprichwörter schildern den guten, glücklichen Menschen in folgender Weise: er arbeitet viel, er fürchtet Gott, und er mißtraut dem leichten Leben. Aber Fräulein Meier arbeitet wenig, sie tut, was sie will (*wants to*), und sie ist doch glücklich. Vielleicht hat sie einen besseren Begriff von der Wirklichkeit als (*than*) die Erzähler der Sprichwörter.

Vocabulary

* **aber** — but
  die **Absicht (-en)** — intention, point
* **bekommen** — to receive
* der **Begriff (-s, -e)** — grasp, understanding
  der **Beruf (-s, -e)** — occupation, job
  besuchen — to visit
* **bleiben** — to stay, remain
* **denn** — for, because
  deshalb — for that reason
* **doch** — nevertheless
  ein wenig — somewhat
  der **Erzähler (-s, -)** — teller, narrator

* **faul** — lazy
  fleißig — hard-working
  folgend — following
  fürchten — to fear
  das **Gespräch (-es, -e)** — conversation
  irgendwo — somewhere
  lebendig — lively
* **leicht** — easy
* **meistens** — mostly
  der **Mensch (-en, -en)** — person, human being
  mißtrauen (i) — to mistrust
  schildern — to portray
  das **Sprichwort (-es, ¨er)** — proverb

* **tun** — to do
* **verschieden** — different
* **vielleicht** — perhaps
* **wegen** — because of
  die **Weise (-n)** — way
* die **Weltanschauung (-en)** — worldview

* **wenig** — little
  die **Wirklichkeit** — reality
  wohnen — to live, reside
  die **Zeitung (-en)** — newspaper

Chapter Six

Basic Verb Placement (Part I)

In German, the conjugated verb is placed inflexibly in the sentence or clause in one of three places: (1) it can be the second element in the sentence; (2) it can begin the sentence, or (3) it can appear at the end of the clause.

6.1. The verb usually is the second element in the sentence, with the subject appearing either before or after it. Therefore, one can say either:

Ich sehe den Hund — I see the dog.

or

Den Hund sehe ich — The dog, I see. (This sentence is more emphatic, stressing that it is *the dog* that I see.) This inverted word order with the object appearing first is crucial to recognize, as it can change the entire meaning of the sentence. Obviously *Der Kakerlak* tötet Fräulein Meier — *The cockroach* kills Fräulein Meier — is very different from *Den Kakerlak* tötet Fräulein Meier — Fräulein Meier kills *the cockroach.*

In this respect, *recognition of correct case endings is particularly important*. Whenever you see a sentence beginning with *den* or *dem*, the subject will have to be on the "other side" of the verb. The subject will also have to be on the other side of the verb if the first noun is plural and the verb is singular (*Die Bücher liest* die Frau — The woman reads the books) or if the first noun is singular and the verb is plural (*Die Frau töten* die Wölfe — The wolves kill the woman). Also, whenever *man* (*one*) appears in a sentence it will *always* be the subject. Note that other pronouns can also be nominative, even though they are not capitalized:

Dem kranken Mann ist *nichts* angenehm — *Nothing* is agreeable to the sick man.
Der Frau ist *alles* interessant — *Everything* is interesting to the woman.

Whenever the sentence begins with an adverb or with a prepositional phrase, or even a string of prepositional phrases, the verb will *still* appear in "second" place and the subject will *always* appear *after* the verb.

Überall *sieht* man Kinder — One *sees* children everywhere.

Auf und ab *tanzt* das Glück wie ein Blatt — Fortune *dances* back and forth like a leaf.

Jetzt *ist* dieses Sprichwort klar — Now this proverb *is* clear.

Auf dem Fußpfad *wächst* kein Gras — No grass *grows* on the footpath.

Durch Gebet und Müh' *erhält* man Ochsen und Küh' — Through prayer and effort one *keeps* well oxen and cows.

Im kalten Ofen *bäckt* man kein Brot — In a cold oven one *bakes* no bread.

In der Mitte der schönen kleinen Stadt mit roten Blumen und großen Brunnen *schreibt* die Frau (*nominative*) eine Ansichtskarte — In the middle of the beautiful small city with red flowers and large fountains *the woman writes* a picture postcard.

6.2. The verb will also appear in second place in sentences containing interrogatives. The most common interrogatives are: *wer* (*who*), *wann* (*when*), *wo* (*where*), *warum* (*why*), *wie* (*how*), and *was* (*what*).

Wer is declined like the masculine definite article *der*. Here are examples:

Wer (*nominative*) ist der neue Student? — *Who* is the new student?

Wen (*accusative*) kennt der Briefträger? — *Whom* does the mailman know?

Wem (*dative*) schreibt der Student den Brief? — *To whom* does the student write the letter?

Wann kommt der Briefträger? — *When* is the mailman coming?

Wo ist er jetzt? — *Where* is he now?

Warum spricht der Tierarzt mit Fräulein Meier? — *Why* is the veterinarian speaking with Fräulein Meier?

Wie alt ist die Schildkröte? — *How* old is the tortoise?

Was schreibt der Student? — *What* is the student writing?

6.3. Translate these sentences:

1. Dem Arbeiter hilft Gott.
2. Arme Leute kennt niemand (*no one*).
3. Wohltaten (*good deeds*) schreibt man nicht in den Kalender.
4. Die Gebete (*prayers*) der Bettler (*beggars*) verjagt (*chases*) der Wind.
5. Ein vorwitziges (*impertinent*) Schäflein frißt (*eats*) der Wolf.
6. Der Tugend (*virtue*) ist kein Ziel (*goal*) zu hoch. (Note: **Tugend** is feminine.)
7. Dem Angeklagten (*accused*) gehört der letzte Satz.
8. Gift findet man nicht in der Küche armer Leute.
9. Den Schuldigen (*guilty one*) erschreckt eine Maus.
10. Einen fröhlichen Geber hat Gott gern.

11. Einem faulen Bauer (*farmer*) ist kein Pflug (*plow*) gut genug.
12. Der Wolle wegen schert (*shears*) man die Schafe.
13. Auf der Erde ist nichts ohne Furcht.
14. Wen kennt die alte Frau?
15. Wer spricht alle Sprachen und behält (*retains*) immer das letzte Wort? Ein Echo.
16. Warum sind die Fußspuren (*footprints*) vom Elefanten rund? Damit (*so that*) seine (*his*) Füße hineinpassen.
17. Wie heißt das Weib von Herkules? Antwort: Fraukules!

Vocabulary

* **all** — all
  der **Angeklagte** (-n, -n) — accused
  die **Antwort** (-en) — answer
* **arm** — poor
* der **Arbeiter** (-s, -) — worker
  der **Bauer** (-s, -n) — farmer
  der **Bettler** (-s, -) — beggar
  damit — so that
  der **Elefant** (-en, -en) — elephant
  die **Erde** (-n) — earth
* **erschrecken** — to frighten
* **faul** — lazy
  fröhlich — joyous
  der **Fuß** (-es, ̈e) — foot
  die **Fußspur** (-en) — footprint
  die **Furcht** — fear
  der **Geber** (-s, -) — giver
  das **Gebet** (-es, -e) — prayer
* **gehören** (i) — to belong to
  genug — enough
* **gern haben** — to like
  das **Gift** (-es, -e) — poison
* **glauben** (i) — to believe
  heißen (i) — to be called
  hineinpassen — to fit in
* **hoch** — high
* **immer** — always
  der **Kalender** (-s, -) — calender
* **kennen** — to know
  die **Küche** (-n) — kitchen

* **letzt** — last
* die **Leute** (pl.) — people
* **man** — one
  die **Maus** (̈e) — mouse
* **nichts** — nothing
* **niemand** — no one
* **ohne** — without
  rund — round
* der **Satz** (-es, ̈e) — sentence
  das **Schaf** (-es, -e) — sheep
  das **Schäflein** (-s, -) — little sheep, lamb
  der **Schuldige** (-n, -n) — guilty one
* **schreiben** — to write
  die **Sprache** (-n) — language
* **sprechen** — to speak
  die **Tugend** (-en) — virtue
  verjagen — to chase
* **wann** — when
* **warum** — why
* **was** — what
* **wegen** — because of
  das **Weib** (-es, -er) — wife
* **wer, wen, wem** — who, whom
* **wie** — how
* **wo** — where, what
  die **Wolle** — wool
  das **Ziel** (-s, -e) — goal
* **zu** — too

6.4. Occasionally, the sentence can begin with the verb. At this point in your reading, a sentence beginning with a verb will be either a question or a command.

I. Questions

For simple questions (which do not begin with an interrogative), the verb will begin the sentence, and the subject will follow it. Examples are:

Kennt der Professor seine Studenten? — *Does* the professor *know* his students?
Ist der Tierhüter beim Zoo? — *Is* the zookeeper at the zoo?
Kommt heute der Briefträger? — *Is* the mailman *coming* today?

II. Commands (the imperative)

Although you will not encounter the imperative too often in scholarly German (unless you tend to read Nietzsche, the *Bible*, or German literature in general), you should at least be familiar with it. The familiar singular imperative is the same as the stem of the verb; verb stems ending in *-d* or *-t* and some other consonants add *-e*. Here are examples in comparison with the interrogative:

Gehst du oft? — *Do* you often *go*?
Geh oft! — *Go* often!
Siehst du den Seiltänzer? — *Do* you *see* the tightrope walker?
Sieh den Seiltänzer! — *Watch* the tightrope walker!
Beantwortest du die Frage? — *Are* you *answering* the question?
Beantworte die Frage! — *Answer* the question!

The imperative form of *sein* (*to be*) is *sei*:

Sei vorsichtig! — *Be* careful!
Sei glücklich! — *Be* happy!

The familiar plural imperative is generally the same as the familiar plural indicative. Here are examples in comparison with the interrogative:

Seht ihr den hellen Stern? — *Do* you *see* the bright star?
Seht den hellen Stern! — *Look at* the bright star!
Seid ihr nicht ungeduldig? — *Are* you not being impatient?
Seid nicht ungeduldig! — *Do* not be impatient!

In both the informal forms (*du* and *ihr*), the pronouns are omitted for the imperative form.

For the formal (*Sie*) imperative, the *Sie* form will be used, and the verb will be in the same form as the infinitive. This form will be identical to the interrogative. However, the interrogative will always be punctuated by a question mark, and the imperative will often be punctuated by an exclamation point. Here are examples:

Gehen Sie heute? — *Are* you *going* today?
Gehen Sie heute! — *Go* today!
Sprechen Sie oft mit Ihrer Mutter? — *Do* you often *talk* to your mother?
Sprechen Sie oft mit Ihrer Mutter! — *Talk* to your mother often!

The imperative formal of *sein* is *seien Sie*! Here are examples:

Seien Sie vorsichtig! — Be careful! (*command*)
Seien Sie nicht ungerecht! — Do not be unfair! (*command*)
Compare: *Sind Sie* nicht ungerecht? — Aren't you being unfair? (*question*)

6.5. Translate these sentences:

1. Frevle (*violate*) nicht an Gottes Wort, es bringt Strafe (*punishment*) hier und dort.
2. Sei eine Schnecke (*snail*) im Raten (*advice*), ein Vogel in Taten!
3. Fürchte Gott, tue recht, scheue niemanden!
4. Nimm deine (*your*) Sorgen (*worries, cares*) nicht mit (*with you*) in das Bad (*bath*)!
5. Pfau (*peacock*), schau auf deine (*your*) Beine!
6. Scherze nur mit deinesgleichen (*people like you*)!
7. Sei nicht aller Welt Freund!
8. Ein Trinklied:
   Trink, trink, Brüderlein trink,
   Laß doch die Sorgen (*worries*) zu Haus,
   Trink, trink, Brüderlein trink,
   Laß doch die Sorgen zu Haus!
   Meide (*avoid*) den Kummer (*sorrow*) und meide den Schmerz (*pain*),
   Dann ist das Leben ein Scherz (*joke*)!
   Meide den Kummer und meide den Schmerz,
   Dann ist das Leben ein Scherz.
9. Einige Fragen:
   Glauben Sie an Liebe auf den ersten Blick?
   Wird der Irrtum eines Augenblickes zur Sorge (*worry*) eines Lebens? (In this context, *Leben* means *lifetime*.)
   Ist ein Lehrer (*teacher*) ohne Leben wie eine Wolke (*cloud*) ohne Regen? (In this context, *Leben* means *animation*.)
   Läßt Fräulein Meier oft die Katze aus dem Sack?
   Hat der Briefträger ein Herz aus Gold?
   Ist der alte Professor blind wie ein Maulwurf (*mole*)?

Vocabulary

der **Augenblick** (-s, -e) — moment
das **Bad** (-es, ¨er) — bath
das **Bein** (-es, -e) — leg
der **Blick** (-es, -e) — glance
das **Brüderlein** (-s, -) — little
brother
* **dann** — then
* **doch** — still, just
* **dort** — there
* **einige** — some
* **erst** — first
* die **Frage** (-n) — question
freveln (an) — to violate
* **fürchten** — to fear
* **glauben** — to believe
* das **Herz** (-ens, -en) — heart
der **Irrtum** (-s, ¨er) — error
der **Kummer** (-s) — grief,
sorrow
* **lassen (läßt)** — to let, leave
* das **Leben** (-s, -) — life
* der **Lehrer** (-s, -) — teacher
* die **Liebe** (-n) — love

meiden — to avoid
* **nehmen (nimmt)** — to take
* **niemand** — no one
* **nur** — only, just
das **Raten** (-s) — advice
recht — right
der **Regen** (-s, -) — rain
der **Sack** (-es, ¨e) — sack, bag
schauen (auf) (i) — to look at
scherzen (i) — to joke
scheuen — to avoid
der **Schmerz** (-es, -en) — pain
die **Sorge** (-n) — care
die **Strafe** (-n) — punishment
die **Tat** (-en) — deed
das **Trinklied** (-es, -er) — drinking
song
* **tun** — to do
* die **Welt** (-en) — world
* **werden** (i) — to become
* **wie** — like
die **Wolke** (-n) — cloud
zu Hause — at home

6.6. In dependent clauses, the verb will appear at the end of the clause.
Here are examples:

Kehre erst vor deiner Tür, *ehe* du über andere *redest* — First sweep in front of
your door *before* you *talk* about others.
Herren bleiben Herren, *auch wenn* sie bis zum Mittag *schlafen* — Masters are
masters, *even if* they *sleep* until noon.
Jedes Gleichnis hinkt, *sobald* es über einen gewissen Grad *hinausgeht* — Every
comparison limps *as soon as* it *goes beyond* a certain point.

When the sentence begins with a dependent clause, the main clause usually will
begin with a verb as the second element in the sentence. Here are examples:
Was in einer Wurst *ist, weiß* nur Gott und der Schlächter — What *is* in a
sausage, only God and the butcher *know*.
Wer Geld *hat, hat* auch Freunde — He who *has* money also *has* friends.

Dependent clauses will always be separated from main clauses by commas.

Although you should begin to recognize this construction, I will explain it to you in more detail in Chapters Twenty-two - Twenty-four. Therefore I have given you no practice sentences for this section.

6.7. Vocabulary aid: memorize the words in the following sentences:

1. Um der vollen Wahrheit willen läßt Fräulein Meier die Katze aus dem Sack.
2. Ist die Liebe immer schön?
3. Den Historiker erschreckt das Böse.
4. Der Studentin ist die Wahrheit sehr wichtig.
5. Diesen Irrtum macht man oft.
6. Glauben Sie an die Wahrheit dieses Sprichwortes?
7. Die Studenten kennt der Professor.
8. Wer singt gern das Trinklied?
9. Was ist die erste Tat eines fröhlichen Gebers?
10. Nur der faule Arbeiter glaubt an Wunder (*miracles*).
11. Warum liest der Briefträger keine Ansichtskarten (*picture postcards*)?
12. Wen fürchtet der Student?
13. Wem gehört das neue Auto?
14. Dort kennt niemand den alten Professor.

Reading Selection: *Meeresstrand* **(Theodor Storm)**

Ans Haff (*lagoon*) nun fliegt die Möwe (*seagull*),
Und Dämmrung *bricht hinein* (*arrives*);
Über die feuchten Watten (*shoals*)
Spiegelt der Abendschein (*evening glow*).

Graues Geflügel (*fowl*) huschet (*scurries*)
Neben dem Wasser her;
Wie Träume liegen die Inseln
Im Nebel (*fog*) auf dem Meer.

Ich höre des gärenden (*swirling*) Schlammes (*sand*)
Geheimnisvollen (*secret*) Ton,
Einsames Vogelrufen —
So war es immer schon. (*It was always like that*)

Noch einmal schaudert (*shudders*) leise
Und schweiget dann der Wind;
Vernehmlich (*clear*) werden die Stimmen,
Die (*which*) über der Tiefe sind.

Vocabulary

dann — then

die **Dämmerung** (-en) — twilight

einsam — lonely

feucht — wet, damp

fliegen (i) — to fly

grau — grey

her — hither

die **Insel** (-n) — island

leise — quietly

der **Meeresstrand** (-es, ⸚e) — seashore

noch einmal — once again

schweigen (i) — to be silent

spiegeln — to reflect, to mirror

die **Stimme** (-n) — voice

die **Tiefe** (-n) — depth

der **Ton** (-es, ⸚e) — tone

der **Traum** (-es, ⸚e) — dream

das **Vogelrufen** (-s, -rufe) — bird call

Chapter Seven

The Pronouns

7.1. German pronouns are declined in a way similar to articles. Here are the forms:

nominative	accusative	dative
ich (*I*)	mich (*me*)	mir (*me, to me*)
du (*you*)	dich (*you*)	dir (*you, to you*)
er (*he*)	ihn (*him*)	ihm (*him, to him*)
es (*it*)	es (*it*)	ihm (*it, to it*)
sie (*she*)	sie (*her*)	ihr (*her, to her*)
wir (*we*)	uns (*us*)	uns (*us, to us*)
ihr (*you*)	euch (*you*)	euch (*you, to you*)
sie (*they*)	sie (*them*)	ihnen (*them, to them*)
Sie (*you*)	Sie (*you*)	Ihnen (*you, to you*)

At this point, it is very important for you to learn the declensions of *er* (*he*), *es* (*it*), and *sie* (*she* and *they*) because they are also the pronouns for masculine, neuter, feminine and plural nouns.

7.2. Notice the similarity between the declensions of these four pronouns and the definite articles. In each case, the pronoun either rhymes with the definite article, or it has the same last letter. Compare:

	masculine	neuter	feminine	plural
nominative	der	das	die	die
	er	es	sie	sie
accusative	den	das	die	die
	ihn	es	sie	sie
dative	dem	dem	der	den
	ihm	ihm	ihr	ihnen

7.3.   Here are sentences including these four pronouns in nominative, accusative and dative cases: Note that when an inanimate masculine or feminine noun is used, it is still replaced with a masculine or feminine pronoun in German, even though it is translated into English as *it*.

Nominative

Der Kuchen riecht gut — The cake smells good.
Er riecht gut — It smells good.

Das Brot schmeckt gut — The bread tastes good.
Es schmeckt gut — It tastes good.

Die Lampe ist hell — The lamp is bright.
Sie ist hell — It is bright.

Die Handschuhe sind warm — The gloves are warm.
Sie sind warm — They are warm.

Accusative

Der Mann ißt *den* Apfel — The man eats the apple.
Der Mann ißt *ihn* — The man eats it.

Das Kind ißt *das* Brot — The child eats the bread.
Das Kind ißt *es* — The child eats it.

Die Frau singt *die* Melodie — The woman sings the melody.
Die Frau singt *sie* — The woman sings it.

Die Kinder tragen *die* Handschuhe — The children wear the gloves.
Die Kinder tragen *sie* — The children wear them.

Dative

Der Mann schreibt *dem* Arzt — The man writes the doctor.
Der Mann schreibt *ihm* — The man writes him.

Die Mutter hilft *dem* Kind — The mother helps the child.
Die Mutter hilft *ihm* — The mother helps him.

Die Mutter traut *der* Tochter — The mother trusts the daughter.
Die Mutter traut *ihr* — The mother trusts her.

Der Professor glaubt *den* Studen*ten* — The professor believes the students.
Der Professor glaubt *ihnen* — The professor believes them.

7.4. Replace all the nouns in the following sentences with pronouns:

1. Der Briefträger findet das Stinktier.
2. Die Frau geht ohne den Mann.
3. Das Kind ist glücklich mit der Katze.
4. Der Professor sieht die Frau mit den Studenten.
5. Außer den Katzen sehen die Tiere die Mäuse nicht.
6. Die Frau sitzt dem Fußballspieler nicht gegenüber.
7. Der Pfadfinder (*Boy Scout*) hilft der alten Dame.
8. Das Mädchen trinkt die Milch.

7.5. Here are the masculine, neuter, feminine and plural pronouns and their possibilities. Note which pronouns are identical.

er	**only** masculine nominative (*he*)
es	neuter nominative (*it*) and accusative (*it*)
sie	feminine and plural nominative (*she, they*) and feminine and plural accusative (*her, them*)
ihn	**only** masculine accusative (*him*)
ihm	masculine dative (*him*) and neuter dative (*it*)
ihr	feminine dative (*her*); also informal you plural nominative
ihnen	**only** plural dative

7.6. Translate the following sentences (vocabulary is on pp. 71-72):

1. Wenn Fräulein Meier den Briefträger mit einer anderen Dame sieht, wird sie böse auf ihm.
2. Er hilft ihnen oft.
3. Wann sprechen sie mit ihr?
4. Ihn kennt sie.
5. Es ist ihm nicht klar.
6. Die Äpfel schmecken gut; er ißt sie gern.
7. Ihm helfen sie.
8. Wenn der Briefträger eine Studentin sieht, sagt er ihr: "Guten Tag."
9. Wo ist der Kugelschreiber (*pen*)? Ich sehe ihn nicht.

7.7. The pronouns *du, ihr,* and *sie*

The informal pronouns *du* (*singular*) and *ihr* (*plural*) are seldom encountered in most reading material; therefore you do not need to pay too much attention to them. However, do not confuse *ihr* (*informal you plural*) with *ihr* (*feminine dative*). Compare:

Ihr helft den Kindern oft — *You* often help the children; and
Der Mann hilft *ihr* — The man helps *her*.

Also note that *Sie* (formal you) and *sie* (third person plural) are declined in the same way. However, *Sie* (the formal you) will **always** be capitalized. Compare:

Nominative: Wann gehen *Sie* — When are *you* going?
Wann gehen *sie* — When are *they* going?

Accusative: Wer kennt *Sie* — Who knows *you*?
Wer kennt *sie* — Who knows *them*?

Dative: Wer hilft *Ihnen* — Who is helping *you*?
Wer hilft *ihnen* — Who is helping *them*?

When the sentence begins with *Sie* and the verb is plural, the pronoun will be translated either *you* or *they* depending on context.

7.8. The possessive adjectives

Possessive adjectives in English are the words *my*, *your*, *his*, *her*, *its*, *our*, and *their* placed **directly in front of a noun**:

My friend is brilliant.
His cat is obnoxious.
Her mother is a friend of **their father**.

They are **not** to be confused with **pronouns**, which aren't attached to nouns, even though *her* sometimes appears as a possessive adjective and sometimes as a "simple" pronoun:

He sees **her** often. **Her** in this context is **not** a possessive adjective, it is **only** a pronoun.

This difference is crucial, because possessive adjectives have **two** equally important functions whenever they are used.

1) Like **der** and **ein** words, they are adjectives, which must indicate the gender and case of the noun: Er sieht seinen <u>Freund</u> oft (*Freund* is masculine, accusative)
2) Like possessive adjectives in English, they indicate possession: <u>Er</u> sieht seinen Freund oft (*sein* indicates that the friend is related to <u>er</u>).

Here are all the possessive adjectives in the masculine nominative case:

mein	(*my*)	unser	(*our*)
dein	(*your*)	euer	(*your*)
sein	(*his, its*)	ihr	(*their*)
ihr	(*her*)		

Ihr (*your — formal*)

These possessive adjectives will have exactly the same adjective endings as *ein* words. Here is the complete declension of *mein* in comparison with *ein*:

	masculine	**neuter**	**feminine**	**plural**
nominative	ein Mann	ein Kind	eine Frau	—
	mein Mann	mein Kind	meine Frau	meine Kinder
accusative	einen Mann	ein Kind	eine Frau	—
	meinen Mann	mein Kind	meine Frau	meine Kinder
genitive	eines Mannes	eines Kindes	einer Frau	—
	meines Mannes	meines Kindes	meiner Frau	meiner Kinder
dative	einem Mann	einem Kind	einer Frau	—
	meinem Mann	meinem Kind	meiner Frau	meinen Kindern

7.9. As with all other adjectives, the ending of a possessive adjective is determined by the noun that immediately follows it:

Sein Kind (*neut. nom.*) ist hier — *His child* is here.
Der Mann liebt *seinen Sohn* (*mas. acc.*) — The man loves *his son*.
Der Hund *seiner Mutter* (*fem. gen.*) ist alt — The dog *of his mother* is old.
Er schreibt *seinen Freunden* (*pl. dat.*) oft — He writes *his friends* often.

The form of the possessive adjective (whether it is *my, your, his, its, her, our, your,* or *their*) is determined by the noun to which it refers. Here are examples:

Ich liebe *meine* Katze — *I* love *my* cat. (meine indicates that *Katze* is feminine accusative.)
Liebst *du deinen* Hund? — Do *you* love *your* dog? (deinen indicates that *Hund* is masculine accusative.)
Er hilft *seiner* Mutter — *He* helps *his* mother. (seiner indicates that *Mutter* is feminine dative.)
Sie liebt *ihre* Tochter — *She* loves *her* daughter. (ihre indicates that *Tochter* is feminine accusative.)

Es hat *seine* Schwierigkeiten — *It* has *its* problems (seine indicates that *Schwierigkeiten* is plural accusative.)

Wir glauben *unseren* Freunden — *We* believe *our* friends. (unseren indicates that *Freunden* is plural dative.)

Seht *ihr euer* Kind? — Do *you* see *your* child? (euer with no ending indicates that *Kind* is neuter accusative.)

Kennen *sie ihren* Briefträger? — Do *they* know *their* mailman? (ihren indicates that *Briefträger* is masculine accusative.)

Kennen *Sie Ihre* Nachbarin? — Do *you* know *your* neighbor? (Ihre indicates *Nachbarin* is feminine accusative.)

7.10. It is particularly important to memorize the possessive adjectives for his and its (*sein*) and for her and their (*ihr*), because these are the adjectives most often encountered. Note that these possessive adjectives also will be used for inanimate nouns, depending on whether the nouns are masculine, neuter, feminine, or plural. Here are examples:

Jeder Tag (*masculine*) hat *seinen* Abend — Every day has *its* evening.

Jedes Dach (*neuter*) hat *sein* Ungemach — Every roof (or household) has *its* adversity.

Die Schule (*feminine*) hat *ihre* Regeln — The school has *its* rules.

Die Länder (*plural*) haben *ihre* eigenen Sitten — The countries have *their* own customs.

Note that *sein* (*his, its*) as a possessive adjective has nothing to do with the verb *sein* (*to be*).

7.11. Translate these sentences:

1. Folget meinen Worten, nicht meinen Taten!
2. Die Freundschaft hat ihre Grenzen (*limits*).
3. Lerne Ordnung, übe (*practice*) sie; Ordnung spart dir Zeit und Müh' (*effort*)!
4. Wie (*as*) du mir, so ich dir!
5. Ein weiser Sohn macht seinem Vater Freude, ein törichter (*foolish one*) macht seiner Mutter Kummer (*trouble*). (Proverbs)
6. Jede Flut (*flow*) hat ihre Ebbe.
7. Der Horcher (*listener*) an der Wand hört seine eigne (*own*) Schand'.
8. Wenn der Briefträger Fräulein Meier sieht, fragt er sie nach ihrem Kurs im Korbflechten (*basket-weaving*).
9. Die Reue (*repentance*) ist ein hinkender (*limping*) Bote (*messenger*); sie kommt langsam, aber sicher (*certainly*).

10. Jedes Haar hat seinen Schatten (*shadow*), und jede Ameise (*ant*) hat ihren Zorn (*wrath*). (Even the smallest object is of some consequence.)
11. Faulheit geht so langsam, daß Armut (*poverty*) sie einholt (*catches up with*).
12. Der Briefträger ist der erstgeborene Sohn seiner Eltern (*parents*).
13. Die Schule, wie (*as*) sie ist, verblödet (*dulls*) die Kinder, da (*since*) sie ihre geistigen Fähigkeiten (*capabilities*) verzerrt (*distorts*).
14. Manchmal trägt Fräulein Meier einen purpurroten (*purple*) Mantel, aber er gefällt dem Briefträger gar nicht.
15. Wahrlich, ich sage euch . . .
16. Liebe ist wie Tau (dew), sie fällt auf Rosen und auf Nesseln (nettles).
17. Jede Wolke hat ihren Silberstreifen (silver lining).
18. Arme Gäste sendet uns Gott.
19. Dein Hirtenstab (*shepherd's crook*) und Stock (*staff*), sie sind mein Trost (*comfort*).
    Du deckst für mich einen Tisch angesichts (*in the face of*) meiner Gegner. (Note: is **Gegner** singular or plural?)
    Du salbst (*anoint*) mein Haupt mit Öl.
    Mein Becher (*cup*) ist übervoll. (Aus dem 23. Psalm)

Vocabulary

* **all** — all, every
die **Ameise (-n)** — ant
* **ander** — other
die **Armut** — poverty
* **außer** — except for
der **Becher (-s, -)** — cup
* **böse** — angry, evil
der **Bote (-n, -n)** — messenger
* **da** — since
* **daß** — that
decken — to set, cover
* **dein** — your
die **Ebbe (-n)** — ebb
eigen — own
einholen — to catch up with
die **Eltern (pl.)** — parents
* **essen (ißt)** — to eat
* **euer** — your (informal)
die **Fähigkeit (-en)** — ability

die **Faulheit** — laziness
* **folgen** (i) — to follow
die **Flut (-en)** — flood
* **fragen nach** — to ask about
* die **Freude (-n)** — joy
die **Freundschaft (-en)** — friendship
gar nicht — not at all
der **Gast (-es, ̈e)** — guest
* **gefallen** (i) — to please
der **Gegner (-s, -)** — opponent
geistig — spiritual, intellectual
die **Grenze (-n)** — limit
das **Haar (-s, -e)** — hair
das **Haupt (-s, ̈er)** — head
der **Hirtenstab (-es, ̈e)** — shepherd's crook
der **Horcher (-s, -)** — listener
* **hören** — to hear

* **ihr** — her, their
* **Ihr** — your
* **kennen** — to know
  der **Kummer** — trouble
  der **Kurs** (**-es, -e**) — course
  langsam — slow, slowly
* **lernen** — to learn
* die **Liebe** — love
* **machen** — to make, to do
* **manchmal** — sometimes
  der **Mantel** (**-s, ¨**) — coat
* **mein** — my
  die **Mühe** (**-n**) — effort, trouble
* **nicht** — not
  das **Öl** (**-s, -e**) — oil
  die **Ordnung** (**-en**) — order
  die **Reue** — repentance
  die **Schande** — disgrace
  der **Schatten** (**-s, -**) — shadow
* **schmecken** (**i**) — to taste

  die **Schule** (**-n**) — school
* **sehen** (**sieht**) — to see
* **sein** — his, its
* **sicher** — certain
  sparen — to save
  die **Tat** (**-en**) — deed
  das **Tier** (**-s, -e**) — animal
  der **Tisch** (**-es, -e**) — table
* **tragen** — to wear, carry
  übervoll — overflowing
* **unser** — our
  wahrlich — verily
  die **Wand** (**¨e**) — wall
* **weise** — wise
* **wenn** — if, when
* **wie** — like
  die **Wolke** (**-n**) — cloud
* die **Zeit** (**-en**) — time
  der **Zorn** (**-s**) — wrath

7.12. Vocabulary aid: use these sentences to help you memorize the pronouns.

1. Sie macht ihn glücklich.
2. Es ist ihr eine Freude.
3. Es gefällt ihnen nicht.
4. Vorsicht (*caution, cf. foresight*) spart dir Zeit.
5. Wo sind sie?
6. Sie erzählt ihrem Freund die Geschichte.
7. Die Faulheit des Kindes ist seinem Vater unerklärlich (*inexplicable*), und er versteht (*understands*) sie gar nicht.
8. Das Kind trägt immer seinen blauen Mantel, denn er gefällt ihm.
9. Ihn kennt sie nicht.
10. Ihr helfen sie oft.
11. Ist das Ihnen klar?
12. Sie kauft ihm ein interessantes Buch.
13. Meinen Freund sieht sie oft.
14. Kennt er uns nicht?
15. Wo findet ihr die Antwort?
16. Unsere Freundschaft ist mir sehr wichtig.
17. Ihm glauben sie.
18. Ihre Antwort versteht er nicht. (There are three correct translations for *Ihre Antwort*)

Chapter Eight

Weak Nouns and Adjectives Used as Nouns

8.1. Weak nouns

There are some masculine and a very few neuter nouns which are called "weak nouns." These nouns will require an *-en* or *-n* ending to every case but the nominative singular. Some of these nouns will end in *-e* — such as der Junge (*boy*), der Kollege (*colleague*), der Soziologe (*sociologist*). Other common masculine weak nouns are: Der Mensch, der Student, der Herr (*man, lord*), and der Philosoph. Here are four sentences indicating how the noun *Student* appears in all four cases:

Nominative: *Der Student* kennt die Werke Spinozas — *The student* knows the works of Spinoza.

Accusative: Die Eltern sehen *den Studenten* selten — The parents see *the student* seldom.

Genitive: Der Freund *des Studenten* kennt die Werke Nietzsches — The friend *of the student* knows the works of Nietzsche.

Dative: Seine Kurse sind *dem Studenten* wichtig — His courses are important *to the student*.

Most weak nouns — *der Mensch* (*person*), *der Theologe* (*theologian*), *der Bär* (*bear*), *der Löwe* (*lion*) — are animate. However, there are also a few inanimate weak nouns — *der Name, der Gedanke* (*thought*), *der Friede* (*peace*), *das Herz* (*heart*) — which are declined like animate weak nouns, except that they add *-ens* rather than *-en* to the genitive singular. Here is an example:

Nominative: *Der Gedanke* des Philosophen ist interessant — *The thought* of the philosopher is interesting.

Accusative: Auch der dumme Student begreift *den Gedanken* — Even the dumb student grasps *the thought*.

Genitive: Der Kern *des Gedankens* gefällt dem Studenten — The essence *of the thought* pleases the student.

Dative: Man hört sehr viel von *dem Gedanken* des Professors — One hears very much about *the thought* of the professor.

8.2. Weak nouns always have *-en* plural endings. Consequently, whether such a noun is singular or plural can be determined **only** by the preceding article. Compare the following:

	der Mensch	*der Junge*	*der Name*	*das Herz*
nominative				
singular	*der* Mensch	*der* Junge	*der* Name	*das* Herz
plural	*die* Menschen	*die* Jungen	*die* Namen	*die* Herzen
accusative				
* singular	*den* Menschen	*den* Jungen	*den* Namen	*das* Herz
plural	*die* Menschen	*die* Jungen	*die* Namen	*die* Herzen
genitive				
singular	*des* Menschen	*des* Jungen	*des* Namens	*des* Herzens
plural	*der* Menschen	*der* Jungen	*der* Namen	*der* Herzen
dative				
singular	*dem* Menschen	*dem* Jungen	*dem* Namen	*dem* Herzen
* plural	*den* Menschen	*den* Jungen	*den* Namen	*den* Herzen

* Note that the forms of the dative plural and masculine accusative singular are identical; therefore, only your knowledge of cases will tell you if a masculine weak noun is singular or plural. Compare: Er sitzt *zwischen den* Propheten (*plural dative*) — He sits between the *prophets*; Er *wartet auf den* Propheten (*masculine accusative*) — He waits for the *prophet*.

8.3. Translate these sentences (vocabulary is on pp. 76-77):

1. Das Auge ist des Herzens Zeiger (*indicator*).
2. Man erkennt den Löwen an den Klauen (*claws*).
3. Das Unglück spricht gewaltig (*powerfully*) zu dem Herzen.
4. Feuer im Herzen bringt Rauch in den Kopf.
5. Der Wunsch ist oft der Vater des Gedankens.
6. Des Menschen Wille ist sein Himmelreich (*kingdom of heaven*).

7. Wenn der Berg nicht zum Propheten kommt, so kommt er zu ihm.
8. Manchmal spricht der Professor mit den Studenten.
9. Oft hat der Briefträger einen Brief für den englischen Studenten.

8.4. Adjectives used as nouns

German adjectives often can be used as nouns. For example, *faul* (*lazy*) can be changed into *der Faule* (*the lazy one*); *glücklich* (*happy*) can be changed into *der Glückliche* (*the happy one*); and *gelehrt* (*learned*) can be changed into *der Gelehrte* (*the learned one, or the scholar*). These adjectives are capitalized and function as nouns; however, they still retain adjective endings according to whether they modify an understood masculine or feminine noun, or whether they are plural. Compare:

	masculine	feminine	plural
nominative			
adjective	der *gute* Mann	die *gute* Frau	die *guten* Leute
adjectival noun	der *Gute*	die *Gute*	die *Guten*
accusative			
adjective	den *guten* Mann	die *gute* Frau	die *guten* Leute
adjectival noun	den *Guten*	die *Gute*	die *Guten*
genitive			
adjective	des *guten* Mannes	der *guten* Frau	der *guten* Leute
adjectival noun	des *Guten*	der *Guten*	der *Guten*
dative			
adjective	dem *guten* Mann	der *guten* Frau	den *guten* Leuten
adjectival noun	dem *Guten*	der *Guten*	den *Guten*

Because the adjectival noun *der Guten* can be either feminine genitive, plural genitive, or feminine dative, you will be able to tell the case only by context. However, when it is genitive, *der Guten* will usually be plural rather than feminine.

Whenever a masculine adjectival noun is preceded by *ein* (which will happen only in the nominative case), its ending will be *-er*: ein Deutsch**er**; ein Gut**er**; ein Glücklich**er**.

When translating these nouns, be sure to specify the gender of the person or persons modified: *der* Gute — the good *man* or the good *one*; *die* Gute — the good *woman*; *die* Guten — the good or the good *ones*.

8.5. Adjectives also can be turned into neuter nouns, which are generally abstract: *das Schöne* — the beautiful; *das Gute* — the good; *das Wahre* — the true; *das Gewöhnliche* — the usual.

8.6. Translate the following sentences, stating the gender and case of each of the adjectival nouns:

1. Die Deutsche hat eine dicke Katze.
2. Ein Geliebter ist oft glücklich.
3. Das Wahre ist dem Briefträger sehr wichtig.
4. Die Fehler des Weisen sind erstaunlich.
5. Der Unglückliche beneidet die Glücklichen.
6. Das Neue ist für aktuelle Leute immer interessant.
7. Dem Kranken ist nichts angenehm.
8. Kennen Sie die Klugen?

8.7. Translate these sentences as well:

1. Dem Kühnen gehört die Welt.
2. Im Hause eines Faulen ist es immer Feiertag (*holiday*).
3. Des Narren Unfall ist des Weisen Warnung.
4. Kleine Feinde und kleine Wunden verachtet kein Weiser.
5. Abends wird der Faule fleißig.
6. Die Gesunden und die Kranken haben verschiedene Gedanken.
7. Des Faulen Werktag ist morgen; sein Ruhetag ist heute.
8. Neue Heilige werfen die alten ins Gerümpel (*junk pile*).
9. Dem Reinen ist alles rein.
10. Den Alten gegenüber sitzt Fräulein Meier.
11. Wer kennt den Alten?
12. Hoffnung ist das Brot des Elenden.

Vocabulary

* **abends** — evenings
* **aktuell** — current, modern, up-to-date
* **alles** — everything
  angenehm — agreeable
* das **Auge** (**-s, -n**) — eye

  beneiden — to envy
  der **Berg** (**-s, -e**) — mountain
* **deutsch** — German
* **dick** — fat
  elend — miserable
* **erkennen** —to recognize

erstaunlich — astonishing
* faul — lazy
der **Fehler** (-s, -) — error
der **Feiertag** (-es, -e) — holiday
* der **Feind** (-es, -e) — enemy
* fleißig — industrious
der **Gedanke** (-ns, -n) — thought
* gegenüber — opposite
* gehören (i) — to belong to
geliebt — loved
* gesund — healthy
gewaltig — powerfully
heilig — holy, saintly
* das **Herz** (-ens, -en) — heart
* heute — today
die **Hoffnung** — hope
* immer — always
* kennen — to know
die **Klaue** (-n) — claw
* klug — clever
der **Kopf** (-es, ⁻e) — head
krank — sick
kühn — daring, bold
der **Löwe** (-n, -n) — lion
* manchmal — sometimes

* der **Mensch** (-en, -en) — person
* morgen — tomorrow
der **Narr** (-en, -en) — fool
* nichts — nothing
* nie — never
der **Prophet** (-en, -en) — prophet
der **Rauch** (-s) — smoke
rein — pure
der **Ruhetag** — day of rest
der **Unfall** (-s, ⁻e) — accident
das **Unglück** (-es, -e) —
misfortune
verachten — to despise
verschieden — different
* wahr — true
die **Warnung** (-en) — warning
* weise — wise
* die **Welt** (-en) — world
werfen — to throw
der **Werktag** (-es, -e) — work day
* wichtig — important
* der **Wille** (-ns, no pl.) — will
die **Wunde** (-n) — wound
der **Wunsch** (-es, ⁻e) — wish
der **Zeiger** (-s, -) — indicator

Chapter Nine

The Various Uses of Es

Although *es* is the pronoun for *it*, there are several instances in which it will not be translated literally.

9.1. *Es gibt*

Es gibt (*literally*: *it gives*) means either *there is* if the object is singular, or *there are* if the object is plural. Examples are:

Es gibt keinen Rauch ohne Feuer — *There is* no smoke without fire.
Es gibt leider kein Bier mehr — Unfortunately, *there's* no more beer.
Es gibt viele Antworten auf diese Frage — *There are* many answers to this question.
Niemand stirbt jetzt an tödlichen Wahrheiten: *es gibt* zu viele Gegengifte — No one now dies from deadly truths: *there are* too many antidotes. (Nietzsche)

9.2. *Es ist* and *es sind*

Es ist and *es sind* are both used in a similar way. *Es ist* will mean *there is* (and the predicate nominative will be singular), and *es sind* will mean *there are* (and the predicate nominative will be plural). Examples are:

Es ist eine Katze im Haus — *There is* a cat in the house.
Es sind keine Mäuse in der Nähe — *There are* no mice near by.

9.3. The "pay attention" *es*

Occasionally, the subject of a German sentence will appear later in the sentence so that it can receive emphasis; therefore the sentence will begin with *es* merely in order to gain the reader's attention. In these cases, *es* is best left untranslated. You can recognize these sentences because
(1) they will always begin with *es*;
(2) the "real" subject of the sentence will be in the nominative case; and
(3) occasionally the verb will be plural.

Here are examples of the "pay attention" *es*:

Es ist *nicht jede schwarze Katze* eine Hexe — *Not every black cat* is a witch.
Es fällt *kein Baum* beim ersten Streich — *No tree* falls from the first blow.
Es hat *alles* einen Anfang und ein Ende — *Everything* has a beginning and an end.
Es gehen viele geduldige Schafe in einen Stall — *Many patient sheep* go into a stable. (Because the sheep are patient, the stable can accommodate all of them.)

9.4. Translate these sentences:

1. Es gibt keine Regeln ohne Ausnahmen (*exceptions*).
2. Es beißt kein Wolf den anderen. (i.e. There is honor among thieves.)
3. Es hilft keine Krone für das Kopfweh. (No matter how powerful you are, a *Kopfweh* still hurts!)
4. Es gehören nicht zwei Sättel (*saddles*) auf ein Roß (*horse*).
5. Es gibt keine Würde (*dignity*) ohne [eine] Bürde.
6. Es sind zu viele Köche in der Küche.
7. Es findet auch (*even*) ein Blinder ein Hufeisen (*horseshoe*).
8. Es fallen keine Äpfel weit vom Baum.
9. Es hofft der Mensch, solang (*as long as*) er lebt.
10. Es gibt kein häßliches Liebchen und kein schönes Gefängnis (*prison*).
11. Die Herrscher (*rulers*) wechseln nie; es wechseln nur die Namen.
12. Es gehen viele Freunde in ein Haus.
13. Es fällt kein Gelehrter vom Himmel. (In other words, no one is born well-educated.)

Vocabulary

* **ander** — other
  der **Apfel** (-s, -̈) — apple
* **auch** — also, even
  die **Ausnahme** (-n) — exception
  der **Baum** (-es, -̈e) — tree
  beißen — to bite
  blind — blind
  die **Bürde** (-n) — burden
* **fallen (fällt)** (i) — to fall
* der **Freund** (-es, -e) — friend
  das **Gefängnis** (-ses, -se) — prison
* **gehen** (i) — to go
* **gehören** (i) — to belong to
  gelehrt — learned, scholarly

* **es gibt** — there is, there are
  häßlich — ugly
  das **Haus** (-es, -̈er) — house
  der **Herrscher** (-s, -) — ruler
  der **Himmel** (-s, -) — heaven, sky
* **hoffen** (i) — to hope
  das **Hufeisen** (-s, -) — horseshoe
  der **Koch** (-es, -̈e) — cook
  das **Kopfweh** (-s) — headache
  die **Krone** (-n) — crown
  die **Küche** (-n) — kitchen
  leben (i) — to live
  das **Liebchen** (-s, -) — little loved one

* **nie** — never
* **nur** — only
  die **Regel** (-n) — rule
  das **Roß** (-sses, -sse) — horse,
  steed
  der **Sattel** (-s, ⸚) — saddle
  schön — beautiful
  solang — as long as

* **viel** — much, many
  wechseln — to change
* **weit** — far
  der **Wolf** (-s, ⸚e) — wolf
  die **Würde** — dignity
* **zu** — too
* **zwei** — two

Reading Selection: *Das Sprichwort*[1]

In jedem Land hört man Sprichwörter. Die folgenden Sprichwörter sind Ihnen wahrscheinlich schon bekannt (*familiar*): "Blut ist dicker als Wasser"; "Ein Vogel auf der Hand ist besser als zwei im Busch", und so weiter.

Die meisten Sprichwörter sind sehr alt — viele erscheinen sogar in der Bibel. Die typischen Gestalten der Sprichwörter sind der Bauer, der König, der Fürst (*prince*), die gehorsame (*obedient*) Frau, der Arzt, der Dieb, der Heilige (*saint*), Gott und der Teufel. Die Sprichwörter beschreiben oft das wünschenswerte Benehmen (*behaviour*) eines anständigen (*decent, respectable*) Menschen. Solch ein Mensch arbeitet viel, er hilft seinen Nachbarn, er fürchtet (und liebt) Gott, und er ist vorsichtig. Er ist auch der Meinung, sein Glück möge (*may*) nicht lange dauern (*last*).

In den Sprichwörtern begegnet man auch vielen Tieren. Typische Tiere sind das Huhn, die Kuh (und ihr Kalb), das Pferd, der Esel, der Hund, die Katze, die Maus, der Wolf und der Fuchs. Manche Sprichwörter beschreiben das Verhältnis (*relationship*) zwischen dem Menschen und dem Tier. Beispiele sind: "Wenn der Reiter nichts taugt (*amount to*), gibt er dem Pferd die Schuld"; "Wer zwei Hasen (*rabbits*) auf einmal jagt (*hunts*), fängt keinen"; "Alte Hühner machen gute Suppen"; "Bellende (*barking*) Hunde beißen nicht".

Man findet oft in den Tiersprichwörtern eine Personifizierung des Tieres. Hier sind einige wiederkehrende (*recurring*) Themen solcher Sprichwörter. (1) Man kann nicht anders sein, als man ist: "Wenn der Esel eine Löwenhaut (*lionskin*) trägt, <u>gucken</u> die Ohren <u>hervor</u> (*peek out from under it*)"; "Ein Pudel, dem man eine Mähne geschoren hat (*that one has sheared so that it has a mane*), ist noch kein Löwe (*lion*)." (2) Ein behindertes (*handicapped*) Geschöpf (*creature*) hat manchmal Glück: "Auch (*even*) eine blinde Sau findet eine Eichel (*acorn*)." (3) Irren ist "menschlich": "Auch der beste Gaul (*nag, horse*) stolpert

---

1 Vocabulary for this section can be found in the back of the book, pp. 285-356. Or you may wish to use a dictionary in order to increase your speed in looking up words.

(*stumbles*) einmal"; "Auch kluge Hühner legen (*Eier*) einmal in Nesseln." (4) Das Prahlen (*bragging*) taugt nichts: "Hühner, die (*who*) viel gackern (*cackle*), legen keine Eier."

Die kleinen Tiere (zum Beispiel das Schäflein und das Kalb) symbolisieren meistens menschliche Kinder: "Ein vorwitziges (*impertinent*) Schäflein frißt der Wolf"; "Eine gute Kuh hat manchmal ein übles Kalb"; "Wer als (*as a*) Kalb in die Fremde (*abroad*) geht, kommt als Kuh heim (*home*)".

Natürlich findet man noch weitere wiederkehrende Themen in den Sprichwörtern. Die Beobachtungen über Hoffnung, Glück, Armut und Alter sind besonders interessant. Wenn Sie die Sprichwörter jetzt lesen, beachten Sie, wie (*how*) verschiedene Themen behandelt werden (*are treated*)!

Chapter Ten

The Future Tense

10.1. There is less use of the future tense in German than in English. For example, whenever a sentence contains a future adverb in German, the present tense will be used, even though the sentence will be translated into English as a future tense. Examples are:

Morgen kommt der Briefträger — *Tomorrow* the mailman *will come.*
Übermorgen kommt der Bibelverkäufer — *The day after tomorrow* the Bible salesman *will come.*
Fräulein Meier *fliegt nächstes Jahr* nach Wuppertal — Fräulein Meier *will fly* to Wuppertal *next year.*

10.2. However, when the time sequence is unclear, the verb *werden* will be used in conjunction with another verb in order to form the future tense. Note that *werden* is conjugated and appears in "second" place in the sentence while the other verb appears in its infinitival form at the end of the clause:

Vielleicht *wird* Fräulein Meier nach Wuppertal *fliegen* — Perhaps Fräulein Meier *will fly* to Wuppertal.
Die Studenten *werden* bestimmt viel *lernen* — The students *will* certainly *learn* a lot.

Here is a chart:

Ich *werde* hier *sein* (*I will be here*)	Ich *werde* das *singen* (*I will sing that*)
Du *wirst* hier *sein* (*you will be here*)	Du *wirst* das *singen* (*you will sing that*)
Er *wird* hier *sein* (*he will be here*)	Sie *wird* das *singen* (*she will sing that*)

Wir *werden* hier *sein*
(*we will be here*)

Wir *werden* das *singen*
(*we will sing that*)

Ihr *werdet* hier *sein*
(*you will be here*)

Ihr *werdet* das *singen*
(*you will sing that*)

Sie *werden* hier *sein*
(*they will be here*)

Sie *werden* das *singen*
(*they will sing that*)

Sie *werden* hier *sein*
(*you will be here*)

Sie *werden* das *singen*
(*you will sing that*)

In dependent clauses, the word order will be as follows:

Sie weiß nicht, wann der Briefträger *kommen wird* — She does not know when the mailman *will come*.
Es ist nicht klar, ob Fräulein Meier viele Zeitungsartikel *schreiben wird* — It is not clear if Fräulein Meier *will write* many newspaper articles.

10.3. From now on be careful when you see the verb *werden*! When it is the **only** verb in the sentence, it will **only** mean *to become, to grow*. When *werden* is used with any infinitive (which will appear at the end of the clause), it will **always** mean *will*. Compare the following:

Der Mann *wird* alt — The man *grows* old. (**present**)
Der Mann *wird* den Film *sehen* — The man *will see* the film. (**future**)

Now, whenever you see *werden*, be on the lookout for verb infinitives lurking at the end of the clause; if there are any, the sentence will have to be translated in the future tense.

10.4. Translate these sentences. Be particularly aware of verb tenses!

1. Ein dreitägiger Gast wird zu einer Last.
2. Der Briefträger wird mit Fräulein Meier in den Zoo gehen.
3. Morgen früh (*tomorrow morning*) besucht ein Bibelverkäufer (*Bible salesman*) Fräulein Meier.
4. Irgendwann (*at some point*) wird der Student eine Fremdsprache (*foreign language*) lernen.
5. Die Ersten werden die Letzten und die Letzten werden die Ersten sein. (Note: *sein* is the infinitive for both *werden* auxiliaries)
6. Wird Fräulein Meier die Weltanschauung des Briefträgers je verstehen?

7. Es wird dem Gerechten kein Leid (*sorrow*) geschehen; aber die Gottlosen werden voll (*filled with*) Unglücks sein. (Proverbs)
8. Wer wird der Spatzen (*sparrows*) wegen das Säen (*sowing*) unterlassen (*neglect*)?
9. Wanderers Nachtlied

    Über allen Gipfeln (*mountain peaks*)
    Ist Ruh,
    In allen Wipfeln (*tree tops*)
    Spürest du
    Kaum (*barely*) einen Hauch (*breath*):
    Die Vögelein schweigen im Walde.
    Warte nur, balde
    Ruhest du auch.
    (Goethe)

Vocabulary

* **auch** — also
* **bald** — soon
  besuchen — to visit
  dreitägig — three day
  endlich — finally
* **erst** — first
  fliegen (i) — to fly
  die **Fremdsprache** (-n) — foreign language
  der **Gast** (-es, ̈e) — guest
  gerecht — righteous
* **geschehen (geschieht)** (i) — happen, to occur
  gottlos — godless
  der **Hauch** (-es, -e) — breath
  irgendwann — at some point
  je — ever
  kaum — hardly, barely
  die **Last** (-en) — burden
  das **Leid** — sorrow
* **letzt** — last
  morgen früh — tomorrow morning

das **Nachtlied** (-es, -er) — night song
* **nur** — only, just
  die **Ruhe** — peace
  ruhen (i) — to rest, sleep
  ruhig — quiet
  schweigen (i) — to be silent
  spüren — to feel
* **über** — over
  das **Unglück** (-s, -e) — misfortune
* **unter** — among
* **verstehen** — to understand
* **vielleicht** — perhaps
  der **Vogel** (-s, ̈) — bird
  der **Wald** (-es, ̈er) — woods, forest
* **warten** (i) — to wait
* **wegen** — because of
* die **Weltanschauung** (-en) — worldview
* **werden (wird)** — to become; will
* **wissen (weiß)** — to know

10.5. Vocabulary aid: continue to be aware of verb tenses!

1. Ich werde die Dramen Georg Kaisers nie verstehen.
2. Vielleicht werden die Kinder dem alten Mann helfen.
3. Endlich wird das Kind ruhig.
4. Vielleicht werden die Studenten die Philosophie Schopenhauers studieren.
5. Niemand von diesen Studenten wird den langen Film sehen.
6. Morgen fliegen sie nach Europa.
7. Wer weiß, was der Abend bringt?
8. Sage mir, mit wem du umgehst (*go around*), und ich sage dir, wer du bist.

Chapter Eleven

Comparison of Adjectives
and Adverbs

Note: this chapter is trickier than it looks. The recognition of comparatives requires a careful observation of adjectival and adverbial endings.

11.1. Comparison of adjectives

There are three basic forms of the adjective, both in German and in English: **regular** (happy), **comparative** (happier), and **superlative** (happiest). Here are examples:

regular	**comparative**	**superlative**
nett (*nice*)	netter (*nicer*)	nettest-* (*nicest*)
warm (*warm*)	wärmer (*warmer*)	wärmst-* (*warmest*)
lang (*long*)	länger (*longer*)	längst-* (*longest*)

* The dash at the end of the superlative adjectives indicates that these adjectives must have adjective endings following the superlative (**-st**) ending. An example is: "der wärmste Tag" — The warmest day.

Monosyllabic adjectives with stem vowels *a*, *o*, or *u* generally will take an umlaut. Here are examples:

alt (*old*)	älter (*older*)	ältest- (*oldest*)
kalt (*cold*)	kälter (*colder*)	kältest- (*coldest*)
dumm (*dumb*)	dümmer (*dumber*)	dümmst- (*dumbest*)

11.2. Like regular adjectives, adjectives with comparative and superlative endings will also take the traditional adjective endings (see 4.1-4.3 for review). The comparative or superlative ending is added to the adjective before the usual ending that indicates the declension. Here are examples:

der nettere Mann — the nicer man (*masculine nominative comparative*)
der netteste Mann — the nicest man (*masculine nominative superlative*)

die netteren Frauen — the nicer women (*plural nominative or accusative comparative*)
die nettesten Frauen — the nicest women (*plural nominative or accusative superlative*)

Because adjectives following **der** and most **ein** words will have **-e** or **-en** endings, sometimes the comparative or superlative ending will seem hidden. Note:

der ärmere Mann — the poorer man; der ärmste Mann — the poorest man
den netteren Mann — the nicer man; den nettesten Mann — the nicest man
des längeren Briefes — the longer letter; des längsten Briefes — the longest letter

Do not mistake the strong masculine adjective ending for the comparative! "Ein *netter* Mann" is **only** "a *nice* man." The correct form for "a *nicer* man" would be "ein *netterer* Mann."

Here are other instances in which **-er** endings are not comparative:

Alt*er* Wein ist gut*er* Wein — Old wine is good wine.
Die Suppen arm*er* Leute sind dünn — The soups of poor people are thin.
Die Frau ist bei schlecht*er* Laune — The woman is in a bad mood.

11.3. Note the following regular and comparative adjective endings:

Regular:	der alte Freund — the old friend
	ein alter Freund — an old friend
Regular Predicate Adjective:	der Freund ist alt — the friend is old
Comparative:	der ältere Freund — the older friend
	ein älterer Freund — an older friend
Comparative Predicate Adjective:	der Freund ist älter — the friend is older

When the superlative form of the adjective is a predicate adjective, it will appear in the following way:

Das kleine Kind ist *am nettesten* — The small child is *the nicest*.
Or:
Das kleine Kind ist *das netteste* — The small child is *the nicest*.
Die ältesten Lieder sind *am schönsten* (or *die schönsten*) — The oldest songs are *the most beautiful*.

11.4. Common adjective combinations

The most common adjective combination is *als* (*than*):

Geben ist *seliger als* Nehmen — Giving is *more blessed than* receiving.

When this construction is used, the comparative adjective is always a predicate adjective and therefore always ends in **-er**.

Here are more examples:

Eine Biene ist *besser als* tausend Fliegen — One bee is *better than* a thousand flies.
Der Arzt ist oft *gefährlicher als* die Krankheit — The doctor is often *more dangerous than* the disease.

Other comparative adjective combinations are: *so . . . wie* (*as . . . as*), *je . . . desto* (*the . . . the*), and *immer* with a comparative adjective.

Here are examples:

Das kaiserliche Wort ist *so* kräftig *wie* ein Eid — The imperial word is *as* strong *as* an oath.
Das Huhn ist nicht *so* klug *wie* der Fuchs — The hen is not *as* clever *as* the fox.
Je höher der Kirchturm, *desto schöner* das Geläute — *The higher* the church tower, *the more beautiful* the chimes.
Fräulein Meier und der Briefträger werden *immer freundlicher* — Fräulein Meier and the mailman are becoming *friendlier and friendlier*.
Wenn die Katze aus dem Haus ist, werden die Mäuse *immer frecher* — When the cat is out of the house, the mice become *bolder and bolder*.

Hint: Whenever an adjective with an **-er** ending appears right **before a noun**, it will **rarely** be comparative; whenever an adjective with an **-er** ending is **not** directly in front of a noun, it will **almost always** be comparative. Note:

Ein alt**er** Mann — an old man
Der Mann ist ält**er** als die Frau — The man is old**er** than the woman.

11.5. The following adjectives will have irregular forms:

regular	comparative	superlative
groß (*large, tall*)	größer (*taller*)	größt- (*tallest*)
gut (*good*)	besser (*better*)	best- (*best*)
hoch (*high*)	höher (*higher*)	höchst- (*highest*)
nah(e) (*near*)	näher (*nearer*)	nächst- (*nearest*)
viel (*many*)	mehr (*more*)	meist- (*most*)

11.6. Comparison of adverbs

The forms of the adverb in the comparative and superlative are the same as the forms of the predicate adjective:

Das Kind läuft *schnell* — The child runs *fast*. (Regular)
Der Student läuft *schneller* — The student runs *faster*. (Comparative)
Der Wanderer läuft *am schnellsten* — The hiker runs *the fastest*. (Superlative)

The superlative adverb will always have the *am . . . -en* form, regardless of where it appears in the sentence. Here is an example of a superlative adverb modifying an adjective:

Die *am frühesten* erscheinenden Erdbeeren schmecken am besten — The *earliest* appearing strawberries taste the best.

11.7. The adjective formulas also apply to adverbs:

Ein Doktor und ein Bauer wissen *mehr als* ein Doktor allein — A doctor and a farmer know *more than* a doctor alone.
Sie lieben einander *so* zärtlich *wie* Tristan und Isolde — They love one another *as* tenderly *as* Tristan and Isolde.
Je tiefer ich grabe, *desto* mehr Wasser finde ich — *The* deeper I dig, *the* more water I find.
Ich grabe *immer tiefer* — I dig *more and more deeply*.

11.8. The adverbs *bald* (soon) and *gern* (gladly) have irregular forms:

bald *(soon)*;	eher *(sooner)*	am ehesten *(soonest)*
gern *(likes to, gladly)*	lieber *(prefers to, preferably)*	am liebsten *(best of all, most preferably)*

Gern and its comparative forms are translated as follows:

Der Briefträger trinkt *gern* Wasser — The mailman *likes* to drink water, aber er trinkt Coca-Cola *lieber* — but he *prefers* to drink Coke,
und er trinkt Wein *am liebsten* — and he *likes* to drink wine *the best*.

Note that *lieber* means *preferably* rather than *lover*.

11.9. Translate these sentences:

1. Je magerer der Hund, desto fetter die Flöhe.
2. Die süßesten Trauben (*grapes*) hängen am höchsten.

3. Die Augen sind größer als der Magen (*stomach*).
4. Es ersaufen (*drown*) mehr Leute im Wein als im Rhein.
5. Doktor Maß (*moderation*), Doktor Stille und Doktor Frohmann (*good cheer*) sind die größten Ärzte.
6. Es gibt kein süßeres Leiden als Hoffen.
7. Die Liebe der Bürger ist des Landes stärkste Mauer (*wall*).
8. Die Kühe fremder Leute haben größere Euter.
9. Der faulsten Sau gehört immer der größte Dreck (mud).
10. Erfahrung (*experience*) ist ein langer Weg.
11. Schlaf nach dem Mittagstisch ist so gesund wie ein fauler Fisch.
12. Dem Schuster (*cobbler*) ist der Schuh wichtiger als der Fuß.
13. Der Spaß (*fun*) kostet mehr, als er wert ist. (A killjoy proverb!)
14. Überzeugungen (*convictions*) sind gefährlichere Feinde der Wahrheit als Lügen. (Nietzsche)
15. Die Lüge ist ein Schneeball; je länger man sie wälzt (*rolls*), desto größer wird sie. (Luther)
16. Wird Fräulein Meier immer schöner mit jedem Tag?
17. Ein guter Ruf (*reputation*) ist köstlicher als großer Reichtum, und anziehendes (*attractive*) Wesen (*character*) [ist] besser als Silber und Gold. (Proverbs)

Vocabulary

* **allein** — alone
* **als** — than
* **alt, älter, am ältesten** — old
* **der Arzt (-es, ⸚e)** — doctor
* **auch** — even
* **das Beispiel (-s, -e)** — example
* **böse** — bad
  der **Bürger (-s, -)** — citizen
  dumm, dümmer, am dümmsten — dumb
  dunkel — dark
  die **Erfahrung (-en)** — experience
  ersaufen (ersäuft) — to drown
  das **Euter (-s, -)** — udder
  faul — rotten, lazy
* der **Feind (-es, -e)** — enemy
  fett — fat
  der **Fisch (-es, -e)** — fish
  der **Floh (-es, ⸚e)** — flea
  fremd — strange, other

* der **Fuß (-es, ⸚e)** — foot
  gefährlich — dangerous
* **gefallen (i)** — to please
* **gehören (i)** — to belong to
* **gelten (gilt)** — to be valid, worth
* **gern, lieber, am liebsten** — likes to, preferably, best
  gesund — healthy
* **gleich** — same, equal
* **groß, größer, am größten** — tall, large, great
* **gut, besser, am besten** — good
  hängen (i) — to hang
* **hoch, höher, am höchsten** — high
* das **Hoffen (-s)** — hope
* **immer** — always
* **immer (& comparative)** — more and more
  immer wieder — again and again
* **je ... desto** — the ... the

kosten — to cost
köstlich — costly
die **Kuh** (¨e) — cow
das **Land** (-es, ¨er) — country
das **Leiden** (-s, -) — sorrow
die **Lüge** (-n) — lie
der **Magen** (-s, -) — stomach
mager — thin
die **Mauer** (-n) — wall
der **Mittagstisch** — lunch
* der **Morgen** (-s, -) — morning
* **nach** — after
* das **Pfund** (-es, -e) — pound
das **Recht** (-es, -e) — justice
der **Reichtum** (-s) — wealth
der **Rhein** — Rhine river
der **Ruf** (-es, -e) — reputation,
calling
die **Sau** (¨e) — sow
der **Schlaf** (-es) — sleep
der **Schneeball** (-es, ¨e) —
snowball

der **Schuster** (-s, -) — cobbler
* **schwer** — heavy, hard
* **so . . . wie** — as . . . as
der **Spaß** (-es, ¨e) — fun
* **stark** — strong
die **Stille** — quiet
* **süß** — sweet
die **Traube** (-n) — grape
die **Überzeugung** (-en) —
conviction
* die **Unze** (-n) — ounce
* **viel, mehr, am meisten** — many
wälzen (wälzt) — to roll
* der **Weg** (-es, -e) — way
der **Weintrinker** (-s, -) — wine
drinker
* **wert** — worth
das **Wesen** (-s, -) — being,
character
* **wichtig** — important
* **wiederholen** — to repeat

11.10. Vocabulary aid

1. Alte Freunde und alter Wein sind am besten.
2. Eine Hand voll (*full of*) Gold ist schwerer als ein Sack voll Recht und Wahrheit.
3. Er ist so hungrig wie eine Kirchenmaus.
4. Ein Dummer findet zehn Dümmere.
5. Es gibt mehr alte Weintrinker als alte Ärzte.
6. Eine Unze guten Beispiels gilt mehr als ein Pfund Worte.
7. Der Briefträger bleibt lieber allein als in böser Gemeinschaft (*company*).
8. Ein kluger Mann ist interessanter als ein dummer Mann.
9. Je dunkler die Nacht, desto schöner der Morgen.

Chapter Twelve

Da- and Wo-Compounds

Da- and *wo*- compounds are used as placeholders in place of pronouns when inanimate objects are dealt with as objects of prepositions. They are called compounds because they combine with the preposition to become one word.

12.1. *Da*-compounds

As a compound, *da*- generally means *it*, *this*, *that*, or *them*. Here are examples:

Er schreibt *mit* dem Bleistift — He writes *with* the pencil.
Er schreibt *damit* — He writes *with it*.
Fräulein Meier denkt manchmal *an ihre Arbeit* — Fräulein Meier sometimes thinks *about her work*. Denkt sie *daran*? — Does she think *about it*?
Der kleine Hund hat Angst *vor dem Donner* — The small dog is afraid *of the thunder*.
Der kleine Hund hat Angst *davor* — The small dog is afraid *of it*.

However, while *da* will virtually always mean *it*, the same *da*- compound can be translated differently depending on the *verb* in the clause. Here is an example:

Fräulein Meier wartet *auf den Bus* — Fräulein Meier is waiting *for the bus*.
Fräulein Meier wartet *darauf* — Fräulein Meier waits *for it*.
Fräulein Meier sitzt *auf dem Sofa* — Fräulein Meier sits *on the sofa*.
Fräulein Meier sitzt *darauf* — Fräulein Meier sits *on it*.
Fräulein Meier hört nicht *auf die Warnungen* — Fräulein Meier does not listen *to the warnings*.
Fräulein Meier hört nicht *darauf* — Fräulein Meier does not listen *to them*.

Therefore, be careful to understand the entire context of the sentence before you translate the *da*-compound.

If a preposition begins with a vowel, an "r" is added for purposes of pronunciation. Here are examples:

Er denkt an das Buch — He thinks of the book.
Er denkt *daran* — He thinks *of it*.
Sie lacht über ihren Lieblingswitz — She laughs at her favorite joke.
Sie lacht *darüber* — She laughs *at it*.

12.2. Translate the following (memorize the verbs and prepositions if you aren't already familiar with them):

1. Sie fragt danach.
2. Glauben Sie daran?
3. Er spricht davon.
4. Schreiben sie darüber?
5. Wir helfen ihr damit.
6. Haben sie keine Zeit dafür?
7. Er spricht dagegen.
8. Sie hofft darauf.

12.3. When prepositions normally follow verbs in German (in set phrases such as *denken an, warten auf*, etc.), a *da*-compound will be used as a placeholder in an independent clause which will indicate the arrival of a dependent clause:

Fräulein Meier denkt oft *daran*, daß der Briefträger ihr schöne Gedichte schreibt — Fräulein Meier often thinks *about the fact* that the mailman writes beautiful poems to her.
Der Briefträger wartet *darauf*, daß er eine Antwort bekommt — The mailman waits *so* that he will get an answer.

In these cases, the *da*-compound may be translated, or it may be left out, whichever sounds smoother.

12.4. Note that *damit* can be a subordinating conjunction as well as a *da*-compound:

Fräulein Meier liest viel, *damit* sie über viele Sachen informiert ist — Fräulein Meier reads a lot *so that* she will be knowledgeable in many matters.
Der Student lernt Deutsch, *damit* er Goethes *Faust* lesen kann — The student learns German *so that* he can read Goethe's *Faust*.

12.5. *Wo* is used as an interrogative, generally meaning "which" or "what:"

Worauf wartet er? — *For what* is he waiting?

Worüber lacht sie? — *At what* is she laughing?
Womit schreiben Sie? — *With what* are you writing?

A *wo*-compound can also be used in the middle of a sentence:

Hier ist der Bleistift, *womit* er schreibt — Here is the pencil *with which* he is writing.
Hier ist die Antwort, *worauf* sie wartet — Here is the answer *for which* she is waiting.

12.6. Translate these sentences:

1. Der Reichtum (*wealth*) gleicht dem Seewasser; je mehr man davon trinkt, desto durstiger wird man. (Schopenhauer)
2. Die Heirat (*marriage*) gleicht einem Vogelhaus; wer darin ist, will (*wants*) hinaus.
3. Die Henne legt (*lays*) gern ins Nest, worin Eier (*eggs*) schon sind.
4. Wo Gott eine Kirche baut, stellt der Teufel eine Kapelle (*chapel*) daneben (nämlich ein Wirtshaus [*tavern*]).
5. Der Mund sagt es, aber das Herz weiß nichts davon.
6. Wer (*whoever*) nach dem Kranze (*wreath*) strebt, bekommt eine Blume daraus (as a consolation prize!).
7. Höre darauf, was andere sagen, und sei vorsichtig, ehe (*before*) du sprichst.
8. Die Furcht des Herrn [Gott] ist ein gesegneter (*blessed*) Garten; die schönsten Blumen wachsen darin.
9. Der junge Arzt weiß nicht immer, wovon er spricht.
10. Worauf wartet Fräulein Meier? Auf wen wartet der Briefträger?

Vocabulary

* **andere** — others
  bauen — to build
* **bekommen** — to receive
  die **Blume (-n)** — flower
* **da** — it
  durstig — thirsty
  ehe — before
  das **Ei (-s, -er)** — egg
* **fragen nach** — to ask about
  die **Furcht** — fear
  der **Garten (-s, ⁻)** — garden
* **gegen** — against
  gesegnet — blessed

* **glauben (i)** — to believe
* **gleichen (i)** — to resemble
  die **Heirat (-en)** — marriage
  die **Henne (-n)** — hen
* **hinaus** — out
* **hoffen auf** — to hope for
* **immer** — always
* **je ... desto** — the ... the
  die **Kapelle (-n)** — chapel
  die **Kirche (-n)** — church
  der **Kranz (-es, ⁻e)** — wreath
* der **Mund (-es, ⁻er)** — mouth
* **nämlich** — namely

* **schön** — beautiful
* **schon** — already
  schreiben über — to write about
  das **Seewasser (-s, -)** — sea water
* **stellen** — to place
  streben nach — to strive for
  das **Vogelhaus (-es, ¨er)** — birdhouse

* **vorsichtig** — careful
  wachsen (i) — to grow
* **warten auf** — to wait for
* **was** — what
* **wer** — who, whoever
* **wissen (weiß)** — to know
* **wo** — which, what, where

Reading Selection: *Der Elefant*
(Eine Umarbeitung einer Kurzgeschichte von Slawomir Mrozek)

Der Direktor des Zoos ist kein redlicher Mann. Die Tiere benutzt er lediglich (*merely*) als [die] Mittel (*means*) seiner eigenen Karriere. In seinem Zoo hat die Giraffe einen kurzen Hals (*neck*); das Stachelschwein hat keine Stacheln; und der Waschbär (*raccoon*) wäscht sich nicht. Dieser Zustand ist um so bedauerlicher, weil (*because*) oftmals viele Schulkinder in diesen Zoo gehen.

Der Zoo liegt in einem kleinen Dorf, und es fehlt ihm an manchen (*some*) der wichtigsten Tiere. Zum Beispiel fehlt es ihm an einem Elefanten. (Denn dreitausend Kaninchen [*rabbits*] sind kein guter Ersatz dafür!) Aber endlich bekommt der Zoo das Geld für den Kauf (*purchase*) eines Elefanten. Alle Bewohner (*inhabitants*) des Dorfs erwarten die Ankunft (*arrival*) des Elefanten mit Freude.

Aber der Direktor des Zoos hat einen heimlichen (*secret*) Plan. Elefanten sind allerdings (*to be sure*) sehr teuer. Statt eines lebendigen Tiers wird der Zoo also einen Elefanten aus Gummi (*rubber*) bekommen. Denn jeder weiß, Elefanten sind sehr träge (*sluggish*); so wird man ein Plakat (*sign*) vor den Gummielefanten stellen, worauf man schreibt: "Besonders träge."

So kauft der Direktor des Zoos einen Elefanten aus Gummi. Dann haben zwei Angestellte (*employees*) die Aufgabe (*task*), <u>ihn aufzublasen</u> (*of inflating it*). Aber diese Aufgabe ist ihnen unmöglich (*impossible*), weil das Gummitier einfach zu groß ist. Als die zwei Männer ruhen (*rest*), bemerken sie ein Gasrohr (*gas pipe*), und sie kommen auf eine wunderbare Idee. Sie werden den Gummielefanten mit dem Gas von dem Gasrohr aufblasen. Sie tun das, und der Elefant wird sofort sehr groß. Die Angestellten betrachten (*observe*) das Tier mit Freude. Weil es jetzt sehr spät ist, kehren (*return*) die Angestellten zufrieden (*satisfied*) nach Hause.

Am anderen (*next*) Morgen stellt der Direktor des Zoos den Elefanten neben den Affenkäfig (*monkey cage*). Das Plakat "Besonders träge — läuft überhaupt nicht" steht vor ihm. Nach der Meinung des Direktors ist der Elefant großartig (*splendid*).

Unter den ersten Besuchern (*visitors*) des Zoos sind viele Schulkinder und ihr Lehrer. Der Lehrer hat eine gute Kenntnis der Tierkunde (*zoology*). Er erzählt viel über die Größe und die Macht des Elefanten.

Aber während der Rede (*lecture*) des Lehrers geschieht etwas. Der Wind setzt den Elefanten in Bewegung (*motion*), und so springt er immer höher in die Luft (*air*). Eine Weile lang betrachten die Schulkinder die vier Kreise (*circles*) der Füße, den herausragenden (*bulging*) Bauch und den Rüssel (*trunk*). Aber dann verschwindet (*vanishes*) das Tier über die Baumkronen. Sogar die Affen sind erstaunt (*astonished*) darüber.

Endlich findet man das Gummitier in dem benachbarten botanischen Garten. Es liegt zerschmettert (*smashed to pieces*) auf der Erde in der Nähe einer Kaktuspflanze.

Die Schulkinder des Dorfes machen jetzt keine Schularbeiten mehr. Und sie werden Rowdys. Wahrscheinlich trinken sie jetzt Wodka, und sie zerschmettern Fenster. Und jetzt glauben sie nicht mehr an Elefanten.

Vocabulary

* **als** — when, as
* **also** — thus, so
  der **Angestellte (-n, -n)** — employee
  aufblasen — to inflate
  die **Aufgabe (-n)** — task
  der **Bauch (-es, ̈e)** — belly
  die **Baumkrone (-n)** — treetop
  bedauerlich — deplorable, regrettable
* **zum Beispiel** — for example
* **bekommen** — to get, receive
  bemerken — to notice
  benachbart — neighboring
  benutzen — to use
* **besonders** — especially
  betrachten — to observe

  botanisch — botanical
* **dann** — then
* **denn** — because, for
  das **Dorf (-es, ̈er)** — village
  eigen — own
* **einfach** — simple
  der **Elefant (-en, -en)** — elephant
* **endlich** — finally
* die **Erde (-n)** — earth, ground
  der **Ersatz (-es)** — substitute
* **erwarten** — to await, expect
* **erzählen** — to explain, tell
* **etwas** — something
* **fehlen** — to lack; **es fehlt ihm an etwas** — he is lacking something
* die **Freude (-n)** — joy
  das **Gasrohr (-s, -e)** — gas pipe

* das **Geld** (-es, -er) — money
* **geschehen** (i) — to happen
* **glauben** (i) — to believe
  die **Größe** (-n) — size, magnitude, greatness
* **jeder** — each, every, everyone
* **jetzt** — now
  die **Karriere** (-n) — career
  der **Kauf** (-es, ⸚e) — purchase
  die **Kenntnis** (-sse) — knowledge
  kurz — short
  die **Kurzgeschichte** (-n) — short story
* **lang** (prep.) — for
  laufen (i) — to run; to move
* **lebendig** — living
* **liegen** (i) — to lie, be situated
  die **Macht** (⸚e) — strength, power
* die **Meinung** (-en) — opinion
* das **Mittel** (-s, -) — means
  nach Hause — home
  die **Nähe** — vicinity
* **nicht mehr** — no longer
  oftmals — often
  das **Plakat** (-es, -e) — sign, placard
  redlich — honest
  der **Rowdy** (-s, -s) — scoundrel

die **Schularbeit** (-en) — schoolwork
* **sofort** — immediately
* **sogar** — even
* **spät** — late
  der **Stachel** (-s, -n) — quill
  das **Stachelschwein** (-s, -e) — porcupine
* **statt** — instead of
* **stellen** — to place
* **teuer** — expensive
* das **Tier** (-s, -e) — animal
* **tun** — to do
  überhaupt nicht — not at all
* **um so** (& comp.) — all the more
  die **Umarbeitung** (-en) — adaptation
* **vier** — four
* **während** — during
* **wahrscheinlich** — probably
  waschen (r) — to wash
* **weil** — because
  die **Weile** — while
* **wichtig** — important
  der **Wodka** — vodka
  zerschmettern — to smash
  der **Zustand** (-es, ⸚e) — condition, situation
* **zwei** — two

Chapter Thirteen
Verb Prefixes

In German, it is possible to form new meanings to a verb by adding a prefix to the root. While *steigen* means *to climb*, *einsteigen* means *to board* (a train or plane), and *umsteigen* means *to change* (trains, etc.); and while *lernen* means *to learn*, *verlernen* means *to forget what one has learned*. There are both separable and inseparable verb prefixes.

13.1. Separable verb prefixes

The separable verb prefixes are more numerous and more complicated than the inseparable. For, in independent clauses, and in sentences beginning with a verb, the verb root appears in its usual place, while the prefix appears at the end of the clause. Here are examples:

Der Letzte *macht* die Türe *zu* — The last one closes the door.
Heute *sieht* Frau Schneider gut *aus* — Today Frau Schneider looks good.
Steht Fräulein Meier früh *auf*? — Does Fräulein Meier get up early?
Hören die Kinder ihrer Mutter *zu*? — Do the children listen to their mother?

In order to find the infinitive in such sentences, you must attach the prefix at the end of the sentence to the conjugated verb, and then look up the prefixed verb. In the sentences used as examples, the infinitives are: *zumachen, aussehen, aufstehen*, and *zuhören*.

13.2. A complete list of verb prefixes (and other prefixes and suffixes as well) can be found in: *A German Word Family Dictionary* (Howard Keller, The University of California Press, 1978). However, here is a list of the most common verb prefixes and their most common meanings:

ab	away, downwards: *abgehen* — to go away; start; resign
an	at, on, to: *angehen* — to begin, open
auf	up, open: *aufgehen* — to rise; break up; open
aus	out, out of, with: *ausgehen* — to go out, come to an end

durch	through: *durchgehen* — to walk, go, pass through, pierce
ein	into: *eingehen* — to go in; enter; arrive; decay
fort	away, continuing: *fortgehen* — to go away, to continue
her	motion towards a speaker: *hergehen* — to go here, proceed
hin	motion away from a speaker: *hingehen* — to go there, pass away
mit	with: *mitgehen* — accompany, go along
nach	away from, imitating, toward: *nachgehen* — follow; investigate
nieder	down, low: *niedergehen* — go down; fall
über	over, more: *übergehen* — to pass over, to overflow
um	around, embracing: *umgehen* — to by-pass, circulate
unter	under: *untergehen* — to perish; to set
vor	before, forward: *vorgehen* — to advance; occur
weg	away, gone: *(hin)weggehen* — to go away
weiter	to continue: *weitergehen* — to continue
zu	to, towards, closed: *zugehen* — go on; shut; happen
zurück	back: *zurückgehen* — to go back, fall back
zusammen	together: *zusammengehen* — to go together, close; diminish

13.3. Whenever you find any of these prefixes isolated at the end of a clause, you should identify them as separable prefixes. Then you *must* attach the prefix to the verb root in order to translate the infinitive correctly. Because most of these prefixes are short, they are sometimes easy to overlook; therefore, watch out for them!

Sometimes a verb prefix can change the meaning of a verb radically. For example, while *bringen* means *to bring*, *umbringen* means *to kill*; while *hören* means *to hear*, *aufhören* means *to stop*; while *fangen* means *to capture*, *anfangen* means *to begin*. Consequently it is crucial to look up a verb with its prefix in order to discover its correct meaning in the sentence you are translating.

13.4. However, at other times, the prefixed verb may not appear in your dictionary. In this case, you should look up both the verb and its prefix and combine them in a logical manner. For example, if you had to translate the sentence, "Die zwei Menschen *gehören* nicht *zusammen*," and you could not find the verb *zusammengehören*, you could still translate the sentence accurately if you realized that *zusammen* meant *together* and *gehören* meant *to belong to* and if you then translated the verb as *to belong together*. But before you resort to this method, first look in your dictionary for the verb with its prefix.

13.5. In clauses when the verb appears at the end, the prefix will no longer be separated from the verb. Here are examples:

Wann wird der alte Mann mit seiner langen Rede *aufhören* — When will the old man end his long tirade?
Wo Verdacht *einkehrt*, nimmt die Ruhe Abschied — When suspicion enters, peace leaves.

13.6. Do not confuse verb and preposition combinations with verb prefixes. Compare "Er *hört auf* diese Frage" — He *listens to* this question (a verb and preposition combination) with "Er *hört* mit dieser Frage *auf*" — He *ends* with this question (*auf* is now a verb prefix). A separable verb prefix will nearly always be at the end of the clause, and it will **never** be immediately followed by a noun without at least some intervening punctuation, such as a comma.

13.7. *Hin* and *her* are two common directional prefixes. Wo geht er *hin*? means "Where is he going *to*" and Wo kommt er *her*? means "Where is he coming *from*?" Often they do not need to be translated into English. Also, they are often used in conjunction with another prefix for emphasis. Examples are: *hinein* (*into*), *heraus* (*out of*), and *hindurch* (*through*).

13.8. Translate these sentences. Underline the whole verb in each sentence (vocabulary is on p. 102):

1. Die Dummen sterben nie aus.
2. Wer (*he who*) mit Hunden zu Bett geht, steht mit Flöhen auf.
3. Ein kleiner Topf (*pot*) kocht bald über.
4. Wo man Liebe aussät (*sows*), dort wächst Freude hervor.
5. Hin geht die Zeit, her kommt der Tod.
6. Wo Elefanten tanzen, bleiben die Ameisen weg.
7. Mache den Mund zu und die Augen auf.
8. Furcht steckt an.
9. Liebe deine Nachbarn, aber lege den Zaun (*fence*) nicht nieder.
10. Schlächter (*butchers*) und Schwein stimmen nicht überein.
11. Beinah (*almost* — this is used as a noun, meaning *a half-way measure*) bringt keine Mücke (*gnat*) um.
12. Ein Stein, der (*that*) rollt, setzt kein Moos an.
13. Wann kommt der Professor von seiner Reise zurück?
14. Wegen ihrer fruchtbaren Gespräche lernen Fräulein Meier und der Briefträger nie aus.

13.9. Inseparable verb prefixes

There are seven common inseparable verb prefixes — *be-, ent-* (or *emp-*), *er-, ge-, miß-, ver-,* and *zer-*. Unfortunately, the meanings of these prefixes are not always consistent. However, here are some of the more common meanings of some of them:

be- commonly changes an intransitive verb into a transitive. Examples are: antworten, **be**antworten (*to answer*); achten, **be**achten (*to pay attention to*); dienen, **be**dienen (*to serve*); gehen, **be**gehen (*to walk on, commit*).

er- indicates the beginning of an action (**er**bleichen — to begin to turn pale) or an achievement of the aim set by the action (**er**kennen — to recognize; **er**reichen — to reach). And the prefix *er-* attached to the verbs of violence means that the action is fatal: **er**schießen — to shoot to death; **er**stechen — to stab fatally.

miß- corresponds to the English *mis-* or *dis-*. Examples are: **miß**brauchen — to misuse; **miß**deuten — to misinterpret; and **miß**fallen — to displease.

ver- has a wide range of meanings. It can mean a variety of "negative" things such as waste, or disappearance, or errors in action. Examples are: **ver**sprechen — to misspeak; **ver**gehen — to disappear, pass, elapse; **ver**schlafen — to oversleep. On the other hand, it can also mean *to intensify* or *to come together* when added to a verb. Examples are: **ver**sprechen — to promise; **ver**bessern — to improve; **ver**mischen — to mix together.

zer- denotes the destruction resulting from the root verb, and it means *to pieces, in pieces*. Examples are: **zer**brechen — to break into pieces; **zer**reißen — to rip to shreds; and **zer**stören — to destroy.

13.10. Translate these sentences:

1. Der Vater des Briefträgers beklagt das Benehmen (*behavior*) seines Sohnes.
2. Gute Schwimmer ersaufen zuerst. (Because they venture into the deepest water!)
3. Die Rosen verblühen, die Dornen bleiben.
4. Wenn die Sonne scheint, erbleicht der Mond.
5. Den Elefanten erschreckt die Maus.
6. Wann erwartet Fräulein Meier den Briefträger?
7. Die Furcht vergrößert die Gefahr.
8. Ein junges Kind mißtraut niemandem.

9.　Wer zerschneidet das häßliche Photo?
10.　Der Student zertritt den Kakerlak (*cockroach*).

Vocabulary (In this section, verb prefixes are hyphenated.)

die **Ameise** (-n) — ant
an-setzen — to accumulate, to gather
an-stecken — to contaminate, to be catching
* **auf-machen** — to open
* **auf-stehen** (i) — to get up
aus-lernen — to finish learning
aus-säen — to sow
aus-sterben (i) — to die out
* **bald** — soon
* **beinah** — almost
be-klagen — to complain about
das **Benehmen** (-s) — behavior
* **bleiben** (i) — to remain
* **dick** — thick
* **dort** — there
der **Dorn** (-es, -en) — thorn
er-bleichen (i) — to pale
er-saufen (i) — to drown
er-schrecken (**erschrickt**) — to frighten
* **er-warten** — to expect
der **Floh** (-s, ̈e) — flea
* die **Freude** (-n) — joy
fruchtbar — fruitful
* die **Furcht** — fear
die **Gefahr** (-en) — danger
das **Gespräch** (-es, -e) — conversation
häßlich — ugly
* **her** — whence (from)
hervor-wachsen (i) — to grow forth
* **hin** — whither (to)
* **klein** — small

* **klug** — clever
* **lieben** — to love
* **miß-trauen** (i) — to mistrust
der **Mond** (-es, -e) — moon
das **Moos** (-es, -e) — moss
der **Mund** (-es, ̈er) — mouth
* der **Nachbar** (-s, -n) — neighbor
* **nie** — never
nieder-legen — to take down, to give up
* **niemand** — no one
die **Reise** (-n) — trip
* **scheinen** (i) — to shine; to seem
das **Schwein** (-s, -e) — swine
der **Schwimmer** (-s, -) — swimmer
der **Stein** (-es, -e) — stone
der **Tod** (-es, -e) — death
der **Topf** (-es, ̈e) — pot
überein-stimmen — to agree
über-kochen (i) — to boil over
um-bringen — to kill
ver-blühen (i) — to wither
* **ver-größern** — to enlarge, increase, magnify
* **wann** — when
weg-bleiben (i) — to stay away
* **wegen** — because of
* **wo** — where, when
* die **Zeit** (-en) — time
zer-schneiden — to cut into pieces
zer-treten (**zertritt**) — to stomp on
zu-erst — first of all
* **zu-machen** — to close
* **zurück-kommen** (i) — to return

Chapter Fourteen

Verb Tenses (Part I)

14.1. The four German verb forms

German has only four indicative verb forms — present, past, present perfect, and past perfect. They are:

present: Er *hört* den Lärm — He *hears* (or *is hearing*) the noise.
past: Er *hörte* den Lärm — He *heard* (or *was hearing*) the noise.
present perfect: Er *hat* den Lärm *gehört* — He *has heard* (or *heard*) the noise.
past perfect: Er *hatte* den Lärm *gehört* — He *had heard* the noise.

The present and past perfects are formed by using an auxiliary (helping verb) with a participle.
English grammar review: a **participle** is a verb which requires a helping verb: has <u>seen</u>; have <u>made</u>; had <u>written</u>; are <u>rung</u>; was <u>done</u>; were <u>lost</u>

14.2. The German past is used much less frequently than the English past; primarily it is used for narration or story-telling. However, the past also is used with the two most common German verbs, *sein* (to be) and *haben* (to have), and with the modals (which are discussed in Chapter Nineteen — 19.1-19.8).

Gestern *war* der Student glücklich — Yesterday the student *was* happy.
Gestern *hatte* Fräulein Meier Kopfschmerzen — Yesterday Fräulein Meier *had* a headache.

14.3. The present perfect tense (has seen, has heard) is used much more often in German than in English, and it can be translated either as a simple past (*saw, heard*), or as the present perfect (*has seen, has heard*) depending on context. It is more common to translate the present perfect into English as a simple past tense:

Gestern *hat* die Studentin den Professor *gesehen* — Yesterday the co-ed *saw* the professor.

Er *hat* die Frage nicht *gehört* — He *did* not *hear* the question.
Er *hat* mit ihr *getanzt* — He *danced* with her.

14.4. The present and past perfect tenses will always require an auxiliary verb — *haben* (*to have*) or *sein* (*to be*) — which will be conjugated, while the participle (as in English) will remain the same. Here is an example, using the infinitive *sehen*:

Ich *habe* den Film *gesehen*	— I *have seen* the film.
Du *hast* den Film *gesehen*	— You *have seen* the film.
Sie *hat* den Film *gesehen*	— She *has seen* the film.
Wir *haben* den Film *gesehen*	— We *have seen* the film.
Ihr *habt* den Film *gesehen*	— You *have seen* the film.
Sie *haben* den Film *gesehen*	— They *have seen* the film.
Sie *haben* den Film *gesehen*	— You *have seen* the film.

14.5. While most verbs will take *haben* as an auxiliary, as all verbs do in English, some verbs will take *sein* as an auxiliary. Verbs of motion (which are intransitive) such as *fliegen* (*to fly*), *kommen* (*to come*), *steigen* (*to climb*), and *gehen* (*to go*) will take *sein* as an auxiliary, as do the verbs *sein, werden* (*to become*), and *bleiben* (*to remain*). Your dictionary will note in parentheses if a verb takes *sein* with the symbol (aux. s.). Here is a paradigm using the infinitive *fliegen*:

Ich *bin* nach Kalifornien *geflogen*	— I *have flown* to California.
Du *bist* nach Kalifornien *geflogen*	— You *have flown* to California.
Er *ist* nach Kalifornien *geflogen*	— He *has flown* to California.
Wir *sind* nach Kalifornien *geflogen*	— We *have flown* to California.
Ihr *seid* nach Kalifornien *geflogen*	— You *have flown* to California.
Sie *sind* nach Kalifornien *geflogen*	— They *have flown* to California.
Sie *sind* nach Kalifornien *geflogen*	— You *have flown* to California.

Whenever *sein* is used as an auxiliary, it **must** be translated into English as *has* or *have* — it can **never** be translated as *is* or *are*. Here are more examples:

Ich *bin* oft nach Berlin *gefahren* — I *have* often *gone* to Berlin.
Schon *ist* er nach Hause *gegangen* — Already he *has gone* home.
Selten *ist* sie hier *gewesen* — She *has* seldom *been* here.
Oft *sind* wir zu Hause *geblieben* — We *have* often *stayed* home.

14.6. Placement of the auxiliaries *sein* and *haben* in the present and past perfect tenses

In sentences containing the present or past perfect tenses, the auxiliary verb will be conjugated and will appear in "second" place in the clause while the participle will appear at the end of the clause:

Er *hat* schon viele Gedichte von Goethe *gelesen* — He *has* already *read* many of Goethe's poems.
Sie *ist* noch nicht *gekommen* — She *has* not yet *arrived*.

Note that the past perfect is formed in German by using the past tense of either *sein* or *haben* with a participle:

Er *hatte* den Film schon *gesehen* — He *had* already *seen* the film.
Sie *war* nach Bern *geflogen* — She *had flown* to Bern.

14.7. Conjugations of *sein* and *haben*:

sein (*to be*)	present (*he is*)	past (*he was*)	present perfect (*he has been*)	past perfect (*he had been*)
ich	bin	war	bin gewesen	war gewesen
du	bist	warst	bist gewesen	warst gewesen
er, sie, es	ist	war	ist gewesen	war gewesen
wir	sind	waren	sind gewesen	waren gewesen
ihr	seid	wart	seid gewesen	wart gewesen
sie	sind	waren	sind gewesen	waren gewesen
Sie	sind	waren	sind gewesen	waren gewesen

haben (*to have*)	present (*he has*)	past (*he had*)	present perfect (*he has had*)	past perfect (*he had had*)
ich	habe	hatte	habe gehabt	hatte gehabt
du	hast	hattest	hast gehabt	hattest gehabt
er, sie, es	hat	hatte	hat gehabt	hatte gehabt
wir	haben	hatten	haben gehabt	hatten gehabt
ihr	habt	hattet	habt gehabt	hattet gehabt
sie	haben	hatten	haben gehabt	hatten gehabt
Sie	haben	hatten	haben gehabt	hatten gehabt

14.8. Weak (or "regular") verbs

Weak verbs are verbs which require no vowel change for their past and perfect forms. Comparable English verbs are: look, looked, looked; close, closed, closed; enjoy, enjoyed, enjoyed. In German, the first and third person past will end in -te, and the participle will usually end in ge-...-t. Here are examples:

present infinitive	past (first and third person singular)	present perfect (third person singular)
hören (*to hear*)	hörte (*heard*)	hat gehört (*has heard*)
lachen (*to laugh*)	lachte (*laughed*)	hat gelacht (*has laughed*)
sagen (*to say*)	sagte (*said*)	hat gesagt (*has said*)
leben (*to live*)	lebte (*lived*)	hat gelebt (*has lived*)

Here are all the conjugations of the weak verb *leben* (*to live*):

	present	past	present perfect	past perfect
ich	lebe	lebte	habe gelebt	hatte gelebt
du	lebst	lebtest	hast gelebt	hattest gelebt
er, sie, es	lebt	lebte	hat gelebt	hatte gelebt
wir	leben	lebten	haben gelebt	hatten gelebt
ihr	lebt	lebtet	habt gelebt	hattet gelebt
sie	leben	lebten	haben gelebt	hatten gelebt
Sie	leben	lebten	haben gelebt	hatten gelebt

14.9. If a verb has an inseparable prefix — be-, emp-, er-, ge-, ver-, or zer-, or if the verb ends in -*ieren*, the participle will have no *ge*- prefix. Example are: verlernen, verlernte, hat verlernt; beantworten, beantwortete, hat beantwortet; studieren, studierte, hat studiert. Here is the conjugation of *erwarten* (*to expect, await*):

	present	past	present perfect	past perfect
ich	erwarte	erwartete	habe erwartet	hatte erwartet
du	erwartest	erwartetest	hast erwartet	hattest erwartet
er, sie, es	erwartet	erwartete	hat erwartet	hatte erwartet
wir	erwarten	erwarteten	haben erwartet	hatten erwartet
ihr	erwartet	erwartetet	habt erwartet	hattet erwartet
sie	erwarten	erwarteten	haben erwartet	hatten erwartet
Sie	erwarten	erwarteten	haben erwartet	hatten erwartet

When the verb has an inseparable prefix or ends in *-ieren*, the third person singular present will be the same as the participle. Here is an example:

Sie *studiert* Deutsch — She *is studying* German.
Sie *hat* Deutsch *studiert* — She *studied* German.

However, the participle usually can be recognized as a participle because (1) it will be accompanied by an auxiliary verb, and (2) it will appear at the end of the clause.

14.10. Finding an infinitive of a weak verb

In order to find the infinitive when you encounter the past tense of a weak verb, simply eliminate the final *-te* and add *-en*:

past	hörte	lachte	wohnte	sagte	schaute
infinitive	hören	lachen	wohnen	sagen	schauen

In order to find the infinitive when you encounter the participle of a weak verb, eliminate the initial *ge-* and the final *-t* and add *-en* to the ending:

participle	gelobt	gelacht	gemacht	gesagt	gefragt
infinitive	loben	lachen	machen	sagen	fragen

14.11. State the infinitives of the following weak verbs:

glaubte, gelacht, lernte, geschaut, studiert, gehörte, erinnerte, geantwortet, setzte, legte, gewohnt, lobte, machte

14.12. Translate these sentences:

1. Armut (*poverty*) hat viele Städte gebaut.
2. Der alte Ochs (*ox*) ist auch ein Kalb (*calf*) gewesen.
3. Wer auf Hoffnung traut, hat auf Eis gebaut.
4. Das Goldene Zeitalter (*age*) existierte damals (*at that time*), als das Gold noch nicht vorhanden war.
5. Der Teufel war schön in seiner Jugend.
6. "Gut und Böse sind die Vorurteile (*prejudices*) Gottes", sagte die Schlange. (Nietzsche)
7. Fräulein Meier hat die Antwort des Briefträgers nicht erwartet.
8. Nachdem der Student in Deutschland gewohnt hatte, studierte er die Romane Grimmelshausens.
9. Sind die Gänslein ihrer Mutter gefolgt?
10. Wer hat darüber gelacht?
11. Die klügsten Studenten hörten darauf.

12. Wo wohnte Fräulein Meier vor drei Jahren?
13. Dabei hat Sie die ganze Zeit eine nette Frau bedient.
14. (ich) Habe nun, ach!* Philosophie,
    Juristerei (*law*) und Medizin
    und leider auch Theologie
    durchaus studiert mit heißem Bemühn (*effort*).
    Da steh'** ich nun, ich armer Tor (*fool*)!
    und bin so klug als wie zuvor (*none the wiser*) . . .

    (Goethe — *Faust*)

*   This is just an exclamation — it does not indicate the end of the sentence.
** The apostrophe stands for an "e": *steh' — stehe*

Vocabulary

ach — alas
* als — when
* die **Antwort (-en)** — answer
die **Armut** — poverty
* auch — also, even
bauen — to build
bedienen — to wait on, serve
* das **Böse** — evil
* da — there
dabei — at that time; then
* damals — then, at that time
durchaus — thoroughly
das **Eis (-es, -)** — ice
* erwarten — to expect
existieren (i) — to exist
folgen (i., aux. s.) — to follow
das **Gänslein (-s, -)** — little goose
* ganz — entire
* gewesen — been
Grimmelshausen — a Baroque
German writer
* haben, hatte, hat gehabt — to have
* heiß — hot, ardent
herrschen — to rule
* die **Hoffnung** — hope
hören auf — to listen to
die **Jugend** — youth

* klug — clever
lachen (i) — to laugh
leider — unfortunately
die **Medizin** — medicine
* nachdem — after
nett — nice
* noch nicht — not yet
* nun — now
* der **Roman (-s, -e)** — novel
die **Schlange (-n)** — snake
* schön — beautiful
* sein, war, ist gewesen (i) — to be
die **Stadt (-̈e)** — city
* stehen (i) — to stand
der **Teufel (-s, -)** — devil
die **Theologie** — theology
der **Tor (-en, -en)** — fool
trauen (auf) — to trust (in)
* vor (with time) — ago
vorhanden — available;
vorhanden sein — to exist
das **Vorurteil (-s, -e)** — prejudice
* wer — who
* wohnen (i) — to live, dwell
* die **Zeit (-en)** — time
das **Zeitalter (-s, -)** — age

Chapter Fifteen

Verb Tenses (Part II)

15.1. Strong (or "irregular") verbs

Strong verbs are verbs which require a vowel change for their past and perfect forms. Comparable English strong verbs are: see, saw, seen; ring, rang, rung; fight, fought, fought.

present infinitive	past (first and third person singular)	present perfect (third person singular)
singen (*to sing*)	sang (*sang*)	hat gesungen (*has sung*)
fallen (*to fall*)	fiel (*fell*)	ist gefallen (*has fallen*)
ziehen (*to draw*)	zog (*drew*)	hat gezogen (*has drawn*)
schreiben (*to write*)	schrieb (*wrote*)	hat geschrieben (*has written*)

There are seven different types of verb changes which are listed in the appendix on pp. 246-248, and eventually these patterns should become familiar to you. But until then, if you look up the past or participle of a strong verb, most dictionaries (except the paperback Cassells) will give you the infinitive.

15.2. While weak verbs end in -*te* in the past tense and in -*t* in the perfect tenses, strong verbs usually will end in a consonant in the past tense, and in -*en* in the perfect tenses. Compare the following:

	weak (-*te*, -*t*)		strong (*consonant*, -*en*)	
present infinitive	fragen	loben	geben	greifen
past	fragte	lobte	gab	griff
present perfect	gefragt	gelobt	gegeben	gegriffen

Whenever a verb for first or third person singular ends in a consonant other than -t (stand, ging, schrieb), it will always be past (unless it is a

modal or the verb *wissen*)! Whenever a verb ends in -t, it **usually** will be present.

15.3. Here are all the conjugations of the strong verb *singen*:

	present	past	present perfect	past perfect
ich	singe	sang	habe gesungen	hatte gesungen
du	singst	sangst	hast gesungen	hattest gesungen
er, sie, es	singt	sang	hat gesungen	hatte gesungen
wir	singen	sangen	haben gesungen	hatten gesungen
ihr	singt	sangt	habt gesungen	hattet gesungen
sie	singen	sangen	haben gesungen	hatten gesungen
Sie	singen	sangen	haben gesungen	hatten gesungen

15.4. Whether it is weak or strong, if a verb has an inseparable prefix (see 13.9; 14.9) **the participle will have no** *ge-* **prefix.** Here are examples:

present indicative	past	present perfect
vergessen (*to forget*)	vergaß (*forgot*)	hat vergessen (*has forgotten*)
bestehen (*to consist*)	bestand (*consisted*)	hat bestanden (*has consisted*)
erfinden (*to invent*)	erfand (*invented*)	hat erfunden (*has invented*)

When a strong verb has an inseparable prefix, the infinitive and the participle can sometimes be the same. Examples are: *vergessen, erfahren, verlesen,* and *gefallen*.

Wir *erfahren* viel — We *experience* a lot.
Wir *haben* viel *erfahren* — We *have experienced* a lot.

However, as with weak verbs, the participle usually can be recognized as a participle because (1) it will be accompanied by an auxiliary verb, and (2) it will appear at the end of the clause.

15.5. Moreover, the following steps are needed for finding an infinitive in your dictionary when you encounter a participle with an inseparable prefix:

(1) eliminate the prefix temporarily,
(2) add *ge-* to the rest of the verb,
(3) look up the participle to find the verb stem,
(4) reattach the prefix to the stem.

Here are examples:

Participle: **erstochen**. Look up **gestochen** to discover the stem infinitive *stechen*, then look up **erstechen**.

Participle: **ent**nommen. Look up **genommen** to discover the infinitive *nehmen*, then look up **ent**nehmen.

Participle: **zer**ronnen. Look up **geronnen** to discover the stem infinitive *rinnen*, then look up **zerrinnen**.

15.6. State the infinitives of the following strong verbs:

blieb, geflogen, las, geritten, gestohlen, ging, versprochen, nahm, erfunden, getrunken, trug, rief, beschrieben, fiel, schien, zerrissen, bog, aß, gekommen, mißverstanden.

15.7. Irregular weak verbs

There are also some "irregular weak" verbs which have both vowel changes and the standard weak endings. The most important of these verbs are:

definition	present infinitive	past	present perfect
to be acquainted with	**kennen**	kannte	hat gekannt
to bring	**bringen**	brachte	hat gebracht
to think	**denken**	dachte	hat gedacht
to know	**wissen**	wußte	hat gewußt

15.8. There are also some verbs with a ge-prefix which can be confused with verbs with the same stem and no prefix. Compare:

gebrauchen	(*to use*)	vs.	brauchen	(*to need*)
gefallen	(*to please*	vs.	fallen	(*to fall*)
gehorchen	(*to obey*)	vs.	horchen	(*to hear*)
gehören	(*to belong to*)	vs.	hören	(*to hear*)
geraten	(*to land, succeed*)	vs.	raten	(*to advise*)
gestehen	(*to confess*)	vs.	stehen	(*to stand*)

Because verbs with a *ge*-prefix look the same in the participial form as their non-*ge*-stems, meanings can be ambiguous and determined only by context. For example, "Fräulein Meier hat dem Briefträger gehorcht" can mean either that Fräulein Meier has listened to the mailman, or that she has obeyed him.

15.9. Here is the conjugation of a separable verb, *ansehen* (*to look at*):

	present	past	present perfect	past perfect
ich	sehe an	sah an	habe angesehen	hatte angesehen
du	siehst an	sahst an	hast angesehen	hattest angesehen
er, sie, es	sieht an	sah an	hat angesehen	hatte angesehen
wir	sehen an	sahen an	haben angesehen	hatten angesehen
ihr	seht an	saht an	habt angesehen	hattet angesehen
sie	sehen an	sahen an	haben angesehen	hatten angesehen
Sie	sehen an	sahen an	haben angesehen	hatten angesehen

Here are sentences containing each of the four tenses:

Das Kind *sieht* die Katze *an* — The child *looks at* the cat.
Das Kind *sah* die Katze *an* — The child *looked at* the cat.
Das Kind *hat* die Katze oft *angesehen* — The child *has* often *looked at* the cat.
Das Kind *hatte* die Katze oft *angesehen* — The child *had looked at* the cat often.

15.10. The participle of a separable verb can be recognized because the *ge-* **prefix will always separate the prefix** (*an*) **from the stem** (*sehen*)**.**

To find the infinitive of a weak separable verb, eliminate the *ge-* in the middle and replace the final *t-* with *-en*. Examples are:

Participle	angehört	aufgefaßt	ausgefragt	niedergelegt
Infinitive	an-hören	auf-fassen	aus-fragen	nieder-legen

To find the infinitive of a strong separable verb,

(1) eliminate the prefix temporarily,
(2) look up the participle in your dictionary to find the verb stem,
(3) re-attach the prefix to the stem.

Here are examples:

Participle: *angegriffen*. Look up *gegriffen* to discover the stem infinitive *greifen*, then look up the infinitive *angreifen*.
Participle: *ausgezogen*. Look up *gezogen* to discover the stem infinitive *ziehen*, then look up the infinitive *ausziehen*.
Participle: *aufgenommen*. Look up *genommen* to discover the stem infinitive *nehmen*, then look up the infinitive *aufnehmen*.

15.11. Give the infinitive of the following separable verbs; state whether the verbs are strong, weak, or irregular weak: (Hint: participles ending in -en are **always** strong!)

ausgeholt, aufgestanden, abgestiegen, zugemacht, aufgebaut, eingegriffen, eingebrochen, zuerkannt, umgedeutet, umgebracht, mitgegangen, zugedacht, vorgewiesen, ausgeflippt.

Note: not all of the above verbs can be found in a small dictionary.

15.12. Translate these sentences:

1. Die Hoffnung ist in den Brunnen (*well*) gefallen. (In other words, *Hoffnung* is irretrievably lost!)
2. Dankbarkeit ist in den Himmel gestiegen und hat die Leiter (*ladder*) mitgenommen. (*Dankbarkeit* is as hard to retrieve as Hoffnung!)
3. Als der Tag anbrach, noch ehe (*before*) die Sonne aufgegangen war, schrieb der Briefträger ein langes, romantisches Gedicht.
4. Ein Wolf im Schlaf fing nie ein Schaf.
5. Heute erfährt man, was man gestern nicht gewußt hat.
6. Ein süßer Gesang hat <u>manch einen</u> (*many a*) Vogel betrogen.
7. Es sind mehr Leute aus Überfluß (abundance) als aus Armut gestorben.
8. Das Lernen hat kein Narr erfunden.
9. Als er böse wurde, bot der Vater des Briefträgers ein Bild starken Zorns, und er erschreckte Fräulein Meier.
10. Sind sie der Gefahr entgangen?
11. Wer ist nach Zürich gezogen?
12. Das Genie haben die Räuber umgebracht.

15.13. Note that as in English a participle can be used as an adjective or an adverb. Here are examples:

Gestohlene Äpfel schmecken am besten — *Stolen* apples taste best.
Wer eine Frau nur des Geldes wegen nimmt, bekommt *ungeratene* Kinder — Whoever takes (marries) a wife only because of her money ends up with *spoiled* children.
Der Briefträger läuft *erregt* auf und ab — The mailman walks back and forth *excitedly*.

Although these participles are to be translated as adjectives, their infinitival forms still must sometimes be found before they can be translated accurately.

Note: verbs can be found <u>only</u>:

1) at the beginning of the clause (for questions or commands);
2) in "second" place (for indicative clauses, and for conjugated verbs);
3) at the end of the clause (for infinitives, participles, or dependent clauses —
cf. chapters 23-25)

A word found in any other place can <u>not</u> be a verb!

15.14. Translate these sentences, being particularly aware of participles used as adjectives:

1. Gelehrte Narren sind die besten.
2. Eine gezähmte Zunge ist ein seltsamer Vogel.
3. Gemalte Fenster machen die Stube (*room*) nicht hell. (In other words, superficial measures aren't very effective.)
4. Ungeladene Gäste gehören nicht zum Feste.
5. Mit jeder neu gelernten Sprache erwirbst (*gain*) du eine neue Seele. (Is the first *neu* an adjective or an adverb?)

Vocabulary

an-brechen, brach an, ist ange-brochen — to begin, to break
die **Armut** — poverty
auf-gehen, ging auf, ist aufgegangen — to rise
betrügen, betrog, hat betrogen — to deceive
bieten, bot, hat geboten — to present
das **Bild (-es, -er)** — picture, image
* **bringen, brachte, hat gebracht** — to bring
der **Brunnen (-s, -)** — well
die **Dankbarkeit** — thankfulness
daraus — from it
* **einst** — once
enorm — enormous
entgehen, entging, ist entgangen — to escape
erfahren, erfuhr, hat erfahren — to learn, to discover
* **erfinden, erfand, hat erfunden**

— to invent
erschrecken — to frighten
* **erwarten** — to expect
* **fallen, fiel, ist gefallen** (i) — to fall
fangen, fing, hat gefangen — to catch
der **Gast (-es, -̈e)** — guest
das **Gedicht (-es, -e)** — poem
die **Gefahr** — danger
* **gehören** (i) — to belong to
das **Genie (-s, -s)** — genius
der **Gesang** — song
* **gestern** — yesterday
hell — bright
* **heute** — today
* der **Himmel** — sky, heaven
die **Hoffnung** — hope
* **kennen, kannte, hat gekannt** — to know
laden, lud, hat geladen — to invite
lehren — to teach
* **lernen** — to learn
malen — to paint

mit-nehmen, nahm mit, mitgenommen — to take with
der **Narr** (-en, -en) — fool
* **nie** — never
* **noch** — still
der **Räuber** (-s, -) — robber
* **schreiben, schrieb, hat geschrieben** — to write
* die **Seele** (-n) — soul
* **seltsam** — strange, rare
die **Sprache** (-n) — language
* **stark** — strong
steigen, stieg, ist gestiegen — to climb

* **sterben, starb, ist gestorben** — to die
um-bringen, brachte um, hat umgebracht — to murder
* **werden, wurde, ist geworden** — to become, grow
* **wissen, wußte, hat gewußt** — to know
zähmen — to tame
ziehen, zog, ist gezogen — to move
der **Zorn** (-s) — wrath
die **Zunge** (-n) — tongue

15.15. Vocabulary aid

1. Sie hat die Antwort nicht gewußt.
2. Der Professor ist nie reich geworden.
3. Die Philosophie Wittgensteins kannte der Student nicht.
4. Sind sie nicht hier gewesen?
5. Die Kaktuspflanze ist enorm gewachsen.
6. Der Briefträger hat Fräulein Meier ein seltsames Geschenk (*gift*) gebracht. Sie hatte es nicht erwartet.
7. Dem Studenten gehört das neue Auto.

Reading Selection: *Abraham and Isaak*

[Gott versuchte] Abraham und sprach zu ihm: Abraham! Und er antwortete: Hier bin ich.

Und er sprach: Nimm Isaak, deinen einzigen Sohn, den (*whom*) du liebst, und geh hin in das Land Morija und opfere (*sacrifice*) ihn dort zum Brandopfer (*burnt offering*) auf einem Berge, den (*which*) ich dir sagen werde.

Da stand Abraham früh am Morgen auf und gürtete (*saddled*) seinen Esel und nahm mit sich (*him*) zwei Knechte (*servants*) und seinen Sohn Isaak und spaltete (*split*) Holz zum Brandopfer, machte sich auf (*set out*) und ging an den Ort, von dem Gott ihm gesagt hatte.

Am dritten Tag hob Abraham seine Augen auf und sah die Stätte von ferne (*afar*) und sprach zu seinen Knechten: Bleibt hier mit dem Esel. Ich und der Knabe werden dorthin gehen, und wenn wir gebetet haben (*have prayed*) werden wir wieder zu euch kommen.

Und Abraham nahm das Holz zum Brandopfer und legte es auf seinen Sohn Isaak. Er aber nahm das Feuer und das Messer (*knife*) in seine Hand; und die beiden gingen miteinander.

Dann sprach Isaak zu seinem Vater Abraham: Mein Vater! Abraham antwortete: Hier bin ich, mein Sohn. Und er sprach: Siehe, hier ist Feuer und Holz; wo ist aber das Schaf zum Brandopfer?

Abraham antwortete: Mein Sohn, Gott wird <u>sich ersehen</u> (*select*) ein Schaf zum Brandopfer. Und die beiden gingen miteinander.

Und als (*when*) sie an die Stätte kamen, die (*which*) ihm Gott gesagt hatte, baute Abraham dort einen Altar und legte das Holz darauf und band seinen Sohn Isaak, legte ihn auf den Altar oben auf das Holz.

Und er streckte seine Hand aus und faßte das Messer, so daß er seinen Sohn schlachten konnte (*would be able to slay*).

Dann rief ihn der Engel des Herrn vom Himmel und sprach: Abraham, Abraham! Er antwortete: Hier bin ich!

Er sprach: Lege deine Hand nicht an den Knaben und tu ihm nichts; denn nun weiß ich, daß du Gott fürchtest und hast deines einzigen Sohnes nicht verschont (*spared*) <u>um meinetwillen</u> (*for my sake*).

Dann hob Abraham seine Augen auf und sah einen Widder (*ram*) hinter sich (*him*) in der Hecke (*hedge*) mit seinen Hörnern hängen und ging hin und opferte ihn an seines Sohnes statt.

Vocabulary

auf-heben, hob auf, hat aufgehoben — to raise
* **auf-stehen, stand auf, ist aufgestanden** — to get up
aus-strecken — to reach out, to stretch
* **beide** — both
der **Berg (-es, -e)** — mountain
beten, betete, hat gebetet — to pray
binden, band, hat gebunden — to bind

das **Brandopfer (-s, -)** — burnt offering
* **denn** — for, because
* **dort** — there
einzig — only
fassen — to seize
* **fern** — far
das **Feuer (-s, -)** — fire
* **früh** — early
fürchten — fear
* **gehen, ging, ist gegangen** — to go
hängen — stuck

das **Holz** (**-es**) — wood
der **Knabe** (**-n, -n**) — boy
legen — to lay
das **Messer** (**-s, -**) — knife
miteinander — with each other
* **nehmen, nahm, hat genommen** —
to take
* **nun** — now
* **oben** — above
opfern — to sacrifice
der **Ort** (**-es, -e**) — place

rufen, rief, gerufen — to call
das **Schaf** (**-es, -e**) — sheep
schlachten — to slay
* **sehen, sah, hat gesehen** — to see
* **sprechen, sprach, hat gesprochen**
— to speak
die **Statt** (**-**) — place, stead
die **Stätte** (**-n**) — place
um meinetwillen — for my sake
* **versuchen** — to try

Chapter Sixteen

The Plurals

16.1. German nouns regularly form the plural in five ways. Although I have already listed the plurals in 1.5 of the introduction, here is a review. Plurals of German nouns are indicated by the use of the definite article *die* plus one of the following endings:

1. the ending *-e* (sometimes with, sometimes without an umlaut):

Singular	die Nacht	der Traum	der Hund	das Schaf
Plural	die Nächte	die Träume	die Hunde	die Schafe

2. the ending *-er* (with an umlaut, providing the vowel is a, o, u):

Singular	das Ei	das Kind	der Gott	der Wald
Plural	die Eier	die Kinder	die Götter	die Wälder

3. the ending *-(e)n* (never with an umlaut):

Singular	der Mensch	die Übung	die Frage	die Blume
Plural	die Menschen	die Übungen	die Fragen	die Blumen

4. a few nouns of non-Germanic origin will form the plural by adding *-s*. Many of these will end in a vowel:

Singular	das Auto	das Sofa	das Restaurant
Plural	die Autos	die Sofas	die Restaurants

5. there are also some nouns (ending in -er, -el or -en) which have **no plural endings**. Some of them will have an umlaut added to the medial vowel:

Singular	der Großvater	der Apfel	die Tochter
Plural	die Großväter	die Äpfel	die Töchter

   However, many of these nouns will have neither an ending nor an umlaut:

Singular	der Dichter	das Ringen	der Meister
Plural	die Dichter	die Ringen	die Meister

Therefore, be suspicious whenever you see a noun ending in -l, -e, -r, or -n!

All other nouns (except for a few ending in -s) **will always be singular!** Please **le(a)rn** this!

16.2. How to determine grammatically if a noun is singular or plural

1. Nominative plural nouns will **always** have plural verbs:

   Die Bäume *wachsen* nicht in den Himmel — Trees do not *grow* into the sky. (The English equivalent is: There is a limit to everything.)
   Die Briefträger *lesen* viele Ansichtskarten — The mailmen *read* many picture postcards.

2. Any nominative or accusative plural noun with an adjective following a definite article can be identified as a plural because the adjective ending will **always** be *-n*:

Plural	die schönen Karten	die roten Lampen	die alten Pflanzen
cf. **Singular**	die schöne Karte	die rote Lampe	die alte Pflanze

3. Any dative plural will automatically have an *-n* ending on the definite article and on the end of the noun as well (provided that the plural is not *-s*):

   den Bäumen, **den** Briefträgern, **den** Karten, **den** Kindern

4. Most nouns which end in *-en* or *-er* and which have a *die* article will be plural. The main exceptions are *Mutter, Tochter, Schwester*, and *Butter*. Here are examples:

Plural	die Dichter	die Briefträger	die Häuschen
cf. **Singular**	der Dichter	der Briefträger	das Häuschen

5. If the noun does not have an article, it often will be plural:

   Selten sieht man *Schuhmacher, Briefträger*, oder *Milchmänner* — One seldom sees *shoemakers, mailmen*, or *milkmen*.
   Dichter, Kritiker, und *Romantiker* haben interessante Ideen — *Poets, critics*, and *romanticists* have interesting ideas.
   On the other hand, if you see the article *ein*, the noun will **always** be singular.

16.3. Singular nouns that can look plural:

1. Genitive singular nouns often look plural to American students because of the *-s* ending on masculine and neuter nouns. However, an *-s* usually will signal a singular construction. Examples are:

Singular	der Geist *des* Dichters	die Freundin *des* Briefträgers
cf. **Plural**	der Geist *der* Dichter	die Freundin *der* Briefträger
Singular	die Mutter *des* Kindes	das Buch *des* Professors
cf. **Plural**	die Mutter *der* Kinder	das Buch *der* Professoren

2. Some masculine and neuter dative nouns take an *-e* ending. Examples are: *dem* Briefe; nach Hause; *dem* Hunde; *dem* Kinde.
However, the *dem* or the dative preposition (*aus, außer, bei, mit, nach, seit, von, zu*) is the clue that the noun has to be singular.

3. Adjectives used as nouns can be confusing. Here are the declensions of both the singular and plural cases of *Deutsche*:

	singular (*the German*)	**plural** (*the Germans*)
nominative	**der** Deutsche	**die** Deutschen
accusative	**den** Deutschen	**die** Deutschen
genitive	**des** Deutschen	**der** Deutschen
dative	**dem** Deutschen	**den** Deutschen

Because the form *den Deutschen* can be either accusative singular (Er kennt *den Deutschen* — He knows *the German*) or dative plural (Er spricht mit *den Deutschen* — He speaks with *the Germans*), it is important for you to know whether such a noun is in the accusative or the dative case.

4. Other common nouns which take the *-n* endings in the accusative, genitive and dative cases are: der Student, der Mensch, der Herr, etc. (For a review of weak nouns and adjectives used as nouns, see 8.1-8.4)

Note also appendix E (p. 253) which lists common genitive and plural endings.

16.4. Translate these sentences:

1. Advokaten und Soldaten sind des Teufels Spielkameraden.
2. Ein böses Gewissen hat die Zähne eines Wolfs.
3. Die dümmsten Bauern ernten die dicksten Kartoffeln. (There's no justice!)
4. Hunde, Bauern und Edelleute machen keine Türen zu.

5. Eine fleißige Mutter hat faule Töchter.
6. Anderer Fehler sind gute Lehrer.
7. Die Augen suchen, was dem Herzen gefällt.
8. Viele Streiche fällen (*fell, cut down*) die große Eiche.
9. Die schönsten Äpfel sieht der Wurm zuerst.
10. Ein Kind — kein Kind
    Zwei Kinder — Spielkinder
    Drei Kinder — viele Kinder
    Vier Kinder — ein ganzes Haus voller Kinder!
11. Die Beobachtungen der Historiker haben Fräulein Meier überrascht.
12. Dem Glücklichen schlägt keine Stunde. ("Time flies, when you're having fun!" Note: do not translate *der Glückliche* as *happiness*. Why not?)
13. Die Schlange lauert im Grase.
14. Gute Lehrer haben gute Schüler.
15. Sogar in den Pelz (*fur*) eines Herrenhundes kommen Flöhe.
16. Esel essen Nesseln nie. Nesseln essen Esel nie. (This is a tongue twister which makes virtually no sense. Try saying it as quickly as possible.)

Vocabulary

der **Advokat** (-en, -en) — lawyer
* **ander** — other
der **Apfel** (-s, ⸚) — apple
der **Bauer** (-s, -n) — farmer
die **Beobachtung** (-en) — observation
die **Edelleute** (pl.) — noblemen
die **Eiche** (-n) — oak
* **erkennen** — to recognize
ernten — to reap, harvest
der **Esel** (-s, -) — donkey
* **essen** — to eat
fällen — to fell, to cut down
* **faul** — lazy
* der **Fehler** (-s, -) — error
fleißig — industrious
der **Floh** (-s, ⸚e) — flea
* **ganz** — whole, entire
* **gefallen** (**gefällt**) (i) — to please
* das **Gewissen** (-s, -) — conscience
* **glücklich** — happy
das **Gras** (-es, ⸚er) — grass

der **Herrenhund** (-es, -e) — aristocrat's dog
die **Kartoffel** (-n) — potato
lauern (i) — to lurk
* der **Lehrer** (-s, -) — teacher
die **Nessel** (-n) — nettle
* **nie** — never
der **Pelz** (-es, -e) — fur
schlagen — to strike
die **Schlange** (-n) — snake
* der **Schüler** (-s, -) — student, disciple
* **sogar** — even
der **Soldat** (-en, -en) — soldier
das **Spielkind** (-es, -er) or
der **Spielkamerad** (-en, -en) — playmate
der **Streich** (-es, -e) — blow
die **Stunde** (-n) — hour
* **suchen** — to seek
die **Tochter** (⸚) — daughter
die **Tür** (-en) — door

überraschen — to surprise

voll — full, full of

der **Wurm** (-s, ¨er) — worm

der **Zahn** (-s, ¨e) — tooth

* **zuerst** — first of all

zumachen — to close

Chapter Seventeen

How to Use a German Dictionary

17.1. It is extremely important for you to learn to use a German dictionary correctly. For if you are unable to find a word, or if you choose an improper definition, your translation will be wrong even if you have correctly understood all the grammatical constructions. Therefore, read this section carefully, and refer to it whenever you have trouble finding words.

First I will explain what to look for when you are looking up different parts of speech (and I have listed the parts of speech and other dictionary features in alphabetical order). Note: the advantages and disadvantages of various German-English dictionaries are described in the appendix, pp. 254-260.

17.2. Abbreviations

Abbreviations are found in a separate section of most dictionaries. In the large Cassells, they are found after the center divider, immediately before the English-German section; in the large Langenscheidts, they are found before the center divider, immediately after the German-English section; in the small Langenscheidts, they are found at the very end of the dictionary, after the English-German section. In the Oxford Duden and the Collins dictionary, they are found in the text. There is **no** list of abbreviations in the small Cassells.

The most common abbreviations which are worth memorizing are:

d.h. — *das heißt* (*i.e.* — *that is*)
usw. — *und so weiter* (*etc.* — *and so forth*)
vgl. — *vergleiche* (*cf.* — *compare*)
z.B. — *zum Beispiel* (*for example*)

17.3. Adjectives and adverbs

Adjectives will be indicated by the abbreviation *adj.* and **adverbs** will be indicated by the abbreviation *adv.* Although this seems straightforward, problems arise because some German words can be used both as adjectives and as adverbs. If an adjective has essentially the same meaning when used as an adverb, it will only be listed as an adjective, although it can also be used adverbially. For example, *glücklich* is listed as an adjective even though it can mean both *happy* and *happily*. In contrast to other dictionaries, however, the Oxford Duden often does list both adjectival and adverbial definitions, so *glücklich* is also listed as an adverb meaning *happily*.

Sometimes the same word will have a radically different meaning depending on whether it is used as an adjective or as an adverb. For example, *lauter* as an adjective means *pure*, but as an adverb it means *nothing but*. **The adjectival meaning will always be listed first.** Therefore, if you are looking up an adverb, make sure you have the correct adverbial definition.

Some adjectives will have different meanings depending on the word that they modify. For example, *faul* means *rotten* when it refers to fruit, but it means *lazy* when it refers to people.

17.4. Translate these sentences:

1. Der Student war eben hier.
2. Sein Verwandter ist ihm gar nicht ähnlich.
3. Sie sieht ihn glücklich an.
4. Die linden Brisen sind ihr angenehm.

17.5. Nouns

Nouns will be followed by the symbols *m.* (*masculine*), *f.* (*feminine*) or *n.* (*neuter*). The inflectional forms (genitive singular / nominative plural) will follow in parentheses immediately after the indication of the gender. In the Oxford Duden, however, nouns are followed by the article **der, das**, or **die** in bold faced type.

Because feminine nouns have no form for genitive singular, the first notation in parentheses will be a dash; the second notation will be the plural. (In some dictionaries, only the plural will be indicated.) Here are examples of two feminine nouns:

Nadel f. (-; -n)   Therefore, the plural of Nadel is Nadeln.
Braut f. (-; ̈e)   Therefore, the plural of Braut is Bräute.

In the Oxford Duden, if an umlaut is added to the medial vowel, the entire plural form will be written out. Here is an example: **Braut die; ~, Bräute**

Here are examples of neuter nouns, which have genitive singular forms:
Grab n. (-[e]s, ⁻er) The genitive singular of Grab is either Grabes or Grabs, and the plural is **Gräber**.
Modell n. (-s, -e) The genitive singular of Modell is Modells, and the plural is Modelle.
Mädchen n. (-s, -) The genitive of Mädchen is Mädchens, and there is **no** plural ending.

Some masculine and neuter nouns are known as *weak nouns* (cf. 8.1-8.2). These nouns can be identified because their genitive form will be listed as *-en* (for animate masculine nouns) or *-ens* (for inanimate masculine and neuter nouns). Here are examples of three such nouns and their singular declensions:

Mensch, m. (-en, -en) (plural is: Menschen);
Name, m. (-ens, -n) (plural is: Namen);
Herz, n. (-ens, -en) (plural is: Herzen)

Nominative	der Mensch	der Name	das Herz
Accusative	den Menschen	den Namen	das Herz
Genitive	des Menschen	des Namens	des Herzens
Dative	dem Menschen	dem Namen	dem Herzen

Some nouns will be spelled the same, but their meanings will vary according to their gender and according to their plurals. Here are examples:

Band n. (-s; ⁻er)   ribbon, riband, tape, string
Band n. (-s, -e)   bond, fetter, chain
Band m. (-es, ⁻e)   volume
Tor m. (-en, -en)   fool, simpleton
Tor n. (-[e]s, -e)   gate

Also a noun sometimes can have radically different meanings according to context. For example, *Einsatz* means *stake* when it refers to a game, and it means *lace insert* when it refers to a dress, and its military definition is *mission*.

Also be wary of expressions which include parts of the body (eye, nose, head, heart, etc.), but which do not make sense initially. Such phrases usually will be idiomatic. Examples are: *ein flammendes Herz* (literally: a *flaming* heart) — a bleeding heart; *auf freiem Fuß* (literally: *on a free foot*) — at liberty; *unter vier Augen* (literally: *under four eyes*) — face-to-face. Whenever an idiomatic meaning seems likely, check the definitions of the body part in question.

17.6. Translate these sentences:

1. Fräulein Meier hat Schwierigkeiten mit ihrer Jalousie.
2. Aus einem kleinen Reis wird ein großer Baum.
3. Das Buch besteht aus drei Bänden.
4. Auf keinen Fall wird Fräulein Meier ihre Katze aufgeben.
5. Die lange Erklärung hatte weder Hand noch Fuß.

17.7. Compound nouns

Compound nouns often are not listed as separate entries; instead, *Meister-stück* will be found somewhere after *Meister, Gegensatz* may be found somewhere after *gegen*, and the like. Moreover, compound nouns won't always be listed in your dictionary. Whenever you encounter such a compound, divide it into its separate parts (watch for s's, as they may be used as connectives). For a rough, literal definition, translate each word within the compound, then hyphenate your English translation. Examples are: *Kartenspiel* (Karten-Spiel) — card game; *Kinderfreundlichkeit* (Kinder-Freundlichkeit) — child-orientation; *Herzentzündung* (Herz-Entzündung) — heart-inflammation. Once you have understood the concept, you may wish to add an "of" or a "for" to make the translation smoother. Examples are: *der Freiheitsbegriff* (Freiheits-Begriff) — the concept *of* freedom; *die Gerechtigkeitslehre* (Gerechtigkeits-Lehre) — the doctrine *of* justice; *die Unfallversicherungsgesellschaft* (Unfall-Versicherungs-Gesellschaft) — the society *for* accident insurance.

17.8. Translate these compounds:

die Unabhängigkeitserklärung; die Erdentstehungslehre; die Seinserfahrung; die Formveränderung; die Sättigungspunktsbestimmung.

17.9. Proper nouns

German proper nouns (including names of countries) will be listed in the back of the small Langenscheidts (after the English-German section), and they also will be listed in a separate section in the large Cassells published before 1978. They will be listed in the text in most other dictionaries. Unlike English, a proper noun turned into an adjective will **not** be capitalized. Here is an example:

die *deutsche* Schreibmaschine — the *German* typewriter.

Sometimes people's names will coincidentally also have a common noun meaning, which should be ignored. Examples are: Spengler (plumber) — a

German philosopher; Fichte (pine tree) — a German philosopher; Walther von der Vogelweide (bird pasture) — a German poet. For a list of proper German names, see page 357.

17.10. Prepositions

Prepositions will be indicated by the abbreviation *prep.* Since prepositions take either accusative, dative, genitive, or dative or accusative cases, the case they take will be indicated in parentheses. When a preposition takes either dative or accusative, your dictionary will list definitions associated with the dative case first. Because preposition entries generally are long, they can be a nuisance, as it is hard to find the meaning sought. If a preposition seems to be joined with a specific verb, the correct idiom generally can be found more quickly if the verb is looked up instead. Examples of verb-preposition combinations are: **bestehen aus** (*to consist of*), **fragen nach** (*to ask about*), **erinnern an** (*to remind of*), and **warten auf** (*to wait for*).

For the most common meanings of prepositions, consult my preposition list (Chapter Five, pp. 239-240 of the Appendix) or my Humanities Vocabulary.

17.11. Translate these sentences:

1. Vielleicht wird man das Gesetz außer Kraft setzen.
2. Der Briefträger besteht auf der Wahrheit.
3. Kant hatte einen wichtigen Einfluß auf Kleist.
4. Was verstehen Sie unter diesem Begriff?

17.12. Verbs

Verbs will be followed by the abbreviation *v.t.* (or *v.a.* or *tr. V.*) which will indicate that the verb is transitive (it can have a direct object), or it will be followed by the abbreviation *v.i.* (or *v.n.* or *itr. V.*) which will indicate that the verb is intransitive (it cannot have a direct object). If a verb has no other symbols following it, you can assume that it is conjugated regularly, and that it takes **haben** as its auxiliary verb.

Therefore, if you look up **lachen**, it will be conjugated as follows: lachen, **lach**te, **hat ge**lacht.

If you look up a verb such as **folgen**, you will see the following symbols: *v.i.* (*aux. sein* or *mit sein*). The notation *aux. sein* indicates that **folgen** is to be conjugated as follows; folgen, folg**te**, and **ist ge**folgt. A large dictionary will also note that while **folgen** (aux. sein) means *to follow*, **folgen** (aux. h.) means *to obey.* A large dictionary will also have (Dat.) in parentheses to indicate that the verb *folgen* only takes a dative object. (Er folgt *mir* — He follows *me*.)

Irregular verbs will be listed as *irr. v.* or as *unr.* And a list of irregular verbs is included in most dictionaries. An irregular verb which has *sein* as its auxiliary will be listed as follows: *irr. v. i. (aux. sein).* Verbs which take *sein* as an auxiliary will be intransitive.

A verb which is **reflexive** will be listed as follows: *v.r.* or *refl. V.* The reflexive meaning of a verb will usually be listed second, except in the Oxford Duden where the reflexive meaning may be listed first if it is more common than the non-reflexive meaning. While the non-reflexive definition of **erinnern** is "to remind," the reflexive definition is "to remember." (Reflexive verbs will be explained in Chapter Twenty-six.)

Some verbs will even have different definitions depending on whether they are used transitively or intransitively. For example, *heißen* as a transitive verb means *to command*, while as an intransitive verb, it means *to be called*. When verbs have both transitive and intransitive definitions, the transitive meaning will usually be given first, except in the Oxford Duden, where the more common definition will be given first.

When a verb combined with a preposition has a radically different meaning, it will be listed in italics or bold face type. For example, *bestehen auf* means *to insist on* while *bestehen aus* means *to consist of*.

Some verbs also have different definitions depending on whether they are separable or inseparable. While *übersetzen* (separable) means *to set over*, *übersetzen* (inseparable) means *to translate*. While *wiederholen* (separable) means *to fetch back*, *wiederholen* (inseparable) means *to repeat*.

Be cautious of verbs (often with prefixes) which have both literal and figurative meanings. The literal meaning is usually given first, while the more "figurative" meanings — which are generally used in scholarly writings — are listed later, as a third or fourth definition. For example, among other things, *einfallen* means both *to collapse* and *to occur to someone*; *zugehen* means both *to close* and *to happen*.

17.13. Translate these sentences:

1. Wer traut dem alten Wahrsager?
2. Wann sind die Ereignisse eingetreten?
3. Wenn ihre Uhr nachgeht, kommt Fräulein Meier oft zu spät.

4. Die Verhandlungen gehen um Leben und Tod!
5. Mutter sein heißt Märtyrerin sein.

17.14. Added cautions, false cognates

Be careful when looking up all words. Small carelessnesses such as mistaking *kein* for *klein*, *Lied* for *Leid*, or *Freude* for *Freunde* can seriously affect your translation, regardless of how well you understand German grammar. Whenever a sentence seems unusually awkward or incomprehensible, you should probably double check the definitions of the words in it!

Also, beware of the following false cognates:

also — therefore (*not* "also")
Art — manner, way (*not* "art")
bekommen — to receive (*not* "to become")
brav — honest, good (*not* "brave")
breit — wide, broad (*not* "bright")
Christ — Christian (*not* "Christ")
denn — because, for (*not* "then")
Geld — money (*not* "gold")
human — humane (*not* "human")
konkurrieren — to compete (*not* "to concur")
Konvent — meeting, convention (*not* "convent")
pathetisch — lofty, elevated, expressive (*not* "pathetic")
Prägnanz — precision (*not* "pregnant")
Rapport — report (*not* "rapport")
sensibel — sensitive (*not* "sensible")
Sinn — sense, meaning (*not* "sin")

17.15. A final note: If you have trouble memorizing words, you might find it helpful to mark common words and definitions in your dictionary so you can find them more easily whenever you need to look them up.

In case you have skimmed this chapter, please make sure you have done the exercises 17.4; 17.6; 17.8; 17.11; and 17.13.

Chapter Eighteen
Common Suffixes

18.1. Common Suffixes (Note: a list of prefixes can be found on 13.2 and 13.9. A complete list of suffixes can be found in *A German Word Family Dictionary*: Howard Keller, The University of California Press, 1978)

-bar generally means *ible*. It is added to verbs to turn them into adjectives. Examples are: *denkbar* (*thinkable*), *eßbar* (*edible*), *trennbar* (*separable*).

-chen and *-lein* are diminutives which are added to nouns. Examples are: *Vögelchen* (*little bird*), *Häuslein* (*little house*), *Fräulein* (*literally: little woman*), *Rotkäppchen* (*Little Red Riding Hood*).

-d changes a verb into a present participle which will always be an adjective or adverb. Examples are: *singend* (*singing*), *lachend* (*laughing*), *spielend* (*playing*).

-e added to an adjective (adding an umlaut to the stem vowel) will change it into a noun. Examples are *Güte* (*goodness*) from *gut*; *Kälte* (*coldness*) from *kalt*; *Treue* (*loyalty*) from *treu*; *Schwäche* (*weakness*) from *schwach*.

-fach means *fold*, *times*. Examples are: *dreifach* (*three times*), *vielfach* (*many times*).

-haft means having the quality of the word expressed in the stem. Do not confuse this with *Haft* which means *imprisonment*. Examples are: *lehrhaft* (*didactic*; cf. *Lehre* — *teaching*), *rätselhaft* (*puzzling*; cf. *Rätsel* — *puzzle*), *zweifelhaft* (*doubtful*; cf. *Zweifel* — *doubt*).

-heit, -keit, -igkeit are added to adjectives to form abstract nouns corresponding to English nouns ending in *-ity* or *-ness*. Examples are: *Ewigkeit* (*eternity*; cf. *ewig* — *eternal*), *Krankheit* (*sickness*; cf. *krank* — *sick*), *Genauigkeit* (*exactness*; cf. *genau* — *exact*).

-ig is like the English *y*. Examples are *hungrig* (*hungry*), *durstig* (*thirsty*), *völlig* (*fully*).

-isch is added to nouns to turn them into adjectives. Examples are: *neidisch* (*envious*; cf. *Neid* — *envy*), *launisch* (*moody*; cf. *Laune* — *mood*), *kindisch* (*childish*; cf. *Kind* — *child*).

-lich is added to verbs and nouns to turn them into adjectives. When it is added to verbs, *-lich* means *-able*, and when it is added to nouns, it means *-ly*. Examples are: *nützlich* (*useful*; cf. *nützen*), *glaublich* (*believable*; cf. *glauben*), *freundlich* (*friendly*; cf. *Freund*), *monatlich* (*monthly*; cf. *Monat*).

-los means *without, less*. Examples are: *hilflos* (*helpless*), *farblos* (*colorless*), *herzlos* (*heartless*).

-mal means *time, times*. Examples are: *manchmal* (*sometimes*), *einmal* (*once*), *zehnmal* (*ten times*).

-ung is added to a verb, and it corresponds to nouns ending in *-ing, -tion*, and *-ment*. Examples are: *Übung* (*practice*; cf. *üben*), *Trennung* (*separation*; cf. *trennen*), *Vertreibung* (*banishment*; cf. *vertreiben*).

18.2. Translate these sentences:

1. Jedes Häuslein hat sein Kreuzlein.
2. Das Geld geht hinkend ein und geht tanzend fort.
3. Baue dem fliehenden Feind eine goldene Brücke.
4. Ein lebendiger Hund ist besser als ein toter Löwe.
5. Im Spiel gibt es keine Freundschaft.
6. Wenn man die Gerechtigkeit biegt (*bends*), so bricht sie.
7. Alles ist flüchtig, nur das Ewige [ist] wichtig.
8. Bei Gott ist kein Ding unmöglich.
9. Einmal ist keinmal.
10. Die Dichter sind gegen ihre Erlebnisse schamlos; sie beuten sie aus. (Nietzsche) (How do you know that *schamlos* does *not* modify *Erlebnisse*?)

Vocabulary

* **alles** — everything
  aus-beuten — to exploit
  aus-gehen (i) — to exit
* **bauen** — to build
* **brechen** — to break
  die **Brücke** (-n) — bridge
* der **Dichter** (-s, -) — writer, poet

ein-gehen (i) — to enter
* **einmal** — once, one time
  das **Erlebnis** (-sses, -sse) — experience
  ewig — eternal
* der **Feind** (-es, -e) — enemy
  fliehen — to flee

flüchtig — fleeting
fort-gehen (i) — to go away
die Freundschaft — friendship
* das Geld (-er) — money
* gegen — against, with regard to
* die Gerechtigkeit — justice
hinken (i) — to limp
keinmal — no time
das Kreuz (-es, -e) — cross

* lebendig — living
der Löwe (-n, -n) — lion
* nur — only
* schamlos — shameless
* das Spiel (-s, -e) — game
* tot — dead
* unmöglich — impossible
* wichtig — important

Chapter Nineteen

The Modal Auxiliaries

19.1. In German, there are six modals, known superficially as "helping verbs." Since modals usually express an attitude towards the action expressed by an infinitive rather than a specific action themselves, they seldom appear alone in a sentence. For example, in the English sentence, "I *must* work," the modal *must* causes the infinitive *work* to be perceived as a necessity. In the sentence, "I *can* work," the modal *can* indicates that the work is capable of being done, but is no longer a necessity. And in the sentence, "I *want* to work," the modal *want* indicates that the work is in fact desirable.

The modals are:

dürfen — to be permitted to, may
können — can, to be able to
mögen — to like to, may
müssen — to have to, must
sollen — to be supposed to, is to
wollen — to want to, to intend to

19.2. Here are the present tense forms for all six modals. Note that the singular form is significantly different from the infinitive for the modals *dürfen, können, mögen*, and *wollen*. Also note that the first and third person singular are identical for all modals:

	dürfen	*können*	*mögen*	*müssen*	*sollen*	*wollen*
ich	darf	kann	mag	muß	soll	will
du	darfst	kannst	magst	mußt	sollst	willst
er	darf	kann	mag	muß	soll	will
wir	dürfen	können	mögen	müssen	sollen	wollen
ihr	dürft	könnt	mögt	müßt	sollt	wollt
sie	dürfen	können	mögen	müssen	sollen	wollen
Sie	dürfen	können	mögen	müssen	sollen	wollen

19.3. **In a simple indicative sentence with a modal, the modal will be in "second" place, and the infinitive will be at the end of the clause.** Here are sentences with each of the six modals:

Wenn sie eine Karte hat, *darf* sie in die Bibliothek *gehen* — If she has a card, she *is permitted* to go to the library.

Der Briefträger *kann* die lesbare Schrift leicht *lesen* — The mailman *can* easily read the legible handwriting. (Note: *kann* should **not** be translated as *to know*!)

Fräulein Meier *mag* das nicht *tun* — Fräulein Meier does not *like* to do that.

Jeden Tag *muß* der Student viel *studieren* — The student *has to* study a lot each day.

Was *soll* sie *tun*? — What *should* she do?

Der Student *will* ins Theater *gehen* — The student *wants to* go to the theater.

19.4. Common idioms involving modals (memorize the asterisked sentences — they are used as often as the more standard meanings):

Er *kann* Deutsch — He speaks German.

* Das *mag* sein — That *may* be.
An example: Der Professor *mag* krank *sein* — The professor *may be* ill.

Er *soll* gelehrt *sein* — He *is reputed to be* educated.

* Heute abend *soll* der Professor seine berühmte Vorlesung halten — This evening the professor *is to* give his famous lecture.
Another example: Das Gebäude *soll* ein Museum werden — The building *is to* become a museum.
Soll das wahr sein? — *Can* that be true?

Mögen often appears in its subjunctive form — *möchte*, which is best translated *would like to*:
Fräulein Meier *möchte* Zoologie studieren — Fräulein Meier *would like to* study zoology.

19.5. Sometimes the modals can be difficult to translate because they look so much like English cognates. For example *muß* sometimes is better translated as *have to* rather than *must*, and *sollen* sometimes is better translated *is to* rather than *should*. Here is a graphic example: Da ihr Mann im Kriege gefallen war, *sollte* das Kind der armen Frau keinen Vater haben — Because her husband had been killed in the war, the child of the poor woman *was to* have no father.

19.6. The past and present perfect tenses of modals

The pasts of the modals are formed in the following ways:

Modal	Past
dürfen — to be permitted	*durfte* — was permitted
können — to be able to, can	*konnte* — was able to, could
mögen — to like to, may	*mochte* — liked to, might
müssen — to have to, must	*mußte* — had to
sollen — is to, should	*sollte* — was to, was supposed to
wollen — to want to	*wollte* — wanted to

The past tense of *müssen* is always translated as *had to*:

Sie *mußte* Finnisch studieren — She *had to* study Finnish.

The modals almost never appear in their participial forms. Instead, the following construction is much more common:

Er *hat* nicht gehen *dürfen* — He was not permitted to go.
Er *hat* viel dazu sagen *können* — He was able to say a lot about that.
Sie *hat* ihrem Freund helfen *müssen* — She had to help her friend.
Es *hat* eben nicht sein *sollen* — That just should not have been (that way).
Sie *haben* essen *wollen* — They wanted to eat.

19.7. Modals in combination with other verbs

Modals can be used in combination with (1) the future, (2) the past, and (3) other modals. When you are confronted with any of these combinations, you should translate the modal first, the verb at the end of the clause second, and the penultimate verb last. Here is an example:

Sie *konnte* das *getan haben* — She could have done that.
    1   3   2

(1) The future combination with a modal is formed as follows:

Sie *wird* das *tun können* — She will be able to do that.
  1   3   2

Wir *werden* alles *wissen wollen* — We will want to know everything.
  1   3   2

Er *wird* viele Briefe *schreiben müssen* — He will have to write several letters.
  1   3   2

(2) Here are modals in combination with the past infinitive:

Ein Dilettant **kann** das Buch nicht **geschrieben haben** — An amateur can not
have written the book.

Ehe du Gott suchst, **muß** dich Gott schon **gefunden haben** — Before you look
for God, he already must have found you.

(3) Here are examples for modals in combination with other modals:

Der alte Mann **soll** nicht immer zu Hause **bleiben wollen** — The old man
should not always want to stay at home.

Das Kind **muß** endlich **schlafen wollen** — The child must finally want to
sleep.

**19.8. Sometimes when a modal is used with a verb of action, that verb will
be omitted, and only the modal will be used:**

Wenn wir nicht [tun] **können**, was wir [tun] **wollen**, so **müssen** wir [tun], was
wir [tun] **können** — If we *can* not *do* what we *want to do*, then we *have to do*
what we *can (do)*. Although the **tun** is omitted in German, *do* is added in
English. Here are further examples:

Darf ich ins Kino? — *May* I *go* to the movies?
Er **kann** nichts dazu — He *can do* nothing (or: can't do anything) about it.
Wo **wollen** Sie hin — Where do you *want to go*?

19.9. Additional verbs which occasionally function as modals

(1) The verb **lassen** also can function as a type of modal when it means
(a) to let, to permit, to allow, or
(b) to have something done, to cause, to make. Here are examples:

Der Briefträger **läßt** Fräulein Meier viel **klatschen** — The mailman *lets* Fräulein
Meier *gossip* a lot.
Ach du großer Gott! Was für kleine Kartoffeln **läßt** du **wachsen**! — Alas great
God! What kind of small potatoes do you *let grow*! (In other words, why do
you make so many stupid little things when you are capable of magnificent
creations?)
Der Professor **läßt** sich einen neuen Anzug **machen** — The professor *has* a new
suit *made*.

(2) Other verbs which occasionally function as modals are: **heißen** (*to order, to
bid*), **hören** (*to hear*), **lernen** (*to learn*), **machen** (*to make*), and **sehen** (*to see*).
Here are examples:

Der Professor *heißt* den Studenten *hereinkommen* — The professor *asks* the student *to come in.*

Die Mutter *hörte* ihr Kind *singen* — The mother *heard* her child *sing.*

Im Zoo *sahen* die Leute den Bären *tanzen* — At the zoo, the people *saw* the bear *dance.*

Wer will *schwimmen lernen* — Who wants to *learn to swim?*

19.10. Translate these sentences:

1. Den Alten muß man glauben. (Note: *glauben* is intransitive.)
2. Liebe und Husten (*coughing*) kann man nicht verbergen (*conceal*).
3. Das Werk zeigt an, was der Mann kann.
4. In den Monaten ohne "r" (Mai, Juni, Juli, August) soll man wenig küssen und viel trinken. (... because it is so hot then.)
5. Um eines faulen Astes (*branch*) willen soll man den Baum nicht umhauen (*cut down*). (Do not confuse *um ... willen* with *wollen*!)
6. Ein Mann, der (*who*) will, kann mehr als zehn, die (*who*) müssen.
7. Wer befehlen (*command*) will, muß erst gehorchen (*obey*) lernen.
8. Not lehrt den Affen geigen (*to fiddle*). (When he is desperate, an ape or person can do *anything*.)
9. Die Hexen haben rote Augen und können nicht weit sehen, aber sie haben eine feine Witterung (sense of smell) wie die Tiere und merken es, wenn Menschen herankommen. (aus *Hänsel und Gretel*)
10. Wer das Wasser des Lebens sucht, muß lange dürsten (*to thirst*) können.
11. Spucke (*spit*) nicht in den Brunnen (*well*), wenn du noch daraus trinken mußt.
12. Die Behauptung (*assertion*) des Briefträgers über Fräulein Meier mag wahr sein.
13. Fräulein Meier will sich (*herself*) bessern; also belegt sie einen Fernkurs (*correspondence course*), und sie studiert Erdkunde (*geography*).
14. Der Briefträger hat Fräulein Meier bei ihren Schularbeiten (*homework*) helfen müssen.
15. Von allen Bäumen des Gartens darfst du essen, nur vom Baum der Erkenntnis von Gut und Böse darfst du nicht essen; denn am Tage, an dem du davon ißt, mußt du sterben.
16. Willst du immer weiter schweifen (*roam*)?
    Sieh, das Gute liegt so nah.
    Lerne nur, das Glück ergreifen (*grasp*),
    Denn das Glück ist immer da.
    (Goethe)

Vocabulary

der **Affe** (-n, -n) — ape
* der **Alte** (-n, -n) — old man
* **also** — therefore
  an-zeigen — to indicate
  der **Ast** (-es, ⁻e) — branch
* der **Baum** (-es, ⁻e) — tree
  die **Behauptung** (-en) — assertion
  belegen — to take; to enroll in
* **bessern** — to improve
* das **Böse** — evil
  der **Brunnen** (-s, -) — well
* **da** — there; then
* **denn** — for, because
* **dürfen** (darf) — to be permitted to
  dürsten (i) — to thirst
  die **Erdkunde** — geography
  ergreifen — to grasp
* die **Erkenntnis** — knowledge
  erzählen — to tell
* **essen** (ißt) — to eat
  faul — rotten
  das **Gedicht** (-es, -e) — poem
* **glauben** (t. & i.) — to believe
  herankommen (i) — to approach
* **heute abend** — this evening
  die **Hexe** (-n) — witch
  das **Husten** (-s, -) — coughing
* **können** (kann) — can, to be able to
  küssen — to kiss
* **lange** — for a long time

* **lassen** (läßt) — to let
* das **Leben** (-s) — life
* **lehren** — to teach
* **lernen** — to learn
* die **Liebe** — love
* **liegen** (i) — to lie
* **manchmal** — sometimes
* **merken** — to notice
* **mögen** (mag) — like to, may
* der **Monat** (-s, -e) — month
* **müssen** (muß) — to have to
* **nah** — near
* **nehmen** — to take
  die **Not** (⁻e) — need
* **nur** — only, just
  die **Schularbeit** (-en) — school
  work
* **sollen** (soll) — should; is to
  spucken — to spit
* **sterben** (i) — to die
* **suchen** — to seek
  das **Tier** (-s, e) — animal
* **um . . . willen** — for the sake of
  verbergen — to conceal
  vor-lesen — to read
* **weit** — far
* **weiter** — further
* **wenig** — little
* **wollen** (will) — want to
* **zehn** — ten

19.11. Vocabulary aid

1. Die Katze mag hungrig sein.
2. Heute abend soll der Professor uns seine neuesten Gedichte vorlesen.
3. Er will glücklich sein.
4. Sie mußte lange da bleiben.
5. Wer hat den Apfel nicht essen dürfen?
6. Die Mutter läßt das Kind die Geschichte (*story*) erzählen.
7. Können Sie ihnen glauben?
8. Sie will die Philosophie Spinozas studieren.

9. Einen Monat lang hat der Briefträger schlechtes Wetter erleiden (*put up with*) müssen.
10. Unseren Freunden kann sie helfen.

Reading Selection: *November*
(Peter Bichsel)

Er <u>fürchtete sich</u> (*was afraid*) und wenn er zu jemandem sagte: "Es ist kälter geworden", erwartete er Trost (*comfort*).

"Ja, November", sagte der andere.

"Bald ist es Weihnachten", sagte er.

Er hatte Heizöl eingekauft, er besaß einen Wintermantel, er war versorgt (*prepared*) für den Winter, aber er fürchtete sich. Im Winter ist man verloren. Im Winter ist alles Schreckliche möglich, Krieg zum Beispiel. Im Winter <u>kann die Stelle gekündigt werden</u> (*one can lose one's job*), im Winter <u>erkältet</u> man <u>sich</u> (*catches cold*). Man kann sich (*himself*) schützen gegen die Kälte, Halstuch (*scarf*), Mantelkragen (*coat collar*), Handschuhe. Aber es könnte (*could*) noch kälter werden.

Es nützt nichts, jetzt "Frühling" zu sagen.

Die Schaufenster sind beleuchtet (*lit up*), sie täuschen Wärme vor. Aber die Kirchenglocken klirren (*clank*). In den Wirtschaften (*taverns*) ist es heiß, zu Hause öffnen die Kinder die Fenster und lassen die Wohnungstür offen, im Geschäft (*office*) vergißt man seinen Hut.

Man bemerkt nicht, wie die Bäume die Blätter fallen lassen. Plötzlich haben sie keine mehr. Im April haben sie wieder Blätter, im März vielleicht schon. Man wird sehen, wie sie Blätter bekommen.

Bevor er das Haus verläßt, zählt er sein Geld nach.

Schnee wird es keinen geben, Schnee gibt es nicht mehr.

Frierende Frauen sind schön, Frauen sind schön.

"Man muß <u>sich</u> an die Kälte <u>gewöhnen</u> (*accustom oneself*)", sagte er, "man muß tiefer atmen (*breathe*) und schneller gehen." — "Was soll ich den Kindern zu Weihnachten kaufen?" fragte er.

"Man wird sich an die Kälte gewöhnen", sagte er zum anderen. "Ja, es ist kälter geworden, November", sagte der andere.

Vocabulary

alles Schreckliche — everything (that is) terrible	**besitzen** — to own
* **ander** — other	**das Blatt (-es, ¨er)** — leaf, page
* **bald** — soon	**ein-kaufen** — to buy
* **bekommen** — to get, receive	**frierend** — freezing
bemerken — to notice	**der Frühling (-s)** — spring
	fürchten (sich) — to fear

gewöhnen (sich) — to accustom oneself
heiß — hot
das **Heizöl** — heating oil
der **Hut (-es, ̈e)** — hat
* **ja** — yes, indeed
* **jemand** — someone
* **jetzt** — now
* **kaufen** — to buy
die **Kirchenglocke (-n)** — church bell
* der **Krieg (-es, -e)** — war
lassen — to let
März — March
* **möglich** — possible
nach-zählen — to count again
(es) **nützt nichts** — it is not worth it

* **plötzlich** — suddenly
das **Schaufenster (-s, -)** — show window
* **schnell** — fast, quick
* **schon** — already
schützen — to protect
* **tief** — deep
vergessen — to forget
verlassen — to leave
verlieren — to lose
* **vielleicht** — perhaps
vor-täuschen — to feign
Weihnachten — Christmas
* **wieder** — again
die **Wohnungstür (-en)** — apartment door
zum Beispiel — for example

Chapter Twenty

The Zu Construction

20.1. In German, a verb is seen in its infinitival form with a _zu_ in front of it if it is found in a sentence with another verb which is not a modal. Here are examples:

Es _macht_ Spaß, ins Kino _zu gehen_ — It is fun to go to the movies.
Er _hat_ Angst, das _zu tun_ — He is afraid to do that.
Er _denkt_ daran, auf seine Freundin _zu warten_ — He thinks about waiting for his girlfriend.
Fräulein Meier _hält_ es für gut, ihrer Katze Thunfisch _zu füttern_ — Fräulein Meier thinks it good to feed her cat tuna.

In this construction, there usually will be a comma separating each clause, and the infinitival form of the verb will appear at the end of the clause. If the infinitive is an inseparable verb, the _zu_ construction will appear as follows: _zu gehen, zu wissen, zu verstehen, zu beschreiben_.

If the verb is separable, however, the _zu_ will appear between the prefix and the verb root — _aufzumachen, fortzuwerfen, anzusehen_ are examples. And here is a sample sentence:

Manchmal ist es schwer, früh _aufzustehen_ — Sometimes it is difficult to get up early.

Therefore, in order to find the infinitive, simply eliminate the _zu_ in the middle.

20.2. Placement of the _zu_ construction when translated into English

When the noun appearing in the infinitival clause is nominative, the _zu_ and the infinitive usually will remain at the end of the clause in your English translation. Here are examples:

Der Fuchs (_nominative_) ist schwer zu fangen — _The fox_ is hard to capture.
Die Theologie Schleiermachers (_nominative_) ist interessant zu lesen — _The theology of Schleiermacher_ is interesting to read.

But if the noun in the infinitival clause happens to be accusative or dative, the *zu* and the infinitive should be placed in front of that noun in your English translation. Here are examples:

Es hilft nicht, **den Dieb** (*accusative*) zu beschreiben — It does not help to describe *the thief*.

Es ist nicht der Mühe wert, **dem Dilettanten** (*dative*) zuzuhören — It is not worth the effort to listen *to the amateur*.

Die Katze versucht **den Vogel mit großen Flügeln** (*accusative*) zu fangen und **ihn** (*accusative*) zu töten — The cat tries to capture *the bird with large wings* and to kill *it*.

Sometimes, the phrase before the fragment will contain a *da*-compound, which you should ignore in your translation:

Das Publikum wartet ungeduldig *darauf*, die berühmte Schauspielerin zu sehen — The public is impatiently waiting to see the famous actress.

20.3. Three common phrases using *zu*: *um...zu, ohne...zu,* and *anstatt...zu*

The most common of these constructions is **um...zu**, which will always mean *in order to*. Here are examples:

Er will hier sein, **um** den Professor kennen**zu**lernen — He wants to be here *in order to* meet the professor.

Fräulein Meier belegt einen Briefwechselkursus, **um** etwas **zu** lernen — Fräulein Meier takes a correspondence course *in order to* learn something.

Er gibt einen Taler aus, **um** einen Pfennig **zu** sparen — He spends a dollar *in order to* save a penny.

The other two phrases are **anstatt...zu** which means *instead of*, and **ohne . . . zu** which means *without*. Here are examples:

Anstatt das Schauspiel **Sappho** von Grillparzer **zu lesen**, ging der Student ins Kino — *Instead of reading* Grillparzer's play, *Sappho*, the student went to the movies.

Sie tut das, **ohne** ihren Freund **zu fragen** — She does that *without asking* her friend.

20.4. The negation of *müssen* (to have to) is *nicht brauchen zu* (not to have to). Here are examples:

Du *brauchst* das *nicht zu* tun — You do not have to do that.

Wer die Sonne hat, *braucht nicht* nach den Sternen *zu* fragen — Whoever has the sun (i.e. good things) need not ask about the stars.

20.5. *Zu* in combination with *sein*

Note that *zu* used with an infinitive following all forms of the verb *sein* will be translated into English with a passive meaning. Here are examples:

Von einem Rind *ist* nicht mehr als Rindfleisch *zu erwarten* — From a cow, nothing other than beef *is to be expected.*
Im Zoo *war* nur ein Flußpferd *zu sehen* — In the zoo, only one hippo *was to be seen.*
When used with a negation, this construction can be used to indicate something that cannot be done, and therefore should be translated passively with *cannot.* Here are examples:

Die Antwort *ist nicht zu verstehen* — The answer *cannot be understood.*
Die Bärin *war nicht zu finden* — The she-bear *could not be found.*

However, whenever an adjective (rather than an adverb or a noun) follows any form of the verb *sein*, the clause will not be translated passively, but rather like a normal *zu* construction:

Auch im Paradies *ist* es nicht *gut*, allein zu sein — Even in Paradise it is not good to be alone.
Es *ist klug*, schlafende Hunde liegen *zu lassen* — It is wise to let sleeping dogs lie.

20.6. Translate these sentences:

1. Im Haus eines Diebes ist es schwer zu stehlen.
2. Der Wolf drückte auf die Klinke, die Türe ging auf, und er ging, ohne ein Wort zu sprechen, gerade zum Bett der Großmutter und verschluckte sie. (aus *Rotkäppchen*)
3. Es kann kein Wahrsager (*prophet*) den anderen ansehen, ohne zu lachen.
4. Es ist besser, eine Laus im Kohl zu finden, als gar kein Fleisch.
5. Gott schließt keine Tür, ohne eine andere aufzumachen.
6. Geschehene Dinge (*things which have happened*) sind nicht zu ändern.
7. Man muß zeitig (*on time*) aufbrechen (*leave*); dann braucht man nicht zu rennen (*run*).
8. Nicht wenn es gefährlich ist, die Wahrheit zu sagen, findet sie am seltensten Vertreter, sondern wenn es langweilig ist. (Nietzsche)
9. Drei Dinge sind nicht aufzuhalten: Wasser, Feuer, die Menschenmenge.
10. Der Briefträger geht manchmal zehn Schritte, um einen zu sparen.
11. Der Journalist liebte es, die Schwächen anderer boshaft und treffend zu karikieren.

12. Curt zertrat seine Zigarette, und Nikolaus nützte den Augenblick, um vor ihm einzusteigen (*to get on [a bus]*) und Recha die Hand zu reichen und ohne aufdringliche (*urgent*) Hast den Platz neben ihr zu nehmen. (Brigitte Reimann)

13. Alles hat seine Stunde, und es gibt eine Zeit für jegliche (*every*) Sache unter der Sonne. Eine Zeit für die Geburt und eine Zeit für das Sterben, eine Zeit zu pflanzen und eine Zeit, das Gepflanzte (*that which is planted*) auszureißen, eine Zeit zu töten und eine Zeit zu heilen, eine Zeit einzureißen (*rend*) und eine Zeit aufzubauen, eine Zeit zu weinen und eine Zeit zu lachen, eine Zeit zu klagen (*mourn*) und eine Zeit zu tanzen, eine Zeit, Steine wegzuwerfen, und eine Zeit, Steine zu sammeln, eine Zeit zu umarmen und eine Zeit, <u>sich</u> der Umarmung zu <u>enthalten</u> (*to refrain from*), eine Zeit zu suchen und eine Zeit zu verlieren, eine Zeit aufzubewahren (*protect*) und eine Zeit fortzuwerfen, eine Zeit zu zerreißen und eine Zeit zu nähen (*sew*), eine Zeit zu schweigen und eine Zeit zu reden, eine Zeit zu lieben und eine Zeit zu hassen, eine Zeit des Krieges und eine Zeit des Friedens. (**Ecclesiastes 3**)

Vocabulary

* **alles** — everything
* **ander** — other
* **ändern** — to change
* **an-sehen** — to look at
* **anstatt ... zu** — instead of
  auf-bauen — to build up
  auf-bewahren — to protect
  auf-brechen (i) — to leave
  auf-gehen — to open
  auf-halten — to stop
* **auf-machen** — to open
  der **Augenblick** (-s, -e) — moment
  aus-reißen — to rip up
  boshaft — malicious
* **brauchen nicht** — need not
  der **Dieb** (-es, -e) — thief
  drücken — to press
  ein-reißen — to take down, rend
  enthalten (r) — to refrain from
  das **Fleisch** (-es) — meat, flesh
  fort-werfen — to cast away
  die **Freiheit** — freedom

der **Friede** (-ns) — peace
gar kein — not at all
* die **Geburt** (-en) — birth
  gefährlich — dangerous
  gerade — straight
  geschehen (i) — to happen
* **hassen** — to hate
  die **Hast** — haste
  heilen — to heal
  karikieren — to caricature
  klagen — to mourn
  die **Klinke** (-n) — latch
  der **Kohl** (-es, -e) — cabbage
* der **Krieg** (-es, -e) — war
* **lachen** (i) — to laugh
  die **Laus** (-̈e) — louse
  langweilig — boring
* **manchmal** — sometimes
  die **Menschenmenge** (-n) — crowd
  nehmen (nimmt) — to take
  nützen — to use
  ohne ... zu — without

der **Platz (-es, -e)** —place, seat
reden — to speak
reichen — to reach
* die **Sache (-n)** — matter
sammeln — to collect
* **schließen** — to close
* der **Schritt (-es, -e)** — step
die **Schwäche (-n)** — weakness
schweigen (i) — to be silent
* **schwer** — difficult
* **selten** — seldom
* **sondern** — but rather, on the contrary
* die **Sonne (-n)** — sun
sparen — to save
stehlen (stiehlt) — to steal
* das **Sterben (-s, -)** — dying
* die **Stunde (-n)** — hour
* **suchen** — to seek

töten — to kill
treffend — accurate
* die **Tür (-en)** — door
* **um ... zu** — in order to
umarmen — to embrace
die **Umarmung (-en)** — embrace
* **verlieren** — to lose
verschlucken — to swallow
der **Vertreter (-s, -)** — representative, adherent
der **Wahrsager (-s, -)** — prophet
weg-werfen (wirft weg) — to throw away
* **weinen** (i) — to cry
zeitig — on time, early
zerreißen — to rip up
zertreten (zertritt) — to step on, crush, put out

20.7. Vocabulary aid

1. Der alte Mann sitzt, ohne zu reden.
2. Es <u>fällt</u> dem Kind <u>schwer</u> (*to be difficult*), zu schweigen.
3. Anstatt zu arbeiten, will Fräulein Meier ein Liebesgedicht schreiben.
4. Fräulein Meier braucht nicht zu viel zu studieren.
5. Fräulein Meier macht die Tür auf, um den Briefträger zu grüßen (*greet*).
6. Die Freiheit ist nicht zu verlieren.

Chapter Twenty-one

Co-ordinating Conjunctions

21.1. Co-ordinating conjunctions connect words, phrases, or clauses of the same value. They do not have any effect on word order.

> The most common co-ordinating conjunctions are:
>
> | | |
> |---|---|
> | *aber* | but, however |
> | *denn* | for, because |
> | *oder* | or |
> | *sondern* | rather, on the contrary |
> | *und* | and |

Happily, co-ordinating conjunctions are always translated literally. However, note that *denn* as a conjunction means *for, because*; **it does not mean *then***. Also note that both *aber* and *denn* can be used as flavoring particles. Examples are:

Das ist *aber* klar — That is (quite) clear.
Wo ist er *denn* — Where (on earth) is he?

> Here are two word combinations which also function as conjunctions:
>
> | | |
> |---|---|
> | *entweder...oder* | either...or |
> | *weder...noch* | neither...nor |

21.2. If an *und* connects two clauses which do not share a subject or a verb, a comma will appear before the *und*: Ein Narr wirft einen Stein in den Brunnen, *und* zehn Vernünftige können ihn nicht herausholen — A fool throws a stone into the well, and ten wise people cannot get it out.

If there is **no** comma before an *und*, however, it generally means that the subject, and even part of the verb can be carried over into the second clause: *Mache* den Mund *zu* und die Augen *auf* — Close (*zumachen*) your mouth and open (*aufmachen*) your eyes; Im Augenblick der großen Erderschütterung *versank* der größte Teil der Stadt mit einem Gekrache und *begrub* alles unter seinen Trümmern — At the moment of the great earthquake, the greatest part of the city *sank* with a crash and *buried* everything under its ruins.

If other co-ordinating conjunctions are used, however, a comma may appear between clauses, even if the subject of the first clause is carried over into the second clause: Man lernt nicht für die Schule, *sondern* für das Leben — One does not learn (only) for school, but for life.

21.3. Translate these sentences:

1. Osten oder Westen, zu Hause ist es am besten.
2. Entweder bekennen (*confess*) oder brennen!
3. Hör und sei nicht taub (*deaf*), aber langsam glaub. (Do you remember the imperative? If not, review 6.4.)
4. Nicht nur Fräulein Meier, sondern auch der Briefträger wollte ein paar Tage nicht arbeiten.
5. Armut ist weder Schande noch Unehre (*dishonor*).
6. Such eine Frau nicht auf dem Ball, sondern im Stall (*stable*). (Unfortunately, most proverbs regarding women seem to have been created by male chauvinists!)
7. Die Psychologie hatte unbekannte Tiefen und Abgründe der Seele entdeckt, aber auch das feste zielsichere (*unerring*) Selbstbewußtsein aufgelöst. (Fritz Martini)
8. . . . ohne nach rechts oder links zu blicken, überschritt er die Trägerstraße und stieg die Stufen der Kathedrale hinan.
9. Das Kind ist bis zum fünften Jahr der Mutter Herr, bis zum zehnten Jahr ihr Knecht (*servant*), bis zum fünfzehnten Jahr ihr Geheimrat (*confidant*), und dann ist es entweder ihr Freund oder ihr Feind.
10. Der König von Frankreich ist ein König der Esel; denn seine Untertanen (*subjects*) müssen tun, was er ihnen auferlegt (*imposes*); der König in England ist ein König der Leute; denn sie genehmigen (*consent to*) das, was er ihnen auferlegt; aber der Kaiser ist ein König der Fürsten; denn sie tun, was ihnen gefällt. (Luther)

Vocabulary

* **aber** — but, however
der **Abgrund (-s, ∹e)** — abyss
* **auch** — also, even
auf-erlegen — to impose

auf-lösen — to dissolve
bekennen — to confess
* **bis zu** — until
* **blicken** (i) — to look, glance

brennen — to burn
* **dann** — then
* **denn** — for, because
entdecken — to discover
* **entweder...oder** — either...or
der **Esel** (-s, -) — donkey
der **Feind** (-es, -e) — enemy
fest — firm
* das **Frankreich** (-s) — France
fünfzehn — fifteen
der **Fürst** (-en, -en) — prince
* **gefallen** (i) — to please
der **Geheimrat** (-s, ⸚e) — confidant
hinan-steigen (i) — to climb
* **langsam** — slow
* die **Leute (pl.)** — people
* **links** — left
der **Magen** (-s, ⸚) — stomach
* **oder** — or

der **Osten** (-s) — East
* **paar** — couple
* **rechts** — right
die **Schande** — scandal
das **Selbstbewußtsein** (-s) — self-confidence, self-awareness
* **sondern** — but, on the contrary
der **Stall** (-es, ⸚e) — stable
die **Stufe** (-n) — step
suchen — to seek
die **Tiefe** (-n) — depth
die **Trägerstraße** — a street name
* **tun** — to do
überschreiten — to cross over
unbekannt — unknown, unfamiliar
* **weder...noch** — neither...nor
der **Westen** — West

Chapter Twenty-two
Basic Verb Placement (Part II)

22.1. In an earlier chapter on "Basic Verb Placement," you were told that in indicative sentences, the conjugated verb appears in "second" place (cf. 6.1, 6.2):

Oft *geht* der Student ins Theater — The student often goes to the theater.

Since then, you have encountered more complex verbs, and you have discovered that part of the verb can also appear at the end of the clause in the following cases:

(1) Whenever there is a separable verb prefix (cf. 13.1-13.7):

Er *steht* morgens früh *auf* — He gets up early in the morning.
Sie *macht* die Tür *zu* — She closes the door.

(2) Whenever there is a future tense (cf. 10.1-10.3):

Sie *wird* nicht hier *bleiben* — She will not stay here.
Vielleicht *werden* wir das *tun* — Perhaps we will do that.

(3) Whenever the verb is in the present or past perfect tense (cf. 14.6):

Er *hat* das nicht *gewußt* — He did not know that.
Sie *ist* nach Berlin *geflogen* — She has flown to Berlin.
Er *hatte* das oft *getan* — He had often done that.
Sie *war* früher *angekommen* — She had arrived earlier.

(4) Usually whenever a modal appears in a clause (cf. 19.3):

Das Kind *darf* das nicht *sagen* — The child is not permitted to say that.
Sie *kann* gut *schreiben* — She can write well.
Er *mag* nicht hier *sein* — He may not be here.
Er *muß* viel *studieren* — He has to study a lot.
Du *sollst* nicht *töten* — Thou shalt not kill.
Der Student *will* den neuen Film *sehen* — The student wants to see the new film.

22.2. Translation of complex verbs

Therefore, whenever you see most verbs, check the end of the clause for any prefixes, then, if there are any, attach them to the verb root, and look up the complete verb.

Whenever you see *werden*, check the end of the clause for a verb infinitive. If there is one, then *werden* must be translated as *will*.

Er *wird* nicht *gehen* — He *will* not go.

Whenever you see any form of *sein* or *haben*, check the end of the clause for participles. Be particularly suspicious of forms of *sein*, as they sometimes must be translated as a form of *to have*.

Sie *ist* oft *geflogen* — She *has* often *flown*.
Leider *waren* wir niemals dort *gewesen* — Unfortunately we *had* never *been* there.

Whenever you see any form of *dürfen, können, mögen, müssen, sollen* or *wollen*, check the end of the clause for infinitives and translate accordingly:

Er *will* Kafkas Romane *lesen* — He *wants to read* Kafka's novels.

22.3. Whenever three verbs occur in a clause, the conjugated verb is always translated first, the final verb is translated second, and the penultimate verb is translated last (cf. 19.7). Here are examples:

Er *wird* das *getan haben* — He will have done that.
  1   3   2

Er *wird* das *wissen wollen* — He will want to know that.
  1   3   2

Sie *werden* das *abschreiben müssen* — They will have to copy that.
  1   3   2

Sie *hat* den Aufsatz *schreiben müssen* — She had to write the essay.
  1   3   2

Man *hatte* das Unglück nicht *sehen wollen*, weil es so schrecklich war — One
  1   3   2
had not wanted to see the accident because it was so horrible.

22.4. Whenever the zu construction is accompanied by auxiliaries, the auxiliary will always appear after the *zu*, and it will be translated first, while the verb appearing before the *zu* will be translated second. Here are examples:

Es ist unangenehm, nicht *schlafen* zu *können* — It is unpleasant not to be
                              2   1
able to sleep.

Das Kind weckt die Katze, anstatt sie *liegen* zu *lassen* — The child awakens
                                       2   1
the cat, instead of letting it lie (sleep).

Er sprach, ohne die Tatsachen *gewußt* zu *haben* — He spoke without having
                               2   1
known the facts.

22.5. Translate these sentences:

1. Aber es gehört mehr Mut (*courage*) dazu, ein Ende zu machen, als einen
   neuen Vers: das wissen alle Ärzte und Dichter. (Nietzsche)
2. Lerne Schweigen! Leben und Tod hängen davon ab.
3. Lob (*praise*) ist leichter zu erlangen (*attain*) als zu erhalten.
4. Vorschläge gehen mit der Sonne auf und nieder.
5. Die Natur hängt überall ihr Schild heraus.
6. Vor vielen Jahren hatte Fräulein Meier Schauspielerin werden wollen, aber
   ihre Mutter war dagegen.
7. Es war ihm peinlich, dieses deutsche Wort nicht aussprechen zu können.
8. Nur Gott sieht die geheimsten Gedanken. Aber warum sollen diese so
   wichtig sein? Manche sind wichtig, nicht alle. Und müssen alle Menschen
   sie für wichtig halten? (Wittgenstein)
9. In diesem Sinn hat der dionysische (*Dionysian*) Mensch Ähnlichkeit mit
   Hamlet: beide haben einmal einen wahren Blick in das Wesen (*essence*)
   der Dinge getan (*taken*), sie haben erkannt, und es ekelt (*disgusts*) sie zu
   handeln; denn ihre Handlung kann nichts am ewigen Wesen der Dinge
   ändern, sie empfinden (*perceive*) es lächerlich oder schmachvoll
   (*humiliating*), daß ihnen zugemutet wird (*is expected*), die Welt, die aus
   den Fugen ist (*that is out of joint*), wieder einzurichten (*to fix, to set right*).
   Die Erkenntnis tötet das Handeln, zum Handeln gehört das Umschleiertsein
   (*veil — literally: being veiled*) durch die Illusion — das ist die Hamlet-
   lehre. (Nietzsche)

Vocabulary

ab-hängen von — to depend on
die **Ähnlichkeit (-en)** —
resemblance
ändern — to change
auf-gehen (i) — to rise

aus-sprechen — to pronounce
* **beide** — both
* der **Blick (-es, -e)** — look, glance
dazu-gehören — to take
* der **Dichter (-s, -)** — writer, poet

* **einmal** — once
ein-richten — to adjust, to fix
ekeln — to disgust
empfinden — to perceive
erhalten — to keep, to preserve
* **erkennen** — to recognize
* die **Erkenntnis (-sse)** — recognition
erlangen — to attain
* **ewig** — eternal
* der **Gedanke (-ns, -n)** — thought
geheim — secret
* **halten für** — to consider
* **handeln** (i) — to act
die **Handlung** — action
heraus-hängen — to hang out
lächerlich — laughable
* die **Lehre (-n)** — doctrine, teaching

das **Lob (-es)** — praise
* **manche** — some
nieder-gehen (i) — to set
peinlich — embarrassing
der **Schauspieler (-s, -)** — actor
das **Schild (-es, -er)** — sign, label
schmachvoll — disgraceful, humiliating
* **schweigen** (i) — to be quiet
* der **Sinn (-es, -e)** — meaning, sense
* **töten** — to kill
der **Vers (-es, -e)** — verse
der **Vorschlag (-es, ∸e)** — suggestion
* **warum** — why
das **Wesen (-s, -)** — essence
* **wichtig** — important
* **wieder** — again

Reading Selection: *Die zehn Jungfrauen*[*]
(Matthäus 25.1-13)

Das Himmelreich wird gleich zehn Jungfrauen sein, die (*who*) ihre Lampen nahmen und ausgingen, <u>dem Bräutigam zu begegnen</u> (*to meet the bridegroom*).

Aber fünf unter ihnen waren töricht (*foolish*), und fünf waren klug.

Die Törichten nahmen ihre Lampen, aber sie nahmen kein Öl mit (*with them*).

Die Klugen aber nahmen Öl in ihren Gefäßen (*vessels*) samt (*together with*) ihren Lampen.

Weil <u>sich</u> der Bräutigam <u>verspätete</u> (*delayed*), wurden alle schläfrig, und sie schliefen ein.

Zur Mitternacht aber hörte man ein Geschrei: Seht, der Bräutigam kommt; geht, ihm entgegen!

Dann standen die Jungfrauen alle auf und schmückten (*trimmed*) ihre Lampen.

Die Törichten aber sprachen zu den Klugen: Gebt uns von eurem Öl, denn unsre Lampen verlöschen (*are going out*).

Da antworteten die Klugen und sprachen: Nein, das Öl reicht nicht für uns und für euch; geht aber hin zu den Krämern (*merchants*) und kauft für euch selbst.

---

[*] If you don't wish to use a dictionary, vocabulary for this section is given on pp. 285-356.

Und als sie hingingen, zu kaufen, kam der Bräutigam; und sie, die (*who*) bereit waren, gingen mit ihm hinein zur Hochzeit (*wedding*); und die Tür wurde (*was*) verschlossen.

Zuletzt kamen auch die anderen Jungfrauen und sprachen: Herr, Herr, tue uns auf!

Er antwortete aber und sprach: Wahrlich, ich sage euch, ich kenne euch nicht.

Darum wachet; denn ihr wißt weder Tag noch Stunde, in welcher des Menschen Sohn kommen wird.

Chapter Twenty-three

Dependent Clauses (Part I)

A dependent clause (which also is sometimes called a subordinate clause) **is simply one that cannot function alone as a complete sentence.** Common dependent clauses in English begin with the conjunctions *that, when, if, because*, or similar conjunctions.

23.1. Verb placement in dependent clauses

In German sentences which contain only an independent clause, the verb always appears in "second" place. Examples are:

Große Fluten *sind* Gottes Ruten — Large floods *are* God's rods.
Ein hungriger Magen *ist* ein schlechter Ratgeber — A hungry stomach *is* a poor advisor.

In all dependent clauses, in contrast, the verb appears at the **end** of the German clause:

Es mag wahr sein, *daß* große Fluten Gottes Ruten *sind* — It may be true *that* large floods *are* God's rods.

Here are both independent and dependent clauses for the most common verb combinations:

Er *sieht* heute gut *aus* — He looks good today. (Independent)
Wenn er heute gut *aussieht*, sieht er auch morgen gut aus — *If* he looks good today, he will also look good tomorrow.
Er *wird* heute hier *sein* — He will be here today. (Independent)
Es ist wahr, *daß* er heute hier *sein wird* — It is true *that* he will be here today.
Sie *ist* hier *gewesen* — She has been here. (Independent)
Ich weiß nicht, *ob* sie hier *gewesen ist* — I do not know *whether* she has been here.
Sie *kann* nicht hier *sein* — She can not be here. (Independent)
Sie ist traurig, *weil* sie nicht hier *sein kann* — She is sad *because* she cannot be here.

Note that whenever you encounter dependent clauses with two verbs, the last verb in the clause should be translated first.

23.2. When there are three verbs in a sentence, the independent and the dependent clauses are formed in the following ways:

Der Student *hat* das *tun wollen* — The student has wanted to do that. (Independent)
Es ist wahr, *daß* der Student das *hat tun wollen* — It is true *that* the student has wanted to do that.

23.3. The most common subordinating conjunctions

Here are the most common of these conjunctions. The first group is a list which can function **only** as conjunctions. They are:

bevor	before
daß	that
ob	if, whether
weil	because
wenn	when, if

Wenn will mean *when* or *whenever* whenever it refers to a temporal action:

Wenn der Briefträger ihr ein Gedicht schreibt, wird Fräulein Meier sehr glücklich — *Whenever* the mailman writes her a poem, Fräulein Meier becomes quite happy.

Wenn will mean *if* if the verb is subjunctive (which will be examined in 31.5) or if the first phrase of the next clause is *so* or *dann*:

Wenn die Armut zur Tür eingeht, *so* fliegt die Liebe zum Fenster hinaus — *If* poverty comes in the door, *then* love flies out the window.
Wenn einer, was er tut, nicht muß, *dann* tut er es mit Hochgenuß — *If* one does not have to do what he is doing, *then* he does it with pleasure.

Otherwise, there are no other ways to determine whether *wenn* means *if* or *when*, as long as *wenn* refers to the future. For example, "Wenn sie bei ihrem Freund ist, ist die Studentin glücklich" can be translated as "*When* she is with her friend, the student is happy," or "*If* she is with her friend, the student is happy."

23.4. The following subordinating conjunctions also have other definitions when used as a different part of speech. Therefore, be particularly careful when you encounter them. The following can be recognized as subordinating conjunctions when:

(1) they begin the clause, **and**
(2) the verb appears at the end of the clause.

These conjunctions are:

als	- when*	(after a comparative, it means *than*)
bis	- until	(as a preposition, it also means *until*)
da	- since*	(as an adverb, it means *there, then*)
damit	- so that	(as a da-compound, it means *with it*)
nachdem	- after*	(as an adverb, it means *afterwards*)
während	- while	(as a preposition, it means *during*)

---

* See also "Troublesome Words," 35.5; 35.7; 35.16

Here are examples of each of these conjunctions:

Als der Briefträger Fräulein Meier besuchte, photographierte er ihre Katze — *When* the mailman visited Fräulein Meier, he photographed her cat.
Note that **als** as a subordinating conjunction when the verb is in the past should be translated as *when* and **not** as *as*.
Manchmal schreibt der Professor Gedichte, *bis* er einschläft — Sometimes the professor writes poetry *until* he falls asleep.
Da Fräulein Meier nicht zu Hause war, suchte der Briefträger sie beim Zoo — *Since* Fräulein Meier was not at home, the mailman looked for her at the zoo.
Der Student studiert Finnisch jeden Abend, *damit* er finnische Philosophie lesen kann — The student studies Finnish every evening *so that* he will be able to read Finnish philosophy.
Nachdem er seinen Schicksalsschlägen glücklich entronnen war, starb er — *After* he had luckily escaped his blows of fate, he died.
Während die zwei um ein Ei zanken, steckt es der dritte ein — *While* the two quarrel over an egg, the third one is pocketing it.

23.5. The trick to translating a dependent clause

(1) First identify the dependent clause:
(a) commas will always separate it from the main clause,
(b) it will always begin with a subordinating conjunction,
(c) and the verb will always be at the end of the clause.

(2) Place the verb at the end of the clause along with any adverbs which modify it after the **complete** subject (which may have prepositional phrases) and before any existing object. **This is crucial for correct translation.** Once you develop the habit of doing this, dependent clauses will seem quite manageable. But make sure you know exactly what the subject is before you move the verb. And remember to shift only the verb and any adverbs modifying it. **Then the rest of the clause will remain intact.**

Here are some examples:

Wenn *der April* wie ein Löwe *kommt,* / so geht er wie ein Lamm — If *April*
       S   V
comes like a lion, it leaves like a lamb.

Da *der Marchese* durch Krieg und Mißernte in bedenkliche Vermögens-
      S
umstände *geraten war,* wollte er sein Schloß verkaufen — Because *the*
          V
Marquis, through war and bad harvest, *had gotten* into serious financial difficulties, he wanted to sell his castle.

Wenn *der Teufel* Heilige *fangen will,* / so steckt er Heilige an die Angel — If
       S   V
the devil wants to capture saints, then he uses saints as bait. (Literally: ...
then he puts saints on the fishhook)

23.6. Other subordinating conjunctions are:

auch wenn	-	even if
ehe	-	before
obschon and *obwohl*	-	although
sobald	-	as soon as

23.7. Translate these sentences, being particularly aware of verb placement:

1. Was nützt es, wenn die Kuh (*cow*) viel Milch gibt, wenn sie nachher den Milchkrug (*milk jug*) umwirft (*knocks over*)?
2. Der Affe (*ape*) bleibt ein Affe, obwohl er eine goldene Kette (*chain*) anhat. (In other words, "once an ape, always an ape.")
3. Man muß Heu machen, während die Sonne scheint.
4. Wenn Gewalt (*force*) kommt, so geht das Recht auf Krücken (*crutches*).
5. Wirf die alten Schuhe nicht weg, ehe du neue hast.
6. Nachdem der Vater des Briefträgers Fräulein Meier ein ganzes Jahr gekannt hatte, mußte er gestehen, sie sei (*was*) wenigstens amüsant und gutherzig.

7. Solange ein Narr schweigt, hält man ihn für klug.
8. Manche Leute rennen dem Glücke nach und wissen nicht, daß sie es zu Hause haben.
9. Die Narbe (*scar*) bleibt, auch wenn die Wunde heilt.
10. Denn das war Rilkes schmerzliche Erfahrung, daß in dieser gegenwärtigen Wirklichkeit die Kräfte des Herzens nicht mehr die Dinge beleben, daß Welt und Leben immer geringer werden. (Fritz Martini)
11. Sobald wir an die Moral glauben, verurteilen (*condemn*) wir das Dasein. (Nietzsche)
12. Als er das hörte, wurde der Briefträger wütend (*furious*).
13. Da der Briefträger wütend war, wollte Fräulein Meier nicht mit ihm in den Zoo gehen.

Vocabulary

* **als** — when
  amüsant — amusing
  an-haben — to have on
* **auch wenn** — even if
  beleben — to animate
* **da** — since, because
* **damit** — so that
* **das Dasein (-s)** — existence
* **daß** — that
* **denn** — for, because
  ehe — before
  die Erfahrung (-en) — experience
* **ganz** — quite, entirely
  gegenwärtig — present
  gering — negligible
  gestehen — to confess
  die Gewalt (-en) — power
  gutherzig — good-natured
* **halten für** — to consider
  heilen — to heal
  das Heu (-s, -) — hay
* **kennen** — to know
* **die Kraft (-̈e)** — power, force, strength
  die Krücke (-n) — crutch

* **manche** — some
  die Moral (-) — morality
* **nachdem** — after
  nachher — afterwards
  nach-rennen (i) — to pursue
  der Narr (-en, -en) — fool
* **nicht mehr** — no longer
  nützen — to be of use
* **ob** — if, whether
* **obwohl** — although
* **das Recht** — justice
* **scheinen (i)** — to seem, to shine
  schmerzlich — painful
  sobald — as soon as
* **solange** — as long as
  um-werfen — to knock over
  verurteilen — to condemn
* **während** — while
  weg-werfen — to throw away
* **weil** — because
  wenigstens — at least
* **wenn** — if, when
* **die Wirklichkeit (-en)** — reality
  die Wunde (-n) — wound
  wütend — furious

Chapter Twenty-four

Dependent Clauses (II) — Subordinating Conjunctions Wer, Was, Wie, Wo, Warum

The interrogatives *wer, was, wie, wo,* and *warum* also can be used as subordinating conjunctions. Dependent clauses beginning with any of these interrogatives are translated like any other, with the dependent verb being placed at the end of the clause.

24.1. *Wer*

Wer can be translated either as *he who* or as *whoever.* Examples are:

Wer nichts im Glaubenssäcklein *hat*, bekommt eine dreckige Himmelfahrt — *He who* has nothing in his little sack of faith will have a filthy ascension.
Wer nicht arbeiten will, soll auch nichts essen — *Whoever* does not want to work should also eat nothing.

Since *wer* is always nominative, the verb will always immediately follow it in any English translation.

In the few cases when *wem* or *wen* is used, the verb will be placed after any noun functioning as the subject. Here is an example:

Wem *das Schaf* gehört, dem gehört auch die Wolle — To whom the sheep belongs, to him the wool belongs, too.

24.2. *Was*

Was will usually (but not always) be the subject of the clause when it functions as a subordinating conjunction.

Was will be translated as *what* or *whatever* when it does not have any specific antecedent. Here are examples:

Was nicht ist, kann noch werden — *Whatever* does not exist can still come into being.

Was den Käfern entflieht, fressen die Raupen — The caterpillars eat *whatever* escapes the beetles.

Was should be translated as *which* or *that which* when it refers to the thought of a previous clause. Here are examples:

Heute war das Kind pünktlich, *was* seiner Mutter gefiel — Today the child was punctual, *which* pleased his mother.
Was man gern tut, kommt einem nicht schwer an — *That which* one likes to do is not difficult for one to do.

Moreover, there are three pronouns which take the pronoun *was*; and in this context, *was* should be translated as *that*. The pronouns are: *alles* (*everything*), *etwas* (*something*), and *nichts* (*nothing*). Here are examples of each:

Alles, was wir lernen, ist nützlich — *Everything that* we learn is useful.
Das ist *etwas, was* der Professor vorher nicht wußte — That is *something that* the professor did not know before.
Das Kind nimmt *nichts, was* ihm nicht gehört — The child takes *nothing that* does not belong to him.

24.3. Wie

Wie as a subordinating conjunction generally will be translated as *as*, but it also sometimes will be translated as *how*. Generally, the context will indicate how it should be translated. Examples are:

Wie du mir, so ich dir! — *As* you are to me, so I am to you!
Jeder Bär tanzt, *wie* er es versteht — Every bear dances *as* he understands it (the music).
Wer Unglück gekostet hat, weiß, *wie* es anderen schmeckt — Whoever has sampled misfortune, knows *how* it tastes to others.

24.4. Wo

Wo can be translated either as *where* (when referring to a place) or as *when* (when referring to a time). Here are examples:

Wo der Zaun am niedrigsten ist, dort springt der Teufel hinüber — *Where* the fence is the lowest, the devil springs over it.

Wo es an Liebe mangelt, erkennt man alle Fehler — *When* love is missing, one notices all mistakes.

24.5. *Warum*

Warum can be translated as *why*: Fräulein Meier weiß nicht, *warum* ihre Katze keinen Thunfisch fressen will — Fräulein Meier doesn't know *why* her cat doesn't want to eat tuna.

24.6. Translate these sentences:

1. Wer viel redet, muß viel wissen oder lügen.
2. Wie man fragt, so bekommt man Antwort.
3. Wenn der Teufel krank ist, will er Mönch (*monk*) werden; wenn er gesund ist, bleibt er, wie er ist.
4. Der Gesunde weiß nicht, wie reich er ist.
5. Was aus Armut geschieht, soll man leicht vergeben.
6. Was der Himmel schickt, ist der Erde ein Segen (*blessing*) — auch Blitz und Donner.
7. Man muß die Leute nehmen, wie sie sind.
8. Alles, was gegen das Gewissen ist, hat harte Stacheln.
9. Am längsten behält man das, was man in der Jugend gelernt hat.
10. Glaube nicht alles, was du hörst.
11. Wer nichts an die Angel (*fishhook*) steckt, fängt nichts.
12. Was dir lieb ist, ist mir nicht zuwider (*distasteful*).
13. Wer mit dem Teufel essen will, muß einen langen Löffel (*spoon*) haben.
14. Wer Fräulein Meier liebt, liebt auch ihre Katze.
15. Weisheit ist besser als Perlen, und alles, was man wünschen mag, kann ihr nicht gleichen. (Proverbs)
16. Wer anderen eine Grube (grave) gräbt, fällt selbst hinein.
17. Wer mit Ungeheuern kämpft, mag zusehen, daß er dabei nicht zum Ungeheuer wird. Und wenn du lange in einen Abgrund blickst, blickt der Abgrund auch in dich hinein. (Nietzsche)
18. Vielleicht weiß ich am besten, warum der Mensch allein lacht; er allein leidet so tief, daß er das Lachen erfinden mußte. (Nietzsche) (How do you know that *allein* modifies *Mensch* rather than *lacht*?)

Vocabulary

der **Abgrund** (-s, ¨e) — abyss
* **allein** — alone, only
* **alles** — everything

* die **Antwort** (-en) — answer
die **Armut** — poverty
behalten — to retain

* **blicken** (i) — to look
der **Blitz** (-es, -e) — lightning
der **Donner** (-s, -) — thunder
die **Ehrfurcht** — reverence
* **erfinden** — to invent
* **etwas** — something
fangen — to capture
fassen — to receive
* **geschehen** (i) — to happen, to occur
* **gesund** — healthy
* das **Gewissen** (-s, -) — conscience
* **gleichen** (i) — to compare with
graben — to dig
* der **Himmel** (-s, -) — heaven, sky
hinein-blicken (i) — to look into
hinein-fallen (i) — to fall into
die **Jugend** — youth
kämpfen (i) — to fight, struggle
* **krank** — sick
* **lieb** — dear
* **lügen** (i) — to lie, fib

* **nehmen (nimmt)** — to take
* **nichts** — nothing
die **Perle** (-n) — pearl
* **reden** — to speak
* **schicken** — to send
selbst — himself
der **Stachel** (-s, -n) — thorn
stecken — to stick
das **Ungeheuer** (-s, -) — monster
vergeben — to forgive
* **voller** — full of
* **warum** — why
* **was** — what, whatever, which, that
* die **Weisheit** — wisdom
* die **Welt** (-en) — world
* **wer** — who, whoever, he who
* **wie** — as, how
* **wo** — where, when
* **wünschen** — to wish
zu-sehen — watch, see to it
zuwider — distasteful

Chapter Twenty-Five

Dependent Clauses (III) — Relative Clauses

One of the most common forms of subordinate clauses is introduced by relative pronouns. A relative pronoun is one which refers to some noun which goes before it, and it also connects two clauses which together form a sentence. Here are all the possibilities.

25.1. Nominative relative pronouns

Wer ist der Mann, *der* (*masculine*) hier ist? — Who is the man *who* is here?
Jetzt schläft das Kind, *das* (*neuter*) oft schreit — Now the child *who* often screams is sleeping.
Die Frau, *die* (*feminine*) intelligent ist, ist eine Freundin von ihm — The woman *who* is intelligent is a friend of his.
Wo sind die Kinder, *die* (*plural*) Freunde sind? — Where are the children *who* are friends?

25.2. Accusative relative pronouns

Morgen fliegt der Professor, *den* (*masculine*) ich kenne, nach Genf — Tomorrow the professor *whom* I know will fly to Geneva.
Wo ist das Kind, *das* (*neuter*) wir jeden Tag sehen? — Where is the child *whom* we see every day?
Die Frau, *die* (*feminine*) der Mann kennenlernen wollte, war eine bekannte Bürgermeisterin — The woman *whom* the man wanted to meet was a famous mayor.
Die Studenten, *die* (*plural*) der Professor unterrichtet, studieren Deutsch fast jeden Tag — The students *whom* the professor teaches study German almost every day.

25.3. Genitive relative pronouns

Hier ist der Student, *dessen* (*masculine*) Ideen mir wichtig scheinen — Here is the student *whose* ideas seem important to me.
Wo ist das Kind, *dessen* (*neuter*) Spielzeug am Strand liegt? — Where is the child *whose* toy is lying on the beach?

Die Frau, **deren** (*feminine*) Roman einen Preis erhielt, ist eine Freundin von ihnen — The woman *whose* novel won a prize is a friend of theirs.

Die Professoren, **deren** (*plural*) Vorlesungen interessant sind, lehren gern — The professors *whose* lectures are interesting like to teach.

25.4. Dative relative pronouns

Wo ist der Student, **dem** (*masculine*) der rote Sportwagen gehört? — Where is the student *to whom* the red sportscar belongs?

Das Kind, **dem** (*neuter*) die Mutter ein Lied vorsang, schläft jetzt — The child *to whom* the mother sang a song is now sleeping.

Die Frau, **der** (*feminine*) das Schulkind einen Apfel gab, ist Lehrerin — The woman *to whom* the school child gave an apple is a teacher.

Die Kinder, **denen** (*plural*) er die Wahrheit sagt, glauben ihm nicht — The children *to whom* he tells the truth do not believe him.

25.5. Note that the gender of the relative pronoun is determined by the noun to which it relates, and the case of the relative pronoun is determined by its place in the subordinate clause. The relative pronoun does <u>not</u> have to be in the same case as the noun to which it relates:

Der Mann (*nominative*), **den** (*accusative*) die Frau liebte, war Dichter — The man *whom* the woman loved was a poet.

Note also that the declensions of the nominative, accusative and dative (with the exception of the dative plural) relative pronouns are the same as the declensions of the definite article. Therefore the only new pronouns you need to learn are the genitive pronouns **dessen** (masculine and neuter) and **deren** (feminine and plural) and the plural dative pronoun **denen**.

Relative pronouns can also sometimes appear after a preposition:

Die Städte, in **denen** er wohnte, waren interessant — The cities in *which* he lived were interesting.

Die Frau, von **der** er sprach, war schön — The woman about *whom* he spoke was beautiful.

25.6. Here is a chart

	masculine	neuter	feminine	plural
nominative	der	das	die	die
accusative	den	das	die	die
genitive	*dessen	*dessen	*deren	*deren
dative	dem	dem	der	*denen

25.7. Tips for translating relative clauses

In any sentence, a relative clause can be identified because:
(1) it will be set apart from the main clause by commas,
(2) the clause will begin with a relative pronoun,
(3) the last word at the end of a clause will be a verb.

In order to translate the relative clause correctly, first translate the relative pronoun, making certain you know which noun in the main clause it relates to, and which case it is in.

25.8. If the relative pronoun is the subject of the clause

(1) use it as the first word of your translation,
(2) translate the verb at the end of the clause (as well as any adverbs modifying it), and place it next to the subject pronoun,
(3) finally translate the rest of the clause word for word. Here are examples:

Fräulein Meiers Lieblingstier ist ein Elefant, der immer sehr träge ist —
Fräulein Meier's favorite animal is an elephant which is always very sluggish.

Before you pick up the verb in the dependent clause, also make sure you are aware of any prepositional phrases which might go with the subject, and place the verb after them and before the object.

So wurde "Faust" zum Erlösungsdrama, das durch alle Schuld und Abgründe des Lebens zur Läuterung und transzendierenden Befreiung führt — Thus "Faust" became a drama of redemption that through all guilt and abysses of life leads to a purification and to a transcendent liberation. (Fritz Martini)

25.9. If the relative pronoun is not the subject of the clause

(1) still use it as the first word of your translation,
(2) then translate the subject (which generally will follow the relative pronoun);
(3) translate the verb at the end of the clause and place it next to the subject,
(4) finally translate the rest of the clause word for word.

Here are examples:

Wer ist der Mann, <u>den</u> <u>Fräulein Meier</u> <u>vor vielen Jahren</u> <u>liebte</u>? — Who is
the man, <u>whom</u> <u>Fräulein Meier</u> <u>loved</u> <u>many years ago</u>?

Friedrich Schlegels Leistungen lagen in der Fülle der Anregungen, <u>die er</u>
<u>während</u> <u>seines erfahrungsreichen Lebens</u> <u>freigebig</u> <u>ausstreute</u> — Friedrich
Schlegel's achievements lay in the abundance of initial ideas <u>which he</u> <u>gen-</u>
<u>erously</u> <u>circulated</u> <u>during his life which was rich in experiences</u>. (Fritz Mar-
tini)

**25.10. Genitive relative pronouns will be attached to nouns which can be in
nominative, accusative, or dative case.** If they are attached to nominative
nouns, they are to be translated like the sentences in category A. Here is an
example:

In Deutschland hatte der Sieg und die Reichsgründung von 1870/71 zu
einem gewaltigen Aufschwung der Wirtschaft . . . geführt, <u>dessen geistige</u>
<u>und politische Problematik</u> <u>einsichtigen Geistern</u> <u>nicht verborgen blieb</u> —
In Germany the victory and the foundation of the empire of 1870/71 had led
to a powerful rise of the economy, <u>whose spiritual and political problematics</u>
<u>did not remain hidden</u> <u>from insightful minds</u>. (Fritz Martini)

If the genitive relative pronouns are attached to dative or accusative nouns, they
are to be translated like the sentences in category B. Here are examples:

Kafka, <u>dessen Romane</u> <u>der Student</u> <u>gern liest</u>, ist selbstverständlich ein
           1 (accusative)   *2*   *3*
großer Dichter. — Kafka, <u>whose novels</u> <u>the student</u> <u>likes to read</u>, is obviously a great writer.

Die Studentin, <u>deren Freund</u> <u>wir</u> <u>schreiben wollen</u>, studiert Erdkunde —
                1 (dative)   *2*   *3*
The student, <u>whose friend</u> <u>we want to write</u>, studies geography.

**25.11. Each relative clause is a unit unto itself as if it were set off in paren-
theses and having its own subject and its own verb.** Therefore, you may wish
to isolate it from the rest of the sentence by placing brackets around it so that it
will not distract you from locating the subject and the verb of the main clause.
Here are two difficult sentences:

Die geheime Bestellung, die dem alten Don, nachdem er die Tochter nach-
drücklich gewarnt hatte, durch die hämische Aufmerksamkeit seines stolzen
Sohnes verraten worden war, machte den alten Mann böse — The secret
rendezvous — which had been betrayed to the old Don (after he had
emphatically warned his daughter) by the malicious vigilance of his proud
son — made the old man angry. (Kleist)

In den Jahren 1812/13 entstanden unter dem Eindruck der kriegerischen
Volksbewegung seine . . . Lieder, die nicht mehr um das individuelle Leben
kreisten, sondern . . . der Ausdruck eines gemeinsamen Fühlens sind, in
(predicate nominative)
dem Tapferkeit und Frömmigkeit, Ehre und Glaube ein umfassendes Ethos
bilden — In the years 1812/1813, under the imprint of the military national
movement, his songs originated, which no longer revolved around the indi-
vidual life, but rather are the expression of a common feeling, in which
bravery and piety, honor and faith create a comprehensive Ethos. (Martini
über Ernst Moritz Arndt)

25.12. Translate, noting the gender and case of each relative pronoun:

1. Falsche Freunde sind Fischer, die das Wasser trüben, ehe sie angeln (*fish*).
2. Ein Weiser ist ein Mensch, dem die Dinge gerade so schmecken, wie sie sind.
3. Die Kühe, die am meisten brüllen, geben die wenigste Milch.
4. Das Feuer, das mich nicht verbrennt, lösche ich nicht.
5. Schließ keinen Brief, den du nicht durchgelesen hast, noch (*nor*) trink Wasser, ohne es gesehen zu haben.
6. Ehre folgt dem Menschen, der sie flieht, und flieht den, der sie jagt.
7. Es gibt keine ärgeren Tauben als die, die nicht hören wollen.
8. E. T. A. Hoffmann war ein Artist des Unheimlichen, der bewußt seine Traumbilder auskostete und sie zugleich ironisch spiegelte. (Martini)
9. Die erste Hälfte des 19. Jahrhunderts steht stark unter dem Eindruck der Enttäuschung der politischen Freiheitsbewegung seit 1815, die die mißlungenen Revolutionen von 1830 und 1848 noch verschärften. (Martini)
10. Der größte Schritt ist der aus der Tür.
11. Weh dem Land, dessen König ein Kind ist.

12. Zeit ist der Stoff, aus dem das Leben gemacht ist.
13. Wer war die Frau, die der Mann liebte?
14. Herzog Wilhelm von Breisach, der seit seiner heimlichen Verbindung (*alliance*) mit einer Gräfin (*countess*) namens Katharina von Heersbruck aus dem Hause Alt-Hüningen, die unter seinem Rang (*rank*) zu sein schien, mit seinem Halbbruder, dem Grafen Jakob dem Rotbart (*redbeard*), in Feindschaft lebte, kam gegen Ende des 14. Jahrhunderts, als die Nacht des heiligen Remigius zu dämmern begann, von einer Zusammenkunft zurück. (Kleist)

Vocabulary

arg — wicked
aus-kosten — to enjoy to the fullest
bewußt — consciously
brüllen (i) — to bellow, moo
dämmern (i) — to grow dark
durch-lesen — to read through
* **ehe** — before
die **Ehre** (-n) — honor
der **Eindruck** (-es, ⸚e) — impression
die **Enttäuschung** (-en) — disappointment
die **Feindschaft** — animosity
der **Fischer** (-s, -) — fisherman
fliehen — to flee
* **folgen** (i) — to follow
die **Freiheitsbewegung** (-en) — independence movement
* **gerade** (adj.) — straight; (adv.) — just
der **Graf** (-en, -en) — count
der **Halbbruder** (-s, ⸚) — half-brother
die **Hälfte** — half
heilig — holy, saint
heimlich — secret
der **Herzog** (-s, -e) — duke
ironisch — ironically
jagen — to hunt
* das **Jahrhundert** (-s, -e) — century

löschen — to extinguish
mißlungen — unsuccessful
* **namens** — by name of
* **noch** — still
* **ohne...zu** — without... -ing
* **scheinen** (i) — to seem
schließen — to close
* **schmecken** (i) — to taste
der **Schritt** (-s, -e) — step
der **Stoff** (-es, -e) — material
* **seit** — since
spiegeln — to reflect
stark — strong
stehen (i) — to stand, to be
taub — deaf
das **Traumbild** (-es, -er) — vision, illusion
trüben — to pollute
unheimlich — uncanny, unearthly
verbrennen — to burn
verschärfen — to heighten, to intensify
weh — woe to
der **Weise** (-n, -n) — wise man
* **wenig** — little
zugleich — at the same time
* **zurück-kommen** (i) — to return
die **Zusammenkunft** (⸚e) — meeting

Reading Selection: Aus dem *Erdbeben in Chili**
(Heinrich von Kleist)

(The following selections are particularly difficult. However, if you work through each sentence carefully, you may find to your surprise and delight that you can actually understand them. Good luck!)

I. Es war am Fronleichnamsfest (*Corpus Christi Festival*), und die feierliche Prozession der Nonnen (*nuns*), welchen die Novizen (*novices*) folgten, nahm eben (*just*) ihren Anfang, als die unglückliche (*unfortunate*) Josephe (*a woman's name*) bei dem Anklang (*ringing*) der Glocken in Mutterwehen (*birth-pangs*) auf den Stufen der Kathedrale niedersank (*collapsed*).

II. In St. Jago, der Hauptstadt des Königreichs Chili, stand gerade (*just*) in dem Augenblick der großen Erderschütterung (*earthquake*) vom Jahre 1647, bei welcher viele tausend Menschen ihren Untergang (*demise*) fanden, ein junger . . . Spanier namens Jeronimo Rugera [the father of the child who had just been born in the previous reading passage] an einem Pfeiler (*column*) des Gefängnisses (*prison*), in welches man ihn eingesperrt hatte, und wollte sich (*himself — accusative*) erhenken (*hang*).

III. [Jeronimo] stand an einem Wandpfeiler (*pilaster*) und befestigte (*fastened*) den Strick (*rope*), der ihn dieser jammervollen (*sorrowful*) Welt** entreißen sollte (*was to*), an eine Eisenklammer (*iron clamp*), als plötzlich der größte Teil (*part*) der Stadt mit einem Gekrache (*crash*) versank und alles (*this is accusative! Note that "der größte Teil der Stadt" is still the subject of this clause — cf. 21.2*), was Leben atmete, unter seinen Trümmern (*ruins*) begrub.

IV. Hier lag ein Haufen (*heap*) Erschlagener, hier ächzte (*moaned*) noch eine Stimme unter dem Schutt (*rubbish*), hier schrien Leute von brennenden Dächern herab, hier kämpften (*battled*) Menschen und Tiere mit den Wellen (*undulations*), hier war ein mutiger (*courageous*) Retter (*rescuer*) bemüht, zu helfen; hier stand ein anderer, bleich wie der Tod, und streckte sprachlos zitternde (*trembling*) Hände zum Himmel.

(However, in the midst of all this destruction, Jeronimo and Josephe, who had been condemned to death prior to the earthquake for producing an illegitimate child, manage to reunite.)

---

*   If you don't wish to use a dictionary, vocabulary for this section is given on pp. 285-356.
**   What is the case of *Welt* in this sentence?

V. Indessen (*in the meantime*) war die schönste Nacht herabgestiegen, voll wundermilden (*wonderfully mild*) Duftes, so silberglänzend und still, wie nur ein Dichter davon träumen mag.

VI. Sie [Jeronimo und Josephe] fanden einen prachtvollen (*magnificent*) Granatapfelbaum (*pomegranate tree*), der seine Zweige voll duftender (*fragrant*) Früchte weit ausbreitete; und die Nachtigall flötete (*whistled*) im Wipfel (*tree-top*) ihr wollüstiges (*delightfully pleasant*) Lied.

(While Jeronimo and Josephe don't quite live happily ever after, they at least enjoy a few good moments together.)

Chapter Twenty-six

The Reflexive

A verb is considered reflexive when its subject and object are the same person(s) or thing(s): *Sie* kauft *sich* eine Schreibmaschine — *She* buys *herself* a typewriter; *Das Kind* wäscht *sich* — *The child* washes *himself*.

26.1. Accusative and dative reflexive pronouns:

Singular (I, you, he, she, it)		**Plural** (we, you, they)	
accusative	*mich* — *myself*	accusative *uns*	—*ourselves*
dative	*mir* — *myself*	dative *uns*	—*ourselves*
accusative	*dich* — *yourself*	accusative *euch*	—*yourselves*
dative	*dir* — *yourself*	dative *euch*	—*yourselves*
accusative	*sich* — *himself,* *herself, itself*	accusative *sich*	—*themselves,* *each other*
dative	*sich* — *himself,* *herself, itself*	dative *sich*	—*themselves,* *each other*

The formal accusative and dative form (yourself, yourselves) is *sich*. This is the only time the formal pronoun (*Sie, Ihnen, Sie*) is not capitalized.

The accusative and dative reflexive pronouns are identical for all persons except the first person singular and the singular form of the informal you. The most common reflexive pronoun is *sich*.

26.2. Some meanings which the reflexive may express are:

(1) An action done by the subject to itself:

Ich amüsiere *mich* — I amuse *myself.*
Ich sehe *mich* in dem Spiegel — I see *myself* in the mirror.

(2) An action done by the subject to itself which also involves an object (in these cases, the dative reflexive pronoun will be used):

Ich kaufe *mir* ein Buch — I buy *myself* a book.
Sie schreibt *sich* eine Liste — She writes *herself* a list.

(3) A reciprocal action:

Sie küssen *sich* — They kiss *each other*.
Sie lieben *sich* — They love *each other*.

26.3. Occasionally the reflexive pronoun is used when only the direct object is used in English:

Er nimmt das Buch mit *sich* — He takes the book with *him*.
Der Briefträger hat eine Freundin bei *sich* — The mailman has a girl friend with *him*.

But in other cases when *sich* is the object of a preposition, it will be translated reflexively, as it would be in English:

Sie weiß viel über *sich* — She knows a lot about *herself*.
Sie tun das für *sich* — They do that for *themselves*.

26.4. Reflexive pronouns also are used in German when English uses possessive pronouns instead:

Er wäscht *sich die* Hände (literally: he washes *to himself the* hands) — He washes *his* hands.

To understand how to translate this construction correctly, consider the following hypothetical sentences:

I wash to myself my hands.
Ich wasche mir meine Hände.

The sentences are grammatically incorrect in both languages because they contain an unnecessary extra indication of possession. In English, *to myself* is eliminated because the adjective *my* already indicates that the hands are mine. In German, on the other hand, the adjective *meine* is omitted because the word *mir* already indicates that the hands belong to me. Therefore, whenever you see this construction in German, it is advisable to substitute the appropriate English possessive adjective (such as *my*) for the corresponding German reflexive pronoun (such as *mir*). Here are more examples:

Ich putze *mir die* Zähne (literally: I brush *to myself the* teeth) — I brush *my* teeth.
Er ist *mir* ein Dorn *im* Auge (literally: he is *to me* a thorn in *the* eye) — He is a thorn in *my* eye.
Küß *mir den* Ellbogen (literally: kiss *to me the* elbow) — Kiss *my* elbow! (Luther was reputed to say this when he was being "polite.")

26.5. *Selbst* **and** *selber*

Selbst and *selber* are sometimes used with reflexive pronouns to emphasize the reflexive meanings. Here are examples:

Sich selbst erkennen ist die größte Kunst — To know *oneself* is the greatest skill.
Arzt, heil *dich selber* — Physician, heal *thyself.*

Following a noun or pronoun, *selbst* and *selber* should be translated as *himself, herself, themselves,* etc. depending on the noun modified. For example, "Fräulein Meier hat den Korb *selbst* geflochten" is translated "Fräulein Meier *herself* wove the basket" while "Der Briefträger hat den Apfelbaum *selbst* gepflanzt" is translated as "The mailman *himself* has planted the apple tree."

Selbst and *selber* used as pronouns are interchangeable. However, **when** *selbst* **precedes a noun or pronoun, it means "even."**
Selbst der Professor hat über den Witz gelacht — *Even* the professor laughed at the joke.

26.6. Translate these sentences:

1. Was man zu sich selbst sagt, hört der Himmel wie Donner. (In other words, you can't have any secrets from God.)
2. Selbst ein Experte hat seinen Meister.
3. Gegen Dummheit kämpfen (*struggle*) Götter selbst vergebens (*in vain*).
4. Das Glück hilft denen nicht, die sich selbst nicht helfen.
5. Das Glück fiel ihm in den Schoß (*lap*).
6. Wer dem anderen Menschen den guten Namen raubt, macht ihn arm und sich nicht reich.
7. Wer sich bei einem Geizigen (*miser*) wärmen will, muß das Feuer mitbringen.
8. Fräulein Meier hat keine Lust, mit ihrem ehemaligen Geliebten in den Zoo zu gehen, denn sie muß sich die Haare waschen.
9. Der wilde Hund ist dem Briefträger ein Dorn im Auge.
10. Nächstenliebe fängt bei sich selbst an.

Vocabulary

* **an-fangen** — to begin
* **bei** — at the home of, with
  der **Donner** (-s, -) — thunder
  der **Dorn** (-s, -en) — thorn
  die **Dummheit** (-en) — stupidity
  ehemalig — former
  der **Experte** (-n, -n) — expert
  der **Geizige** (-n, -n) — miser
  die **Lust** (-̈e) — desire

der **Meister** (-s, -) — master
mit-bringen — to bring with one
die **Nächstenliebe** — charity
der **Schoß** (-es, -̈e) — lap
* **selber** — self
* **selbst** — self, even
* **sich** — self
vergebens — in vain
wärmen — to warm

26.7. Reflexive Verbs

There are several verbs which are reflexive in German but not in English. Here are some examples:

sich beeilen — to hurry
sich freuen — to rejoice, to be pleased
sich handeln um — to deal with, be a matter of
sich irren — to err
sich kümmern um — to worry about, to be concerned with
sich sehnen nach — to long for
sich verlassen auf — to rely upon

When you encounter any of these verbs, **do not translate the *sich*!** For example, "Er *wundert sich* über diese Regel" would be translated as: "He *wonders* about this rule."

26.8. Here are sentences illustrating the use of all the reflexive pronouns in conjunction with the reflexive verb, *sich beeilen*:

ich beeile *mich* oft — I often hurry.
du beeilst *dich* auch — you also hurry.
er beeilt *sich* manchmal — he sometimes hurries.
sie beeilt *sich* selten — she hurries seldom.
es beeilt *sich* abends — it hurries in the evenings.
wir beeilen *uns* morgens — we hurry in the mornings.
ihr beeilt *euch* täglich — you hurry daily.
sie beeilen *sich* mittags — they hurry at noon.
Sie beeilen *sich* nicht — you do not hurry.

Again note that the reflexive pronoun is never translated in any of the above sentences! Doing so indicates an insecurity and unfamiliarity with the intricacies of German grammar.

26.9.   There are also several verbs which have both reflexive and non-reflexive meanings. The non-reflexive meaning will always be listed first in your dictionary. Therefore, if you encounter a sentence with a *sich* form in it in which there is no obvious reciprocal action of the subject, **realize that the** *sich* **(or** *mich, dich,* **etc.) is** *only* **guiding you to the v.r. definition in your dictionary.** Here are some common verbs which have both reflexive and non-reflexive meanings:

non-reflexive	reflexive
denken — to think	*sich denken* — to imagine
erinnern — to remind	*sich erinnern* — to remember
setzen — to set	*sich setzen* — to sit down
benehmen — to take away	*sich benehmen* — to behave
verstehen — to understand	*sich verstehen* — to get along with someone
unterhalten — to sustain	*sich unterhalten* — to converse

Compare the following sentences:

Sie *erinnert* den Briefträger an die Aufgabe — She *reminds* the mailman of the task. (*non-reflexive*)
Er *erinnert sich* jetzt an die Aufgabe — He now *remembers* the task. (*reflexive*)
Er *zieht* nächste Woche nach Kalifornien *um* — He will *move* to California next week. (*non-reflexive*)
Er *zieht sich* oft *um* — He often *changes his clothes.* (*reflexive*)

26.10. Translate these sentences (vocabulary is on pp. 177-178):

1. Wenn sich ein Igel (*hedgehog*) und ein Regenwurm (*earthworm*) paaren, was gibt das? Antwort: zehn Meter Stacheldraht.
2. Wer sich auf dem Schulwege verirrt, findet sich durch das ganze Leben nicht zurecht.
3. Hüte dich vor denen, die Gott gezeichnet hat.
4. Seit es Menschen gibt (*since mankind has existed*), hat der Mensch sich zu wenig gefreut: das allein ist unsre Erbsünde (*original sin*). (Nietzsche)

5. Nietzsches Schriften stellten sich als eine gewaltige (*powerful*) Sammlung kühnster Aphorismen (*aphorisms*) dar, die durch eine einzigartige (*unique*) Wortkunst (*artistic use of words*) faszinierte (*fascinating*) Prägnanz erhalten. (Martini)

6. Mehrere Jahre nachher, da der Marchese (*marquis*) [who was the owner of a castle] durch Krieg und Mißernte (*bad harvest*) in bedenkliche (*critical*) Vermögensumstände geraten war, fand sich ein florentinischer Ritter (*knight*) bei ihm ein, der das Schloß seiner schönen Lage wegen von ihm kaufen wollte. (Kleist)

7. Fräulein Meier verläßt sich immer mehr auf den Briefträger.

8. Gott versalzt uns dieses Leben, damit wir uns nach dem heiligen Feierabend sehnen.

26.11. When *sich* is translated, and when it is left untranslated:

Compare the following first two sentences with the second two:

1. Sie macht *sich* selber unglücklich — She makes *herself* unhappy.
2. Sie macht *sich* das Essen — She fixes *herself* the meal.
3. Sie *wundert sich* über ihren Freund — She *wonders* about her friend.
4. Sie *unterhält sich* mit ihm — She *converses* with him.

In the first two sentences, *sich* is translated as *herself* because the subject *she* needs an object to complete the thought; *sich* explains in #1 whom she makes unhappy and in #2 whom she fixes the meal for. If the *sich* were left untranslated, something serious would be missing from the sentences.

In the second two sentences, however, *sich* is not translated because *sich* **only** serves to indicate that the German verb, unlike the English verb, is reflexive. This will obviously be the case because
(1) a v.r. (or *sich*) definition will be listed in your dictionary,
(2) adding a reflexive pronoun (such as *herself*) would make the sentence sound awkward. For example, no English-speaking person would *ever* say: "She wonders *herself* about her friend."

26.12. Translate this joke (it is not a very good joke, but it is excellent stylistically):

Ein bejahrter (*old*) Münchner kommt auf dem Viktualienmarkt (*marketplace*) mit einer netten Taube (*pigeon*) ins Gespräch. Beide verstehen sich ausgezeichnet (*excellently*) und möchten die Bekanntschaft (*acquaintance*) fortsetzen (*continue*), und so lädt der alte Herr die Taube für den nächsten Nachmittag zu sich zum Kaffee ein. Die Stunde ist gekommen, er hat den Tisch nett gedeckt und extra ein paar Blumen besorgt (*gotten*), aber wer nicht erscheint, ist die Taube. Habe ich mich so in meiner Taubenkenntnis (*pigeon-knowledge*) geirrt, fragt sich der alte Herr, während er vor seinem Kaffee sitzt, der langsam kalt wird. Unruhig schaut er immer häufiger auf die Uhr (*watch*) — endlich, eine Stunde später, klingelt es. Die Taube steht vor der Tür und sagt mit einem reizend verlegenen Lächeln: "Ich bitte Sie, entschuldigen Sie, daß ich so spät komme. Aber es war <u>ein so</u> (*such a*) herrlicher Nachmittag, und so habe ich mich entschlossen, zu Fuß zu gehen!"

Vocabulary

ausgezeichnet — excellently
* **beide** — both
* **bitten um** — to ask for
* **da** — since, because
* **damit** — so that
dar-stellen (r) — to appear
decken — to set, cover
ein-finden (r) — to appear
* **ein so** — such a
ein-laden — to invite
* **endlich** — finally
entschließen (r) — to decide
entschuldigen — to excuse
erhalten — to keep, maintain, receive
* **erscheinen** (i) — to appear
extra (adv.) — specially
der **Feierabend** — quitting time
* **freuen** (r) — to rejoice, be happy
geraten (i) — to land, fall
ins Gespräch kommen — to converse with
gewaltig — powerful
häufig — frequent
herrlich — glorious
hüten (r) (vor) — to be on guard (against)
* **irren** (r) — to err
klingeln (i) — to ring;
es klingelt — the doorbell rings
kühn — bold
das **Lächeln** — smile

die **Lage** (-n) — site, location
* **langsam** — slow
* **mehrere** — several
* **möchte** — would like to
der **Münchner** (-s, -) — inhabitant of Munich
* **nachher** — afterwards
der **Nachmittag** (-s, -e) — afternoon
* **nächst** — next
nett — nice
* **paar** — couple
paaren (r) — to mate
* die **Prägnanz** — precision
reizend — charming
der **Ritter** (-s, -) — knight
die **Sammlung** (-en) — collection
* **schauen** (i) — to look at
das **Schloß** (-sses, ̈-sser) — castle
* die **Schrift** (-en) — writing
der **Schulweg** (-s, -e) — way to school
* **sehnen** (r) (**nach**) — to long (for)
* **seit** — since
* **spät** — late
der **Stacheldraht** — barbed wire
* die **Stunde** (-n) — hour
die **Taube** (-n) — pigeon
* die **Uhr** (-en) — clock
unruhig — restless
verirren (r) — to go astray

verlassen auf (r) — to rely on
verlegen — embarrassed
der **Vermögensumstand (-es, ⸚e)**
— financial condition
versalzen — to spoil
* **verstehen** (r) — to get along with
* **während** — while, during

* **wegen** — because of
zeichnen — to mark, to
distinguish
zu Fuß gehen — to walk
zurecht-finden (r) — to find one's
way
zu sich — at his place

Reading Selection: *Frühlingsglaube*
(Ludwig Uhland)

Die linden Lüfte sind erwacht,
Sie säuseln (*rustle*) und weben Tag und Nacht,
Sie schaffen an allen Enden [der Welt].
O frischer Duft, o neuer Klang!
Nun, armes Herz, sei nicht bang!
Nun muß sich alles, alles wenden.

Die Welt wird schöner mit jedem Tag,
Man weiß nicht, was noch werden mag,
Das Blühen will* nicht enden.
Es blüht das fernste, tiefste Tal:
Nun armes Herz, vergiß der Qual (*torment*)!
Nun muß sich alles, alles wenden.

---

*   This is one of the few instances in which *wollen* should be translated as *will* rather than *want to*
— it means *will* in the sense of *strong desire*.

Chapter Twenty-seven

The Overloaded Adjective Construction

The **overloaded adjective construction** (also known as the "extended adjective" or the "participial" construction) is one of the most difficult constructions in the German language. Therefore, be sure to read this section carefully.

27.1. In this construction, one of two participles generally is used — the present participle, or the past participle.

The present participle is formed by adding a "d" to any German infinitive. *Singen* (*to sing*) can be changed to *singend* (*singing*); *lachen* (*to laugh*) can be changed to *lachend* (*laughing*); and *tanzen* (*to dance*) can be changed to *tanzend* (*dancing*).

The past participle is identical with other past participles — *gesungen* (*sung*), *gelacht* (*laughed*), *getanzt* (*danced*), *geschrieben* (*written*).

Both present and past participles can be used as adjectives:

die *singende* Frau — the *singing* woman
das *geschriebene* Buch — the *written* book

In fact, the present participles are most often used as adjectives, and they are used as adverbs occasionally. They are **never** used as verbs.

27.2. German differs from English to the degree that modifiers can be placed between the introductory word and the present or past participles.
For example, one can say: (*von*) *einer nach dem langen Schlaf wirklich überflüssigen Schläfrigkeit* — an after the long sleep really superfluous sleepiness; or: ... *den wahrscheinlich ein für allemal für Gregor bestimmten Napf* — the probably once and for all for Gregor designated bowl. (Kafka, *Die Verwandlung*)

27.3. Generally, an overloaded adjective can be identified as such when two words appear together in German which cannot be consecutive in English. The most common non-consecutive word combinations are:

(1) **an article** (or a similar strong adjective) and a **preposition** such as *die in* (der Realität unbefriedigt gebliebenen Wünsche des menschlichen Unterbewußten); *mein nach* (Europa oft fliegender Freund); ein *schöner, im* (Winter selten vorkommender Tag).

(2) **two articles** (or similar strong adjectives) such as *die dem* (Lehrer gehorchenden Schulkinder); *ein dem* (Studenten sehr interessantes Buch); or *die neue, den* (meisten Menschen noch fremde Idee).

27.4. When you encounter an overloaded adjective construction, use the following four steps in order to transform it into idiomatic English:

(1) **Locate the modifier which begins the overloaded construction.** (Generally, the modifier will be an article.)

(2) **Locate the noun, or the noun phrase, which the modifier describes.** This noun will be the first "available" noun which agrees with the modifier. For example, in the segment, *die in der Realität unbefriedigt gebliebenen Wünsche des menschlichen Unterbewußten, Wünsche* (des menschlichen Unterbewußten) agrees with *die*, and it is the first available noun. *Realität* is not considered available because it is already the object of the preposition *in*.

(3) **Locate a participle and any accompanying adverbs;** the participle will have a "second" adjective ending (usually either -*e* or -*en*; cf. 4.1-4.3); it will appear before the noun. In the above segment, *unbefriedigt gebliebenen* is an example.

(4) **Read the final clause; do not change the order of the words in this clause** (*in der Realität*). The final clause will often end with a noun.

Therefore, the segment: <u>die</u> <u>in der Realität</u> <u>unbefriedigt gebliebenen</u>
                              1   4   3

<u>Wünsche des menschlichen Unterbewußten</u> should be translated as follows:
                    2

<u>the</u> <u>wishes of the human subconscious</u> <u>which have remained unsatisfied</u> <u>in</u>
  1   2   3   4

<u>reality</u>.
  4

Note: It is sometimes desirable to add a "which" or a "who" and an auxiliary to the participle in order to make the translation sound smoother. By adding a "which," etc., you are merely changing an adjectival clause into a relative one in the same way as you could change the clause "the often discussed topic" into "the topic which has often been discussed" and retain the same meaning.

27.5. While this construction usually contains a participle functioning as an adjective, other adjectives sometimes occur instead. Here are examples: eine mir sehr *angenehme* Idee — an idea very *agreeable* to me; ein den jungen Kindern *wichtiges* Versprechen — a promise *important* to the young children.

Here are more examples of each of the four steps:

Step 1 will consist of finding the <u>adjective</u>, or adjectives which begin this construction:

Der vom Schicksal verfolgte Mann — The man persecuted by fate
Ein vom Schicksal verfolgter Mann — A man persecuted by fate
Ein alter, vom Schicksal verfolgter Mann
Der alte, einsame, vom Schicksal verfolgte Mann
Die Freunde **alter**, vom Schicksal verfolgter Männer — The friends of old men persecuted by fate

Step 2 will consist of finding the <u>noun</u> to which the adjective is attached:

Der vom Schicksal verfolgte **Mann**
Der vom Schicksal verfolgte **Mann der kranken Frau mit vielen Schmerzen** — The husband of the sick woman with many pains who was persecuted by fate
Der vom Schicksal verfolgte **alte Mann**

Step 3 will consist of finding the adjective which is a kind of pivot for step 4. It will appear <u>in front of the noun</u> in step 2, and it will always have an adjective ending. It may be an adjective formed from a verb, or it may be a regular adjective:

Der vom Schicksal **verfolgte** Mann
Der vom Schicksal **oft verfolgte** Mann — The man often persecuted by fate
Der seinem Schicksal **folgende** Mann — The man following his fate
Der mit seinem Schicksal **glückliche** Mann — The man who is happy with his fate

Step 4 will consist of the words located after step 1 and before step 3; they may be translated in the order in which they are found.
Der **vom Schicksal** verfolgte Mann
Der **von einem schrecklichen, fast unglaublichen Schicksal** verfolgte Mann — The man persecuted by a horrible, almost unbelievable fate

27.6. Here are some examples to help you establish this pattern:

Diese von den Ägyptern geschriebenen Erzählungen enthalten wichtige
1   4   3   2   (verb)
Wahrheiten.

These stories written by the Egyptians contain important truths.
1   2   3   4

Ein junger, auf ein Verbrechen angeklagter Spanier namens Jeronimo war
1   4   3   2   (verb)
der Geliebte Josephes.

A young Spaniard named Jeronimo (who was) accused of a crime was
1   2   3   4
Josephe's lover.

Der in den vielen alten Erzählungen oft beschriebene böse König hatte nur
1   4   3   2   (verb)
ein Auge.

The evil King often described in the many old stories had only one eye.
1   2   3   4

When the overloaded adjective is found in the beginning of the sentence, the
appropriate noun to which the article belongs will be found immediately before
the conjugated verb. For in this type of clause, as in all independent German
clauses, the conjugated verb appears in "second" place (cf. "Basic Verb
Placement," 6.1); therefore, all the words preceding it will have to belong
together. The first three examples have followed this pattern.

27.7. More examples of overloaded adjectives:

Wir können beobachten, wie eine des Morgens noch lebhafte Traum-
1   4   3   2
erinnerung im Laufe des Tages dahinschwindet.
2

We can observe how a dream-memory still vivid in the morning fades away
1   2   3   4
in the course of the day.

Shakespeares Werke enthalten eine Fülle zutreffender, der Umwelt
1   4
entnommener Beobachtungen.
3   2

Shakespeare's works contain an abundance of accurate observations taken
1   2   3
from the environment.
3   4

In dem "Naiven" begriff Schiller den natürlichen, wachstümlichen, in der
1   4
Wirklichkeit des Seins gleichsam unbewußt ruhenden antiken Menschen.
4   3   2
(Fritz Martini)

In the "naive," Schiller perceived the <u>natural, growing ancient man who</u>
<u>1   2   3</u>
<u>was, so to speak, unconsciously rooted</u> <u>in the reality of being.</u>
<u>3</u>   <u>4</u>

27.8. It is even possible for several overloaded adjectives to precede the noun:

<u>Der</u> <u>wegen seiner Gedichte</u> <u>gut bekannte,</u> <u>bei vielen Studenten</u> <u>beliebte,</u>
<u>1</u>   <u>4a</u>   <u>3a</u>   <u>4b</u>   <u>3b</u>
<u>viele Sprachen</u> <u>fließend sprechende</u> <u>Professor</u> wurde entlassen.
<u>4c</u>   <u>3c</u>   <u>2</u>
<u>The</u> <u>professor</u> <u>who was well known</u> <u>because of his poems,</u> <u>who was popular</u>
<u>1</u>   <u>2</u>   <u>3a</u>   <u>4a</u>   <u>3b</u>
<u>with his students,</u> and <u>who was fluent</u> <u>in many languages</u> was fired.
<u>4b</u>   <u>3c</u>   <u>4c</u>

Das Volksbuch von Doktor Faustus zeigte die Tragödie <u>des leiden-</u>
<u>1</u>
<u>schaftlichen</u> <u>nach der Welt und nach Erkenntnis</u> <u>verlangenden</u> <u>und so</u>
<u>1</u>   <u>4a</u>   <u>3a</u>   <u>4b</u>
<u>seine Seele</u> <u>preisgebenden</u> <u>Menschen</u>. (Fritz Martini)
<u>4b</u>   <u>3b</u>   <u>2</u>
The chap book of Doctor Faustus showed the tragedy <u>of the suffering</u> <u>man</u>
<u>1</u>   <u>2</u>
<u>longing for</u> <u>the world and knowledge</u> <u>and thus relinquishing</u> <u>his soul</u>.
<u>3a</u>   <u>4a</u>   <u>3b</u>   <u>4b</u>

27.9. This overloaded adjective construction will always contain the four steps I have indicated, and these steps will always follow the same pattern (1, 4, 3, 2) which I have given you in the sample sentences. Moreover, all the words included between the article and the noun **must be included within the overload**; they can **never** be carried over to any other part of the sentence. In fact, you may find it useful to place brackets around this construction to remind yourself that all these words consist of a **single unit** within the sentence.

27.10. When the participle preceding the noun is a past participle, you will have to look up the infinitive in your dictionary, even though the word is used as an adjective. Here are examples:

das *benutzte* Beispiel — look up *benutzen*
der *aufgeklärte* Artikel — look up *aufklären*
die *geschriebene* Regel — look up *schreiben*

After the adjective ending (which generally will be either *-e* or *-en*) is removed, all such participles will end either in *-t* (when they are weak — cf. "benutzt" and "aufgeklärt") or in *-en* (when they are strong — cf. "geschrieben").

Overloaded adjective constructions can be differentiated from relative constructions because they don't have commas preceding the article, and because they end with a noun rather than a verb. Compare:

Der Elefant, *der* in die Luft *stieg*, war aus Gummi — The elephant *which* rose in the air was made of rubber. (*relative*)

Der in die Luft steigende *Elefant* war aus Gummi — The elephant rising in the air was made of rubber. (*overload*)

27.11. Translate these sentences. Indicate the four steps for each overload:

1. Josephe (*a woman*) fand ihren Geliebten in einem dunklen, von Pinien (*pines*) beschatteten Tal (*valley*). (Kleist)
2. Herzog Wilhelm von Breisach kam von einer in Worms mit dem deutschen Kaiser abgehaltenen (*held*) Zusammenkunft (*meeting*) zurück. (Kleist)
3. Am Fuße der Alpen, bei Locarno, im oberen Italien befand sich ein altes, einem Marchese (*marquis*) gehöriges Schloß. (Kleist)
4. Ist der Briefträger ein vom Schicksal (*fate*) verfolgter Mensch?
5. Poseidon wurde überdrüssig (*bored with*) seiner Meere (*seas*). Der Dreizack (*trident*) entfiel (*fell from*) ihm. Still saß er an felsiger (*rocky*) Küste, und eine von seiner Gegenwart (*presence*) betäubte (*dazed*) Möwe (*seagull*) zog schwankende (*precarious*) Kreise um sein Haupt. (Kafka)
6. Solche in seinem gegenwärtigen Zustand (*situation*) ganz nutzlose Gedanken gingen ihm durch den Kopf. (Kafka)
7. Ein auf die Spitze (*point, extreme*) getriebenes Recht kann unter manchen Umständen (*circumstances*) zu einem großen Unrecht werden.
8. Ein von Fräulein Meier sehr oft gebrauchtes Sprichwort lautet (*goes this way*): "Eine gezähmte (*tamed*) Zunge ist ein seltener Vogel."
9. Gegenüber der Tür . . . zeigte sich im Kerzenschein (*candle light*) eine große, in heftigen (*severe*) Strichen (*strokes, outlines*) ausgeführte Kreidezeichnung (*chalk drawing*), die Napoleon darstellte (*represented*), wie er in plumper (*awkward*) und despotischer Haltung seine mit Kanonenstiefeln (*gun-boots*) bekleideten Füße an einem Kamin (*fireplace*) wärmte. (Thomas Mann)
10. Trotz seines Pessimismus wurde der Roman [Thomas Manns *Buddenbrooks*] ein behagliches (*cozy, agreeable*), den Reiz (*charm*) der alten Bürgerlichkeit (*middle-class way of life*) mit Liebe und Humor, geduldiger (*patient*) Breite (*prolixity*) und köstlichem (*exquisite*) Detail ausbreitendes (*depicting*) Buch. (Martini)

11. Am schmalen Bogenfenster (*bow window*) einer Zelle, die nach dem grauen, jetzt vom Morgenlicht beschienenen Schloßturm von Riedberg hinüberschaute, saß die schöne Lukretia Planta. (C. F. Meyer)
12. E. T. A. Hoffmann war ein wegen seiner boshaften Karikaturen gefürchteter Zeichner (*sketcher*) und ein Dichter, der ohne . . . viele Getränke nicht zu arbeiten vermochte. (Martini)
13. Der von dem Jäger (*hunter*) getötete Wolf war der Wolf, der Rotkäppchen gefressen hatte.
14. Ein hoch in die Luft springender Kakerlak (*cockroach*) erschreckte Fräulein Meier, während sie bei dem Briefträger saß.
15. Der Briefträger sah in dem mutigen (*plucky*), vom Zoo neulich entflohenen (*escaped*) Flußpferd (*hippo*) ein Symbol des Drangs der Freiheit aller Menschen und Tiere.

Vocabulary

ab-halten — to hold
die **Alpen** — alps
aus-breiten — to spread out, to depict
aus-führen — to execute, to carry out
* **befinden** (r) — to be located
behaglich — cozy, comfortable
bekleiden — to dress
beschatten — to shade
bescheinen — to light up
betäuben — to daze
boshaft — malicious
die **Breite** — expanse, prolixity
die **Bürgerlichkeit** — middle class way of life
dar-stellen — to represent
despotisch — despotic
der **Drang** (-es, ⸚e) — craving
* **dunkel** — dark
entfallen (i) — to fall away from
erschrecken — to frighten
erstreben — to desire
felsig — rocky
* die **Freiheit** — freedom
* **fürchten** — to fear

ganz — completely
gebrauchen — to use
geduldig — patient
* **gegenüber** — opposite
die **Gegenwart** — present
gegenwärtig — present
gehörig — belonging to
geliebt — loved
das **Getränk** (-es, -e) — drink
* **gewiß** — certain
grau — grey
die **Haltung** — stance, manner
* das **Haupt** (-s, ⸚er) — head
hinüber-schauen (i) — to look over
* das **Italien** (-s) — Italy
der **Kaiser** (-s, -) — emperor
der **Kamin** (-s, -e) — fireplace
die **Karikatur** (-en) — caricature
der **Kopf** (-es, ⸚e) — head
köstlich — precious, exquisite
der **Kreis** (-es, -e) — circle
* **künstlerisch** — artistic
die **Küste** (-n) — coast
lauten (i) — to sound, to say
loben — to praise
* die **Luft** (⸚e) — air

* **manche** — some
das **Meer** (-es, -e) — sea, ocean
die **Möwe** (-n) — seagull
mutig — courageous
neulich — recently
* **nutzlos** — useless
* **ober** — upper
die **Pinie** (-n) — pine
plump — awkward
* das **Recht** (-es, -e) — justice, right
der **Reiz** (-es, -e) — charm,
stimulus
* der **Roman** (-es, -e) — novel
das **Schicksal** (-s, -e) — fate
das **Schloß** (-sses, ⸚sser) —
castle
schmal — narrow
* **selten** — seldom, rare
* **solch** — such
die **Spitze** (-en) — point, extreme
springend — springing
* **still** — quiet
das **Tal** (-es, ⸚er) — valley

das **Tier** (-es, -e) — animal
treiben — to drive
* **trotz** — in spite of
die **Tür** (-en) — door
der **Turm** (-es, ⸚e) — tower
überdrüssig — bored with
verfolgen — to persecute
* **vermögen** — to be able to
* **voll** — full
* **während** — while, during
* **wärmen** — to warm
* **wegen** — because of
der **Zeichner** (-s, -) — sketcher
* **zeigen** (r) — to show
die **Zelle** (-n) — cell
* **ziehen** (zog, hat gezogen) — to
draw, to pull
* **zurück-kommen** (i) — to return
die **Zunge** (-n) — tongue
die **Zusammenkunft** (⸚e) —
meeting
der **Zustand** (-es, ⸚e) —
condition

27.12. Vocabulary aid:

1. Wo befindet sich ein schöner Park?
2. Fräulein Meier will alles über Erdkunde (*geography*) wissen, um einen Aufsatz (*essay*) darüber schreiben zu können.
3. Ein Roman, der auf diese Weise (*way*) anfängt, kann kein gutes Ende haben.
4. Den hoch in die Luft springenden Elefanten sahen die Leute an.
5. Die lange, für den Studenten sehr interessante Geschichte handelt von einem Ringen (*struggle*) nach Freiheit.
6. Die Frau freut sich, mit ihrem Geliebten langsam in dem Park herumzugehen.
7. Vor einem Jahr ging der Student jeden Abend ins Theater, um sein Lieblingsdrama immer wieder zu sehen.

Chapter Twenty-eight

The Passive

28.1. The German passive

In German, the passive is formed by using a conjugation of **werden** with the past participial form (such as **gesagt, geschrieben**) of another verb. Here are examples:

Es **wird geschrieben** — It *is written*.
Das Buch **wird** von ihr **gekauft** — The book *is bought* by her.
Oft **wird** das deutsche Lied **gesungen** — The German song *is sung* often.
Ehrlichkeit **wurde** nie **bereut** — Honesty *was* never *regretted*.
In the passive construction, **werden** will be conjugated, and it will appear in "second" place, while the participle will appear at the end of the clause. The tense of **werden** will determine whether the tense of the passive is present, past, present perfect or past perfect.

28.2. Examples of the passive

(a) Here are all the examples of the present passive:

ich **werde** gesehen —I *am* seen
du **wirst** gesehen —you *are* seen
er **wird** gesehen —he *is* seen
es **wird** gesehen —it *is* seen
sie **wird** gesehen —she *is* seen

wir **werden** gesehen —we *are* seen
ihr **werdet** gesehen —you *are* seen
sie **werden** gesehen —they *are* seen

Sie **werden** gesehen —you *are* seen

(b) Here are all the examples of the past passive:

ich **wurde** gesehen —I *was* seen
du **wurdest** gesehen —you *were* seen
er **wurde** gesehen —he *was* seen
es **wurde** gesehen —it *was* seen
sie **wurde** gesehen —she *was* seen

wir **wurden** gesehen —we *were* seen
ihr **wurdet** gesehen —you *were* seen
sie **wurden** gesehen —they *were* seen

Sie **wurden** gesehen —you *were* seen

(c) Here are all the examples of the present perfect passive:

ich **bin** gesehen **worden**
du **bist** gesehen **worden**

I *have been* seen
you *have been* seen

er, es, sie *ist* gesehen *worden*   he, it, she *has been* seen
wir *sind* gesehen *worden*   we *have been* seen
ihr *seid* gesehen *worden*   you *have been* seen
sie *sind* gesehen *worden*   they *have been* seen
Sie *sind* gesehen *worden*   you *have been* seen

(d) Here are the other passive forms, which appear rarely:

Das Bild *war* gesehen *worden* — The picture *had been* seen. (**Past perfect passive**)
Das Bild *wird* gesehen *werden* — The picture *will be* seen. (**Future passive**)
Das Bild *wird* gesehen *worden sein* — The picture *will have been seen.*
This is the **future perfect passive**, which is seldom used.

28.3. The passive construction can be confusing because *werden* also is used in two other ways with which you are already familiar:

(a) without an infinitive, *werden* simply means "to become:"

Es *wird* dunkel — It *becomes* dark.
Er *wird* alt — He *grows* old.

(b) with an infinitive, *werden* designates the future:

Sie *wird* mit uns *gehen* — She *will go* with us.
Sie *wird* das Gedicht *schreiben* — She *will write* the poem.

(c) Compare the sentences in (a) and (b) with the following passive:

Der Student *wird* von dem Professor *gesehen* — The student *is seen* by the professor.
Das Gedicht *wird* von ihr *geschrieben* — The poem *is written* by her.
Werden used passively will **always** be translated as a form of the verb *to be* and **never** as the verb *to become*.

Worden will **always** be translated as *been* because *worden* is used only as the participial form of the passive. Compare the following two sentences:
Der Hund *ist* alt *geworden* — The dog *has become* old. (**Regular**)
Der Hund *ist* verkauft *worden* — The dog *has been* sold. (**Passive**)

28.4. Whenever you see a form of *werden*, therefore, check for possible verbs at the end of the clause.

If there are **no** verbs, translate *werden* as *become*: Sie *wird* glücklich — She *becomes* happy. Die Leute *werden* reich — The people *become* rich.

If there is a **simple** infinitive, the sentence will be a **simple** future: Er *wird* mit uns *gehen* — He *will go* with us. Sie *werden* den Film *sehen* — They *will* see the film.

Reminder: The infinitive is the verb form found in your dictionaries. It will *always* end in -n or -en.

If there is a **past participle** the sentence will be **passive:** Das Buch *wird* selten *gelesen* — The book *is* seldom *read.* Die Frage *wurde* oft *gestellt* — The question *was* often *asked.*

Reminder: The participle will end in -t if it is a weak verb or -en if it is a strong verb. It will have a ge- prefix **unless** it begins with **be-, ent-, emp-, er-, ver-,** or **zer-.** Here are examples of participles:

ge**schrieben**	(infinitive: schreiben)
ver**standen**	(infinitive: verstehen)
ge**liebt**	(infinitive: lieben)
er**wartet**	(infinitive: erwarten)

Also, sentences with the passive usually will have an inanimate noun (*das Bild, das Gedicht*) for the nominative noun.

28.5. Occasionally, however, a passive sentence should be translated as future passive, as can be shown by the following two sentences:

Morgen *wird* der Film *gesehen* — Tomorrow the movie *will be seen.*
Wann *wird* der Tanzbär *gefüttert?* — When *will* the dancing bear *be fed?*

In each sentence, *wird* makes the sentence **passive only.** The *morgen* in the first sentence and the *wann* in the second sentence rather than the verb point out that the sentences should be translated in the future tense.

Otherwise, the "official" future will be written as follows:

Der Film *wird gesehen werden* — The movie *will be seen.*

28.6. Sometimes the infinitive of the verb and its perfect are identical.

However, you can generally differentiate the future from the passive by context. Here are examples:

Er *wird* den toten Vogel *begraben* — He *will bury* the dead bird. (**Future**)
Der tote Vogel *wird* von ihm *begraben* — The dead bird *is buried* by him. (**Passive**)
Er *wird* seine Kollegen *empfangen* — He *will receive* his colleagues. (**Future**)
Er *wird* von seinen Kollegen *empfangen* — He *is received* by his colleagues. (**Passive**)

28.7. Modals can be combined with the passive in the following way:

Das Buch *muß* unbedingt *gelesen werden* — The book *must* definitely *be read.*
Das Bild *mußte gesehen werden* — The picture *had to be seen.*
Das Bild *hat gesehen werden müssen* — The picture *has had to be seen.*
Das Bild *hatte gesehen werden müssen* — The picture *had had to be seen.*
Das Bild *wird gesehen werden müssen* — The picture *will have to be seen.*

Whenever you have to translate a sentence with three or more verbs, the conjugated verb will always be translated first, the final verb will be translated second, the penultimate verb will be translated third, and any fourth verb will be translated last. Here is an example:

Der Brief <u>wird</u> von dem Professor <u>geöffnet</u> <u>werden</u> <u>müssen</u> — The letter
      1   4   3   2
<u>will</u> <u>have</u> <u>to be</u> <u>opened</u> by the professor.
 1   2   3   4

28.8. Translate these sentences, being particularly aware of how you are translating *werden*:

1. An der Frucht wird der Baum erkannt.
2. Hohe Klimmer (*climbers*) und tiefe Schwimmer werden nicht alt.
3. Esel werden zur Hochzeit geladen (*invited*), nur um Wasser zu tragen.
4. Beim (*at the*) Tanze wird die Unschuld (*innocence*) umgebracht (*murdered*); auf dem Heimwege wird sie begraben. (Obviously, this proverb is amazingly puritanical! I cannot imagine any German-speaking person *ever* saying it.)
5. Rom wurde nicht in einem Tag erbaut.
6. Kein Armer soll verachtet werden, denn Christus war auch arm auf Erden.
7. Unter Räubern wird kein Mord begangen. (There is honor among thieves.)
8. Wer im Frühling nicht sät (*sows*), wird im Herbst nichts ernten (*reap*). (Be careful when translating *nicht* and *nichts*)
9. Freundschaft muß vergolten werden.
10. Wenn der Stein aus der Hand und das Wort aus dem Mund ist, können sie nicht mehr zurückgebracht werden.
11. Liebe wird durch Liebe erkauft.
12. Die liebevolle Katze Fräulein Meiers ist oft gestreichelt worden.
13. Die Erinnerung (*memory*) ist das einzige Paradies, aus welchem wir nicht vertrieben werden können. (Jean Paul)
14. Fräulein Meier wird von einem sensiblen Mann der neunziger Jahre geliebt.

15. Aber die deutschen Revolutionäre (um 1830), die unter dem Sammelnamen "Junges Deutschland" mißverständlich und unfreiwillig zusammengefaßt wurden, waren der Vergangenheit stärker verhaftet, als sie selbst es ahnten und je zugeben wollten. (Martini)
16. Stefan George wollte nicht auf deutschem Boden (*soil*) begraben werden. (Martini)
17. Unterwelt und Abgrund (*abyss*) werden niemals satt (*full*), und der Menschen Augen sind auch unersättlich. (Proverbs)
18. Das schönste Grün wird auch Heu.
19. Wer seine Ohren verstopft vor den Schreien der Armen, der wird einst auch rufen und nicht erhört werden. (Proverbs)
20. Lukas (*Luke*) verbessert (*improved upon*) — Wer sich selbst erniedrigt, will erhöht werden. (Vgl. Lukas 18.14 — Wer aber sich selbst erniedrigt, *wird* erhöht werden.) (Nietzsche)

Vocabulary

ahnen — to suspect
begehen, beging, hat begangen — to commit
begraben, begrub, hat begraben — to bury
der **Boden (-s, ∸)** — ground, soil
* **einst** — once
* **einzig** — only
erbauen — to build
erhöhen — to elevate
erhören — to hear
* die **Erinnerung (-en)** — memory
* **erkaufen** — to buy
* **erkennen, erkannte, hat erkannt** — to recognize
erniedrigen — to lower, humiliate
* die **Freundschaft** — friendship
* der **Frühling (-s)** — spring
das **Grün (-s, -)** — green
der **Heimweg** — way home
der **Herbst (-es, -e)** — fall
das **Heu (-s)** — hay
die **Hochzeit (-en)** — wedding
* **je** — ever
laden, lud, hat geladen — to invite
liebevoll — loving, affectionate

mißverständlich — erroneous, misleading
der **Mord (-s, -e)** — murder
* **neunziger Jahre** — the nineties
* **nicht mehr** — no longer
* **niemals** — never
das **Paradies** — paradise
der **Räuber (-s, -)** — robber, thief
der **Revolutionär (-s, -e)** — revolutionary
* das **Rom (-s)** — Rome
* **rufen, rief, hat gerufen** — to call
der **Sammelname (-ns, -n)** — collective name
satt — satiated, satisfied
der **Schrei (-es, -e)** — scream
* **selber** — self, even
sensibel — sensitive
streicheln — to stroke, pat
um-bringen, brachte um, hat umgebracht — to murder
umgebracht — to murder
unersättlich — insatiable
unfreiweillig — involuntarily
die **Unterwelt** — underworld
verachten — to despise
* **verbessern** — to improve

* die **Vergangenheit** — past
vergelten, vergalt, hat vergolten —
to reward
* **vgl. — vergleiche** — compare (cf.)
verhaftet — dependent, bound up
with
verstopfen — to plug
vertreiben, vertrieb, hat

vertrieben — to drive away
* **worden** — (always) been
zu-geben, gab zu, hat zugegeben
— to admit
* **zurück-bringen, brachte zurück,
hat zurückgebracht** — to bring
back
zusammen-fassen — to combine

Chapter Twenty-nine

Constructions to be Translated Passively in English; the "Fake" Passive

Some constructions which are active in German may be translated into English as passive. The most common of these constructions are: (1) sentences in which *man* is the subject; (2) some verbs which are active in German, but passive in English; (3) some reflexive verbs should be translated passively; *sich lassen* is one of the most common of these reflexive verbs.

29.1. Sentences with *man* (one)

Sentences with *man* as the subject can be translated either actively or passively, depending on personal preference. However, at times, a passive translation may sound smoother in English. Examples are:

Man tut das *nicht* — *One does not do* that, or: That *is not done*.
Man hat Jeronimo Rugera in das Gefängnis *eingesperrt* — *One locked* Jeronimo Rugera in prison, or: Jeronimo Rugera *was locked* in prison.

29.2. Some verbs which are active in German must be translated into English with the verb "to be." The most common of these verbs are *gelten* (*to be valid*), *heißen* (*to be called*), and *schweigen* (*to be silent*). Here are examples:

Eine Unze guten Beispiels *gilt* mehr als ein Pfund Worte — An ounce of a good example *is worth* more than a pound of words.
Der Hund *heißt* Grimmelshausen — The dog *is named* (or called) Grimmelshausen.
Die Vögel *schweigen* im Walde — The birds *are silent* in the woods.

29.3. Some reflexive verbs also should be translated with the verb "to be."
Here are the most common of these verbs:

sich finden	to be found
sich freuen über	to be happy about
sich fürchten vor	to be afraid of
sich interessieren für	to be interested in
sich spiegeln	to be reflected

Here are sample sentences:

Hier *findet sich* ein interessanter Gedanke — Here an interesting thought *is found*.

Fräulein Meier *interessiert sich für* Erdkunde — Fräulein Meier *is interested in* geography.

29.4. *Sich wiederholen* is translated passively whenever the subject is inanimate. Here is an example:

Das *wiederholt sich* immer wieder — That *is repeated* again and again.

29.5. *Sich lassen*

Sich lassen should be translated as *can be* in the present tense, or as *could be* in the past tense. Here are examples:

Das *läßt sich* zeigen — That *can be* shown. (present)
Das Problem *läßt sich* leicht verstehen — The problem *can* easily *be* understood. (present)
Das *ließ sich* sagen — That *could be* said. (past)

However, if the subject is a person rather than an abstraction, *läßt sich* should be translated as *has* or even *lets himself*:

Der Mann *läßt sich* die Haare schneiden — The man *has* his hair cut.
Die Frau *läßt sich* das Auto reparieren — The woman *has* her car repaired.
Man soll *sich* nicht zu viel träumen *lassen* — One should not *let himself* dream too much.

29.6. Translate these sentences (vocabulary is on p. 196):

1. Wer sich fürchtet, sieht Gespenster.
2. Der Bauch (*stomach*) läßt sich nicht vergessen.
3. Der Teufel ist nicht so schwarz, wie man ihn malt (*paints*).
4. Im Gebet (*prayer*) spiegelt sich unser Herz.
5. Für jeden Topf (*pot*) findet sich ein Deckel (*cover*).
6. Fische fängt man mit der Angel (*hook*), Leute fängt man mit Worten.

7. Lieben und Beten (*praying*) lassen sich nicht nötigen.
8. Glück läßt sich finden, Behalten (*keeping it*) ist eine Kunst.
9. Der Expressionismus läßt sich nicht ohne Nietzsches Vorgang (*precedence*) begreifen. (Martini)
10. Was von Stroh ist, muß sich vor dem Feuer hüten.
11. Ein zänkisches (*cranky*) Weib und ein triefendes (*dripping*) Dach (*roof*), wenn es sehr regnet, lassen sich miteinander vergleichen. (Proverbs)
12. Alte Bäume lassen sich nicht biegen.
13. Leoparden brechen in den Tempel ein und saufen (*guzzle*) die Opferkrüge leer. Das wiederholt sich immer wieder. Schließlich kann man es vorausberechnen (*calculate in advance*), und es wird ein Teil der Zeremonie. (Kafka)

29.7. The "fake" passive

The "fake" (or apparent, or statal) passive is conjugated with a form of the verb *sein* plus a past participle. This passive is a fake because the past participle is an adjective rather than a real verb, and it describes the result of a previous action. Here is an example: ***Das Auto ist verkauft*** indicates that the car is sold and that it can no longer be bought by anyone; *verkauft* (*sold*) is an adjective describing the car. ***Das Auto wird verkauft***, on the other hand, indicates that the car is in the process of being sold and that anyone who wants to can still buy it.

The "fake" passive is easy to translate into English because the verb *sein* is translated literally as *to be*, while the participle is translated naturally as a participle. Examples are:

Die Tür *ist geschlossen* — The door *is closed*.
Das Kind *ist* natürlich sehr *erregt* — The child *is* naturally very *excited*.

Note that even though the participle is functioning as a predicate adjective, it still appears at the end of the clause.

29.8. Translate these sentences:

1. Verlobt (*engaged*) ist noch nicht verheiratet.
2. Das Glück ist leichter gefunden als gebunden.
3. Die Süßigkeiten (*sweets*) sind dem Kind verboten.
4. Nachdem die Kuh gestohlen ist, sperrt (*locks*) man den Stall (*stable*).
5. Solange man nährt (*nourishes*), ist man geehrt, und solange man gibt, geliebt.
6. Die Bärenhaut (*bearskin*) soll man nicht verkaufen, ehe der Bär erstochen ist.

Vocabulary

die **Angel (-n)** — fishhook
der **Bär (-en, -en)** — bear
* **begreifen** — to comprehend
behalten — to keep
biegen, bog, gebogen — to bend
das **Dach (-es, ̈er)** — roof
ehe — before
ehren — to honor
ein-brechen — to break in
erstechen, erstach, erstochen — to stab
der **Expressionismus** — Expressionism
fangen (fängt) — to catch
* **finden** (r) — to be found
* **freuen** (r) — to be pleased
* **fürchten** (r) — to be afraid
das **Gespenst (-es, -er)** — ghost
hüten (vor) (r) — to be on guard (against)
* **immer wieder** — again & again
* die **Kunst (̈e)** — art
* **lassen (läßt)** (r) — can be
leer — empty
der **Leopard (-en, -en)** — leopard
malen — to paint
miteinander — with one another
* **nachdem** — after

nähren — to nourish
* **noch nicht** — not yet
nötigen — to force
der **Opferkrug (-s, ̈e)** — sacrificial vessel
saufen — to guzzle
* **schließlich** — finally
* **schwarz** — black
* **solange** — as long as
spiegeln (r) — to be reflected
der **Stall (-s, ̈e)** — stable
stehlen, stahl, gestohlen — to steal
das **Stroh (-s)** — straw
* das **Teil (-s, -e)** — part
* der **Topf (-es, ̈e)** — pot
* **verbieten, verbot, verboten** — to forbid
* **vergessen (vergißt)** — to forget
* **vergleichen** — to compare
verheiraten — to marry
verkaufen — to sell
voraus-berechnen — calculate in advance
das **Weib (-es, -er)** — wife
* **wiederholen** (r) — to be repeated
zänkisch — cranky
die **Zeremonie (-n)** — ceremony

29.9. Vocabulary aid (the vocabulary from 28.8 is also included):

1. Die Liebesgedichte des Briefträgers lassen sich nicht vergessen.
2. Der Frühling ist eine Jahreszeit (*season*), die man mit Freude erwartet.
3. Wann wurde der chinesische Topf Fräulein Meiers gebrochen?
4. Ist der Teufel wirklich nicht so schlecht, wie er gemalt wird?
5. Wem darf man widersprechen (*contradict*)?
6. Der Hund hat den Ball immer wieder zurückgebracht.
7. Das Kind fürchtet sich vor dem Zahnarzt (*dentist*).
8. Nur ein einziger Mensch hörte das Schreien.
9. Der Roman ist längst vergessen worden.
10. Der Vater des Briefträgers ist alt geworden.

11. Kann die Kuh gefunden werden, nachdem sie gestohlen worden ist?
12. Wer will erhöht (*elevated*) werden?
13. Bevor man daran glauben kann, muß das gesehen werden.
14. Man muß laut schreien, um gehört zu werden.

Reading Selection: *Zwei Chassidische* Geschichten*** **(Martin Buber)**

I. Eine arme Apfelhändlerin (*lady apple dealer*), deren Stand nah am Hause Rabbi Chaims von Zans war, kam einst klagend zu ihm: "Unser Rabbi, ich habe noch kein Geld, um für den Sabbat einzukaufen." "Und dein Apfelstand?" fragte der Zaddik (*wise man*). "Die Leute sagen", antwortete sie, "meine Äpfel seien (*are*) schlecht, und sie wollen keine kaufen." Sogleich lief Rabbi Chaim auf die Gasse und rief: "Wer will gute Äpfel kaufen?" Im Nu (*immediately*) sammelte sich die Menge um ihn, die Münzen flogen unbesehen und ungezählt herbei, und bald waren alle Früchte zum doppelten und dreifachen Preis verkauft. "Sieh nur", sagte er zur Frau, als er sich zum Gehen wandte, "deine Äpfel waren gut, die Leute haben es nur nicht gewußt."

II. Am Vorabend des Versöhnungstages (*Yom Kippur*) . . . waren in Sassow alle im Bethaus (*temple*) versammelt und warteten auf den Rabbi. Die Zeit verging, er kam nicht. Eine der Frauen sprach zu sich: "Es dauert wohl noch eine Weile, bis angefangen wird (*the service will begin*), und ich habe mich so sehr beeilt, und mein Kind ist allein zu Hause geblieben, da (*therefore*) will ich doch schnell nach ihm sehen, ob es nicht aufgewacht ist, in ein paar Minuten bin ich wieder hier." Sie lief hinüber, horchte an der Tür, es war still. Leise drückte sie die Klinke (*latch*) nieder (*pressed down*), steckte den Kopf vor, da (*there*) stand der Rabbi und hielt ihr Kind im Arm***, dessen Weinen (*crying*) ihn auf dem Weg zum Bethaus hergelockt (*enticed*) hatte; er hatte mit ihm gespielt und ihm vorgesungen, bis es eingeschlafen war.

---

*   Chassidische — Hasidic
**   If you don't wish to use a dictionary, vocabulary for this section is given on pp. 285-356.
*** Translate *im Arm* as *in his arms*.

Chapter Thirty

The Subjunctive (Part I — Subjunctive I)

30.1. The German subjunctive is not too difficult to translate (although most explanations of the subjunctive may seem long and confusing) because often the context forces the reader to use the subjunctive naturally, whether or not the form is recognized.

There are two types of the subjunctive, one based on the infinitive stem of the verb, and based on the past stem. At this point, it will be crucial for you to learn the infinitive and the past subjunctive forms of *sein* (*sei* — infinitive stem; *wäre* — past stem) and *haben* (*habe* — infinitive stem; *hätte* — past stem), as these are the verbs which appear most frequently in your reading.

30.2. The subjunctive formed from the infinitive stem of the verb (which I will call "subjunctive I")

Here are some examples of the subjunctive based on the infinitive stem of the verb in comparison with the present indicative:

indicative	subjunctive I	subjunctive I	subjunctive I	subjunctive I
(gehen)	*(gehen)*	*(sein)*	*(haben)*	*(werden)*
ich gehe	gehe	sei	habe	werde
du **gehst**	**gehest**	sei(e)st	**habest**	**werdest**
er **geht**	**gehe**	sei	**habe**	**werde**
wir gehen	gehen	seien	haben	werden
ihr **geht**	**gehet**	sei(e)t	**habet**	**werdet**
sie gehen	gehen	seien	haben	werden
Sie gehen	gehen	seien	haben	werden

For virtually all verbs except *sein* and the modals (***dürfen, können, mögen, müssen, sollen,*** and ***wollen***), present indicative and the Subjunctive I will be identical except for second and third person singular and the informal you plural.

30.3. The most common use of this subjunctive form is indirect discourse, that is, whenever a sentence includes what someone has said or thought without using his direct words. Examples are:

Er sagt, er *habe* die Karte — He says, he *has* the ticket.
Sie glaubt, sie *spreche* die Wahrheit — She believes she *is speaking* the truth.

The Subjunctive I generally appears after verbs such as ***sprechen*** (*speak*), ***sagen*** (*say*), ***fragen*** (*ask*), ***antworten*** (*answer*), ***glauben*** (*believe*), ***denken*** (*think*), ***versprechen*** (*promise*), ***meinen*** (*be of the opinion, suppose*), ***erzählen*** (*explain*), ***hoffen*** (*hope*), or even ***schreiben*** (*write*).

A rough equivalent of this in English is shown by adding the word "*that*" after similar verbs:

Er glaubt, er habe viel zu tun — He believes *that* he has a lot to do.

While it is not necessary to add "*that*" to your translation, chances are that if you feel like adding it, you are dealing with a sentence that is in indirect discourse, and therefore you do not need to add any auxiliaries to the verb in your translation to prove that you realize it is subjunctive I.

30.4. Although this form is subjunctive in German, it is not subjunctive in English. Therefore, it is to be translated as an indicative verb. Moreover, it should be translated either present or past tense, depending on whether the supposition verb (*sagen, hoffen,* etc.) is present or past. Here are examples:

Sie *glaubt*, sie *verstehe* den komplizierten Begriff — She *believes* she *understands* the complicated concept. (**present**)
Er *sagt*, er *sei* glücklich — He *says* he *is* happy. (**present**)
Sie *glaubte*, sie *verstehe* den komplizierten Begriff — She *believed* she *understood* the complicated concept. (**past**)
Er *sagte*, er *sei* glücklich — He *said* he *was* happy. (**past**)

30.5. The present perfect is formed by using the Subjunctive I form of either *haben* or *sein* with a participle. Here are examples:

Er sagte, er *habe* den Begriff *verstanden* — He said he *had understood* the concept.

Fräulein Meier glaubte, ihr Kindheitstraum *sei* Wirklichkeit *geworden* — Fräulein Meier believed, her childhood dream *had become* a reality.

30.6. Occasionally, this subjunctive will also be used as a command. A good example is the Lord's Prayer: "Unser Vater im Himmel. Dein Name *werde* geheiligt. Dein Reich *komme*. Dein Wille *geschehe* auf Erden wie im Himmel." — Our Father in Heaven. *Let* thy name be hallowed. *Let* thy kingdom come. *Let* thy will be done . . .

The expletive Gottseidank — *let* God be thanked, or Thank God — also has the command subjunctive within it.

This form can be recognized because the third person singular ends in -*e* rather than -*t* for present tense; moreover, the form *sei* will always be either imperative or subjunctive I.   Also, a straight indicative translation will seem somewhat inappropriate. Here is another example:

Gott *gnade* dem, der mit faulen Leuten haushält — *Let* God bless him who associates with lazy people.

When the verb is followed by *wir* and the sentence has an exclamation point, it is also best translated by *let us*. Examples are:

Vergessen wir nicht, das zu tun! — *Let us* not forget to do that!
Gehen wir jetzt! — *Let us go* now!
Seien wir glücklich! — *Let us be* happy!

30.7. At other times, subjunctive I (which is not indirect discourse) should be translated into English with may, should, or even without an -s ending on the verb. Examples are:

Obwohl es gut *sei*, gefällt es ihr nicht — Although it *may be* good, it does not please her.
Man *vergesse* nicht . . . — One *should* not forget . . .
Gott *helfe* mir! — God *help* me!

Note the difference between the indicative and the subjunctive I:

Man glaubt das nicht — One *does not believe* that. (indicative)
Man glaube das nicht — One *should not believe* that. (subjunctive I)

30.8. Translate these sentences:

1. Ein böses (*guilty*) Gewissen denkt stets (*constantly*), der Wolf sei hinterm Ofen.
2. Der Fuchs meint, daß jeder Hühner stehle, wie er. (How do you know that *jeder* does not modify *Hühner*?)

3. Hoch lebe der König! (You may translate *hoch* as *long*)
4. Wenn alle dir sagen, du seiest betrunken, geh schlafen!
5. Wer Ohren hat, der höre!
6. Kinder meinen, wenn es im Dorf regnet, es regne in der ganzen Welt. (How do you know that *meinen* is *not* an adjective?)
7. Wer einen guten Boten will, gehe selbst.
8. Die Wahrsager erinnern uns: Vergessen wir nicht die Zukunft!
9. Besser, es fresse mich ein Wolf als ein Lamm.
10. Wer nicht mit der Feder schreiben kann, nehme die Mistgabel (*pitch-fork*).
11. Der Bibelverkäufer schlägt vor: Lesen wir die Bibel!
12. Wenn man eines Diebes bedarf (*requires*), so nehme man ihn vom Galgen (*gallows*); wenn man ihn gebraucht hat, so henke man ihn wieder daran.
13. Gott bewahre mich vor meinen Freunden!
14. Wer fürchtet, er tue zu viel, tut immer zu wenig.
15. Die Gelehrten sind gute Uhrwerke: nur sorge man, sie richtig aufzuziehen (*wind*)! Dann zeigen sie ohne Falsch die Stunde an und machen einen bescheidenen (*modest*) Lärm (*noise*) dabei. (Nietzsche) (Nietzsche's view of scholars tends to be as dim as his view of Christians!)

Vocabulary

an-zeigen — to show
auf-ziehen — to wind
bedürfen (bedarf) (with gen.) — to require
bescheiden — modest
bewahren vor — to protect from
der **Bibelverkäufer (-s, -)** — Bible salesman
der **Bote (-n, -n)** — messenger
dabei — in so doing
der **Dieb (-es, -e)** — thief
das **Dorf (-es, ̈er)** — village
* **erinnern** — to remind
(ohne) Falsch — without error
die **Feder (-n)** — pen
fressen — to eat
der **Fuchs (-es, ̈e)** — fox
* **fürchten** — to fear; (r) — to be afraid

der **Galgen (-s, -)** — gallows
* **gebrauchen** — to make use
* der **Gelehrte (-n, -n)** — scholar
henken — to hang
das **Lamm (-s, ̈er)** — lamb
der **Lärm (-es)** — noise
* **meinen** — to be of the opinion, think
die **Mistgabel (-n)** — pitch-fork
der **Ofen (-s, ̈)** — oven
* **regnen** (i) — to rain
* **richtig** — correctly
schlafen (i) — to sleep
* **sei** (from sein) — to be
* **selbst** — self, even
sorgen (i) — to take care
stehlen — to steal
stets — constantly
* die **Stunde (-n)** — hour

das **Uhrwerk (-s, -e)** — clock, clockwork

vergessen — to forget

vor-schlagen — to suggest

der **Wahrsager (-s, -)** — prophet

* **wieder** — again

die **Zukunft** — future

Chapter Thirty-one

The Subjunctive (Part II — Subjunctive II)

31.1. The subjunctive based on the past of the verb (subjunctive II)

The subjunctive II usually is formed by adding an umlaut to the past of strong verbs (if these verbs contain vowels a, o, or u). When weak verbs are encountered, the past indicative and the Subjunctive II are identical. Here are examples:

Past indicative	Subjunctive II	Past indicative	Subjunctive II
singen (strong)		*sagen* (weak)	
ich sang	sänge	sagte	sagte
du sangst	sängest	sagtest	sagtest
er sang	sänge	sagte	sagte
wir sangen	sängen	sagten	sagten
ihr sangt	sänget	sagtet	sagtet
sie sangen	sängen	sagten	sagten
Sie sangen	sängen	sagten	sagten

And here are the Subjunctive II forms of *sein, haben,* and *werden*:

sein	haben	werden
ich wäre	hätte	würde
du wär(e)st	hättest	würdest
er wäre	hätte	würde
wir wären	hätten	würden
ihr wär(e)t	hättet	würdet
sie wären	hätten	würden
Sie wären	hätten	würden

31.2. Here are the most frequent uses of the subjunctive II:

(1) Expressions of events which did not occur:

Es *wäre* nett *gewesen,* wenn er *gekommen wäre* — It *would have been* nice, if he *had come.*

Wenn er das *gewußt hätte, hätte* er die richtige Antwort *gegeben* — If he *had known* that, he *would have given* the right answer.

Wenn Fräulein Meier hier *wäre, gäbe* sie uns eine Erklärung — If Fräulein Meier *were* here, she *would give* us an explanation.

(2) Different degrees of assumption or possibility:

Vielleicht *wäre* das möglich — Perhaps that *would* be possible.

Es *wäre* nett, das zu tun — It *would* be nice to do that.

Wenn ich nur reich *wäre* — If only I *were* rich!

(3) Clauses of conjecture which cannot be confirmed immediately, such as after *als ob* (*as if*), *als wenn,* and *als*:

Er sieht aus, *als ob* er glücklich *wäre* — He looks *as if* he *were* happy.

Arbeite, *als könntest* du ewig leben — Work *as if* you *could* live eternally;

Bete, *als endete* morgen dein Streben — Pray *as if* tomorrow your striving *would end.*

(4) Desires:

Ich *wünschte,* ich *könnte gehen* — I *wish* I *could go.* (Note that *wünschte* also is subjunctive in German, although it is indicative in English.)

Also, *mögen* (*to like*) often appears in its subjunctive form:

Ich *möchte* gehen — I *would like* to go.

(5) Reported speech

such as the words of a third person (the first person being the narrator and the second person being the listener). The subjunctive II is also used if there is the slightest doubt about the accuracy of the statements:

Man sagte, Fräulein Meier *ginge gern* in den Zoo — It was said that Fräulein Meier *liked to go* to the zoo.

Sie behauptet, daß sie hilflos *wäre* — She asserts that she *is* helpless.

31.3. There are both present and past forms of the subjunctive II:

Das *wäre* möglich — That *would be* possible (**present**).

Das *wäre* möglich *gewesen* — That *would have been* possible (**past**).

Wenn er das *wüßte, täte* er das nicht — If he *were to know* (or *knew*) that, he *would not do* that (**present**).
Wenn er das *gewußt hätte, hätte* er das nicht *getan* — If he *had known* that, he *would* not *have done* that (**past**).

Note that in the past form the subjunctive of either *sein (wäre)* or *haben (hätte)* is used as the auxiliary verb.

31.4. How to translate the subjunctive II

(1) When there is only one subjunctive II verb in a sentence, it usually will be translated as **would**, particularly if it appears in the main clause of the sentence:

Es *wäre* schön, einen neuen Wintermantel zu besitzen — It *would be* nice to own a new winter coat.
Ohne ihre getigerte Katze *wäre* Fräulein Meier sehr betrübt — Without her tabby cat, Fräulein Meier *would be* quite sad.
Vielleicht *ginge* er doch mit uns ins Kino — Perhaps he *would go* to the movies with us, after all.

(2) The subjunctive II also will be translated as **would** if the verb refers to some event which can happen only in the future:

Er glaubte, er *flöge* nächstes Jahr nach Berlin — He believed he *would fly* to Berlin next year.
Sie sagte, wir *sähen* sie morgen — She said we *would see* her tomorrow.
Arbeite, als *endete* morgen dein Streben — Work as if tomorrow your striving *would end*.

(3) The subjunctive II will be translated as **were** (or a similar past) whenever it is part of an "if" clause:

Er tat, als ob er das *wüßte* — He acted as if he *knew* that.
Zuviel schmeckt bitter, auch wenn es lauter Honig *wäre* — Too much tastes bitter, even if it *were* pure honey.
Wenn er nur hier *wäre*! — If only he *were* here!

31.5. If...then clauses (the conditional)

In most "if...then" sentences, both verbs will be subjunctive; in the "if" clause, the subjunctive verb should be translated as **were** (or a similar past), while in the main clause, the subjunctive verb should be translated as **would**. Examples are:

Wenn der Student hier *wäre, sänge* er ein Trinklied — *If* the student *were* here, he *would sing* a drinking song.
Wenn der Student ein Trinklied *sänge, wäre* er glücklich — *If* the student *were to sing* a drinking song, he *would be* happy.
Wenn er mich *gefragt hätte, hätte* ich ihm die Antwort *gegeben* — *If* he *had asked* me, I *would have given* him the answer.

Moreover, some subjunctive sentences begin with a verb, and they all follow an "if...then" pattern. Again, the verb in the "if" clause (which is the verb starting the sentence) should be translated as *were* while the other subjunctive II verb should be translated as *would*. Here are examples:

Gäbe es keine Armut, so *gäbe* es keine Kunst — If there *were* no poverty, there *would be* no art.
Hätte ich das *gewußt, wäre* ich nicht *dahingegangen* — *If* I *had known* that, I *would* not *have gone* there.

31.6. The subjunctive in conjunction with the passive:

Whenever the subjunctive II is used in conjunction with the passive, the auxiliary will always be *wäre*.
When a subjunctive passive verb is part of the main clause, it should be translated as *would have been* . . . Examples are:

Es *wäre* von ihm *erwartet worden*, daß er die Antwort wissen würde — It *would have been expected* of him that he would know the answer.
Wenn die Katze sich nicht so gut versteckt hätte, *wäre* sie eher *gefunden worden* — If the cat had not hidden so well, she *would have been found* sooner.

When a subjunctive passive verb is part of an "if" clause, it should be translated as *had been* . . . Examples are:

Wenn es nur eher *gesehen worden wäre* — *If* it *had* only *been seen* sooner!
Sie sieht aus, als *wäre* sie *geküßt worden* — She looks *as if* she *had been kissed*.

31.7. Translate these sentences:

1. Ohne Musik wäre das Leben ein Irrtum. (Nietzsche)
2. Ein Esel bleibt ein Esel, auch wenn er nach Rom käme.
3. Wäre die Wahrheit ein Bach (*brook*), hätten die Menschen Wasserscheu (*hydrophobia*).
4. Wenn er an den ehemaligen (*former*) Geliebten Fräulein Meiers denkt, sieht der Briefträger aus, als hätte er einen Holzapfel gegessen. (He is looking quite annoyed!)

5. Ich wüßte nicht zu leben, wenn ich nicht noch ein Seher wäre dessen, was kommen muß. (Nietzsche)

6. Er sieht aus, als hätten ihm die Hühner das Brot genommen. (In other words, he looks totally worn out and defeated.)

7. Wenn es ein Maul (*mouth*) hätte, so biß' es dich. (It looks mean and hostile. Or, it is quite obviously right in front of you.)

8. Wenn es möglich gewesen wäre, den Turm (*tower*) von Babel zu erbauen, ohne ihn zu erklettern (*climb*), es wäre erlaubt worden. (Kafka) (Note: do not add a *would* to the *if* clause!)

9. Der Dilettant behauptet, er spräche fließend Griechisch.

10. Niemand hätte erwartet, daß der einsichtsvolle, die Zukunft der Erde behandelnde Aufsatz (*essay*) von Fräulein Meier geschrieben worden war.

11. Warum kann der Hund Furcht, aber nicht Reue (*repentance*) empfinden? Wäre es richtig zu sagen, "weil er nicht sprechen kann"? (Wittgenstein) (How do you know that **kann** and **empfinden** have to go together?)

12. Jeronimo war starr (*rigid*) vor Entsetzen; und gleich, als ob sein ganzes Bewußtsein (*consciousness, mind*) zerschmettert worden wäre, hielt er sich jetzt an dem Pfeiler (*column*), an welchem er hatte sterben wollen, um nicht umzufallen. (Kleist)

13. Zarathustra über Jesus:
Wäre er doch in der Wüste geblieben und ferne von den Guten und Gerechten! Vielleicht hätte er leben gelernt und die Erde lieben gelernt — und das Lachen dazu . . . Er starb zu früh: er selber hätte seine Lehre widerrufen, wäre er bis zu meinem Alter gekommen. (Nietzsche)

Vocabulary

* **als ob** — as if
* das **Alter** (-s, -) — age
* **auch wenn** — even if
  der **Aufsatz** (-es, ⸚e) — essay
* **aus-sehen** (i) — to seem, appear
  der **Bach** (-es, ⸚e) — brook
  behandeln — to treat
  behaupten — to assert
* **bis zu** — to the point of
  bisse — subj. of beißen — to bite
  das **Bewußtsein** (-s) — consciousness, mind

* **dazu** — in addition
* **dessen** — of that (review 25.2)
  der **Dilettant** (-en, -en) — amateur
  ehemalig — former
  einsichtsvoll — insightful
  empfinden — to feel, perceive
  das **Entsetzen** (-s) — horror
  erbauen — to build
  erlauben — to allow
* **erwarten** — to expect
  fern — far
  fließend — fluent

* **früh** — early
  gäbe — subj. of geben
  geliebt — loved
  der **Gerechte (-n, -n)** — righteous one
* **gleich** — immediately
  Griechisch — Greek
  halten — to hold
* **hätte** — subj. of haben
  der **Holzapfel (-s, ⁻)** — crabapple
  der **Irrtum (-s, ⁻er)** — error
* **jetzt** — now
  käme — subj. of kommen
* die **Lehre (-n)** — teaching, doctrine
* **möglich** — possible
* **nehmen** (with dat.) — to take *from*

* **niemand** — no one
* **noch** — still
  die **Reue** — repentance
* **selber** — himself
  spräche — subj. of sprechen
  starr (vor) — rigid (with)
* **sterben (i)** — to die
  um-fallen (i) — to fall down
* **wäre** — subj. of sein
* **weil** — because
* **welch** — which, what
  widerrufen — to renounce
  wüßte — subj. of wissen
  die **Wüste (-n)** — desert
  zerschmettern — to smash
  die **Zukunft** — future

Chapter Thirty-two
Other Subjunctive Forms

32.1. The subjunctive forms of the modals

Here are two charts giving the subjunctive forms of the modals:

The subjunctive I (formed from the infinitive stem of the modal)						
	dürfen	*können*	*mögen*	*müssen*	*sollen*	*wollen*
ich	dürfe	könne	möge	müsse	solle	wolle
du	dürfest	könnest	mögest	müssest	sollest	wollest
sie	dürfe	könne	möge	müsse	solle	wolle
wir	dürfen	können	mögen	müssen	sollen	wollen
ihr	dürft	könnt	mögt	müßt	sollt	wollt
sie	dürfen	können	mögen	müssen	sollen	wollen
Sie	dürfen	können	mögen	müssen	sollen	wollen

The subjunctive II (formed from the past stem of the modal)						
	dürfen	*können*	*mögen*	*müssen*	*sollen*	*wollen*
ich	dürfte	könnte	möchte	müßte	sollte	wollte
du	dürftest	könntest	möchtest	müßtest	solltest	wolltest
sie	dürfte	könnte	möchte	müßte	sollte	wollte
wir	dürften	könnten	möchten	müßten	sollten	wollten
ihr	dürftet	könntet	möchtet	müßtet	solltet	wolltet
sie	dürften	könnten	möchten	müßten	sollten	wollten
Sie	dürften	könnten	möchten	müßten	sollten	wollten

The subjunctive formed from the infinitive stem of the modal probably will not appear too often in your reading. Consequently I am giving you the chart primarily as a reference, in case you do come across it.

32.2. The subjunctive II of the modals appears more often; therefore, you should become familiar with it. Here are more sample sentences:

Wenn er einundzwanzig wäre, *dürfte* er Schnaps trinken — If he were twenty-one, he *would be permitted* to drink brandy.
Er *müßte* dahin gehen, wenn er nicht krank wäre — He *would have* to go, if he were not sick.

Möchte generally will be translated as *would like to*: Fräulein Meier *möchte* ein Glas Schnaps trinken — Fräulein Meier *would like to* drink a glass of brandy.

Könnte generally will be translated as *could*: Wenn das Kind singen *könnte*, sänge es mit dem Chor — If the child *could* sing, he would sing with the choir.
Wenn der Wahrsager wirklich wahrsagen *könnte*, hätte er viel Geld verdient — If the prophet really *could* prophesy, he would have earned a lot of money.

32.3. Note the following possible meanings of subjective modals:

dürfte — might be; *wollte* — wished; *sollte* — should

Das *dürfte* möglich sein — That *might be* possible.
Ich *wollte*, ich könnte gehen — I *wished* I could go.
Ich *sollte* studieren, anstatt einen Krimi zu lesen — I *should* study instead of reading a murder mystery.

32.4. Here is a comparison of the present indicative, past indicative, and subjunctive II of the modals *dürfen, können, mögen,* and *müssen*. Note that the infinitive and the third person plural (they) present *indicative* have umlauts, as does the subjunctive. Therefore, whenever you see any of these modals with umlauts, be careful to note whether the verb is indicative or subjunctive, and try not to confuse them. Here is a chart:

	dürfen	*können*	*mögen*	*müssen*
present indicative				
er	darf	kann	mag	muß
sie	dürfen	können	mögen	müssen
past indicative				
er	durfte	konnte	mochte	mußte
sie	durften	konnten	mochten	mußten
subjunctive II				
er	dürfte	könnte	möchte	müßte
sie	dürften	könnten	möchten	müßten

32.5. *Hätte* **in conjunction with a modal will always indicate something that could (would, should) have taken place, but which did not.** Here are examples:

Er *hätte* gehen können — He *could* have gone.

Fräulein Meier *hätte* das nicht sagen sollen — Fräulein Meier *should* not have said that.

32.6. Translate these sentences (vocabulary is on p. 213):

1. Wenn alle Lügner Hafer (*oats*) fräßen, müßten die Pferde verhungern.
2. Wäre dem Mann keine Gehilfin gegeben, er könnte auf Erden nimmer so (wohl) leben.
3. Der Briefträger glaubt, der Wein könne des Menschen Herz erfreuen.
4. Wer möchte mit Fräulein Meier in die Schweiz fahren?
5. Fräulein Meier hätte einen komischen autobiographischen Roman schreiben können, wenn sie viel Zeit dafür gehabt hätte.
6. Spiele nicht mit dem Schießgewehr (*weaponry*), denn es könnte geladen (*loaded*) sein.
7. Der Student wollte, er hätte die Philosophie Kants studiert.
8. Es dürfte nicht möglich sein, Hegels *Phänomenologie des Geistes* völlig zu begreifen.
9. Sie sollten sicher sagen, was sie meinen.

32.7. The conditional, formed by the subjunctive form of *werden* (*würde*)

Occasionally, the subjunctive form of *werden* will be used in conjunction with other verbs. (The conjugation of the subjunctive form of *werden* is given to you in 31.1.) Note that the subjunctive II of **werden** (generally either *würde* or *würden*) will **almost always** mean **would**! Here are examples:

Ich *würde gehen*, wenn ich die Zeit dafür hätte — I *would go* if I had the time for it.
Wir *würden* das *gefragt haben*, wenn wir daran gedacht hätten — We *would have asked* that if we had thought of it.
Er *würde* das *tun müssen*, wenn er hier wäre — He *would have to do* that if he were here.

Note: do *not* confuse würde with its non-subjunctive form wurde, which means *became* when used as the only verb (Es *wurde* dunkel — it *became* dark) or *was* when used passively (Es *wurde* oft *getan* — it *was* often *done*). **The conditional will always have an umlaut** (Er *würde* das getan haben — he *would* have done that . . .).

32.8. Translate these sentences:

1. Zarathustra sagte: "Ich würde nur an einen Gott glauben, der zu tanzen verstünde." (Nietzsche)
2. Wäre Narrheit (*foolishness*) das Zipperlein (*gout*), würde man wenige Leute beim Tanze sehen.
3. Wenn Gott ein Land strafen (*punish*) wollte, würde er den Herren die Weisheit nehmen.
4. Es sind böse Hennen, die dem Nachbarn die Eier zutragen (*to carry to*) würden.
5. Wenn der Magen des alten Mannes satt (*full*) gewesen wäre, so wäre sein Herz fröhlich gewesen.
6. Wenn die Keuschheit (*chastity*) zum Tanze käme, so würde sie auf gläsernen (*glass*) Schuhen tanzen.
7. Der Briefträger würde sich freuen, Fräulein Meier ins Theater begleiten (*accompany*) zu dürfen.
8. Der Professor würde gerne Dichter werden.
9. Eine chassidische (*Hasidic*) Geschichte:
   Rabbi Chajim von Krosno (a place), ein Schüler (*disciple*) des Baalschem (a name), sah einst mit seinen Schülern einem Seiltänzer (*tightrope-walker*) zu. Er war so tief in den Anblick versunken, daß sie ihn fragten, was es sei, das seine Augen an die törichte Schaustellung (*exhibition*) banne (*attract*). "Dieser Mann", antwortete er, "setzt sein Leben aufs Spiel (*gambles with his life*), ich könnte nicht sagen weswegen. Gewiß aber kann er, während er auf dem Seil (*rope*) geht, nicht daran denken, daß er mit seiner Handlung (*action*) hundert Gulden (*guilders*) verdient; denn sowie (*as soon as*) er dies dächte, würde er abstürzen" (*fall off*). (Buber)

Vocabulary

ab-stürzen (i) — to fall off
der Anblick (-es, -e) — spectacle
bannen — to attract
* bauen — to build
begleiten — to accompany
* begreifen — to understand
* dächte — subj. of denken
* dürfte (sometimes) — might be
das Ei (-es, -er) — egg
erfreuen — to please
fräße — subj. of fressen — to eat
like an animal
* freuen (r) — to be pleased
fröhlich — joyous
die Gehilfin — helper, female
companion
* die Geschichte (-n) — story, tale,
history
* gewiß — certain
gläsern — glass
die Handlung (-en) — action
komisch — funny, comic
der Lügner (-s, -) — liar
der Magen — stomach
* meinen — to believe
* möchte — would like to

möglich — possible
der Nachbar (-s, -n) — neighbor
nimmer — never
das Pferd (-es, -e) — horse
* der Roman (-es, -e) — novel
satt — full, satiated
der Schüler (-s, -) — disciple
die Schweiz — Switzerland
* sicher — certain
* sollte (sometimes) — should
spielen — to play
töricht — foolish
* tun — to do; to act
verdienen — to earn
verhungern (i) — to starve
versunken — absorbed
* verstünde — subj. of verstehen —
to understand, to know how to
* völlig — completely
* wenig — few
weswegen — on what account
* wollte (sometimes) — wished
* würde — would
zu-sehen (i) — to watch
zu-tragen — to carry to

Reading Selection: *Der Schwan**
(Slawomir Mrozek)

Im Park befand sich ein Teich. Seine Zierde war ein Schwan. Eines Tages war
der Schwan verschwunden. Halbstarke hatten ihn gestohlen.

Der Vorstand der Städtischen Grünanlagen besorgte einen neuen Schwan.
Um ihm das Los seines Vorgängers zu ersparen, wurde ihm ein eigener Wächter
zugeteilt.

Dieser war ein alter, seit Jahren vereinsamter Mann. Als er seinen Posten
antrat, begann es abends bereits kalt zu werden. Niemand kam mehr in den
Park. Der Alte ging um den Teich herum, paßte auf den Schwan auf und sah

---

*　If you don't wish to use a dictionary, vocabulary for this section is given on pp. 285-356.

manchmal in die Sterne. Ihn fror. Er hatte Lust, auf einen Sprung in die kleine Wirtschaft (*inn*) in der Nähe des Parks zu gehen. Schon wollte er sich auf den Weg machen, als ihm der Schwan einfiel. Er befürchtete, dieser könne während seiner Abwesenheit gestohlen werden. Dann verlöre er seinen Posten. Er verzichtete also auf sein Vorhaben.

Aber die Kälte quälte ihn immer mehr und vertiefte seine Einsamkeit. Schließlich beschloß er, zusammen mit dem Schwan in die Wirtschaft zu gehen. Selbst wenn jemand in den Park käme, um sich der schönen Natur zu erfreuen, würde er das Fehlen des Schwans nicht sofort bemerken. "Die Nacht ist sternklar, aber ohne Mondschein, und wir kommen gleich zurück", dachte er und nahm den Schwan mit.

Die Wirtschaft war voll Wärme und Bratenduft. Der Alte setzte den Schwan sich gegenüber auf einen Stuhl, um ihn im Auge zu behalten. Dann bestellte er ein bescheidenes Mahl und ein Gläschen Wodka, um sich aufzuwärmen.

Als er sein Hammelfleisch mit Lust und Zufriedenheit verzehrte, fiel ihm auf, daß ihn der Schwan ganz eigenartig ansah. Der Vogel tat ihm leid. Solange dieser vorwurfsvolle Blick auf ihm ruhte, konnte er nicht essen. Er rief den Kellner und bestellte für den Schwan eine in warmem, gezuckertem Starkbier aufgeweichte Semmel. Der Schwan wurde fröhlich, und nachdem sie ihr Mahl beendet hatten, kehrten beide munter und zufrieden auf ihren Posten zurück.

Am nächsten Abend war es wieder kalt. Die Sterne glänzten besonders stark, und jeder Stern war wie ein kalter Nagel im warmen, einsamen Herzen des Alten. Aber er kämpfte gegen die Versuchung.

In der Mitte des Teichs schwamm als sanft leuchtender weißer Fleck der Schwan.

Bei dem Gedanken, welch ein Schauer jeden durchdringen müsse, der in einer solchen Nacht mit Wasser in Berührung käme, wurde der Alte ganz gerührt. Sollte der arme Schwan gar nichts vom Leben haben? Bestimmt würde er lieber in einer warmen Ecke sitzen und etwas essen.

Er nahm also den Vogel unter den Arm und begab sich in die Wirtschaft.

Und wieder kam ein Abend, und wieder überfiel Melancholie den Alten. Aber diesmal war er fest entschlossen, nicht in die Wirtschaft zu gehen. Gestern auf dem Nachhauseweg hatte der Schwan getanzt und unglaubliche Sachen gesungen.

Als er am Ufer saß und in den Himmel oder in den leeren, beißend kalten Park blickte, fühlte er plötzlich ein zaghaftes Zupfen an seinem Hosenbein. Der Schwan war ans Ufer geschwommen, um ihn an etwas zu erinnern. Da gingen sie.

Einen Monat später wurde der Alte zusammen mit dem Schwan entlassen. Der Schwan torkelte am hellichten Tage auf dem Wasser. Die Mütter, die mit ihren kleinen Kindern in den Park kamen, um sich zu erholen und den Vogel anzusehen, hatten sich beschwert. Der Kinder wegen. Daraus ersieht man, daß moralische Haltung auch für den bescheidensten Posten erforderlich ist.

Chapter Thirty-three

When the Sentence Starts
with a Verb

33.1. So far, you have been told that a sentence can begin with a verb

(1) if the sentence is a question (cf. 6.4)

Ist Arbeit der beste Schlaftrunk — *Is* work the best sleeping-potion?

(2) or if it is a command (cf. 6.4)

Lerne Geschichte, sonst bleibst du ewig ein Kind — *Learn* history, or else you will remain eternally a child.

(3) or when the verb appears in the subjunctive I form and is followed by *wir*, the verb will be translated *let us* (cf. 30.7)

Studieren wir jetzt — *Let us* study now!

33.2. However, a sentence beginning with a verb can also signal an if . . . then construction.

This type of sentence will always contain two clauses separated by commas; the first clause will begin with a verb and the second clause generally will begin with the word *so* or *dann*. Here is an example:

Sagt Gott ja, *so* spricht die Schlange nein — If God says yes, the snake says no.

33.3. These sentences are to be translated in the following way:

(1) Begin the sentence with *if*;
(2) find the subject of the sentence;
(3) place the verb (found at the beginning of the German sentence) after the subject;
(4) either translate *so* (or *dann*) as *then*, or omit *so* from your translation.

Here are more examples:

Hat der Fuchs den Schwanz verloren, *so* sagt er, er sei unnütz — *If* the fox has lost his tail, *then* he will say it is useless.
Redet das Geld, *so* schweigt die Welt — *If* money talks, (*then*) the world is silent.

33.4. Translate these sentences:

1. Tanzt ein Alter, so macht er viel Staub (*dust*). (This is mean!)
2. Will die Katze nicht mausen ("*to mouse*"), so laß sie draußen (*outside*).
3. Klopft die Not (*need*) an, so tut die Liebe die Tür auf. (At least the person in need hopes this will happen.)
4. Führt ein blinder Mann den anderen, werden beide nicht weit wandern.
5. Bellt (*bark*) ein alter Hund, so soll man aufschauen. (Denn ein alter Hund bellt nicht leichtfertig [*irresponsibly*].)
6. Spricht man vom Wolf, dann lauert er schon hinterm Busch. (The English equivalent for this might be: "Speak of the devil.")
7. Fehlt es dir an Wein, so trinke Bier.
8. Kommt der Berg nicht zu mir, so gehe ich zu ihm.
9. Hab' ich keine Küh', so hab' ich keine Müh'. (Is *Küh'* singular or plural?)
10. Gäbe es keine Narren, so gäbe es keine Weisen. (If you wish to review *es gibt*, please turn to 9.1.)
11. Die Welt ist ein trunkener Bauer; hilft man ihm rechts in den Sattel (*saddle*), so fällt er links hinab.
12. Bekommt der Arme ein Stück Brot, so reißt es ihm der Hund aus der Hand. (Das Glück eines Armen ist allzu kurz!)
13. Fällt der Krug (*jug*) auf den Stein, so zerbricht er; und fällt der Stein auf den Krug, so zerbricht er auch.
14. Ist dein Feind auch nur wie eine Ameise (*ant*), so rechne ihn doch unter den Elefanten. (No *Feind* is harmless!)
15. Bist du heiter (*cheerful*), sag' es weiter.
    Drückt (*pushes, oppresses*) dich ein Stein, trag' ihn allein.
    (In other words, spread your joy and hide your sorrow.)
16. Tonio Kröger ging den Weg, den er gehen mußte, ein wenig nachlässig und ungleichmäßig . . . , und wenn er irrging, so geschah es, weil es für etliche (*many*) einen richtigen Weg überhaupt nicht gibt. Fragte man ihn, was in aller Welt er zu werden gedachte, so erteilte (*imparted*) er wechselnde Auskunft (*information*), denn er <u>pflegte zu sagen</u> (*was in the habit of saying*) . . . , daß er die Möglichkeiten zu tausend Daseinsformen in sich trage, zusammen mit dem heimlichen (*secret*) Bewußtsein, daß es <u>im Grunde</u> (*fundamentally*) lauter Unmöglichkeiten seien. (Thomas Mann, "Tonio Kröger")

Vocabulary

allzu — all too
* der **Alte (-n, -n)** — old man
* **ander** — other
an-klopfen (i) ‿ to knock
auf-schauen (i) — to look up
* **auf-tun** — to open
die **Auskunft** — information
der **Bauer (-s, -n)** — farmer
* **bekommen** — to receive, get
* das **Bewußtsein** — awareness
die **Daseinsform (-en)** — form of
existence
* **doch** — nevertheless
draußen — outside
drücken — to press, oppress
erteilen — to impart
* **fehlen** (i) — to lack
* **führen** — to lead
gedenken (i) — to intend
* **geschehen** (i) — to occur, to
happen
(im) Grunde — fundamentally
heimlich — secret
heiter — cheerful
hinab-fallen (i) — to fall down
irr(e)gehen (i) — to go astray
der **Krug (-es, -̈e)** — jug

die **Kuh (-̈e)** — cow
* **kurz** — short, brief
lauern (i) — to lie in wait; lurk
* **lauter** — nothing but
* **links** — left
die **Möglichkeit (-en)** —
possibility
die **Mühe (-n)** — effort
nachlässig — careless
* der **Narr (-en, -en)** — fool
rechnen — to calculate, to
consider
* **rechts** — right
reißen — to rip, tear
der **Sattel (-s, -̈)** — saddle
* das **Stück (-s, -e)** — piece
überhaupt — at all, generally
ungleichmäßig — irregular
* **wechselnd** — changing
* **weil** — because
* **weit** — far
* **wenig** — little
* die **Welt (-en)** — world
zerbrechen (zerbricht) — to break
into pieces
* **zusammen** — together

Chapter Thirty-four
Other Pronouns

In addition to the pronouns *ich, du, er, sie, es, wir, ihr, sie,* and *Sie,* there are other pronouns which you have encountered already. Here is a summary of them.

34.1. *Alles, etwas,* and *nichts*

Three pronouns are undeclined, regardless of whether they are nominative, accusative, genitive, or dative. They are:

alles — everything; *etwas* — something; and *nichts* — nothing.
Here are examples:
Es hat *alles* seinen Zweck — *Everything* has its purpose.
Etwas fehlt — *Something* is missing.
Was *nichts* kostet, taugt *nichts* — Whatever costs *nothing* amounts to *nothing*.

Occasionally, these three pronouns will be followed by an adjective that is capitalized. Such constructions should be translated as follows:

Alles Schöne gefällt dem Briefträger — *Everything* (that is) *beautiful* pleases the mailman.
Wer will *etwas Neues* hören? — Who wants to hear *something new*?
Zu seiner Überraschung geschah *nichts Außergewöhnliches* auf seiner Reise — To his surprise, *nothing* (that was) *unusual* happened during his trip.

34.2. *Man, alle, jemand, niemand* and *wer*

These pronouns are all declined in a manner similar to *der* words. Here are their declensions:

nominative	*man*	*alle**	*jemand*	*niemand*	*wer*
	(*one*)	(*everyone*)	(*someone*)	(*no one*)	(*who*)
accusative	einen	alle	jemanden	niemanden	wen
genitive	eines	aller	jemandes	niemandes	wessen
dative	einem	allen	jemandem	niemandem	wem

* Note that *alle* is plural in German: Alle *sind* hier — Everyone *is* here.

34.3. *Jeder, ander* and *viel*

These pronouns are technically adjectives, and they are declined as if they were adjectives used as nouns. However, they are never capitalized. Their definitions are: *jeder* — each; *ander* — other; and *viel* — many. Here are examples:

Jeder singt auf seine Weise, der eine laut, der *andere* leise — *Each* (person) sings in his (own) way — the one sings loudly, the *other* sings softly.
Jeder ist seines Glückes Schmied — *Each* one is the smith (creator) of his happiness.
Auch der Unordentlichste verlangt von *anderen* Ordnung — Even the most disorganized one demands order from *others*.
Tadle *andere* nicht deiner Mängel wegen — Do not fault *others* on account of your own failings.
Viele werden Heilige um ihres Magens willen — *Many* become saints for the sake of their stomach.

34.4. *Der, die, das,* and *die*

The definite articles can also occasionally be used as pronouns. This is particularly true when one of the clauses begins with *wer* or *der*. Here are examples:

Wer alte Säcke mit Seide näht, *der* ist verrückt — *Whoever* sews old sacks with silk, *he* (or *that one*) is crazy.
Der ist weise, *der* die Zeit nimmt, wie sie ist — *He* (or *that one*) is wise, *who* takes time as it is.
Die Guten müssen *den* kreuzigen, *der* sich seine eigene Tugend erfindet — The good (i.e. the self-righteous people) must crucify *him* (or *that one*) *who* invents his own virtue for himself. (Nietzsche)
Die Guten nämlich, *die* können nicht schaffen! *Die* sind immer der Anfang vom Ende — The good namely, *they* cannot create! *They* are always the beginning of the end. (Nietzsche)

34.5. Articles also can be used as placeholders for a previously used noun.
Here are examples:

Es gibt keinen Stolz wie *den* eines reich gewordenen Armen — There is no pride like *that* [pride] of a poor person who has become rich.
Ein Geiziger hat zwei Töchter; *die eine* heißt "Bringher", *die andere* heißt "Tragher". — A miser has two daughters; *the one* is called "Bring-here" and *the other* is called "Carry-here."

34.6. *Einer* and *eines*

Although the indefinite article *ein* does not usually have an ending in the masculine nominative or neuter nominative and accusative cases, it will have an ending if it refers to a noun used in a different part of the sentence. Here are examples:

Einer meiner Handschuhe fehlt — *One* of my gloves is missing.
Eines seiner Kinder ist krank — *One* of his children is sick.

Occasionally, *einer* can be used to refer to one specific person:

Inzwischen rede ich als *einer*, der Zeit hat, zu mir selber. Niemand erzählt mir Neues: so erzähle ich mir mich selber — Inbetween I speak to myself as *one* who has time. No one tells me anything new: so I will explain myself to myself. (Nietzsche)

34.7. Translate these sentences:

1. Wer im dreißigsten Jahr nichts weiß, im vierzigsten nichts ist, im fünfzigsten nichts hat, der lernt nichts, wird nichts und kommt zu nichts.
2. Wer allen alles recht machen will, muß früh aufstehen.
3. Wie sich im Wasser das Angesicht (*countenance*) spiegelt, so ein Mensch im Herzen eines anderen.
4. Wer nichts für andere tut, tut nichts für sich.
5. Es ist niemand so alt, daß er nicht noch etwas lernen könnte.
6. Wer weiter will, als sein Pferd kann, der steige ab und gehe zu Fuß.
7. Einer teilt reichlich (*abundantly*) aus und hat immer mehr; ein anderer kargt (*is stingy*), wo er nicht soll, und wird doch ärmer. (Proverbs)
8. Wenn man einem den Finger gibt, so will er gleich die ganze Hand.
9. Seinem Schicksal (*fate*) mag niemand entrinnen.
10. Wer will, dem ist alles möglich.
11. Es hackt keine Krähe der anderen die Augen aus.
12. Es geschieht nichts Neues unter der Sonne.
13. Als es Mittag war, sahen sie [Hänsel und Gretel] ein schönes schneeweißes Vögelchen auf einem Ast (*branch*) sitzen, das sang so schön, daß sie stehenblieben und ihm zuhörten. Und als es fertig war, schwang es seine Flügel und flog vor ihnen her, und sie gingen ihm nach, bis sie zu einem Häuschen gelangten, auf dessen Dach (*roof*) es sich setzte, und als sie ganz nah herankamen, da sahen sie, daß das Häuslein aus Brot gebaut war und mit Kuchen gedeckt; aber die Fenster waren von hellem Zucker.

14. Wenn Hegel alles Wirkliche als vernünftig erklärte, stützte er einen
    Realismus, der die Dichtung, Philosophie und Religion nicht mehr als
    erste Lebensaufgaben empfand, sondern politische, wirtschaftliche und
    wissenschaftliche Interessen in den Vordergrund schob. (Martini)
15. Es ließe sich alles trefflich schlichten (*performed*),
    könnte man die Sachen zweimal verrichten (*execute, do*). (Goethe)

Vocabulary

ab-steigen (i) — to dismount
* **alle** — everyone
* **alles** — everything
* **ander** — other
  der **Ast** (-es, ⸚e) — branch
  aus-hacken — to peck out
  aus-teilen — to share
  das **Dach** (-es, ⸚er) — roof
* die **Dichtung** (-en) — literature
  decken — to cover
* **dreißig** — thirty
  empfinden — to perceive
  entrinnen (i) — to escape
* **entweder...oder** — either...or
* **erklären** — to explain
* **etwas** — something
  fertig — finished, ready
  der **Flügel** (-s, -) — wing
* **fünfzig** — fifty
  gelangen (i) — to reach
  gleich — immediately
  hell — bright
  heran-kommen (i) — to approach

die **Krähe** (-n) — crow
* **lassen** (r) — can be
  die **Lebensaufgabe** (-n) — life's
  work
  nach-gehen (i) — to follow
* **niemand** — no one
* **noch** — still
  der **Realismus** — realism
* die **Sache** (-n) — matter
  schieben — to push
* **spiegeln** (r) — to be reflected
  stehen-bleiben (i) — to stop
  stützen — to support
  trefflich — excellent
  vernünftig — reasonable
* **vierzig** — forty
  der **Vordergrund** (-es, ⸚e) — foreground
* **weiter** — further
* **wirklich** — real
* **wirtschaftlich** — economic
* **wissenschaftlich** — scientific
  der **Zucker** — sugar

Reading Selection: Nietzsche

I. Aus der *Fröhlichen Wissenschaft*

<u>Wie, wenn</u> (*what if*) dir eines Tages oder Nachts ein Dämon in deine einsamste
Einsamkeit nachschliche (*crept*) und dir sagte: "Dieses Leben, wie du es jetzt
lebst und gelebt hast, wirst du noch einmal und noch unzählige Male leben
müssen; und es wird nichts Neues daran sein, sondern jeder Schmerz und jede
Lust und jeder Gedanke und Seufzer (*moan*) und alles unsäglich Kleine und
Große deines Lebens muß dir wiederkommen, und alles in derselben <u>Reihe und</u>

Folge (*order*) — und ebenso diese Spinne (*spider*) und dieses Mondlicht zwischen den Bäumen, und ebenso dieser Augenblick und ich selber. Die ewige Sanduhr des Daseins wird immer wieder umgedreht — und du mit ihr, Stäubchen (*little speck of dust*) vom Staube!" Würdest du dich nicht niederwerfen und mit den Zähnen knirschen (*gnash*) und den Dämon verfluchen, der so redete? Oder hast du einmal einen ungeheuren (*wonderous*) Augenblick erlebt, wo du ihm antworten würdest: "Du bist ein Gott und nie hörte ich Göttlicheres (*anything more divine*)!"

II. Vgl. Aus dem *Willen zur Macht*

Gesetzt (*assumed*), wir sagen ja (*yes*) zu einem einzigen Augenblick, so haben wir damit nicht nur zu uns selbst, sondern zu allem Dasein ja gesagt. Denn es steht nichts für sich [allein], weder in uns selbst, noch in den Dingen: und wenn nur ein einziges Mal unsere Seele wie eine Saite (*lyre*) vor Glück gezittert und getönt hat, so waren alle Ewigkeiten nötig, um dies Eine Geschehen zu bedingen — und alle Ewigkeit war in diesem einzigen Augenblick unseres Jasagens . . . erlöst, gerechtfertigt und bejaht.

Chapter Thirty-five
Troublesome Words

About the only thing that these words have in common is that they are all troublesome. I have included them here so that you can take special note of them. First, here is a list of the words discussed in this chapter (which are arranged alphabetically):

35.1. The Troublesome Words

all — all, every	**lauter** (adj.) — pure,
alle — everyone	(adv.) — nothing but
als — when, than, as	**mehr** — more
also — thus, so	**nachdem** — after
auch — also, even	**nicht** — not
auch wenn — even if	**nicht mehr** — no longer
da — there, since, it	**nichts** — nothing
denn — because, for	**noch** — yet, still
es sei denn — unless	**noch nicht** — not yet
doch — still, nevertheless, after all	**weder...noch** — neither...nor
eben — flat, just	**selbst** — self, even
einige — several	**so** — thus, so, just, then
erst — only, not until, first	**so ein, ein so** — such a
fehlen — to lack	**stehen** — to stand, be,
gefallen — to please	to be written on
gehen — es geht mir gut — I am fine	**trotzdem** — nevertheless
gelingen — to succeed	**um** — at, around
gerade — straight, just	**um...willen** — for the sake of
gleich — equal, immediately	**voll** — full, full of
indem — while, since	**weiter** — further
kennen — to know	**wieder** — again
können — to be able to, can	**zu** — to, too, closed

35.2. *All* is used with or without endings. When there is an ending, it is always strong. The strong singular ending is used rarely; it occurs mainly in stereotyped phrases and in proverbial expressions. Here is an example:

Aller Anfang ist schwer — *Every* beginning is difficult.

All with an ending is the plural of *jeder* (*each, everyone*), and it means *every single one of them*; it precedes nouns and follows pronouns. Here are examples:

Morgen, morgen, nur nicht heute, sagen *alle* faulen Leute — Tomorrow, tomorrow, only not today, say *all* lazy people.
Wir *alle* haben das gewußt — *All of us* have known that.

35.3. *Alle* often will mean *everyone* (cf. 34.2). Examples are:

Es werden nicht *alle* in das Himmelreich kommen — Not *everyone* will come into the Kingdom of Heaven.
Arm und reich, vor Gott sind *alle* gleich — Poor and rich, before God, *all* are equal.

While *everyone* in English is singular, *alle* is plural.

When *alle* is used as a predicate adjective, it will mean *all gone*.
Der Kuchen ist *alle* — The cake is *all gone*.
However, this appears rarely.

35.4. *Auch* generally means *also*. However, *auch* preceding the noun it modifies means *even*.

Auch Fräulein Meier ist manchmal fleißig — *Even* Fräulein Meier is hard-working sometimes.

Auch wenn and *wenn auch* mean *even if* (cf. 23.6).

Auch wenn es Bindfäden (*strings*) regnet, hat Fräulein Meier sich entschieden, den Briefträger zu begleiten — *Even if* it rains cats and dogs, Fräulein Meier has decided to accompany the mailman.

35.5. *Als* is tricky because it can mean *when, than,* and *as*.

As a conjunction, *als* **means** *when* and it introduces dependent clauses referring to a single event or an action in the past. In these clauses, the verb will always be at the end, and will never be in the present tense. Here is an example:

Als der Student jünger *war*, fuhr er oft mit seinem Fahrrad — *When* the student was younger, he often rode his bicycle. (cf. 23.4)

Als **means** *than* **when used with a comparative** (cf. 11.4):

Er ist größer *als* ich — He is taller *than* I.

Als **means** *as* **when it is followed by a noun:**

Fräulein Meier kennt den Briefträger *als* einen sehr empfindsamen Mann —
Fräulein Meier knows the mailman *as* a very sensitive man.
Bei seinen Freunden gilt er *als* großer Dichter — Among his friends, he is
considered (*as*) a great writer.

Als **when used with the subjunctive can also mean** *as if* (cf. 31.2):

Fräulein Meier sieht aus, ***als hätte*** sie viel zu tun — Fräulein Meier looks *as if*
she *had* a lot to do.
Der Student tat, ***als wäre*** er glücklich — The student acted *as if* he *were* happy.

35.6. *Also* **will always** mean *thus, so*; it will never mean *also*.
Remember Nietzsche's ***Also sprach Zarathustra*** (***Thus*** Spoke Zarathustra).

35.7. *Da* **is one of the most troublesome German words because it is so versatile.**

As an adverb, *da* **can mean** *here* **or** *there*.

Da bin ich — *Here* I am.
Da blieb er, bis der Bus kam — He stayed *there* until the bus came.

Da can also mean *then, at that time*. Here are examples:

Da lachte der Briefträger — *Then* the mailman laughed.
Von *da* an — from *that time* on; hier und *da* — now and *then*.

Moreover, *da* **used in conjunction with a preposition will mean** *it* (cf. 12.1-
12.3). An example:

Er hat einen schönen, mit Edelsteinen besetzten Füller, und er schreibt immer
damit — He has a beautiful jewelled pen, and he always writes *with it*.
As a subordinating conjunction, *da* **will mean** *since, because, in as much as,*
while, although (cf. 23.4):

Da Fräulein Meier nicht zu Hause war, konnte ihre Mutter sie nicht besuchen
— *Since* Fräulein Meier was not at home, her mother could not visit her.
When the verb appears at the end of a clause beginning with *da, da* **will**
have to be a subordinating conjunction!

35.8. *Denn* **generally means** *because, for* (cf. 21.1). **It rarely means** *then*.
Sometimes *denn* will appear in the middle of a sentence, in which case it will
be used as a flavoring particle:

Wo ist er *denn* — Where (on earth) is he?
Was ist *denn* los — What's going on?

In these cases, *denn* need not to be translated.

Note that *es sei denn, daß* means *unless, except.*

35.9. *Doch* means *however, yet, still, nevertheless,* and *after all.* It can be used in a sentence in the following ways:

Das ist *doch* wahr — That (*really*) *is* true (even though you don't believe me).
Das kann *doch* nicht dein Ernst sein — You don't *really* mean that, do you?
Er ist dumm, aber sie liebt ihn *doch* — He is dumb, but she loves him nevertheless.

Doch (like the French *si*) also can be used as a one word contradiction to negative questions. Here is an example:

Haben Sie Tante Lotte immer noch nicht geschrieben? — Haven't you written Aunt Lotte yet? *Doch*! — I have *too* written her!

35.10. *Eben* (cf. 4.11) as an adjective generally means *flat*:
Das ist so *eben* wie der Weg über die Berge — That is as *flat* as the way over the mountains.

However, as an adverb, *eben* can also mean *just, precisely, exactly*:

Das Erdbeben geschah *eben* in dem Augenblick des großen Raubes — The earthquake happened *just* at the moment of the great robbery.

35.11. *Einige* means *some*. *Einige* Menschen lesen gern — *Some* people like to read. Do not confuse this word with *einig*, which means *at one, united, in agreement, unanimous.*

35.12. *Erst* when used with age or time references **will always** mean *only* or *not until*. Here are some examples:

Es wurde *erst* heute fertig — It was *not* ready *until* today.
Erst nach seinem Tode wurde der Dichter weltberühmt — *Only* after his death did the poet become world-famous.

Otherwise, *erst* will mean *first*: *Erst* die Arbeit, dann das Vergnügen — *First* the work, then the pleasure.

35.13. *Fehlen, gefallen, gehen* and *gelingen*: Some verbs in German require an *es* as the subject of the clause, while in English the German noun in the dative case would seem to make a more appropriate subject. Here are examples:

Es *fehlt dem Zoo* an einem Elefanten (Literally: it lacks to the zoo an elephant) — The zoo lacks an elephant.
Die Maus *gefällt der Katze* (Literally: the mouse is pleasing to the cat) — The cat likes the mouse.
Es *geht mir* gut (Literally: it goes to me well) — I am fine.
Es *gelingt der Katze*, die Maus zu fangen (Literally: it succeeds to the cat to catch the mouse) — The cat succeeds in catching the mouse.

35.14. *Gerade* (cf. 4.11) as an adjective means *straight, direct, honest*. However, when used adverbially, *gerade* means *quite, exactly, just, directly*. Here is an example:

Das geschah *gerade* in dem Augenblick des großen Erdbebens — That happened *just* at the moment of the great earthquake.

35.15. *Gleich* (cf. 4.11) as an adjective means *equal, same*. Die Studenten sind *gleichen* Alters — The students are the *same* age.

However, when used adverbially, *gleich* means *immediately*.

Ich komme *gleich* wieder — I will return *immediately*.

35.16. *Indem, nachdem, trotzdem*: There are three common words used in conjunction with *dem*, none of which have anything to do with the dative form of *der* or *das*. All three can be either adverbs or subordinating conjunctions.

Indem is best translated as *while, as*.

Indem der Briefträger Fräulein Meier erwartungsvoll ansah, fragte er sie etwas sehr Wichtiges — *While* looking expectantly at Fräulein Meier, the mailman asked her something very important.

Nachdem generally is used as a subordinating conjunction meaning *after* (cf. 23.4).

Nachdem er seinen neuen silbernen Sportwagen gewaschen hatte, fuhr der Briefträger mit Fräulein Meier in die Stadt — *After* he had washed his new silver sportscar, the mailman drove to the city with Fräulein Meier.

Trotzdem occurs most frequently as an adverb meaning *nevertheless*.
Obwohl es regnete, wollte das Kind *trotzdem* draußen spielen — Although it was raining, the child wanted to play outside, *nevertheless*.

Trotzdem also can be a subordinating conjunction meaning *although, even though*.

35.17. *Kennen* (*to be acquainted with*) and *können* (*to be able to*) are often confused. Remember that *kennen* generally will be the only verb in the sentence, while *können* usually will function as a modal. Here are two sentences each containing the two verbs in both present and past tense:

Der Student *kennt* das Kind — The student *knows* the child.
Der Student *kann* viel essen — The student *is able to* eat a lot.
Der Student *kannte* das Kind — The student *knew* the child.
Der Student *konnte* viel essen — The student *was able to* eat a lot.

35.18. *Lauter* as an adjective means *pure, genuine, true*.

Von *lauteren* Brunnen fließen *lautere* Wasser — *Pure* water flows from *pure* wells.

However, as an adverb, *lauter* means *nothing but*.
Er trinkt *lauter* Wein — He drinks *nothing but* wine.
Er sieht den Wald vor *lauter* Bäumen nicht — He does not see the forest for the trees. (Literally: He does not see the forest on account of *nothing but* trees.)

35.19. *Mehr* usually means *more* (cf. 11.5). Das Flußpferd wiegt *mehr* als der Elefant — The hippo weighs *more* than the elephant.

Immer mehr means *more and more*. An example:

Fräulein Meier und der Briefträger bleiben *immer mehr* zusammen — Fräulein Meier and the mailman are together *more and more*.

However, *nicht mehr* can mean both *no more* and *no longer*.

Sie ist *nicht mehr* zu Hause — She is *no longer* at home.

Mehr will occasionally appear at the end of a clause:

Er hat kein Geld *mehr* — He has no *more* money.
Die Tochter des alten Mannes ist kein Kind *mehr* — The old man's daughter is *no longer* a child.

35.20. *Nicht* and *nichts*. Remember that *nicht* is **always** an adverb, while *nichts* is **always** a pronoun. **Do not confuse them!** Compare:

Wer *nichts* an die Angel steckt, fängt *nichts* — Whoever puts *nothing* on the fishhook captures *nothing*.

Der Briefträger ist *nicht* pessimistisch — The mailman is *not* pessimistic.

35.21. *Noch* generally will mean *yet, still, in addition to*. But it has the following meanings as well:

noch einmal — once more
noch nicht — not yet
noch nie — never (before)
weder...noch — neither...nor (cf. 21.1)

Weder Fräulein Meier *noch* der Briefträger ist zu Hause — *Neither* Fräulein Meier *nor* the mailman is at home.

35.22. *Selbst* (cf. 26.5) generally is used with the reflexive pronouns to emphasize their meanings. Examples are:

Arzt, heil dich *selbst* — Physician, heal *thyself*!
Jeder ist sich *selbst* der beste Freund — Everyone is for *himself* his best friend (Or: Everyone is his own best friend).

However, when *selbst* is placed in front of the noun, it will mean *even*.

Selbst der alte Vater des Briefträgers glaubt nicht an die Wahrhaftigkeit aller pessimistischen Sprichwörter — *Even* the old father of the mailman does not believe in the truth of all the pessimistic proverbs.
Selbst unser Herrgott kann es nicht allen recht machen — *Even* our Lord God cannot make it right for everyone.

35.23. *So* has a variety of meanings in addition to *thus, so*.

(1) *So* can be used as a filler word, which sometimes can be translated *just*, or it can be omitted:

Das haben wir *so* zum Spaß gemacht — We have *just* done that for fun.

(2) *So ein* or *ein so* will mean *such a*:

Das Kind hat *ein so* nettes Lächeln — The child has *such a* nice smile.

(3) *So* can be used as a comparative (cf. 11.4):

Der Student liest *so* viel *wie* der Professor — The student reads *as* much *as* the professor.

(4) *So* is often used in "if . . . then" clauses to mean *then* (cf. 23.3 and 33.2).

Here are examples:

Bezahlen wir die Musik, *so* wollen wir dazu tanzen — If we pay for the music, *then* we also want to dance to it.
Wenn die Armut zur Tür eingeht, *so* fliegt die Liebe zum Fenster hinaus — If poverty comes to the door, *then* love flies out the window.

35.24. *Stehen* usually means *to stand*. But it can also mean *be upright, be situated, be, stand still*, and *stop*. Here are examples:

Tränen *stehen* ihm in den Augen — Tears *are* in his eyes.
Es *steht* in ihren Kräften — It *lies* in her powers.
Ich *stehe* nicht allein mit meiner Meinung — I *am* not alone in my opinion.
Orangensaft *stand* im Eisschrank — Orange juice *was* in the refrigerator.

Perhaps the most common meaning of *stehen* which may seem strange to you is *to be written*. Here is an example:

Auf dem Zettel *steht* "Entschuldigung" — On the note *is written* "excuse me."

35.25. *Um* (a review)

(1) As a preposition, *um* can mean either *around*, or *at* (cf. 5.2).

Er geht *um* die Ecke — He goes *around* the corner.

In reference to time, *um* means *at*: Fast jeden Abend *um* zehn Uhr studiert Fräulein Meier Erdkunde — Almost every evening *at* ten o'clock Fräulein Meier studies geography.

(2) However, *um...willen* means *for the sake of* (cf. 5.8).

Er ist hier *um* seines Freundes *willen* — He is here *for the sake of* his friend.

(3) And *um...zu* means *in order to* (cf. 20.3).

Wir sind hier, *um zu* werden — nicht, *um zu* sein — We are here *in order to* become — not *in order to* be.

35.26. *Voll* means *full, filled, complete, entire*. It can be used as an adjective in front of a noun to mean *full*:

Er hat eine *volle* Tasche — He has a *full* pocket.

In these cases, *voll* will have a normal adjective ending.

However *voll* also can appear directly in front of a noun, with either no ending or with an *-er* ending; and then it should be translated as *full of*. Here are examples:

Die Liebe ist *voll* Eifersucht — Love is *full of* jealousy.
Vier Kinder — ein ganzes Haus *voller* Kinder — Four children — a whole house *full of* children.
Das Zimmer ist *voller* Katzen — The room is *full of* cats.

35.27. *Wieder* (*again*) and *weiter* (*further*) are often confused. Here are sentences to help you remember them:

Wir *wieder*holen es immer *wieder*, daß wir uns *wieder*sehen wollen — We repeat *again* and *again* that we want to see each other *again*.
Der Waldläufer muß *weiter* laufen, um aus dem Forst herauszukommen — The hiker has to walk *further* in order to get out of the woods.
Dann kann er *weiter*gehen — Then he can continue.

35.28. *Zu* is encountered most frequently as a preposition (cf. 5.4). However, it has the other following meanings:

(1) When used as a particle with infinitives, it means *to* (cf. 20.1-20.2):

Die Studenten haben viel *zu* lernen — The students have much *to* learn.

(2) As an adverb, *zu* means *to, closed, towards, shut*.

Die Tür des Autos ist noch nicht *zu* — The car door is not yet *shut*.

(3) When preceding an adjective or an adverb, *zu* can mean *too*.

Man kann nicht *zu* viel lachen — One cannot laugh *too* much.
Es ist *zu* schön, um wahr zu sein — It is *too* good to be true.

(4) When *zu* appears with a form of the verb *to be*, the verb following the *zu* must be translated passively (cf. 20.5):

Viel *ist* noch *zu tun* — Much *is* still *to be done*.

35.29. Translate these sentences:

1. Wie man ißt, so arbeitet man auch.
2. Kommt einmal das Glück, so kommen fünf Sturmwinde (*ill winds*) danach.
3. Unter Gleichen ist der beste Friede.
4. Wer Pech hat, den beißt ein Hund, auch wenn er ein Kamel reitet.

5. "Es ist ein eigentümlicher Apparat," sagte der Offizier zu dem Forschungsreisenden und überblickte mit einem gewissermaßen bewundernden Blick auf den ihm doch wohlbekannten Apparat. (Kafka)
6. Jedem Lapp' (native of Lappland) gefällt seine Kapp'.
7. Auf einem von dem Briefträger an Fräulein Meier geschriebenen Zettel (*note*) steht: "Ich liebe Dich."
8. Lieber zweimal fragen als einmal irregehen.
9. Gesundheit schätzt man erst, nachdem man sie verloren hat.
10. Unter der Brücke war der wetterbraune, weißbärtige Kopf eines Ruderers zum Vorschein gekommen, der, aus seinen ungelenken Bewegungen zu schließen, mit der Lagune nicht vertraut war. (C. F. Meyer)
11. Fräulein Meier und der Briefträger sind in die Stadt gefahren, um sich zu verheiraten!
12. Und in der Tat schien mitten in diesen gräßlichen (*horrible*) Augenblicken, in welchen alle irdischen Güter der Menschen zugrunde gingen und die ganze Natur verschüttet zu werden drohte, der menschliche Geist selbst wie eine schöne Blume aufzugehen. (Kleist)
13. Nach meiner Erfahrung braucht man <u>zum Erlernen</u> (for the learning) des Englischen 30 Stunden, des Französischen 30 Tage, des Deutschen 30 Jahre. Entweder reformiere man also diese Sprache, oder man lege sie zu den toten Sprachen, denn nur die Toten haben heutzutage noch Zeit genug, sie zu erlernen. (Twain)

Vocabulary

* **als ob** — as if
* **an-sehen** — to look at
  der **Apparat** (-es, -e) — apparatus
  auf-gehen (i) — to rise
* der **Augenblick** (-es, -e) — moment
* **beißen** — to bite
  die **Bewegung** (-en) — movement
  bewundernd — admiring
  der **Blick** (-s, -e) — glance
* **brauchen** — to need
  die **Brücke** (-n) — bridge
  drohen (i) — to threaten
  eigentümlich — peculiar
  eng — narrow
  entweder...oder — either...or
  die **Erfahrung** (-en) — experience
* die **Erinnerung** (-en) — memory

  erlernen — to learn
* **ernst** — serious
* **fahren** (i) — to drive, to go
* **folgen** (i) — to follow
* der **Friede** (-ns, -) — peace
  der **Forschungsreisende** (-n, -n) — explorer
* **französisch** — French
* **genug** — enough
  gewissermaßen — more or less
  das **Gut** (-s, ¨er) — property
  heutzutage — nowadays
  irdische Güter — worldly goods
  irre-gehen (i) — to go astray
  das **Kamel** (-s, -e) — camel
  die **Kappe** (-n) — cap
  legen — to place
* **lieber** — preferably

der **Offizier (-s, -e)** — officer
das **Pech** — bad luck
reformieren —to reform
reiten (i) — to ride
der **Ruderer (-s, -)** — rower,
oarsman
* **ruhig** — quiet
der **Schatten (-s, -)** — shadow
schätzen — to value
schließen — to conclude, infer
* **schwer** — difficult, heavy
die **Sprache (-n)** — language
* die **Stunde (-n)** — hour, period
die **Tat (-en)** — deed;

in der Tat — in fact
überblicken — to survey
ungelenk — awkward
verheiraten (r) — to marry
* **verlieren** — to lose
verschütten — to bury
vertraut — familiar
zum Vorschein kommen — to
appear
wetterbraun — weather-browned
wohlbekannt — well-known
der **Zettel (-s, -)** — note
zugrunde gehen — to perish

35.30. Vocabulary aid

1. Erst nach vielen Jahren gelang es der Professorin, ihr umfangreiches Buch zu veröffentlichen (*publish*).
2. Um halb fünf können wir wieder abfahren (*depart*).
3. Auf dem Grabstein (*tombstone*) steht eine liebevolle (*affectionate*) Grabschrift (*epitaph*).
4. Sie sieht ihn an, als ob er verrückt (*crazy*) wäre.
5. Da der Student eine Stunde auf den Bus warten mußte, wollte er nicht mehr damit fahren.
6. Fast (*almost*) alles, was Fräulein Meier tut, ist ihrem Bräutigam angenehm (*agreeable*).
7. Wen will der Dichter kennen?
8. Zu dieser Zeit hatte der Student zu viel zu tun.
9. Bei der Hochzeitsfeier (*wedding celebration*) wird viel Sekt (*champagne*) getrunken.
10. Ist jedes Ende so schwer wie aller Anfang?

APPENDIX

Appendix A

A Summary of German Grammar

I. Declensions of the definite (*der*) and indefinite (*ein*) articles
(For a review of case endings, see 3.1-3.13)

	masculine	neuter	feminine	plural
nominative	der	das	die	die
	ein	ein	eine	—
accusative	den	das	die	die
	einen	ein	eine	—
genitive	des	des	der	der
	eines	eines	einer	—
dative	dem	dem	der	den
	einem	einem	einer	—

Note: *dieser* (*this one*), *jener* (*that, that one*), *jeder* (*each, every*), *mancher* (*some, many a*), *solcher* (*such*), and *welcher* (*what, which*) follow the paradigm for *der* words.

Kein and the possessive adjectives *mein* (*my*), *dein* (*your*), *sein* (*his, its*), *ihr* (*her, their*), *unser* (*our*), *euer* (*your*), and *Ihr* (*your*) follow the paradigm for *ein* words.

II. Adjective endings (For a review of adjectives, see 4.1-4.7)

A. Strong adjective endings

	masculine	neuter	feminine	plural
nominative	guter Wein	gutes Brot	gute Milch	gute Tage
accusative	guten Wein	gutes Brot	gute Milch	gute Tage
genitive	guten Weins	guten Brots	guter Milch	guter Tage
dative	gutem Wein	gutem Brot	guter Milch	guten Tagen

B. Weak adjective endings (after *der* or a similar article)

(1) **nominative** masculine, neuter, and feminine; **accusative** neuter and feminine weak adjectives will end in -e: der gute Wein, das gute Brot, die gute Milch

(2) **All other weak adjectives** (masculine accusative, **all** genitives, **all** datives, and **all** plurals) **will end in -en**: den guten Wein, des guten Brots, dem guten Mann, die guten Ideen, etc.)

C. Adjectives following *ein* words in nominative masculine and neuter and accusative neuter will be strong: ein guter Mann, ein gutes Kind

D. Possessive adjectives (cf. 7.8-7.10)

mein	*(my)*	unser	*(our)*
dein	*(your)*	euer	*(your)*
sein	*(his, its)*	Ihr	*(your — formal)*
ihr	*(her)*	ihr	*(their)*

III. Pronouns

A. Personal pronouns (cf. 7.1-7.3)

	nominative	accusative	dative
I	ich (*I*)	mich (*me*)	mir (*to me*)
you (*informal*)	du (*you*)	dich (*thee, you*)	dir (*to thee, to you*)
he	er (*he*)	ihn (*him*)	ihm (*to him*)
it	es (*it*)	es (*it*)	ihm (*to it*)
she	sie (*she*)	sie (*her*)	ihr (*to her*)
we	wir (*we*)	uns (*us*)	uns (*to us*)
you (*informal*)	ihr (*you*)	euch (*you*)	euch (*to you*)
they	sie (*they*)	sie (*them*)	ihnen (*to them*)
you (*formal*)	Sie (*you*)	Sie (*you*)	Ihnen (*to you*)

B. Relative pronouns (For a review, see 25.1-25.8)

	masculine	neuter	feminine	plural
nominative	der	das	die	die
accusative	den	das	die	die
genitive	dessen	dessen	deren	deren
dative	dem	dem	der	denen

C. Reflexive pronouns (For a review, see 26.1-26.4)

singular (I, you, he, it, she)   **plural** (we, you, they)

accusative	*mich* (*myself*)		accusative	*uns*	(*ourselves*)
dative	*mir* (*myself*)		dative	*uns*	(*ourselves*)

accusative	*dich* (*yourself*)		accusative	*euch* (*yourselves*)
dative	*dir* (*yourself*)		dative	*euch* (*yourselves*)

accusative	*sich*	(*himself,*	accusative	*sich*	(*themselves,*
and dative		*itself,*	*and* dative		*each other*)
		herself)			

sich is also the accusative and dative for the formal *you* (*Sie*).

IV. Prepositions (For more definitions, see also Appendix H, pp. 285-356)

A. Prepositions taking the accusative (cf. 5.2)

bis — *until, as far as*
durch — *through, by means of, as far as*
für — *for, instead of;* *halten für* — *to consider;* *was für* — *what kind of*
gegen — *against, towards;* *gegen* acht Uhr — *around* 8:00
ohne — *without*
um — *at, around;* *um* sechs Uhr — *at* 6:00
wider — *against, contrary to*
entlang — *along;* den Fluß *entlang* — *along* the river

B. Prepositions taking the dative (cf. 5.4)

aus — *out of, of, from;* *aus* Berlin — *from* Berlin
außer — *out of, except (for), aside from, in addition to*
bei — *by, near, with, among, at the house of, at;* *beim* — *bei + dem*
mit — *with, by, at*
nach — *after, according to, to* (with regard to direction); *nach* der Vorlesung
    — *after* class; meiner Meinung *nach* — *in* my opinion; fragen *nach* —
    to ask *about*; fahren *nach* — to go *to*
seit — *since, for*
von — *from, of, by, about;* *vom* — *von + dem*
zu — *to, at, in addition to;* *zum* Beispiel — *for* example; *zu* Hause — *at* home;
    zur — *zu + der;* *zum* — *zu + dem*
gegenüber — *vis-à-vis, opposite, in relation to*

C. Prepositions taking either dative or accusative (cf. 5.6)

an — *at, on, to, in, near to;* denken *an* — to think *of*; *am* — *an + dem*
auf — *on, upon, on top of, in, at, to;* warten *auf* — to wait *for*
hinter — *behind;* *hinterm* — *hinter + dem*
in — *in, into;* *ins* — *in + das;* *im* — *in + dem*
neben — *beside, near, next to*
über — *above, over, about, across;* sprechen *über* — to speak *about*
unter — *under, beneath, among, below;* *unter* den Blinden — *among* the blind
vor — *before, in front of, ago;* *vor* sechs Stunden — six hours *ago*; *vor allem* —
    above all; *vor* Freude — *with* joy
zwischen — *between*

D. Prepositions taking the genitive (cf. 5.8)

trotz — *in spite of*
statt — *instead of*
während — *during*
wegen — *because of*
um . . . willen — *for the sake of*

V. Conjunctions

A. Co-ordinating conjunctions (cf. 21.1-21.2)

aber — *but, however*
denn — *for, because* (cf. also 35.8)
oder — *or*
sondern — *rather, on the contrary*
und — *and*
entweder...oder — *either...or*
weder...noch — *neither...nor* (cf. also 35.21)

B. Subordinating conjunctions (cf. 23.3-23.6)

als — *when*
auch wenn — *even if*
bevor — *before*
bis — *until*
da — *since*
damit — *so that*
daß — *that*
ehe — *before*
nachdem — *after*
ob — *if, whether*

obschon, obwohl — *although*
sobald — *as soon as*
während — *while*
weil — *because*
wenn — *when, if*

C. Subordinating relative pronouns (cf. 24.1-24.5)

wer — *he who, whoever*
was — *what, whatever, which, that which, that*
wie — *how, as*
wo — *where, when*
warum — *why*

VI. Verb conjugations — present, past, and present perfect (For a review, see 14.1-15.3)

A. Conjugation of a weak verb and of a strong verb; present, past, present perfect, and subjunctive II

(1) a weak verb: *lachen* (*to laugh*)

	present	past	present perfect		subjunctive II
ich	lache	lachte	habe	gelacht	lachte
du	lachst	lachtest	hast	gelacht	lachtest
er	lacht	lachte	hat	gelacht	lachte
wir	lachen	lachten	haben	gelacht	lachten
ihr	lacht	lachtet	habt	gelacht	lachtet
sie	lachen	lachten	haben	gelacht	lachten
Sie	lachen	lachten	haben	gelacht	lachten

(2) a strong verb: *finden* (*to find*)

	present	past	present perfect		subjunctive II
ich	finde	fand	habe	gefunden	fände
du	findest	fandest	hast	gefunden	fändest
er	findet	fand	hat	gefunden	fände
wir	finden	fanden	haben	gefunden	fänden
ihr	findet	fandet	habt	gefunden	fändet
sie	finden	fanden	haben	gefunden	fänden
Sie	finden	fanden	haben	gefunden	fänden

B. Conjugation of *sein* (*to be*)

	present	past	present perfect		subjunctive II
ich	bin	war	bin	gewesen	wäre
du	bist	warst	bist	gewesen	wärest
er	ist	war	ist	gewesen	wäre
wir	sind	waren	sind	gewesen	wären
ihr	seid	wart	seid	gewesen	wäret
sie	sind	waren	sind	gewesen	wären
Sie	sind	waren	sind	gewesen	wären

C. Conjugation of *haben* (*to have*)

ich	habe	hatte	habe	gehabt	hätte
du	hast	hattest	hast	gehabt	hättest
er	hat	hatte	hat	gehabt	hätte
wir	haben	hatten	haben	gehabt	hätten
ihr	habt	hattet	habt	gehabt	hättet
sie	haben	hatten	haben	gehabt	hätten
Sie	haben	hatten	haben	gehabt	hätten

D. Conjugation of *werden* (*to become*)

ich	werde	wurde	bin	geworden	würde
du	wirst	wurdest	bist	geworden	würdest
er	wird	wurde	ist	geworden	würde
wir	werden	wurden	sind	geworden	würden
ihr	werdet	wurdet	seid	geworden	würdet
sie	werden	wurden	sind	geworden	würden
Sie	werden	wurden	sind	geworden	würden

VII. Modals (For a review, see 19.1-19.9). Charts of the subjunctive forms of the modals can be found on 32.1.

	dürfen (*to be permitted*)	**können** (*to be able to, can*)	**mögen** (*to like, may*)	**müssen** (*to have to, must*)	**sollen** (*is to, should*)	**wollen** (*to want to*)
ich	darf	kann	mag	muß	soll	will
du	darfst	kannst	magst	mußt	sollst	willst
er	darf	kann	mag	muß	soll	will
wir	dürfen	können	mögen	müssen	sollen	wollen
ihr	dürft	könnt	mögt	müßt	sollt	wollt
sie	dürfen	können	mögen	müssen	sollen	wollen
Sie	dürfen	können	mögen	müssen	sollen	wollen

VIII. *werden* (cf. 2.5; 10.2-10.3; 28.1-28.4)

(A) When *werden* appears **alone** in a sentence, it will mean *to become, to grow*:
Er *wird* alt — He *is growing* old.

(B) When *werden* appears **with an infinitive**, it will mean *will* (future):
Er *wird* nicht *gehen* — He *will* not *go*.

(C) When *werden* appears **with a participle**, it will mean *is* (passive):
Es *wird* selten *getan* — It *is* seldom *done*.

IX. Verb placement (cf. 6.1-6.6; 22.1-22.4; 23.1-23.6; 33.1-33.3)

(A) When there is only one verb in the clause:

(1) In a standard main clause, the verb will appear in "second" place: Er *kennt* Fräulein Meier; Heute *kommt* er mit uns; Den Freund *erkennt* man in der Not; Auf dem Fußpfad *wächst* kein Gras.

(2) If the clause begins with a verb,
(i) it may be a question: *Kennt* er den Briefträger? — *Does* he *know* the mailman?
(ii) it may be a command: *Tue* das sofort! — *Do* that immediately! *Vergessen Sie* das *nicht!* — *Do not forget* that!
(iii) when the verb appears in the subjunctive I form and is followed by *wir*, it will be translated *let us*: *Seien* wir tapfer! — *Let* us *be* brave!
(iv) it can signal an "if . . . then" construction: *Fehlt* es dir an Bier, so *trinke* Wein — If you *lack* beer, then *drink* wine; *Wäre* er reich, so *arbeitete* er nicht — If he *were* rich, he *would* not *work*.

(3) If the clause is a subordinate clause, the verb will appear at the end: Es ist wahr, daß sie viel *studiert* — It is true that she *studies* a lot.

(B) When the verb appears with an auxiliary (such as a form of *sein* or *haben* or *werden* or a modal), the auxiliary will be conjugated, and it will appear in "second" place in the clause (if it is a standard main clause — cf. A-1), while the other verb infinitive or participle will appear at the end of the clause: Er *kann* nicht *gehen*; Sie *hat* das oft *gesagt*.

(2) The auxiliary will appear at the beginning of the clause if the clause is a question, or if it is an "if . . . then" construction (cf. A-2), while the other verb infinitive or participle will appear at the end of the clause: *Darf* er das *tun* — Is he permitted to do that?; *Hätte* sie das *gewußt*, so hätte sie darüber gelacht — If she *had known* that, she would have laughed about it.

(3) In dependent clauses, the auxiliary will appear at the end, while the other verb infinitive or participle will be the penultimate word in the clause: Ich glaube, daß wir *gehen werden* — I believe that we will go; Nachdem er das *gesagt hatte*, wurde der alte Mann ruhig — After he had said that, the old man became silent.

(C) Whenever there are three or more verbs in a clause, the conjugated verb will be translated first, the verb at the end of the clause will be translated next, the penultimate verb will be translated third, and any other possible verb will be translated last: Er wird das getan haben — He will
    ¹   ³   ²

have done that; Man hat mich oft tanzen sehen können (Nietzsche) — One
         ¹   ⁴   ³   ²

was often able to see me dance.

X. Verb tenses: here are most of the possible verb combinations of the infinitive *sagen* (*to say*):

present	er sagt — he says
past	er sagte — he said
present perfect	er hat gesagt — he (has) said
past perfect	er hatte gesagt — he had said
future	er wird sagen — he will say
present (with a modal)	er will sagen — he wants to say
past (with a modal)	er wollte sagen — he wanted to say
present perfect (+ a modal)	er hat sagen wollen — he (has) wanted to say
past perfect (+ a modal)	er hatte sagen wollen — he had wanted to say
future (+ a modal)	er wird sagen wollen — he will want to say
present passive	es wird gesagt — it is said
past passive	es wurde gesagt — it was said
present perfect passive	es ist gesagt worden — it has been said
past perfect passive	es war gesagt worden — it had been said
future passive	es wird gesagt werden — it will be said
present passive (+ modal)	es will gesagt werden — it wants to be said
past passive (+ modal)	es wollte gesagt werden — it wanted to be said
present perfect passive (+ modal)	es hat gesagt werden wollen — it has wanted to be said
past perfect passive (+ modal)	es hatte gesagt werden wollen — it had wanted to be said
present + past, subjunctive I	er sage — he may say, says, said
present + past perfect subjunctive I	er habe gesagt — he may have said, he has said, he had said

present + past subjunctive II	er sagte — he would say, he had said
present + past perfect subjunctive II	er hätte gesagt — he would have said, he had said
conditional	er würde sagen — he would say
present + past subjunctive I + modal	er wolle sagen — he may want to say, he wants to say, he wanted to say
present + past perfect subjunctive I + modal	er habe sagen wollen — he might have wanted to say, he has wanted to say, he had wanted to say
present + past subjunctive II + modal	er wollte sagen — he would have wanted to say, he had wanted to say
present + past perfect subjunctive II + modal	er hätte sagen wollen — he would have wanted to say (but didn't)
conditional + modal	er würde sagen wollen — he would want to say
subjunctive I + passive	es sei gesagt worden — it may have been said
subjunctive II + passive	es wäre gesagt worden — it would have been said

Appendix B

Patterns for Strong Verbs

infinitive (and irregular third person singular)	past (first and third person singular)	participle	definition
group I: *ei-ie-ie* or *ei-i-i*			
bleiben	blieb	geblieben	stay, remain
scheiden	schied	geschieden	part, depart
scheinen	schien	geschienen	shine, seem
schreiben	schrieb	geschrieben	write
steigen	stieg	gestiegen	climb
weisen	wies	gewiesen	point
greifen	griff	gegriffen	grasp
leiden	litt	gelitten	suffer
reißen	riß	gerissen	tear
schneiden	schnitt	geschnitten	cut
streiten	stritt	gestritten	fight
group II: *ie-o-o*			
biegen	bog	gebogen	bend
fliegen	flog	geflogen	fly
fliehen	floh	geflohen	flee
fließen	floß	geflossen	flow
genießen	genoß	genossen	enjoy
riechen	roch	gerochen	smell
schließen	schloß	geschlossen	close
verlieren	verlor	verloren	lose
ziehen	zog	gezogen	pull
group III: *i-a-u* or *i-a-o*			
binden	band	gebunden	bind
finden	fand	gefunden	find

infinitive (and irregular third person singular)	past (first and third person singular)	participle	definition
gelingen	gelang	gelungen	succeed
singen	sang	gesungen	sing
trinken	trank	getrunken	drink
verschwinden	verschwand	verschwunden	disappear
zwingen	zwang	gezwungen	force
beginnen	begann	begonnen	begin
gewinnen	gewann	gewonnen	win, gain
liegen	lag	gelegen	lie, situate
schwimmen	schwamm	geschwommen	swim

group IV: *e-a-o*

befehlen	befiehlt	befahl	befohlen	command
brechen	bricht	brach	gebrochen	break
gelten	gilt	galt	gegolten	be valid
helfen	hilft	half	geholfen	help
kommen		kam	gekommen	come
nehmen	nimmt	nahm	genommen	take
sprechen	spricht	sprach	gesprochen	speak
stehlen	stiehlt	stahl	gestohlen	steal

group V: *e-a-e* (note that *sitzen* is somewhat different)

essen	ißt	aß	gegessen	eat
geben	gibt	gab	gegeben	give
geschehen	geschieht	geschah	geschehen	happen
lesen	liest	las	gelesen	read
sehen	sieht	sah	gesehen	see
treten	tritt	trat	getreten	enter, step
sitzen		saß	gesessen	sit

group VI: *a-u-a*

erfahren	erfährt	erfuhr	erfahren	experience
fahren	fährt	fuhr	gefahren	go, travel
schlagen	schlägt	schlug	geschlagen	hit
tragen	trägt	trug	getragen	carry, wear
wachsen	wächst	wuchs	gewachsen	grow

infinitive (and   **past** (first and   **participle**   **definition**
irregular third   third person
person singular)   singular)

group VII: *a-ie-a* (note that *heißen, laufen,* and *rufen* vary)

infinitive		past	participle	definition
blasen	bläst	blies	geblasen	blow
fallen	fällt	fiel	gefallen	fall
fangen	fängt	fing	gefangen	catch
gefallen	gefällt	gefiel	gefallen	please
halten	hält	hielt	gehalten	hold
lassen	läßt	ließ	gelassen	let, permit
raten	rät	riet	geraten	advise
heißen		hieß	geheißen	be called
laufen	läuft	lief	gelaufen	run
rufen		rief	gerufen	call

irregular strong verbs

gehen		ging	gegangen	go
sein	ist	war	gewesen	be
stehen		stand	gestanden	stand
tun	tut	tat	getan	do

irregular weak verbs

brennen		brannte	gebrannt	burn
kennen		kannte	gekannt	know
nennen		nannte	genannt	name
senden		sandte	gesandt	send
bringen		brachte	gebracht	bring
denken		dachte	gedacht	think
wissen	weiß	wußte	gewußt	know

Appendix C

Days of the Week, the Months, and Numbers

I. Days of the week

Sonntag	Sunday	Donnerstag	Thursday
Montag	Monday	Freitag	Friday
Dienstag	Tuesday	Sonnabend	Saturday
Mittwoch	Wednesday	Samstag	Saturday

Heute in acht Tagen — a *week* from today

II. Names of the month

Januar	January	Mai	May	September	September
Februar	February	Juni	June	Oktober	October
März	March	Juli	July	November	November
April	April	August	August	Dezember	December

III. The cardinal numbers

1	eins	9	neun	17	siebzehn	40	vierzig
2	zwei	10	zehn	18	achtzehn	50	fünfzig
3	drei	11	elf	19	neunzehn	60	sechzig
4	vier	12	zwölf	20	zwanzig	70	siebzig
5	fünf	13	dreizehn	21	einundzwanzig	80	achtzig
6	sechs	14	vierzehn	22	zweiundzwanzig	90	neunzig
7	sieben	15	fünfzehn	23	dreiundzwanzig	100	hundert
8	acht	16	sechzehn	30	dreißig	1000	tausend

Also: null — zero; die Million — million; die Milliarde — billion; die Billion — trillion

IV. The ordinal numbers

(1) Numbers 1-19 will have a **-te** added to the cardinal number:
der zwei**te**, der fünf**te**, der achtzehn**te**, etc. Exceptions are:
der erste (first), der dritte (third), and der achte (eighth).
The seventh can be either der sieb**te** or der sieb**ente**.

(2) Numbers 20 and above will have a **-ste** added to the cardinal number:
der zwanzig**ste** (twentieth), der einundfünfzig**ste** (fifty-first), der hundert**ste**
(hundredth), etc.

Appendix D

Time Phrases

German idioms for time are a nuisance because few of them correspond to English idioms. Here are some of the most common time phrases.

I. Times of day

um acht Uhr — *at* eight o'clock; um *halb acht* — at *seven thirty*
gegen acht Uhr — *around* eight o'clock
zu Mittag — *at* noon; *zu* dieser Zeit — *at* this time

II. Note how dates are expressed

am 4. Juli — *on the* 4th of July
Novalis starb *1801* — Novalis died *in 1801*
die *sechziger* Jahre — the *sixties*

III. Three prepositions relating to time

vor drei Jahren — three years *ago*
Seit drei Jahren *studiert* (present tense) sie Erdkunde — *For* three years she *has been studying* (present perfect progressive) geography.

IV. Other time phrases to watch for

drei Jahre *lang* — *for* three years
in acht Tagen — *in* a week
am *anderen* Tag — on the *next* day
Erst gestern bekam er den Brief — *Not until* yesterday did he get the letter.

V. Note also

(1) When definite time is being expressed, the **accusative** case is used when there is no preceding preposition:
Jeden Tag liest er eine Zeitung — He reads a newspaper *every day*.

(2) But when indefinite time is being expressed, the **genitive** is used:
Eines Tages müssen wir ein geregeltes Leben anfangen — *One day* we must get organized (literally: begin a well-ordered life).

(3) Adverbial expressions of time end in **-s** and are not capitalized. Examples are:
morgens, abends, freitags, etc.
Er will *sonntags* nicht arbeiten — He does not want to work *Sundays*.

Appendix E
Genitive and Plural Endings

ending	gender	genitive	plural
-chen (Mädchen)	n.	-s (des Mädchens)	— (die Mädchen)
-e (Blume)	f.	—	-n (die Blumen)
-e (Junge)	m.	-n (des Jungen)*	-n (die Jungen)
-el (Regel)	f.	—	-n (die Regeln)
-el (Titel)	m.	-s (des Titels)	— (die Titel)**
-er (Dichter)	m.	-s (des Dichters)	— (die Dichter)*
-heit (Wahrheit)	f.	—	-en (die Wahrheiten)
-ion (Situation)	f.	—	-en (die Situationen)
-ist (Novellist)	m.	-en (des Novellisten)	-en (die Novellisten)
-ium (Studium)	n.	-s (des Studiums)	-ien (die Studien)
-keit (Möglichkeit)	f.	—	-en (die Möglich- keiten)
-lein (Häuslein)	n.	-s (des Häusleins)	— (die Häuslein)
-ling (Liebling)	m.	-s (des Lieblings)	-e (die Lieblinge)
-nis (Kenntnis)	f.	—	-sse (die Kenntnisse)
-nis (Verhältnis)	n.	-sses (des Verhält- nisses)	-sse (die Verhältnisse)
-schaft (die Gemein- schaft)	f.	—	-en (die Gemeinschaf- ten)
-tät (Universität)	f.	—	-en (die Universitäten)
-ung (Übung)	f.	—	-en (die Übungen)

* While this is not the only possible ending, it is definitely the most common ending.

** The plural may or may not have an umlaut over the medial vowel (der Apfel — singular; die Äpfel — plural).

Appendix F

Specific German Dictionaries

The following is a list of various German dictionaries as of 1996, and the information may change as other dictionaries are published or revised after this date. It is not complete, but it does include the most commonly used dictionaries. Unfortunately (but logically enough), there is no perfect dictionary. In order to translate German competently, you will need a hardback dictionary such as the **Oxford Duden** or the **Cassells** or the **Collins** or the **Langenscheidts**. But, if you have never had German before, you will find that using only a large dictionary will slow down your reading/translation time. Therefore, I would recommend that you use two dictionaries — a hardback dictionary for compound or obscure words, or for a more precise definition of a word, and a paperback dictionary for more common words which you tend to look up over and over again.

Since each German dictionary has a slightly different layout, I would advise you to check out the introductions of your particular dictionaries to discover the specific abbreviations used and the rationales of their formats.

The Oxford Duden

The Oxford Duden, first published in 1990, is an excellent moderately priced German-English dictionary. With over 260,000 words and phrases and 450,000 translations, it is quite comprehensive (although currently not quite as comprehensive as the Harper Collins, which has 280,000 entries). It also has an abundance of information in the back, including grammar explanations, orthography and punctuation, guides to writing letters, useful phrases (for saying thank you, and even for expressing amazement, disappointment, hope and fear), weights and measures, temperature conversion, numbers, and times of day. Its word definitions tend to be more explicitly laid out than those of other German dictionaries. For example, nouns are listed with the appropriate articles **der, das, die**, rather than as **m., n.,** or **f.**, and definitions are often given in order of frequency of usage rather than by automatically listing transitive verb definitions before intransitive verb definitions.

Slight (but minor) disadvantages are that the Duden has such an abundance of material that finding words and their precise definitions can be more time-consuming (but ultimately more rewarding) than using the large Cassells. Moreover, the grammar explanations and synonyms of German words are listed in German, which can be inconvenient for a beginner with a limited vocabulary. For example, **sein** as a possessive pronoun is listed as follows: **sein** *Possessivpron.* **a)** (*vor Substantiven*) (*bei Männern*) his; (*bei Mädchen*) her; (*bei Dingen, Abstrakta*) its; (*bei Tieren*) its; (*bei Männchen auch*) his; (*bei Weibchen auch*) her; (*bei Ländern*) its; her; (*bei Städten*) its; (*bei Schiffen*) her; its; (*nach man*) one's; his (*Amer.*) . . .

The large Cassells

A large Cassells is a good dictionary for a beginning student to have. It has a clearer layout than the other large dictionaries, as it has separate entries for most words, rather than listing *Gleichnis* under the basic heading *gleich*. It also lists idioms in bold face type, which makes them relatively easy to find. It also has several aids for people not totally familiar with German grammar. For example, it lists the third person singular for all verbs which differ from the stem of the infinitive (such as *tritt*, *liest*, and *läßt*), and it also lists the past and participal forms for all irregular verbs in the text, as well as having a separate irregular verb chart. It also gives the past subjunctives within the text, and it gives the declensions for prounouns such as *wer* and *jemand*. The large Cassells also conveniently lists proper nouns within the text, rather than isolating them in a separate section.

The large Cassells has some features not generally found in other German dictionaries. It gives definitions for most prefixes and suffixes, and it indicates whether or not a prefix can be separable or inseparable. It includes some dialect words (such as *Hübel* — hillock) not listed in other dictionaries, and it has a chart of clothing sizes and a list of specialist dictionaries.

But the large Cassells does have some disadvantages. It does not list the plural for nouns when it considers the plural obvious. (For example, it does not tell you that the plural of *Pflanze* is *Pflanzen*, or that the plural of *Übung* is *Übungen*.)

But, more seriously, the large Cassells does not contain as many words as the other large dictionaries. Although the large Cassells was revised in 1978, it does not have the up-to-date words (such as *Hochrechnung* — projection, or *Zwergschule* — one room school) of the large Langenscheidts (last revised in 1973) or of the large Collins (revised in 1991) nor does it have as many technical words. Also, the large Cassells has slightly fewer abbreviations than the large Langenscheidts.

Note also that the large Cassells was revised in 1978. Dictionaries published prior to that time are not as well laid out and they lack many of the advantages of the current Cassells.

The Collins

The Collins German dictionary, first published in 1980, and revised in 1991, has more words and currently has more definitions than any of the other dictionaries mentioned in Appendix F. It also gives complete grammar explanations in the preface, and it includes a list of regular German noun endings, their genders, genitives, and plurals. There is also a handy reference of all the abbreviations, field labels, and style labels on the inside cover. Like the large Cassells, it also includes the past and participial forms for all irregular verbs, and it gives past subjunctives within the text. The Collins also shares the Cassells format of giving declensions for pronouns such as *wer* and *jemand*, and it, too, lists proper nouns within the text. Verbs which differ from the stem of the infinitive are listed in their imperative singular form (*hilf*, *sprich*, etc.).

However, in some ways, the Collins, like the Oxford Duden, contains almost too much information. While both the Cassells and the Langenscheidts have about fifty entries under the word *Auge*, the Collins has about seventy-five entries; yet because there are so many entries, some of which are redundant, it is quite time-consuming to wade through all of them. Moreover, some of the German words need not be listed because they are so obvious. Examples are: *Kleptomanin* (female kleptomaniac) when *Kleptomane* is already given; *Gin-Fizz*; *Herzpatient*. Because the Collins, like the Oxford Duden, is larger and heavier than the Cassells and the Langenscheidts, it is more time-consuming to use than either of them.

While abbreviations are listed in alphabetical order in the text, their definitions are not given to you immediately. For example, if you look up *usf.*, you are told that it is an abbreviation of *und so fort*; then you must look up *fort* to discover that *usf.* means *and so forth*. Moreover, the Collins has no listing of irregular verbs.

Still, the Collins does have a good selection of words and definitions, and it can be a very useful reference, particularly if you need to read specialized texts.

The large Langenscheidts

The large Langenscheidts is a good dictionary for a student who has mastered German grammar thoroughly because it has more words and more precise definitions than the large Cassells, and it is not as unwieldy as the Duden or the Collins. However, for a beginning student, the layout is confusing, as nouns often are listed under root verbs, and the reverse. Since the large Langenscheidts gives more information about precise word usage than the Cassells, and since it has three columns per page rather than two, students find it difficult to locate specific definitions unless they already have a general idea of what they are looking for. Reflexive verbs are particularly poorly indicated. The large Langenscheidts also does not include the third person singular of some verbs, nor does it include past subjunctives.

However, the large Langenscheidts does include more abbreviations than the large Cassells, and its list of proper names, including names of German authors such as Raabe and Novalis, and of German places probably would be quite helpful for students who are unfamiliar with German culture. The large Langenscheidts was revised in 1995.

The German Word Family Dictionary

This dictionary is useful if you wish to gain an understanding of the most common German roots, prefixes, and suffixes. The discussion of prefixes and suffixes is far more complete than in any other dictionary. German root words such as *kommen*, *gehen*, *legen* and *geben* are particularly useful to look up in order to view all the permutations a German word can have, and the corresponding differences in meaning.

However, the German Word Family Dictionary simply cannot be used as a dictionary. Since words are included only if their roots are common and they have at least three prefixed members, this dictionary is quite incomplete. Moreover, the definitions of the words themselves are at times misleading because they are limited to seven defining words, and no context is given. For example, *faul* is defined as *rotten, foul, putrid; brittle metal; decayed teeth* and there is no indication that it can also mean *lazy*, although *Faulheit* is defined as *laziness*.

Moreover, the symbols appearing to the right of the words are not always as helpful as they might be. For example, *a* can mean either *adjective* or *archaic*, yet some of the words marked *a* are neither adjectives nor particularly archaic. (Examples are: *Überhang* — projection and *Übermut* — arrogance.) The symbol *p* can mean either *preposition* or *poetic*, yet a *p* follows relatively common words such as *zugehören* (to belong to) and *schneeig* (snowy).

Although it is not a consistently reliable resource, the German Word Family Dictionary is definitely worth consulting because it is extremely useful for gaining a feel for the German language.

The pocket Cassells

The pocket Cassells is probably the easiest dictionary to use, as its words are more clearly laid out than the words in the pocket Langenscheidts. However, it is disappointingly incomplete, as it has no list of abbreviations, and words with common prefixes (*be-, ent-, zer-*) are not given. It would be very difficult to translate any passage of relatively complex German accurately with the pocket Cassells because it is so incomplete. I would not recommend it.

The pocket Langenscheidts

This dictionary is a better small dictionary than the pocket Cassells because it contains more words, and also has a list of German proper names and of German abbreviations which the small Cassells lacks. The small Langenscheidts also has a clear listing of verbs, particularly for a small dictionary. It lists whether or not a verb is separable, and it also lists whether or not a verb takes *ge-* in its participial form. It also includes the past and participles of irregular verbs. And it tends to have more precise definitions than the small Cassells, as it has symbols indicating whether a word is familiar or rare or botanic, etc. The pocket Langenscheidts also has more up-to-date words (such as *Mondfähre* — lunar module — and *Einwegflasche* — non-returnable bottle) than the small Cassells.

But the pocket Langenscheidts does not have as clear a lay-out as the small Cassells, and many words are poorly arranged. For example, the common verb *suchen* (to seek) is listed under *Suchdienst* (tracing service). However, in recent revisions, the layout *has* become somewhat clearer, and *suchen* does have a separate entry.

Nevertheless, this dictionary is a handy reference for a beginning student, since common words are listed, and it is easier to leaf through than a larger dictionary.

The Bantam New College German & English Dictionary

With approximately 75,000 entries, the Bantam paperback dictionary contains more words than other paperback dictionaries; therefore it is a useful resource when you do not have a large dictionary handy, or when you don't want to go wading through the numerous definitions contained in a larger dictionary. Proper nouns are included in the text rather than in a separate section.

In the middle of the dictionary, there is a brief summary of German grammar, as well as a verb table. Numbers after strong verb entries refer you to the verb table in the middle of the book. The key to the abbreviations (h., coll., fig., etc.) can be found in the back of the dictionary.

While the Bantam is probably the best paperback German dictionary to have, it does have some drawbacks. Occasionally, definitions are misleading. For example, *Christ* seldom means *Christ*, and yet that is the first definition given. While *alle* means *everyone*, this definition cannot be found. Prepositions are not too well defined, and when words have an adverbial as well as a prepositional meaning, the less common adverbial meaning is given first. Moreover, there is no list of common German abbreviations.

The pocket Oxford Duden Dictionary

This dictionary was revised in 1992, and it has 70,000 entries. It is the most expensive of the paperback German dictionaries.

Oddly enough, the revision omitted many of the nicest features which were included in previous editions. It no longer has a summary of German grammar in the front, and the chart of strong verbs no longer includes their English definitions. An etymology for some words has been eliminated, as well as the symbol indicating that a word is a false cognate. Also, the German/English section of the dictionary is now located <u>after</u> the English/ German section, which makes it slightly less handy for translation purposes. Moreover, some of the more colorful idioms are omitted in the new revision. Examples are: *durch die Blume sprechen* — "to speak in a roundabout way" and *um die Ecke bringen* — "to murder".

Abbreviations and proper names are now incorporated in the main text. There are also more current words, such as *der Blues* ("blues"), and the print is larger. On the whole, however, the 1992 revision is a surprising disappointment. It is to be hoped that still another revision will appear soon.

The Collins pocket German Dictionary

This dictionary has about the same number of words (46,000) as the pocket Langenscheidts, and it is an acceptable dictionary, although it probably is not as useful as either the Bantam or the Oxford. It has a plastic cover so that it won't fall apart with frequent use, but the plastic tends to cut into one's hands, which makes it uncomfortable to leaf through. Occasionally, words can be hard to find, as verbs don't always have separate entries (*folgen* is listed under *Folge*, etc.); also, there is no indication of which weak verbs take *sein* as an auxiliary, and the strong verbs that take *sein* are only listed in the back.

However, this dictionary does have some useful features. It contains a list of regular noun endings, it has a summary of German grammar, and it also has a table for "time, dates, and numbers."

There is also a College Edition of the Harper Collins German Dictionary, which is in paperback, but which has over 70,000 entries and 100,000 translations, and is slightly larger than the standard paperback. Although it is larger than the pocket Oxford Duden, it costs slightly less and is a much better value.

Appendix G

Partial Answer Key

Chapter 2 — The present tense of verbs and the personal pronouns

2.8. er nimmt — he takes (*nehmen*); sie sieht — she sees (*sehen*); es bricht — it breaks (*brechen*); du ißt — you eat (*essen*); du wächst — you grow (*wachsen*); sie wäscht — she washes (*waschen*).

2.9. Sentence translations:

2. Complaining fills no stomach.
6. Beautiful faces have many judges.
7. A new doctor needs a new graveyard.
10. A burned child avoids the fire.
12. It is raining sausages.

2.10. Vocabulary aid:

3. The fire grows (or becomes, or is growing, or is becoming) warm.
7. Often they say (or speak) the truth.
8. He eats the *bratwurst* (sing.).

Chapter 3 — The case endings

3.3. Sentence translations — the accusative:

3. A beginning (mas. nom.) is no masterpiece (neut. nom.).
4. Effort (mas. nom.) *breaks* the ice (neut. acc.) (The infinitive of *bricht* is *brechen*.)
5. Truth (fem. nom.) has a beautiful face (neut. acc.), but torn clothing (acc. pl.).
6. A dwarf (mas. nom.) always remains a dwarf (mas. nom.).
7. A sleeping fox (mas. nom.) captures no rooster (mas. acc.).

3.5. Sentence translations — the genitive:

1. The goat (fem. nom.) is the cow (fem. nom.) of the *small man* (mas. gen.). (Do not confuse *klein* — small with *kein* — no)

2. The will (mas. nom.) is the soul (fem. nom.) of work (neut. gen.).
3. Self-knowledge (fem. nom.) is the beginning (mas. nom.) of self-improvement (fem. gen.).
7. The disorderly life (neut. nom.) of the people (pl. gen.) is the well-being (neut. nom.) of the doctors (pl. gen.).
8. The shadow (mas. nom.) of virtue (fem. gen.) is honor (fem. nom.).
11. Rest is the daily reward (mas. nom.) of the workers (gen. pl.)

3.7. Sentence translations — the dative:

2. Patience (fem. nom.) is a shield (mas. nom.) for the soul (dat. fem.).
3. No dress (neut. nom.) is better *for the woman* (fem. dat.) than being silent (neut. nom.).
5. The prayer (neut. nom.) is a wall (mas. nom.) and a hut (fem. nom.) *for the widow* (fem. dat.).
8. The meaning (fem. nom.) of the drama (neut. gen.) remains a riddle (neut. *nom.*) to the viewers (pl. dat.).
11. The professor (mas. nom.) explains the problem (neut. acc.) to the students (pl. dat.).

3.10. More sentence translations:

1. The friend (mas. nom.) of the woman (fem. gen.) gives the books (pl. acc.) to the mother (fem. dat.) of the children (pl. gen.).
2. The mother (fem. nom.) and the children (pl. nom.) see the cow (fem. acc.) and the steers (pl. acc.).
4. The wife (fem. nom.) of the doctor (mas. gen.) doubts the truth (fem. acc.) of the proverb (neut. gen.).

3.14. Translate these sentences, indicating the gender and case of each noun:

2. The earth (fem. nom.) covers the mistakes (pl. acc.) *of the doctors* (pl. gen.).
5. The blessing (mas. nom.) of the parents (pl. gen.) builds houses (pl. acc.) *for the children* (pl. dat.).
8. Perhaps one avoids punishment (fem. dat.), but one does not avoid the conscience (neut. dat.).
12. The stolen bread (neut. nom.) tastes good to the man (mas. dat.); but finally he has *a* mouth full of pebbles (pl. gen.).
15. What flies (pl. nom.) are *to idle knaves* (pl. dat.), that (neut. nom.) are we *to the gods* (pl. dat.).

3.15. Vocabulary aid:

1. The work (fem. nom.) of this good doctor (mas. gen.) is difficult.

8. The solution (fem. nom.) of this problem (neut. gen.) is unclear to the students (pl. dat.).

Chapter 4 — Adjectives and adverbs

4.12. Translate these sentences:

3. Old churches (pl. nom.) have dark windows (pl. acc.).
4. Thin (adj.) gnats (pl. nom.) sting wickedly (adv.).
8. Mute (adj.) dogs (pl. nom.) and still (adj.) waters (pl. nom.) are dangerous (pred. adj.). Compare: stilles Wasser (sing.) with stille Wasser (pl.).
10. Dark thoughts (pl. nom.) are the children (pl. nom.) of a melancholy head (mas. gen.). Note that Kopfes is singular!
17. The historian looks backwards (adv.); finally he also believes (or thinks) backwards (adv.).
19. A foolish son (mas. nom.) is his father's (mas. gen.) suffering (neut. nom.), and a cranky wife (*neut.* nom.) is like a constant*ly* (adv.) dripping (adj.) roof (neut. nom.).

4.13. Vocabulary aid:

3. The children of old people (pl. gen.) also become old (pred. adj.).
5. Many people like to drink wine.
7. The work (fem. nom.) of the historian (mas. gen.) interests the professor (mas. acc.).
8. The collected works (pl. nom.) of the American historians (pl. gen.) please the German critic (mas. dat.).

Chapter 5 — Prepositions

5.3. Prepositions — accusative:

2. Misfortune, nails and hair grow through the entire year (neut. acc.).
4. Fear *considers* all food poison.
5. *For* five years the professor (mas. nom.) fought against windmills (pl. acc.).
6. Fräulein Meier (fem. nom.) wraps the mailman (mas. acc.) around *her* little finger (mas. acc.).
8. The health fanatic (mas. nom.) swims against the stream (mas. acc.) every morning *at* (not *around*!) six o'clock.

5.5. Prepositions — dative

2. Laziness (fem. nom.) is the key to proverty (fem. dat.).
4. Fräulein Meier often makes *an elephant* (mas. acc.) out of a gnat (fem. dat.).

6. For three years, the student *has been reading* Kant's philosophy.
8. Pride (mas. nom.) breakfasts with abundance (mas. dat.), eats at noon (or lunches) with poverty (fem. dat.) and *eats* in the evening with shame (fem. dat.).
10. From "thrift-mountain" one *easily* (adv.) gets *to* "fat city."
14. With regard to God (mas. dat.) the Christian (mas. nom.) has the heart (neut. acc.) of a child (neut. gen.); with regard to the neighbor (mas. dat.) he has the heart (neut. acc.) of a mother (fem. gen.); and with regard to himself he has the heart of a judge (mas. gen.).

5.7. Prepositions — accusative or dative:

2. An old fox (mas. nom.) *never* goes into the trap (fem. acc.).
3. Virtue (fem. nom.) does not sit at the tables (pl. dat.) of great lords (pl. gen.).
4. Envy does not even grant heat (fem. acc.) in hell (dat. fem.) to the devil (mas. dat.)
6. *Man's* (mas. gen.) life hangs *by* a thread (mas. dat.).
12. The mailman (mas. nom.) hit*s* (present tense) the nail (mas. acc.) on the head (mas. acc.) with his observations (pl. dat.) about Fräulein Meier (fem. acc.).
13. Old friends (pl. nom.), old wine (mas. nom.) and old money (neut. nom.) have value (mas. acc.) in all the world (fem. dat.).

5.9. Prepositions — genitive:

1. One suffers (puts up with) the smoke (mas. acc.) on account of the fire (neut. gen.).
6. In spite of the present (neut. gen.) of the mailman (mas. gen.), Fräulein Meier is somewhat sad.

5.10. Vocabulary aid:

1. A young student (mas. nom.) eats two apples (pl. acc.) every morning (mas. acc.) for the sake of his health (fem. gen.).
2. *For* his whole life the mailman lived in Germany.
6. Four years *ago* Fräulein Meier often stayed home alone.
8. For a year, Fräulein Meier *has been working* part-time.
12. Almost every evening *at* 7:30 (literally: half of *eight*), Fräulein Meier receives a letter (mas. acc.) by special delivery.

Reading Selection: Fräulein Meier

Paragraph 2: Fräulein Meier likes to read proverbs, but the purposes of these proverbs are unclear to this woman (neut. dat.). The proverbs portray the good, happy *person* (mas. acc.) in the following way (fem. dat.): he works a lot, he fears God, and he mistrusts the easy life. But Fräulein Meier works little, she does what she wants to, and she is happy, nevertheless. Perhaps she has a better idea (mas. acc.) of reality (fem. dat.) than the proverb-tellers (*pl.*).

Chapter 6 — Verb placement (part 1)

6.3. Translate these sentences:

2. No one (nom.) knows poor people (pl. acc.).
4. The wind (mas. nom.) chases the prayers (pl. acc.) of beggars (pl. gen.).
6. No goal (neut. nom.) is too high *for* virtue (fem. dat.).
10. God likes a cheerful giver (mas. acc.).
11. No plow (mas. nom.) is good enough *for* a lazy farmer (mas. dat.).
14. *Whom* (acc.) does the old woman know?

6.5. Translate — Questions and commands:

2. Be a snail in advice, a bird in deed*s*.
5. Peacock, *look at* your legs!
8. Drink, drink, little brother drink,/Just leave your worries at home . . .
9. Some questions:
   Do you believe in love at first sight?
   Does the error of a moment become the worry of a lifetime? (Note: you do not need to translate the *zur*.)

6.7. Vocabulary aid:

1. For the sake of the whole truth (fem. gen.), Fräulein Meier lets the cat (fem. acc.) out of the bag.
4. Truth (fem. nom.) is very important to the coed (fem. dat.).
6. Do *you* believe in the truth of this proverb (neut. gen.)?
12. *Whom* (acc.) does the student fear?

Reading Selection: Meeresstrand

The seagull now flies to the lagoon,
And twilight arrives;
The evening glow reflects
Over the damp shoals.

Grey fowl scurries forth (*her*)
Next to the water;
The islands lie like dreams
In the fog, upon the sea.

I hear the secret sound
Of the swirling sand.
Lonely birdcall —
It was always like that.

Once again the wind shudders
Softly and then is silent;
The voices (which are) over the depth
Are becoming clear.

Note: this is quite a literal translation. If you feel like it, you may make it more poetic.

Chapter 7 — The pronouns

7.4. Replace all the nouns:

3. *Es* ist glücklich mit *ihr* (dat. fem.).
4. *Er* sieht *sie* mit *ihnen* (dat. pl.).
5. Außer (except for) *ihnen* sehen *sie sie* nicht.
6. *Sie* sitzt *ihm* nicht gegenüber.
8. *Es* trinkt *sie*.

7.6. Translate the following sentences:

3. When do *they* speak with *her*?
4. *She* knows *him*.
6. The apple*s* taste good; he likes to eat *them*.
7. *They* help *him*.

7.11. Translate these sentences:

1. Follow my words (pl. dat.), not my deeds (pl. dat.).
3. Learn order, practice *it*; order saves *you* (dat.) time and effort.
5. A wise son makes joy (fem. acc.) *for his father* (mas. dat.), a foolish one makes trouble *for his mother* (fem. dat.).
12. The mailman is the first born son *of his parents* (pl. gen.).
16. Thy shepherd's crook and staff, they are my comfort —/ You set for me a table in the face of my enem*ies* (pl. gen.)./ You annoint my head with oil,/ My cup is overflowing. (From the twenty-third psalm)

7.12. Vocabulary aid:

2. It is a joy *to her*.
5. Where are *they*?

6. She tells the story *to her* friend (mas. dat.).
7. The laziness of the child is inexplicable to his father, and he does not understand *it* (the laziness) at all.
10. *They* help *her* often.
11. Is that clear *to you* (formal you, dative)?
15. Where do *you* (informal you, nom.) find the answer?
17. *They* believe *him*.
18. He does not understand *their, her,* or *your* answer.

Chapter 8 — Weak nouns and adjectives used as nouns

8.3. Translate (weak nouns):

1. The eye is the indicator of the heart (neut. gen.).
5. The wish is often the father (mas. nom.) of the thought (neut. gen.).
6. *Man's* (mas. gen.) will is his kingdom of heaven.
8. Sometimes the professor speaks with the student*s* (pl. dat.).
9. The mailman often has a letter for the English student (mas. acc.).

8.6. Translate (adjectival nouns):

1. The German *woman* has a fat cat.
3. The *true* is very important to the mailman (mas. dat.).
4. The mistake*s* of the wise person (mas. gen.) are astonishing.
5. The unhappy *one* envies *the happy ones* (pl. acc.).
7. Nothing (nom.) is agreeable to the sick one (mas. dat.).

8.7. Translate these sentences:

1. The world belongs to the bold *one* (mas. dat.).
4. No wise one (mas. nom.) despises small enemies and small wounds.
8. New saints throw the old ones into the junk pile. (If *die alten* had been capitalized — *die Alten*, the sentence would have been translated: New saints throw old *people* into the junk pile!)
9. *Everything* (nom.) is pure to the pure one (mas. dat.).
10. Fräulein Meier sits opposite the *old ones* (pl. dat.).

Chapter 9 — The various uses of *es*

9.4. Translate these sentences:

1. There *are* no rule*s* without exceptions.
4. Two saddles (pl. nom.) do not belong on *one* horse.
8. No apple*s* (pl. nom.) fall far from the tree.
10. There is no ugly little loved one and no beautiful prison.
12. Many friends go into *one* house.

Reading Selection: Das Sprichwort

Paragraph 4: One often finds a personification *of the animal* (neut. gen.) in the animal proverbs. Here are some recurring themes *of* such proverbs. (1) One cannot be other than what one is: "If the donkey wears a lionskin, the ears peek out from under it;" "A poodle that one has sheared so that it has a mane is still no lion." (2) A handicapped creature sometimes has luck (or is lucky): "Even a blind sow finds an acorn." (3) To err is "human:" "Even the best horse stumbles once (or sometimes);" "Even clever hens sometimes lay (eggs) in nettles." (4) Bragging amounts to nothing: "Hens who cackle a lot lay no eggs."

Paragraph 5: The small animals (for example the lamb and the calf) for the most part symbolize human children: "The wolf eats an impertinent little sheep;" "A good cow sometimes has a bad calf;" "Whoever goes abroad as a calf comes home as a cow."

Chapter 10 — The future

10.4. Translate these sentences:

3. Tomorrow morning a Bible salesman will visit Fräulein Meier.
5. The first will be the last, and the last will be the first.
7. No sorrow will happen to *the just person* (dat.); but the godless will be filled with misfortune. (Do not translate the "pay attention" *es* at the beginning of the sentence.)
8. Who will neglect the sowing *because of* the sparrows?
9. Over all mountains peaks/ Is rest (or peace),/ In all the tree tops you (can) feel/ Barely a breath:/ The little birds are silent in the woods./ Just wait, soon/ You also will rest.

10.5. Vocabulary aid:

1. I will never understand the dramas *of* Georg Kaiser.
5. No one among these students will see the long film.
6. Tomorrow *they will fly* to Europe.
8. Tell me with whom you associate, and I'll tell you who you are.

Chapter 11 — Comparison of adjectives and adverbs

11.9. Translate these sentences:

4. *More people* drown in wine than in the Rhine.
6. There is no sweet*er* suffering than hope.
7. The love *of the citizens* (pl. gen.) is the country's strongest wall.

8. The cows *of other people* (pl. gen.) have larg*er* udders.
10. Experience is a *long* way. (*Weg* is mas. nom.; thus *langer* is *not* comparative.)
14. Convictions are more dangerous enemies *of truth* (fem. gen.) than lies.

11.10. Vocabulary aid:

1. Old friends and *old* wine (mas. nom.) are best.
4. One stupid person finds ten stupider people.
6. An ounce of (a) good example is worth more than a pound of words.
7. The mailman prefers to remain alone than in bad company (fem. dat.).

Chapter 12 — *Da-* and *wo*-compounds

12.2. Translate the following:

2. Do *you* believe in it?
4. Do *they* write about it?
5. We help *her* with it.
6. Don't *they* have any time for it?
8. She hopes for it.

12.6. Translate these sentences:

1. Wealth resembles sea water; the more one drinks (of) it, the thirstier one becomes.
3. The hen *likes to* lay (eggs) in the nest, in which eggs already are.
5. The mouth says it, but the heart knows *nothing of it*.
6. Whoever strives *for* a wreath *gets* a flower from it.
7. Hear (or heed) what others say, and reflect before you speak.
8. Fear of the Lord is a blessed garden; the *most beautiful* flowers grow in it.
10. *For what* is Fräulein Meier waiting? *For whom* is the mailman waiting?

Reading Selection: Der Elefant

Paragraph 2: The zoo lies in a small village, and it lacks some *of the most important* animals. For example, it lacks an elephant. (For three thousand rabbits are not a good substitute for it!) But finally the zoo gets the money for the purchase of an elephant. All the inhabitants of the village await the arrival of the elephant with joy.

Paragraph 7: But during the lecture of the teacher, something happens. The wind sets the elephant in motion, and so it rises (springs) *higher and higher* into the air. *For a while* the schoolchildren observe the four circles of the feet, the bulging belly and the trunk. But then the animal vanishes over the tree tops. Even the apes are astonished *by it*.

Paragraph 9: The schoolchildren of the village now do no more schoolwork. And they become scoundrels. Probably they now drink Vodka, and they smash windows. And now they no longer believe in elephants.

Chapter 13 — Verb prefixes

13.8. Translate these sentences (separable verbs):

1. The stupid ones never die out. (*aussterben*)
4. Where one sows love, there joy grows forth. (*hervorwachsen*)
5. There (or away) goes time, here comes death.
7. *Close your* mouth and *open your* eyes. (*zumachen* and *aufmachen*)
11. "Almost" kills no gnat. (*umbringen*)

13.10. Translate these sentences (inseparable verb prefixes):

1. The father of the mailman complains about the behaviour of his son.
2. Good swimmers drown first of all.
5. The mouse frightens *the elephant* (mas. acc.).

Chapter 14 — Verb tenses (part I)

14.12. Translate these sentences:

3. Whoever trusts in hope has built on ice.
4. The golden age was at the time when gold was not yet available.
8. After he had lived in Germany, the student studied the novels of Grimmelshausen.
9. *Did* the little geese *follow* their mother?
11. The *cleverest* students listened to it.
12. Then, a nice woman (fem. nom.) waited on you the whole time.
14. I have now, alas/ thoroughly studied, with ardent effort/ philosophy, law and medicine,/ and unfortunately even theology./ Thus stand I now, I poor fool/ and am none the wiser . . .

Chapter 15 — Verb tenses (part II)

15.6. State the infinitives of the following strong verbs:

bleiben, fliegen, lesen, reiten, stehlen, gehen, versprechen, nehmen, erfinden, trinken, tragen, rufen, beschreiben, fallen, scheinen, zerreißen, biegen, essen, kommen, mißverstehen.

15.11 Give the infinitive of the following separable verbs:

ausholen (weak), aufstehen (strong), absteigen (strong), zumachen (weak), aufbauen (weak), eingreifen (strong), einbrechen (strong), zuerkennen (irr. weak), umdeuten (weak), umbringen (irr. weak), mitgehen (strong), zudenken (irr. weak), vorweisen (strong), ausflippen (weak).

15.12. Translate these sentences:

2. Thankfulness *has climbed* (*steigen*) to heaven and *has taken* the ladder *with it* (*mitnehmen*).
3. When the day *broke* (*anbrechen*), still before the sun *had risen* (*aufgehen*), the mailman *wrote* (*schreiben*) a long, romantic poem.
4. A wolf in sleep never captured (*fangen*) a sheep.
6. A *sweet* song *has deceived* (*betrügen*) many a bird.
8. *No fool* (mas. nom.) has invented learning. (If "fool" had been accusative, the form would have been: *keinen Narren*).
9. When he became angry, the father of the mailman presented an image *of strong wrath* (mas. gen.), and he frightened Fräulein Meier.

15.14. Translate these sentences:

2. A tamed tongue is a rare bird.
5. With each *newly* learned language, you gain a new soul.

15.15 Vocabulary aid:

1. She did not know the answer.
3. The student was not familiar with the philosophy of Wittgenstein.
4. Haven't *they been* here?
5. The cactus plant has grown enormous.
7. The new car belongs to the student.

Chapter 16 — The plurals

16.4. Translate these sentences:

3. The dumbest farmers have the largest potatoes.
4. Dogs, farmers, and nobles close no doors.
6. The errors *of others* (pl. gen.) are good teachers.
9. The worm sees *the most beautiful apples* first.
12. No hour strikes *for the happy one* (mas. dat.).
15. Fleas get even into the fur of an aristocrat's dog.
16. Donkeys never eat nettles. Nettles never eat donkeys. (A comparable English translation might be: "Burros barely eat burrs . . .")

Chapter 17 — How to use a German dictionary

17.4. Adjectives and adverbs

1. The student was *just* here.
2. His relative is not at all similar to him.
3. She looks at him happily.
4. The *gentle* breezes are agreeable *to her*.

17.6. Nouns

1. Fräulein Meier has problems with her *Venetian blinds*.
3. The book *consists of* three volumes.
4. By no means will Fräulein Meier give up her cat.
5. The long explanation did not hold water.

17.8. Compound nouns

Declaration of Independence; doctrine of the origin of the earth; experience of being; change of form; designation of the saturation point.

17.11. Prepositions

1. Perhaps one will *repeal* the law. (*außer Kraft setzen* — to repeal, annul)
2. The mailman insists on the truth.
3. Kant had an important influence on Kleist.

17.13. Verbs

2. When did these events *occur*?
4. The negotiations *are a matter of* life and death. (*gehen* with the preposition *um* means *to be a matter of, to concern.* Although it is hard to find in dictionaries, it is often used in scholarly writings.)
5. To be a mother means to be a martyr.

Chapter 18 — Common suffixes

18.2. Translate these sentences:

2. Money comes in (*eingehen*) limping and goes away (*fortgehen*) dancing.
3. Build a golden bridge *for the* fleeing enemy.
6. If one bends justice, (then) *it* breaks.
7. *Everything* is fleeting, only *the eternal* is important.
9. One time is no time. (Or: Once is not enough.)
10. Poets are *shameless* with regard to their experienc*es*; they exploit (*ausbeuten*) them.

Chapter 19 — The modal auxiliaries

19.10. Translate these sentences:

1. One must believe the old *ones* (pl. dat.).
5. *On account of* a *rotten* branch, one must not cut down the tree.
6. One man who wants to (do something) can do more than ten who have to.
8. Need teaches the ape to fiddle.
12. The assertion of the mailman about Fräulein Meier may be true.
14. The mailman *had to* help Fräulein Meier with her homework.
16. Do you *want to* roam *further and further*?
    See, the good lies so near.
    Only learn to grasp fortune.
    For fortune is always there.

19.11. Vocabulary aid:

2. This evening the professor *is to* read us his *newest* poems.
4. She *had to* remain there for a long time.
5. Who was not permitted to eat the apple?
7. Can *you* believe them?
9. *For a month*, the mailman *had to* put up with bad weather.

Reading Selection: November

Paragraph 1: He was afraid, and when he said to someone: "It *has become colder*," he expected comfort.

Paragraph 7: One does not notice how the trees let the leaves fall. Suddenly they have no more. In April, they will have leaves again, perhaps already in March. One will see how they get leaves.

Paragraph 9: There will be no snow, there is no longer snow.

Paragraph 11: "One must accustom oneself to the snow," he said, "one must breathe *more deeply* and go *more quickly*." — "What should I buy the children for Christmas?" he asked.

Chapter 20 — The *zu*-construction

20.6. Translate these sentences:

1. In the house *of a thief* it is difficult to steal.
3. *No prophet* can look at the other without laughing. (Do not translate the "pay attention" *es*.)

6. Things which have happened *can not be changed*. (This *must* be translated passively.)
8. Not when it is dangerous to speak the truth does it find adherents most rarely, but when it is boring.
9. Three things *cannot be stopped*: water, fire, the crowd.
12. Curt put out his cigarette, and Nikolaus used the moment to get on (the bus) before him and to give Recha his hand, and without insistent haste to take the seat next to her.

20.7. Vocabulary aid:

3. Instead of working, Fräulein Meier wants to write a love poem.
4. Fräulein Meier does not need to study too much.
5. Fräulein Meier opens the door in order to greet the mailman.
6. Freedom *is not* (or cannot) *to be* lost.

Chapter 21 — Co-ordinating conjunctions

21.3. Translate these sentences:

3. Hear and *be* not deaf, but believe slowly.
7. Psychology had discovered unknown depths and abysses of the soul, but had also dissolved the firm, unerring self-awareness.
8. . . . without looking either to the right or to the left, he *crossed over* Trägerstraße and ascended the steps of the cathedral.
10. The King of France is a king of donkeys; for his subjects must do what he imposes on them; the King in England is a king of the people; for they consent to *that which* he imposes to them; but the Kaiser is a king of princes, for they do what pleases them.

Chapter 22 — Basic verb placement (part II)

22.5. Translate these sentences:

1. But it takes (*dazugehören*) more courage to make an end than (to make) a new verse: all doctors and poets know that.
8. Only God sees the *most secret* thoughts . . .
9. In this respect, the Dionysian man has a similarity to Hamlet: both have at one point taken a true look into the essence of things, they have recognized [what the essence of these things is], and it disgusts them to act; for their action can change *nothing* of the eternal essence of things, they consider it laughable or humiliating that it is expected of them to set right again the world that is out of joint. Recognition kills action, (for) the veil by means of illusion belongs to action — that is the lesson of Hamlet.

Chapter 23 — Dependent clauses (part I)

23.7. Translate these sentences:

1. Of what use is it if the cow gives a lot of milk if she knocks over the milk jug afterwards?
5. Do not throw away the old shoes before you have new ones.
6. After the father of the mailman had known Fräulein Meier for an entire year, he *had to* admit (*gestehen*) that she was at least amusing and good-natured.
8. Some people *pursue* (*nachrennen*) fortune and do not know that they have it at home.
10. For it was Rilke's painful experience, that in this present reality *the powers of the heart* (nom.) *no longer* animate the things, that world and life become more and more negligible.

Chapter 24 — Dependent clauses (part II)

24.6. Translate these sentences:

4. The *healthy one* does not know how rich he is.
8. *Everything that* is against the conscience has hard thorns.
9. One retains that which one has learned in youth the longest.
15. Wisdom is better than pearls, and everything that one may wish can not compare with it.
17. Whoever fights with monsters might see to it that in so doing he does not become a monster. And if you look into an abyss for a long time, the abyss also looks back into you.
18. Perhaps I know best why *man alone* laughs: he alone suffers so deeply that he *had to* invent laughter.

Chapter 25 — Dependent clauses (part III), relative clauses

25.12. Translate, noting the gender and case of each relative pronoun:

2. A wise person is a man *to whom* things taste just as they are.
6. Honor follows the person (mas. dat.) who flees it, and flees him, who hunts it.
7. There are no more wicked deaf ones than those who do not want to hear.
8. E. T. A. Hoffmann was an artiste of the uncanny, who consciously enjoyed his visions to the fullest and at the same time ironically reflected *them* (pl. acc.).
9. The first half of the 19th century stands strongly under the impression of the disappointment of the political independence movement since 1815,

which (acc.) *the unsuccessful revolutions of 1830 and 1848* (nom.) still intensified.

11. Woe to the country whose (neut. gen.) king (mas. nom.) is a child.

13. Who was the woman *whom* (acc.) the man loved?

14. Herzog Wilhelm von Breisach, who since his secret alliance with a countess named Katharina von Heersbruck from the house of Alt-Hüningen — who seemed to be beneath his rank — lived in animosity with his half-brother, the count Jacob the Redbeard, *returned* (*zurückkommen*) from a meeting towards the end of the 14th century when the night of Saint Remigius began to grow dark.

Reading Selection: Aus dem Erdbeben in Chili

I. It was at the Corpus Christi Festival, and the solemn procession of nuns, which the novices followed, had just begun, when the unfortunate Josephe, at the time of the ringing of the bells, collapsed in birth-pangs on the steps of the cathedral.

II. In order to translate this sentence, place the main verb (*stand*) immediately *after* the subject (ein junger Spanier namens Jeronimo Rugera). Otherwise, keep the word order essentially as it is.

III. Jeronimo stood by a pilaster and fortified the rope that was to tear him *from* this sorrowful world (fem. dat.) onto an iron clamp, when suddenly the largest part of the city sank with a crash and *buried everything* that breathed under its ruins.

Chapter 26 — The reflexive

26.6. Translate these sentences:

2. *Even* an expert has his master.

5. Luck fell in *his* lap.

6. Whoever robs the other *person* of his good name makes *him* poor and *himself* not rich (or: does not enrich himself).

7. Whoever wants to warm himself at the house of a miser must bring the fire with him.

9. The wild dog is a thorn in the mailman's eye. (Please translate idiomatically rather than literally.)

10. Charity begins with oneself (or: at home).

26.10. Translate these sentences:

3. *Be on guard against* those whom God has marked.

4. Since mankind has existed, man has rejoiced *too little*: that alone is our original sin.

5. Nietzsche's writings *appeared* (*sich darstellen*) as a powerful collection *of boldest* aphorisms, which through a unique artistic use of words maintain (a) fascinating precision.
6. Several years later, because the marquis [who had owned a castle] through war and a bad harvest had fallen into critical financial conditions, a Florentine knight *appeared* (*sich einfinden*) at his place, who wanted to buy the castle from him because of its beautiful location.

26.12. Translate this joke:

An old inhabitant of Munich gets into a conversation at the marketplace with a nice pigeon. Both get along excellently and would like to continue the acquaintance, and so the old man *invites* (*einladen*) the pigeon for the next afternoon for coffee at his place. The hour has arrived, he has set the table *nicely* and *specially* gotten a *few* flowers, but the one who does not appear is the pigeon (or: but the pigeon does not appear). Have I so erred in my pigeon-knowledge? the old man *asks* himself, while he sits with his coffee, which slowly grows cold. *Restlessly* he looks at his watch *more and more* frequently — finally, an hour later, the doorbell rings. The pigeon stands in front of the door and says with a charmingly embarrassed *smile*: "I beg you, excuse me that I have come so late. But it was such a glorious afternoon, and so I decided to walk!"

Reading Selection: Frühlingsglaube (Spring Faith)

The gentle breezes have awakened,
They rustle and weave day and night,
They create everywhere.
O *fresh* scent, oh new sound!
Now, poor heart, be not afraid!
Now everything, everything must change.

The world grows more beautiful with each day,
One doesn't know what still might become.
The blossoming will not end.
The farthest, deepest valley flourishes:
Now, poor heart, forget the torment!
Now everything, everything must change.

Chapter 27 — The overloaded adjective construction

27.11. Translate these sentences:

1. Josephe found her loved one in a dark (1) valley (2) shaded (3) by pines (4).

3. An old (1) castle (2) belonging to (3) a marquis (4) *was located* at the foot of the alps, near Locarno, in upper Italy.
6. Such (1) thoughts (2) which were quite useless (3) in his current situation (4) went through his head.
9. Opposite the door, a large (1) chalk drawing (2) executed (3) in bold strokes (4) was shown in the candlelight, which represented Napoleon, how he, in an awkward and despotic demeanor warmed by a fireplace his (1) feet (2) clad (3) in gun-boots (4). (Note: in order to avoid a misplaced modifier, you may put the verb elsewhere in the sentence.)
10. In spite of *its* pessimism, the novel became an agreeable (1) book (2) depicting (3) the charm of the old middle-class way of life with love and humor, patient prolixity and exquisite detail (4).
12. E. T. A. Hoffmann was a (1) sketcher (2) feared (3) because of his malicious caricatures (4) and a writer who was not able to work without many drinks.

27.12. Vocabulary aid:

1. Where is a beautiful park situated?
2. Fräulein Meier wants to know everything about geography in order to be able to write an essay about it.
4. The people (nom.) *watched* (**ansehen**) the (1) elephant (2) springing (3) high into the air (4).
5. The long (1) story (2) which is very interesting (3) to the student (4) deals with a struggle of freedom.
7. A year *ago* the student went to the theater every evening in order to see his favorite drama again and again.

Chapter 28 — The passive

28.8. Translate these sentences:

1. The tree *is recognized* by its fruit.
3. Donkeys are invited to the wedding only in order to carry water.
4. Innocence *is murdered* at the dance; on the way home, it (or she) *is buried*.
7. No murder *is committed among* thieves.
8. Whoever does not sow in the spring will reap nothing in the fall.
10. When the stone is out of the hand and the word is out of the mouth, they can no longer be brought back.
13. Memory is the only paradise from which we can not *be driven out*.
14. Fräulein Meier is loved by a sensitive man of the nineties.
15. But the German revolutionaries (around 1830), who were erroneously and involuntarily combined under the collective name "young Germany" were

more strongly bound up with the past (*dat.*) than they themselves suspected and ever wanted to admit.

20. Luke improved upon — Whoever lowers himself *wants to* be elevated. (Cf. Luke, 18.14 — But whoever lowers himself *will* be elevated.)

Chapter 29 — Constructions to be translated passively in English

29.6. Translate these sentences:

1. Whoever *is afraid* sees ghosts.
2. The stomach *cannot be forgotten.*
4. Our heart *is reflected* in prayer.
6. Fish are caught with the hook, people are caught with words.
7. Loving and praying cannot be forced.
9. Expressionism cannot be understood without Nietzsche's precedence.
10. Whatever is of straw must be on guard against the fire.
12. Old trees cannot be bent.

29.8. Translate these sentences (the fake passive):

1. Engaged is *not yet* married.
4. After the cow is stolen the stable is locked.
5. As long as one nourishes, he is honored, and as long as one gives, he is loved.

29.9. Vocabulary aid:

1. The love poems of the mailman cannot be forgotten.
2. Spring is a season which is joyously anticipated.
3. When *was* Fräulein Meiers Chinese pot broken?
6. The dog has returned the ball again and again.
7. The child *is afraid of* the dentist.
9. The novel *has* long *been forgotten.*
12. Who *wants to be elevated*?
14. One must scream loudly in order to *be* heard.

Reading Selection: Zwei Chassidische Geschichten

I. A poor lady apple dealer, whose stand was near the house of Rabbi *Chaim* of Zans, once came complaining to him: "Our Rabbi, I still have no money in order to buy for the Sabbath." "And your apple stand?" asked the Zaddik. "The people say," she answered, "my apples are bad, and they don't want to buy any." Immediately, the Rabbi ran to the street and called: "Who wants to buy good apples?" Immediately the crowd *was gathered* around him, the coins flew past (*herbeifliegen*) unseen and uncounted, and soon all the fruits were sold at double and triple the price. "Just see," he said to the woman *when* he turned to go, "your apples were good, the people just didn't know it."

II. On the evening of Yom Kippur, in Sassow everyone was gathered in the temple and was waiting for the Rabbi. The time passed, he did not come. One of the women said to herself: "It probably will still be a while before the service will begin, and I have hurried (so quickly), and my child has stayed home alone, therefore I want to quickly check on him (to see) whether he has not awakened, in a couple of minutes, I'll be back here again." She went there, listened to the door, it was quiet. Softly, she pressed down the latch, stuck her head in, there stood the Rabbi and held her child in his arms, whose crying had enticed him on the way to the temple; he had played with him and sung to him until he fell asleep.

Chapter 30 — The subjunctive (I)

30.8. Translate these sentences (subjunctive I):

2. The fox believes that everyone (mas. nom.) steals hens (pl. acc.) as he does.
4. When everyone says to you, you are drunk, go to sleep.
5. Whoever has ears, let him hear.
6. Children *believe*, when it rains in the village, it is raining in the whole world. (*Meinen* can *not* be an adjective because it does not precede *Kinder*; it *must* be a verb, because otherwise the clause would be without one and because it has a plural verb ending.)
7. Whoever *wants* a good messenger *should go* himself.
8. The *prophets* remind us: *Let us* not forget the future.
9. Better, a wolf should eat me than a lamb.
11. The Bible salesman *suggests* (*vorschlagen*): *Let us* read the Bible.
12. If one requires a thief, then let one take him from the gallows; when one has used (*ge*brauchen) him, then let one hang him up again.
15. The scholars are good clocks: only *let one take care* to wind *them* correctly! Then they indicate (*anzeigen*) the hour without error and in so doing make a modest noise.

Chapter 31 — The subjunctive (II):

31.7. Translate these sentences (subjunctive II):

2. A donkey remains a donkey, *even if* he *came* (or: were to come) to Rome.

4. When he thinks about Fräulein Meier's former sweetheart, the mailman looks *as if* he *had eaten* a crabapple.

5. I *would not know* how to live, were I not still a seer *of that* (*dessen*) which must come.

6. He looks *as if* the hens *had taken* the bread *from him*.

9. The dilettante asserts that he *speaks* Greek fluently.

10. No one *would have expected* that the insightful (1) essay (2) treating (3) the future of the earth (4) *had been written* by Fräulein Meier.

11. Why can the dog experience fear, but not repentance? Would it be correct to say, "Because he cannot speak?"

12. Jeronimo was rigid *with* horror; and immediately, as if his entire consciousness *had been shattered*, he now held onto the column on which he had wanted to die, in order not to fall off.

13. *Had* he only remained in the desert and far from the good and the just! Perhaps he would have learned to live and would have learned to love the earth — and laughter besides. He died too early: he himself would have renounced his teaching, *had* he reached my age.

Chapter 32 — Other subjunctive forms

32.6. Translate these sentences (modals):

1. If all liars ate (or: were to eat) oats, the horses would have to starve.

4. Who would like to go to Switzerland with Fräulein Meier?

7. The student wished he had studied Kant's philosophy.

8. It might not be possible to completely understand Hegel's *Phenomenology of Mind*.

9. They should certainly say what they mean.

32.8. Translate these sentences (conditional):

1. Zarathustra said, "I would only believe in a God who knew how to dance."

3. If God wanted to punish a country, he would take the wisdom from the rulers.

4. They are evil hens who would carry the eggs to the neighbor.

5. If the stomach of the old man *had been* full, his heart *would have been* joyous.

9. A Hasidic Tale:
Rabbi Chaim of Krosno, a disciple of the Baalschem, once *watched* (*zusehen*) a tightrope-walker with his disciples. He was so deeply absorbed in the spectacle that they asked him, what it *was* that attracted his eyes (acc.) to the foolish exhibition. "This man," he answered, "gambles with his life,

I could not say on what account. But certainly, while he goes on the rope, he cannot think about the fact that he is earning a hundred guilders with his action, for as soon as he thought this, he would fall off."

Reading Selection: The Swan

Paragraph 3: This one was an old man who had been lonely for years. When he took his position, it already began to become cold in the evenings. No one else came to the park. The old man went around the park, paid attention to the swan and sometimes looked at the stars. He was freezing. He wanted to just go to the small inn in the vicinity of the park. He was just ready to go when he remembered the swan. He was afraid it could be stolen during his absence. Then he would lose his job. Therefore he gave up his plan.

Paragraph 4: But the cold tormented him more and more and deepened his loneliness. Finally he decided to go to the inn together with the swan. Even if someone came to the park in order to enjoy the beautiful nature, he would not immediately notice the absence of the swan. "The night is starlit, but without moonlight, and we will return immediately," he thought and took the swan with him.

Paragraph 5: When he consumed his mutton with pleasure and contentment, it occurred to him that the swan looked at him quite strangely. He was sorry for the bird. As long as the latter reproachful glance rested on him, he couldn't eat. He called the waiter and ordered for the swan a (1) roll (2) dipped (3) in warm, sugared strong beer (4). The swan became joyous, and after they had ended their meal, both returned to their *post* (sing.) cheerful and satisfied.

Paragraph 8: With the thought of what a shudder must penetrate each one who in such a night came into contact with water, the old man became quite (emotionally) moved. Should the poor swan have nothing at all of life? Certainly he would rather sit in a warm corner and eat something.

Paragraph 11: When he sat by the shore and looked at the sky or at the empty, *bitterly* cold park, he suddenly felt a timid tug on his trouser leg. The swan had swum to the shore in order to remind him of something. So they went.

Chapter 33 — When the sentence starts with a verb

33.4. Translate these sentences:

1. If an old man dances, he makes a lot of dust.
2. If the cat does not want to mouse, let her out.
4. If a blind man leads *the other*, both will not wander far.
7. If you lack wine, then drink beer.
9. If I have no *cows*, then I have no effort.

10. If there were no fools, then there would be no wise ones.
11. The world is a drunken farmer; if one helps him into the saddle on the right, he falls off on the left.
12. If the poor person gets a piece of bread, then the dog tears it from his hand.
14. If your enemy is even only like an ant, then consider (or rank) him among the elephants, nevertheless.
15. If you are cheerful, say it further. If a stone oppresses you, carry it alone.

Chapter 34 — Other pronouns

34.7. Translate these sentences:

1. Whoever in his thirtieth year knows nothing, at forty is nothing, at fifty has nothing, learns nothing, becomes nothing, and comes to nothing.
2. Whoever wants to make everything right for everyone must get up early.
6. Whoever wants to go further than his horse can go should dismount and go on foot.
11. No crow pecks out the eyes of the other.
14. When Hegel explained everything real as reasonable, he supported a realism *that* (mas. nom.) no longer perceived literature, philosophy and religion as first life's works, but pushed political, economic and scientific interests (acc.) into the foreground.
15. Everything *could be* performed excellently, if one could do things twice.

Reading Selection: Nietzsche

Passage 11: Assuming that we say yes to a single moment, then we have with that said yes not only to ourselves but to all existence. For nothing stands for itself alone, neither in ourselves nor in things: and if only a single time our soul has trembled and sounded with joy like a lyre, then all *eternities* (pl.) were necessary in order to bring about this One occurrence — and in this single moment of our affirmation (or: saying yes) all eternity was redeemed, justified and affirmed.

Chapter 35 — Troublesome words

35.29. Translate these sentences:

2. If luck comes once, then five ill winds come after it.
4. A dog bites whoever has bad luck even if he is riding a camel.
5. "It is a peculiar apparatus," said the officer to the explorer and surveyed with a more or less admiring glance the (1) apparatus (2) which was nonetheless well-known (3) to him (4).
7. On a (1) note (2) written (3) by the mailman to Fräulein Meier (4) is written: "I love you."

8. It is better to ask twice than to go astray once.
9. One values health only after one has lost it.
10. Under the bridge, the weather-browned, white-bearded head of an oarsman *had appeared*, who — to infer from his awkward movements — was not familiar with the lagoon.
13. In my experience, one needs 30 hours for the learning of English, 30 days for French, 30 years for German. Either one should therefore reform this language, or one should place it among the dead languages, for nowadays only the dead have time enough to learn it.

35.30. Vocabulary aid:

1. Only after many years did the professor succeed in publishing her voluminous book.
2. *At* 4:30 we can depart again.
4. She looks at him as if he were crazy.
5. Because the student *had to* wait for the bus for an hour, he no longer wanted to travel with it (or: ride it).
7. *Whom* does the writer *want to* know?
8. At this time, the student had too much to do.
9. At the wedding celebration, much champagne *is* drunk.
10. Is each end as hard as every beginning?

Appendix H

General and Humanities Vocabulary

The General and Humanities Vocabulary consists of about 3,200 entries. In addition to the vocabulary words found in the exercise sentences and reading selections it includes several words you are likely to encounter in scholarly readings as well as the definitions most appropriate for such readings. Many of the words (especially those marked *) have been chosen because (1) they have a wide range of radically different meanings (**absetzen, einfallen, zugehen**), (2) they are easily confused with other words (**fordern, fördern**), or (3) they are false cognates (**konkurrieren, Prägnanz, sensibel**). While it is not necessary to memorize such words, you may wish to mark them in your dictionary. Also, take special note of words (**bringen, gehen, stellen, Zeit**) which you know already, but which have a variety of idioms associated with them. Words marked ** are most important for vocabulary building.

Note the following abbreviations:

adj. — adjective
adv. — adverb
aux.s. — auxiliary is **sein**
conj. — conjunction
pref. — prefix

prep. — preposition
suff. — suffix
v.i. — verb, intransitive
v.r. — verb, reflexive
v.t. — verb, transitive

For most nouns, the genitive and the plural endings are given in parentheses.
When verbs are separable, the prefix is hyphenated. Strong verbs are conjugated.
Note that all verbs with **sein** as an auxiliary are intransitive.

A

ab (adv.) — off, down, from; (sep. prefix) — downward motion, attrition, etc.

** der **Abend** (-s, -e) — evening

aber (conj.) — but, however, yet; (emphasis) — indeed

ab-gehen (irr. v.i., aux.s.) — to depart, leave; deviate, diverge

der **Abgrund** (-s, ⁻e) — abyss

ab-halten — to hold (a meeting)

* **ab-hängen (von)** — (irr. v.i.) — to depend on

* **ab-laufen** (irr. v.i.) — to elapse, lapse, expire; flow or run off, ebb

ab-lehnen (v.t.) — to decline, refuse; reject

* **ab-nehmen** (irr. v.t.) — to remove, take off; (v.i.) — to decrease, diminish, decline

der **Absatz** (-es, ⁻e) — pause, paragraph

ab-schließen (irr. v.t.) — to conclude, to settle

* der **Abschnitt** (-s, -e) — paragraph

* **ab-setzen** (v.t.) — to put down; to dismiss; to delete; (v.i.) — to pause, stop; (v.r.) — to settle, contrast

die **Absicht** (-en) — intention, purpose; **mit Absicht** — on purpose, deliberately

ab-sitzen — to get down, dismount

ab-sondern (v.t.) — to separate, isolate

ab-stürzen (i.) — to fall off

ab-weichen (irr. v.i., aux.s.) — to deviate, digress, depart

die **Abwesenheit** — absence

ab-ziehen (irr. v.t.) — to take off, remove; (v.i.) — to go away, leave, depart

ach — alas

achten (v.t.) — to consider; respect; (v.i.) **(auf)** — to pay attention or regard or heed to, take notice of

der **Advokat** (-en, -en) — lawyer

der **Affe** (-n, -n) — ape

ähneln (v.i.) (dat.) — to resemble

** **ahnen** (v.t.) — to suspect, surmise

ähnlich (adj.) — alike

** **aktuell** (adj.) — relevant, up-to-date

** **all** — all, every

** **alle** (pl.) — everyone; **alles** — everything

** **allein** (indecl. pred. adj.) — alone; (adv.) — only, merely, solely; (conj.) — but, however, nevertheless

allerdings (adv.) — to be sure

** **alles** — everything (34.1)

allgemein (adj.) — general

allzu — all too

die **Alpen** — alps

** **als** (conj.) — than; when; as

** **also** — so, thus

** **alt** — old

das **Alter** (-s, -) — age

das **Altertum** (-s, ⁻er) — antiquity

die **Ameise** (-n) — ant

amüsant — amusing

an (prep.) — with dat. or acc. (dat.) — **am 4. Juli** — on the 4th of July; **an sich** — in itself; (acc.) — on, onto

an-beten — to worship

an-bieten — to offer

der **Anblick** (-s, -e) — sight, view

an-brechen — to begin, start

****ander** (adj., pron.) — other; **am anderen Morgen** — on the next morning; **nichts anderes als** — nothing else but

****ändern** — to alter, change
anders (adv.) — differently

der **Anfang (-s, ⁻e) — beginning
an-fangen (irr. v.t.) — to begin, to do

der **Angeklagte** (-n, -n) — accused

die **Angel** (-n) — fishhook

* **angenehm** — agreeable

das **Angesicht** — face, countenance

* **an-führen** (v.t.) — to lead, to quote; deceive

* **an-gehen** (irr. v.i., aux.s.) to commence; (v.t.) — to concern

an-greifen (irr. v.t. & i.) — to seize, grasp; undertake; attack

die **Angst** (⁻e) — fear, anxiety

an-haben — to have on

der **Anhang** (-s, ⁻e) — appendix, addendum; supporters

an-klopfen (i.) — to knock

* **an-kommen** (irr. v.i. aux.s.) — to arrive; **(auf)** — to depend on, be a matter of; come upon

die **Anlage** (-n) — structure; outline; predisposition

der **Anlaß** (-sses, ⁻sse) — cause

an-legen (irr. v.t.) — to apply; to invest; to use; to arrange, establish

* **an-nehmen** (irr. v.t.) — to adopt; to take; to assume, suppose

die **Anrede** (-n) — speech, form of address

* der **Anschlag** (-es, ⁻e) — stroke; plan; estimate

der **Anschluß** (-sses, ⁻sse) — connection, contact

****an-sehen** — to look at

an-setzen (v.t.) — to attach, estimate; (v.i.) — to start

der **Anspruch** (-s, ⁻e) — claim, demand

anständig — decent, respectable

anstatt (prep., gen.) — instead of

an-stecken — to contaminate, be catching

die **Antike** — antiquity

der **Antrag** (-s, ⁻e) — proposition, proposal, petition

der **Antrieb** (-s, -e) — impulse, drive

die **Antwort (-en) — answer

antworten (tr. & i.) — to answer

an-wenden — to use

die **Anzeige** (-n) — notice; announcement; review

an-zeigen — to show

* **an-ziehen** — to pull; to attract

der **Apfel** (-s, ⁻) — apple

die **Arbeit (-en) — work

der **Arbeiter** (-s, -) — worker

arg — wicked

der **Arm** (-es, -e) — arm

****arm** — poor

die **Armut** — poverty

* die **Art** (-en) — species; class, type, kind; behavior

* **-artig** (suff.) — like, sembling

der **Arzt** (-es, ⁻e) — doctor, physician

der **Ast** (-es, ⁻e) — branch

der **Atem** (-s, -) — breath

der **Ästhet** (-en, -en) — aesthete

atmen — to breathe

auch (adv.) — also, too; (emph.) even; **auch wenn** — even if

auf (prep.) with dat. or acc. — on, onto, on top of; **auf diese Weise** — in this way; **auf jeden Fall** — in any event

auf (pref.) — up, upward, opening; end something; sudden or brief action

auf-bauen (v.i.) — to erect, construct; (v.r.) — to be based on

auf-bewahren — to protect

auf-blasen — to inflate

auf-brechen — (i., aux.s.) — to leave

auf-bringen (irr. v.t.) — to raise, bring up; procure, summon; enrage

auf-erlegen (i.) — to impose

* **auf-fallen** (irr. v.i., aux.s.) — to attract notice or attention; to strike

auf-fassen (v.t.) — grasp, view, comprehend, regard, interpret

* **auf-führen** (v.t.) — present, perform; quote

die **Aufgabe** (-n) — task; giving up

auf-geben (irr. v.t.) — to give; to give up, surrender

auf-gehen (irr. v.i., aux.s.) — to rise; to open; to become apparent

auf-halten — to delay, to stop

auf-heben (irr. v.t.) — to lift or raise up; to terminate, to repeal

auf-hören (v.i.) — to stop

die **Aufklärung** — the Enlightenment

die **Auflage** (-n) — edition

auf-lösen (v.t.) — to dissolve, resolve; (v.r.) — to disperse

auf-machen —to open

die **Aufnahme** (-n) — adoption, acceptance; inclusion

auf-passen (v.i.) — to pay attention to

auf-prägen (v.t.) — to impress

auf-räumen (v.t.) — to do away with

* der **Aufriß** (-sses, -sse) — outline, summary

der **Aufsatz** (-es, ̈-e) — essay, article, treatise

auf-schauen (i.) — to look up

auf-schieben (irr. v.t.) — to delay

der **Aufstand** (-es, ̈-e) — revolt, rebellion

auf-stehen (i., aux.s.) — to get up

auf-stellen (v.t.) — to erect, assemble; (v.r.) — place or position oneself; to nominate

auf-treten (irr. v.i., aux.s.) — to tread; to appear; to occur

auf-tun — to open

auf-wärmen — to warm up

auf-wecken — to wake up

auf-weichen — to soften

auf-ziehen — to wind

aufs Spiel setzen — to gamble

das **Auge** (-s, -n) — eye

der **Augenblick** (-es, -e) — moment

** **aus** (prep.) with dat. out of, from; **aus Berlin kommen** — to come from Berlin; **aus Erfahrung lernen** — to learn by or from experience; **aus verschiedenen Gründen** — for various reasons; **von Grund aus** — thoroughly

aus (pref.) — movement away from; movement forward; completion; choice from several possibilities

aus-beuten — to exploit

aus-breiten — to stretch (v.r.) — to extend

aus-drücken (v.r.) — to express oneself

auseinander-setzen (v.t.) — to explain; (v.r.) — to come to terms with; to argue

* der **Ausfall** — result, outcome; attack

aus-führen — to carry out, execute; to explain

ausführlich — detailed

* die **Ausgabe (-n)** — giving out, distribution; edition (of a book)

* **aus-gehen** (irr. v.i., aux.s.) — to go out; to end; ... **auf** — to aim at; ... **von** — to start with

ausgezeichnet (adj.) — excellent

aus-hacken — to peck out

aus-kosten — to experience

die **Auskunft** (⁻e) — information

das **Ausland (-s)** — foreign countries

aus-legen (v.t.) — to lay out; to explain, interpret

aus-lernen (i.) — to finish learning

aus-machen (v.t.) — to make up, form; decide, determine, agree on

die **Ausnahme (-n)** — exception

aus-reichen (i.) — to be enough

aus-reißen — to pull out

der **Ausruf (-s, -e)** — exclamation; proclamation

der **Ausschnitt (-s, -e)** — extract, excerpt, detail (from an illustration)

****aus-sehen** (irr. v.i.) — to appear

****außer** (prep.) with dat. — out of, outside, except

****außerdem** (adv.) — besides, moreover

das **Äußere** — outward appearance

äußern (v.t.) — to express; (v.r.) to express oneself

äußerst (attrib., adj.) — farthest, utmost, extreme; (adv.) — extremely

aus-sprechen (irr. v.r.) — to speak one's mind; to grant

aus-stehen (irr. v.t.) — to endure, bear; (v.i.) — to be overdue

aus-strecken — to extend

aus-teilen — to distribute, share

der **Austritt (-s, -e)** — escape, resignation, withdrawal

aus-üben (v.t.) — to practice, carry out; to exert

der **Ausweg (-s, -e)** — way out, solution

B

der **Bach (-es, ⁻e)** — brook

backen, bäckt, backte, hat gebacken — to bake

das **Bad (-es, ⁻er)** — bath

die **Bahn (-en)** — path; arena; train, course

****bald** (adv.) — soon; almost

* der **Band (es, ⁻e)** — volume

das **Band (-es, -e)** — tie, bond

bang — anxious

bannen (v.t.) — to banish; to charm; to captivate; to excommunicate

der **Bär (-en, -en)** — bear

barfuß — barefoot

der **Bart (es, ⁻e)** — beard

der **Bauch (-es, -e)** — stomach

bauen (v.t.) — to build, construct; (v.i.) — to build; to depend on

der **Bauer (-n or -s, -n)** — farmer, peasant

die **Baukunst** (-̈e) — architecture

der **Baum** (-es, -̈e) — tree

die **Baumkrone** (-n) — treetop

be- (pref.) — turns v.i. into v.t.; completion; around, on all sides; supply

beachten — to notice, regard, heed

beanspruchen (v.t.) — to claim, have a claim to

der **Becher** (-s, -) — cup, mug

bedauerlich — deplorable

bedenken (irr. v.t.) — to consider, remember (v.r.) — to reflect

bedeuten (v.t.) — to mean, signify

die **Bedeutung (-en) — meaning, significance; importance

* **bedingen** (v.t.) — to cause, determine, condition; to demand

bedürfen (v.i.) — to need, want, require (with gen.)

beeilen (t. & r.) — to hurry

beenden — to end

* **befassen** (v.r.) — to occupy or concern oneself with, engage in

befehlen, befiehlt, befahl, hat befohlen — to command

****befinden** (irr. v.t.) — to find, deem, consider; (v.r.) — to be, to be situated

befürchten — to fear

begeben — to negotiate (v.r.) — to proceed; **es begab sich, daß** — it happened . . .

begegnen (v.i. aux.s.) with dat. — to meet; to occur; (v.r.) — to concur

begleiten — to accompany

begraben, begräbt, begrub, hat begraben — to bury

begreifen, begriff, hat begriffen (v.t.) — to understand, grasp

der **Begriff** (-s, -e) — idea, notion; concept, understanding

begründen (v.t.) — to found, establish; to substantiate

behaglich — comfortable, cozy

* **behalten, behält, behielt, hat behalten** — to retain

****behandeln** (v.t.) — to treat, deal with

behaupten (v.t.) — to maintain, assert

die **Behauptung** (-en) — assertion

beherrschen (v.t.) — to rule over, to control, govern, dominate

behindert — handicapped

bei (prep.) with dat. — at, while, during

bei (pref.) — beside, additional; nearness; tendency toward; add something in addition

****beide** — both (adj.)

der **Beifall** (-s) — approval, applause

bei-legen (v.t.) — to add, join; to attribute, ascribe, bestow

beinah(e) (adv.) — almost

beiseite (adv.) — aside

das **Beispiel (-s, -e) — example; **zum Beispiel** (**z.B.**) — for example

beißen (**biß, hat gebissen**) — to bite

der **Beitrag** (-̈s, -e) — contribution; article

bejahen — to affirm

bekannt (adj.) — known, familiar

bekennen (irr. v.t.) — to admit, confess

beklagen — to lament, complain about

**bekommen (irr. v.t.) — to receive, get

bekümmern (v.t.) — to worry; (v.r.) — to concern oneself with

bekunden (v.t.) — to express, state; (v.r.) — to become evident

belasten (v.t.) — to burden

beleben — to animate

belegen (v.t.) — to occupy, impose; to take, enroll in

beleuchten (v.t.) — to light; to illuminate, to elucidate

beliebt (-s, -e) — popular

bellen (i.) — to bark

bemächtigen (v.r.) — to seize

**bemerken (v.t.) — to notice

bemühen (v.t.) — to trouble; (v.r.) to concern oneself

benachbart — neighboring

benehmen (v.r.) — to behave

das Benehmen (-s) — conduct, agreement

beneiden — to envy

benutzen (v.t.) — to use

beobachten (v.t.) — to observe; to adhere to

die Beobachtung (-en) — observation

berechnen (v.t.) — to calculate; to mean, intend

der Bereich (-s, -e) — district, region; field, range, extent

bereit (adj.) — willing, prepared

bereiten (v.t.) — to make ready, to prepare; to give, offer, cause

bereits — already

der Berg (-es, -e) — mountain

der Bericht (-es, -e) — report, survey, commentary

berücksichtigen (v.t.) — to consider, take into account

der Beruf (-es, -e) — vocation, calling, profession

beruhen (v.i.) — to be based or founded on

berühmt (adj.) — famous

* berühren (v.t.) — to touch, allude or refer to; concern; (v.r.) — to touch; to be in accord with

die Berührung (-en) — touch, contact

beschäftigen (v.t.) — to occupy

beschatten — to shade

der Bescheid (-es, -e) — information, answer

bescheiden — modest

beschließen (r.) — to conclude

beschreiben (irr. v.t.) — to describe

beschwerlich (adj.) — troublesome

besinnen (irr. v.t.) — to think about, consider

besitzen, besaß, hat besessen — to possess

besonder — particular, special

**besonders (adv.) — especially

besorgen — to procure

besprechen (irr. v.t.) — to discuss; to review; (v.r.) — to confer

bessern — to improve

die Besserung (-en) — improvement

beständig (adj.) — constant, invariable, lasting

bestätigen (v.t.) — to confirm

* bestehen (irr. v.t.) — to encounter, undergo; overcome (v.i.) — to be, exist, continue; bestehen auf — to insist on; bestehen aus — to consist of

bestellen (v.t.) — to order; to arrange, prepare

bestimmen (v.t.) — to determine; to grant; to designate; to allocate; to specify, define

bestimmt — definitely

besuchen — to visit

betätigen (v.t.) — to operate, bring about

betäuben — to daze

beten (i.) — to pray

das **Bethaus** — temple

betonen (v.t.) — to emphasize

* der **Betracht** — **in Betracht kommen** — to be possible; **außer Betracht lassen** — to disregard; **in Betracht ziehen** — to take into account

betrachten (v.t.) — to look at; to examine

betreffen (irr. v.t.) — to concern

der **Betrieb** (-es, -e) — business, work, operation

betrügen, betrog, hat betrogen — to deceive

der **Bettler** (-s, -) — beggar

beurteilen (v.t.) — to judge, assess

die **Bevölkerung** (-en) — population

bevor (conj.) — before

bevorzugen (v.t.) — to prefer, to favor

bewahren (v.t.) — to guard; to preserve; to keep, to protect

bewähren (v.r.) — to prove one's ability; to prove effective

die **Bewegung** (-en) — movement

der **Beweis** (-es, -e) — proof

bewilligen (v.t.) — to grant

bewußt (adj. & adv.) — conscious, deliberate, aware

das **Bewußtsein** (-s) — consciousness

bezahlen (v.t.) — to pay

bezeugen (v.t.) — to attest

* **beziehen** (irr. v.t.) — to enter, to adopt; to get; **beziehen auf** — to relate to

die **Beziehung** (-en) — relationship

* der **Bezug** (-es, ̈e) — reference

die **Bibel** (-n) — Bible

der **Bibelverkäufer** (-s, -) — Bible salesman

bieder (adj.) — honest, conventional, conservative

biegen, bog, hat gebogen — to bend

bieten (irr. v.t.) — to offer; to present

das **Bild (-es, -er) — picture, image; portrait; metaphor

bilden (v.t.) — to form, shape; to educate, develop; (v.r.) — to arise, be created

der **Bildhauer** (-s, -) — sculptor

die **Bildung** (-en) — education, culture; form, organization

billig (adj.) — just, fair; cheap, reasonable

binden, band, hat gebunden — to bind

binnen (prep.) with gen. or dat. — within

* der **Biograph** (-en, -en) — biographer

die **Biographie** (-n) — biography

bis (prep.) with acc. — as far as; until; (conj.) — until

bisher (adv.) — until now

bißchen (adj.) — little bit

bitten (irr. v.t.) — to ask (**um**) for

bitter — bitter

* **blank** (adj.) — shining, bright

das **Blatt** (-s, ̈er) — page, leaf; newspaper

bleiben, blieb, ist geblieben (v.i.)
— to remain, stay, continue; to
be left over

bleich — pale

der **Blick** (-es, -e) — look, view,
glance

blicken (v.i.) — to view

blind — blind

der **Blitz** (-es, -e) — lightning

* **bloß** (adj.) — bare; (adv.) —
merely, only, solely, simply

blühen (v.i.) — to blossom, to
flourish

die **Blume** (-n) — flower

das **Blut** (-es) — blood

bluten (i.) — to bleed

der **Boden** (-s, ⸚) — ground,
foundation; **zu Boden schlagen**
— to strike down, to shatter

der **Bogen** (-s, -or ⸚) — sheet of
paper; curve; arch

****böse** (adj.) — bad, evil, wicked,
angry

boshaft — malicious

botanisch — botanic

der **Bote** (-n, -n) — messenger

die **Botschaft** (-en) — message;
news

das **Brandopfer** — burnt offering,
sacrifice

der **Bratenduft** — smell of cook-
ing

die **Bratwurst** (⸚e) — sausage

****brauchen** (v.t.) — to need, want,
require; **brauchen nicht zu** —
to not have to

der **Bräutigam** (-s, -e) —
bridegroom

* **brav** (adj.) — honest, good

brechen, brach, hat gebrochen
— to break; (v.r.) — to refract

****breit** (adj.) — broad, wide

die **Breite** — width, expanse

brennen, brannte, hat gebrannt
— to burn

der **Brief (-es, -e) — letter, epis-
tle, document

der **Briefträger** (-s, -) — mailman

die **Brille** (-n) — eyeglasses

* **bringen, brachte, hat gebracht**
(v.t.) — to bring, to take; to
produce; **an den Tag bringen**
— to expose; **in Gang bringen**
— to start; **in Verdacht bringen**
— to cast suspicion on; **ihn um
etwas bringen** — to deprive
him of something; **zu Ende
bringen** — to finish; **etwas
zustande bringen** — to get
something done

das **Brot** (-es, -e) — bread

die **Brücke** (-n) — bridge

brüllen (i.) — to roar

der **Brunnen** (-s, -) — spring,
well

* das **Buch** (-es, ⸚er) — book

die **Bühne** (-n) — stage, scene,
arena

der **Bund** (-es, ⸚e) — agreement,
bond, alliance

Bundes- (in compounds) — federal

der **Bürger** (-s, -) — citizen,
bourgeois

bügerlich (adj.) — civic, civil;
middle class

die **Bürgerlichkeit** — conven-
tionality, plainness

der **Bürgermeister** (-s, -) —
mayor

der **Busch** (-es, ⸚e) — bush

die **Buße** (-n) — penitence

C

der **Chef** (-s, -s) — boss, chief

* der **Christ (-en, -en)** — Christian
das **Christentum (-s)** — Christianity

D

** **da** (adv.) — there; here; then, in that, for that reason; (conj.) — since, because
dabei (adv.) — near it, at the same time; in addition, moreover; yet
das **Dach (-es, ⸚er)** — roof
dafür (adv.) — for it or them; for that reason; in favor of
dagegen (adv.) — against it or them; (conj.) — on the contrary
* **daher** (adv.) — from that place; therefore; that is why
dahin (adv. and pref.) — there, to that place
dahinter-kommen (v.i., aux.s.) — to get at the truth of
damalig (adj.) — of that time, then
** **damals** (adv.) — then; **erst damals** — only then; **schon damals** — even then
die **Dame (-n)** — woman, lady
** **damit** (adv.) — with it or them; thereupon; (conj.) — so that
dämmern (i.) — to dawn; to grow dark
die **Dämmerung** — twilight
der **Dämon (-s, -en)** — demon
danach (adv.) — after that, towards it; accordingly
die **Dankbarkeit** — thankfulness
danken (v.i.) — to thank; (v.t.) — to owe
** **dann** (adv.) — then, at that time, besides

dar-stellen (v.t.) — to represent, depict; (v.r.) — to appear, to be apparent or obvious
* **darum** (adv.) — around it or them; (conj.) — therefore
* das **Dasein (-s)** — existence, being
die **Daseinsform (-en)** — form of existence
** **daß** (conj.) — that; so that
* **dauern** (v.i.) — to last
dazu (adv.) — for it or them; besides, in addition
dazu-gehören — to take
decken (v.t.) — to cover
** **dein** — your
dementsprechend (adj.) — appropriate; (adv.) correspondingly
demnach (adv., conj.) — accordingly, consequently; therefore
** **denken, dachte, hat gedacht** (v.t. or i.) — to think; consider; imagine; mean; (v.r.) — to think, imagine, believe
** **denn** (conj.) — for, because; **es sei denn** — unless, except
dennoch (conj.) — yet, still, however, nevertheless
** **der** — the
derart (adv.) — in such a way or manner
** **derselbe (dieselbe, dasselbe, dieselben)** — the same
** **deshalb** (adv.) — on this account; (conj.) — therefore
despotisch — despotic
desto (adv.) — all the (more); **je ... desto** — the ... the
deswegen — for that reason

deuten (v.t.) — to explain, interpret; (v.i.) — to point, indicate, signify

deutlich — distinct, clear (adj.)

deutsch (adj.) — German

Deutschland — Germany

dicht (adj.) — dense, compact; (adv.) — near, close

* der **Dichter** (-s, -) — poet, writer

die **Dichtung** (-en) — poetry, literary works; fiction; imagination

* **dick** — thick, fat

der **Dieb** (-es, -e) — thief

dienen (v.i.) — to serve

dieser (m.), **diese** (f.), **dieses** (n.) (dem. adj.) — this; **diese** (pl.) — these

* die **Diktatur** (-en) — dictatorship

das **Ding** (-es, -e) — object, thing, matter

der **Direktor** (-s, -en) — director

der **Diskurs** (-es, -e) — discourse

doch (conj.) — but, though, nevertheless; (adv.) — of course; (part.) — just; **wenn doch** — if only.

der **Dom** (-s, -e) — cathedral, dome

der **Donner** (-s) — thunder

das **Donnerwetter** — scene

doppelt (adj.) — double; (adv.) — twice

das **Dorf** (-s, ¨er) — village

der **Dorn** (-s, -en) — thorn

** **dort** (adv.) — there, over there

das **Drama** (-s, -men) — drama

der **Drang** (-es, ¨e) — pressure; urge, craving; **Sturm und Drang** — Storm and Stress

draußen — outside

drehen (v.t.) — to turn; (v.r.) — **es dreht sich um** — it is a question of

drei — three

dreifach — threefold

dreitägig — three day

* **dringen, drang, ist gedrungen** (v.i.) — to penetrate, enter; (aux.h.) — to beg, plead, insist on

drohen (i.) — to threaten

drücken (v.t.) — to press; to push stamp; (v.i.) — to be oppressive

der **Druckfehler** (-s, -) — misprint

** **du** — you

der **Duft** (-es, ¨e) — scent, smell

dumm — dumb

die **Dummheit** (-en) — stupidity

dumpf (adj.) — dull; vague; stifling

** **dunkel** (adj.) — dark, dim, gloomy, sinister; vague; dubious

dünken (v.i.) — to seem, look, appear

durch (prep.) — with acc. — through, throughout, as a result of, by means of; (adv.) — thoroughly

durch- (pref.) — through; across; thoroughness

durchaus (adv.) — throughout, thoroughly, by all means; quite; **durchaus nicht** — by no means

durch-dringen (irr. v.i., aux.s.) — to penetrate; win acceptance; (v.t. insep.) — to permeate, pervade

durcheinander — at random; mixed up

durch-führen (v.t.) — accomplish, execute

durch-gehen (irr. v.i., aux.s.) — to pass through; **durchgehen lassen** — to let pass, to overlook; (v.t. sep.) — read over or through; to check

durchgehend (adj.) — continuous

durch-kommen (irr. v.i., aux.s.) — to pass or get through; to appear, to reveal itself; to succeed

durch-lesen — to read through

durch-machen (v.t.) — to finish, accomplish; undergo, suffer

der **Durchschnitt (-s, -e)** — cross-section, profile

durchschnittlich — average

* **durch-setzen** (v.t.) — to accomplish; (insep.) — to permeate, pervade; (v.r. sep.) — to be successful

durchsichtig (adj.) — clear

** **dürfen** (modal v.) — may, might; be allowed or permitted to; **dürfte** (subj. II) — conjecture — might, could

dürsten — to thirst

durstig — thirsty

E

die **Ebbe (-n)** — ebb

* **eben** (adj.) — even, level; (adv.) — just, precisely, exactly; **eben erst** — only just, just now

ebenso (adv.) — likewise, in the same way

echt (adj.) — genuine, authentic

die **Ecke (-n)** — corner

edel (adj.) — noble

die **Edelleute** — nobles, noblemen

egal (adj.) — equal, alike, all the same

die **Egalität** — equality

** **ehe** (conj.) — before

die **Ehe** — marriage

ehemalig — former

* **eher** (adv.) — sooner; more likely; rather; **eher als** — rather than; more

die **Ehre (-n)** — honor

die **Ehrfurcht** — reverence

ehrlich (adj.) — honest

das **Ei (-s, -er)** — egg

die **Eiche (-n)** — oak

der **Eid (-es, -e)** — oath

der **Eifer (-s)** — eagerness, zeal

die **Eifersucht** — jealousy

eigen (adj.) — own; peculiar, characteristic

* **-eigen** (suff.) — property of, belonging to

eigenartig — peculiar, odd

die **Eigenschaft (-en)** — quality, attribute

** **eigentlich** (adj.) — actual; (adv.) — actually, really

eigentümlich (adj.) — belonging to; peculiar to; strange

eignen (v.r.) — to be suitable; (v.i.) — to be characteristic of

ein- (pref.) — motion into

** **ein** — a, an, one; **ein so** — such a

einander — one another; each other

ein-bilden (v.t.) — to imagine; to be conceited

ein-brechen — to break in

eindeutig (adj.) — clear, plain, unequivocal; definite

* **ein-dringen** (irr. v.i., aux.s.) — to penetrate; to study closely; to attack; to entreat

der **Eindruck (-es, ˵e)** — impression

****einfach** (adj.) — simple; single
der **Einfall** (-s, ⸚e) — sudden
idea, brain-wave; collapse
* **ein-fallen** (irr. v.i., aux.s.) — to
occur to; to collapse, to invade
ein-finden (r.) — to appear
* der **Einfluß** (-sses, ⸚sse) —
influence
ein-führen (v.t.) — to introduce;
to insert in
die **Einführung** — introduction
der **Eingang** (-s, ⸚e) — entrance;
introduction; beginning
ein-gehen (irr. v.i., aux.s.) — to
understand; to arrive; to die;
to be credible to; to consider
carefully; (v.t.) — to enter
into
ein-greifen (irr. v.i.) — to influence; to interfere in; to intrude
die **Einheit** (-en) — unity
ein-holen — to catch up with; to
gather
einig (adj.) — united
****einige** (adj.) — some, a few
ein-kaufen — to buy
der **Einklang** — harmony, agreement
ein-laden — to invite
ein-lassen (irr. v.t.) — to let in;
(v.r.) — to become involved
with
****einmal** (adv.) — once; **auf einmal**
— at once; **nicht einmal** — not
even; **noch einmal** — once
again
**ein-nehmen, nahm ein, hat ein-
genommen** (v.t.) — to take in;
to seize, to take up
ein-ordnen (v.t.) — to arrange; to
classify, fit in
ein-prägen (v.t.) — to imprint, to
impress

ein-reißen — to pull down
ein-richten (v.t.) — to arrange,
adjust; (v.r.) — to settle down,
to establish oneself; to prepare
for
****einsam** — lonely
die **Einsamkeit** — loneliness
ein-schlafen (i.) — to fall asleep
* **ein-schließen, schloß ein, hat
eingeschlossen** (v.t.) — to lock
up; to surround; to include, to
contain
ein-sehen (irr. v.t.) — to realize,
see
einsichtsvoll — insightful
ein-sperren — to lock up
ein-setzen (v.t.) — to appoint; to
use; (v.i.) — to start
****einst** (adv.) — once; some day
ein-stellen (v.t.) — to stop, to discontinue; to adjust; (v.r.) — to
appear; to adopt
einstimmig (adj.) — unanimous
ein-treten (irr. v.i., aux.s.) — to
occur, happen; to enter, step in;
eintreten für — to intercede for
der **Einwand** (-s, ⸚e) — objection
ein-wirken (v.i.) — influence,
affect
* der **Einwurf** (-s, ⸚e) — objection;
insertion
einzeln (adj.) — single, individ-
ual; isolated; (adv.) — sepa-
rately, one at a time; **im
einzelnen** — in detail
****einzig** (adj.) — only, absolute;
(adv.) — only
das **Eis** (-es) — ice
ekeln — to disgust
der **Elefant** (-en, -en) — elephant
elend — miserable
die **Eltern** (plural) — parents

empfänglich (adj.) — susceptible, receptive

empfehlen, empfahl, hat empfohlen (v.t.) — to recommend; (v.r.) to recommend oneself

empfinden, empfand, hat empfunden (v.t.) — to feel, perceive

das Ende (-s, -n) — end, conclusion; **letzten Endes — in the long run; **Ende der zwanziger Jahre** — in the late 20's

**endlich (adj.) — ultimate, final; (adv.) — finally

eng — narrow

engagiert (adj.) — committed, involved

der **Engel (-s, -)** — angel

ent- (pref.) — negation, reversal, removal; separation; emergence; initiation; intensification

entblößen (v.t.) — to uncover

entdecken (v.t.) — to discover

entfallen (irr. v.i., aux.s.) — to not apply; **jemandem entfallen** — to slip one's mind

entfalten (v.t.) — to unfold; to develop

entfernen (v.t.) — to move away; to remove; (v.r.) — to withdraw, to depart

entfremden (v.t.) — to alienate

entgegen (adv., prep.) with dat. — towards; against

entgegen- (pref.) — approach or opposition

entgegen-setzen (v.t.) — to oppose

entgegen-stellen (v.t.) — to contrast; (v.r.) — to oppose

entgegen-treten (irr. v.i. aux.s.) — to oppose, to confront

entgegnen (v.t. and v.i.) — to answer

entgehen, entging, ist entgangen (v.i.) — to escape, avoid, elude

enthalten (t.) — to contain; (r.) — to refrain (from)

entlang (adv. prep) with acc. — along

entlassen — to dismiss, fire

entnehmen, entnahm, hat entnommen (v.t.) — to deduce, infer; to take from

entreißen — to tear away from

entrinnen (i., aux.s.) — to escape

entsagen (v.i.) — to renounce

entscheiden (irr. v.t., i. & r.) — to decide

entschließen (irr. v.r.) — to decide

entschuldigen — to excuse

das **Entsetzen (-s)** — horror, terror

entsetzen (v.t.) — to horrify

entsprechen, entsprach, hat entsprochen (v.i.) — to agree, to correspond

* **entstehen, entstand, ist entstanden** (v.i.) — to originate; to result; to develop

die **Enttäuschung** — disappointment

**entweder . . . oder — either . . . or

entwerten (v.t.) — to devalue

entwickeln (v.t.) — to develop, to evolve

entziehen, entzog, hat entzogen (v.t.) — to remove, withdraw, to deprive; (v.r.) — to elude

der **Epigone (-n, -n)** — undistinguished descendent or follower

er- (pref.) — to produce, bring about, die, kill

**er — he, it

erbauen — to build

der **Erbe (-n, -n)** — heir, successor

das **Erbe (-s)** — heritage, inheritance

erbleichen (i., aux.s.) — to turn pale

** die **Erde (-n)** — earth, ground, world

das **Ereignis (-sses, -sse)** — event

* **erfahren, erfuhr, hat erfahren (v.t.)** — to experience, discover, undergo, learn

die **Erfahrung (-en)** — experience; empirical knowledge

erfassen (v.t.) — to seize, grasp; to understand; to include

erfinden, erfand, hat erfunden (v.t.) — to invent

der **Erfolg (-es, -e)** — success, result, outcome, effect

erforderlich — necessary

erforschen (v.t.) — to investi-gate

erfreuen — to delight, (r) (with gen.) to enjoy

erfüllen (v.t.) — to fill; to fulfill (v.r.) — to come true

ergänzen (v.t.) — to complete, supplement

* **ergeben, ergab, hat ergeben (v.t.)** — to produce, yield; (v.r.) — to be result of, ensue; to surrender

das **Ergebnis (-ses, -se)** — result, outcome

ergreifen — to seize, to grasp

erhaben (adj.) — elevated, lofty

erhalten — to preserve; to receive

erheben (irr. v.t.) — to raise, ascertain; (v.r.) — to rise up, revolt

erhöhen — to elevate

erholen (r) — recover, relax

erhören — to hear

** **erinnern (v.t.)** — to remind; (v.r.) — to remember

die **Erinnerung** — memory

erkaufen — to buy

** **erkennen, erkannte, hat erkannt (v.t.)** — to recognize; **erkennen lassen** — to make clear; **es läßt sich nicht erkennen** — one cannot tell

die **Erkenntnis (-se)** — knowledge; perception, realization

** **erklären (v.t.)** — to explain, interpret; to declare, state

erkundigen (v.r.) — to inquire

erlauben (v.t.) — to permit

erläutern (v.t.) — to explain, comment

erleben (v.t.) — to experience

* das **Erlebnis (-sses, -sse)** — occurrence, experience

erledigen (v.t.) — to deal with; settle

erlösen (v.t.) — to save, free, redeem; liberate

erniedrigen — to lower, humble

ernst (adj.) — earnest, serious

eröffnen (v.t.) — to open, to start; to disclose or make known

erregen (v.t.) — to excite, provoke

** **erreichen (v.t.)** — to reach, attain

der **Ersatz (-es)** — substitute

ersaufen (i., aux.s.) — to drown

** **erscheinen (irr. v.i., aux.s.)** — to seem, appear

die **Erscheinung (-en)** — phenomenon

erschlagen (past participle) — slain

erschließen (irr. v.i.) — to develop, infer

erschrecken (t. & i.) — to frighten

erst (adj.) — first; (adv.) — not until, only; **eben erst — just now

erstaunlich — astonishing

erstechen, erstach, hat erstochen — to stab

erstehen, erstand, ist erstanden (v.i.) — to arise, to result

ertappen — to catch

erteilen (v.t.) — to give; impart

erwachsen, erwuchs, ist erwachsen (v.i.) — to grow up; to develop; to result; to arise

erwähnen (v.t.) — to mention

**erwarten (v.t.) — to expect, anticipate; await

erwecken — to wake

erweisen, erwies, hat erwiesen (v.t.) — to prove, establish; to show

erwidern (v.t.) — to answer

erzählen (v.t.) — to tell, narrate

die Erzählung (-en) — story, tale

erzeugen (v.t.) — produce, beget

erziehen, erzog, hat erzogen (v.t.) — to bring up, educate

es — it; **es gibt — there is, there are

der Esel (-s, -) — donkey

* essen, ißt, aß, hat gegessen — to eat

die Ethik (-en) — ethics, moral philosophy

etlicher (m), **etliche** (f), **etliches** (n) — quite a few

**etwa (adv.) — approximately, perhaps; for instance

**etwas (pron.) — something; (adv.) — somewhat, a little

euer — your

das Europa (-s) — Europe

das Euter (-s, -) — udder

das Evangelium (-s) — gospel

* eventuell (adj.) — possible

ewig (adj.) — eternal; (adv.) — always

**die Ewigkeit — eternity

das Exemplar (-s, -e) — copy (of a book), sample

existieren (i.) — to exist

der Experte (-n, -n) — expert

der Expressionismus — Expressionism

extra (adj.) — extra; (adv.) — specially

die Extrapost — special delivery

F

* das Fach (-es, ⁼er) — field, subject; division

-fach (suff.) — fold

das Fachgebiet (-s, -e) — specialty

das Fachwort (-s, ⁼er) — technical term

die Fachzeitschrift (-en) — trade journal

fähig (adj.) — able, capable

die Fähigkeit (-en) — ability

* fahren, fährt, fuhr, ist gefahren — to ride, drive, go

der Fall (-es, ⁼e) — case, instance, matter, affair; **auf jeden Fall — in any case; fall, decline, ruin

* fallen, fällt, fiel, ist gefallen — to fall

fällen — to fell, chop down

das Falsch — error

fangen, fing, hat gefangen (v.t.) — to capture; (v.r.) — to get caught, to take hold

die Farbe (-n) — color

fassen (v.t.) — to grasp, seize, apprehend; include; understand

* die **Fassung (-en)** — draft, formulation; setting, frame; composure

****fast** — almost, nearly

****faul** (adj.) — lazy; rotten

die **Faulheit** — laziness

die **Feder (-n)** — feather, quill

fehlen (v.i.) — to be missing or wanting; to be absent

der **Fehler (-s, -)** — fault, error

der **Feierabend (-s, -e)** — quitting time

feierlich — solemn, festive

der **Feiertag (-s, -e)** — holiday

fein (adj.) — fine, precise; acute

der **Feind (-es, -e)** — enemy

die **Feindschaft** — animosity

das **Feld (-es, -er)** — field, area

felsig — rocky

das **Fenster (-s, -)** — window

****fern** (adj.) — far, distant

fertig (adj.) — ready, finished

****fest** (adj. and adv.) — firm, solid; permanent

fest-stellen (v.t.) — to establish; to discover, to stress

fett — fat

feucht — damp

das **Feuer (-s, -)** — fire

der **Film (-s, -e)** — film, movie

finden, fand, hat gefunden (v.t.) — to find; to think, to consider

finster (adj.) — dark, sinister; grim

der **Fisch (-es, -e)** — fish

der **Fischer (-s, -)** — fisherman

fix (adj.) — fixed, firm; quick

die **Fläche (-n)** — surface, area

flechten, flocht, hat geflochten — to weave

der **Fleck (-es, -e and -en)** — spot

das **Fleisch (-es)** — flesh, meat

der **Fleiß (-sses)** — diligence; **mit Fleiß** — intentionally

fleißig — diligent

die **Fliege (-n)** — fly

****fliegen, flog, ist geflogen** — to fly

fliehen, floh, ist geflohen — to flee

* **fließen, floß, ist geflossen** (v.i.) — to flow; **fließen aus** — to proceed or result from

fließend — flowing; fluent

der **Floh (-es, ⁻e)** — flea

der **Fluch (-es, ⁻e)** — curse

die **Flucht (-en)** — flight, escape

flüchtig — fleeting

flüssig (adj.) — flowing, fluid

die **Flut (-en)** — flood, flow

die **Folge (-n)** — sequence, series; consequence; **zur Folge haben** — to lead to

folgen (v.i., aux.s.) — to follow, ensue; (aux.h.) — to obey, to listen to

folgend — following

folgerichtig (adj.) — consistent

der **Folgeschluß (-sses, ⁻sse)** — logical consequence

* **fordern** (v.t.) — to demand, challenge

* **fördern** (v.t.) — to further, promote

die **Formel (-n)** — formula

forschen (v.i.) — search, investigate, do research on; der **Forscher** — research worker, scholar

fort (adv.) — away, gone, forth

* **fort-fahren, fort-führen** — to go away; to continue

fort-gehen (i., aux.s.) — to go away

der **Fortschritt (-s, -e)** — progress

fort-setzen — to continue; **Fortsetzung folgt** — to be continued

fort-werfen — to throw away

die **Frage (-n) — question, problem, issue; **fragen (nach)** — to ask about

die **Fraktur** — Gothic print

Frankreich — France

der **Franzose (-n, -n)** — Frenchman

die **Frau (-en) — woman, Mrs.

das **Fräulein (-s, -s) — young woman, Miss

frei (adj.) — free, independent; die **freien Künste** — the liberal arts

die **Freiheit (-en) — freedom

die **Freiheitsbewegung (-en)** — freedom movement

freilich (adv.) — to be sure; indeed

fremd (adj.) — someone else's; strange; foreign

die **Fremde** — foreign country; **in der Fremde** — abroad

die **Fremdsprache (-n)** — foreign language

fressen — to eat like an animal

die **Freude (-n) — joy

freuen (r) — to be pleased

der **Freund (-es, -e) — friend

die **Freundschaft (-en)** — friendship

freveln (i.) — to violate, blaspheme

der **Friede (-ns, -n)** — peace

friedlich — peaceful

frieren, fror, hat gefroren (i.) — to freeze

frisch (adj.) — fresh, bright

die **Frist (-en)** — period, deadline; extension

fröhlich — joyous

* die **Frucht (-̈e)** — fruit

fruchtbar (adj.) — fruitful, prolific

****früh** (adj.) — early; **früher** — former

der **Frühling** — spring

das **Frühstück (-s)** — breakfast

* **fügen** (v.t.) — to ordain; formulate; to add; (v.r.) — to comply; to be proper, to come to pass

****fühlen** (v.t. & r.) — to perceive

führen (v.t.) — to lead, direct

die **Fülle** — abundance, wealth

füllen — to fill

der **Fund (-es, -e)** — finding

fünf — five

für (prep.) with acc. — for

die **Furcht** — fear (**vor**) — of

fürchten (v.t.) — to fear; (v.r.) — to be afraid

der **Fürst (-en, -en)** — prince; ruler

der **Fuß (-es, -̈e)** — foot, base

die **Fußspur (-en)** — footprint

die **Fußnote** — footnote

G

die **Gabe (-n)** — gift

gackern (i.) — to cackle

der **Galgen (-s, -)** — gallows

* der **Gang (-es, -̈e)** — motion; **im Gang bleiben** — to keep going; **in Gang setzen** or **bringen** — to set in motion; path, aisle, passage

die **Gans (-̈e)** — goose

****ganz** (adj.) — whole, entire, complete; (adv.) — very, quite, entirely; **ganz anders** — quite different

gar (adv.) — entirely; even

gar nicht — not at all

der **Garten (-s, ̈-)** — garden

die **Gasse (-n)** — side street

der **Gast (-es, ̈-e)** — guest

der **Gaul (-s, -e)** — horse, nag

gebären, gebar, geboren (v.t.) — to bear, bring forth

das **Gebäude (-s, -)** — building, structure, framework

** **geben, gab, hat gegeben** (v.t.) — to give, impart, grant; **es gibt** — there is, there are; (v.r.) — to submit, yield, abate, to pass oneself off as

das **Gebet (-s, -e)** — prayer

das **Gebiet (-es, -e)** — district, territory, area; field

gebieten (irr. v.t.) — to demand (v.i.) — to govern, rule over

geboren (adj.) — born

das **Gebot (-es, -e)** — command

der **Gebrauch (-es, ̈-e)** — use; custom

gebrauchen — to use

die **Geburt (-en)** — birth

das **Gedächtnis (-ses, -se)** — memory

der **Gedanke (-ns, -n)** — thought, conception, idea, notion

gedeihen, gedieh, ist gediehen (v.i.) — to develop; prosper

gedenken, gedachte, hat gedacht (v.i.) — to bear in mind; recall (with gen.)

das **Gedicht (-es, -e)** — poem

die **Geduld** — patience

geeignet (adj.) — suitable

die **Gefahr (-en)** — danger, risk

gefährlich — dangerous

** **gefallen, gefiel, hat gefallen** (v.i.) — to please; **es hat ihm**

gefallen — it pleases him or he likes it

** **gefallen** (adj.) — killed in action

das **Gefängnis (-sses, -sse)** — prison

das **Gefühl (-es, -e)** — feeling, touch, instinct, intuitive grasp

gegen (prep.) with acc. — towards; against; **gegen fünf Uhr** — around five o'clock

die **Gegend (-en)** — region, area, neighborhood

gegeneinander-stellen (v.t.) — to compare

der **Gegensatz (-es, ̈-e)** — antithesis; contrast

der **Gegenstand (-s, ̈-e)** — object, thing; subject (matter)

gegenüber (prep.) with dat. — opposite, vis-à-vis; with regard to

die **Gegenwart** — presence; the present (time); **gegenwärtig** — present day

der **Gegner (-s, -)** — opponent

* der **Gehalt (-s, -e)** — contents, capacity

geheim (adj.) — secret, confidential

der **Geheimrat (-s, ̈-e)** — confident

** **gehen, ging, ist gegangen** (v.i.) — to go, walk, proceed; **in sich gehen** — to take stock of one's position; **es geht** — it is possible; **es geht um** — it is a matter of

** **gehören** (v.i.) — to belong to

gehörig (adj.) — belonging to; proper, requisite

gehorsam — obedient

der **Geist (-es, -er) — spirit, wit, intellect, genius, essence, ghost

die **Geistesgeschichte** — history of ideas

geistig — spiritual, intellectual

geizig — avaricious, stingy

das **Gelände (-s, no pl.)** — tract of land, area, region

gelangen (v.i.) — to gain, acquire, reach, arrive at

das **Geld (es, -er)** — money, capital

* **gelegen** (adj.) — situated, located; convenient, opportune

die **Gelegenheit (-en)** — opportunity

gelehrt — educated, scholarly

****gelingen, gelang, ist gelungen** (v.i.) — to succeed, to be successful

****gelten, galt, hat gegolten** (v.i.) — to mean; be valid; count; **gelten für** or **als** — to be considered as; **das gilt nicht** — that is not allowed; (v.t.) — to be worth

gemäß (adj.) — suitable; (prep.) with dat. according to

gemein (adj.) — common, general; low, vulgar, mean

die **Gemeinde (-n)** — community; municipality

gemeinhin (adv.) — generally

gemeinsam (adj.) — common

* die **Gemeinschaft (-en)** — community

das **Gemüt (-s, -er)** — disposition, soul

gemütlich (adj.) — good-natured; agreeable; cosy, comfortable

genannt (adj.) — called

****genau** (adj.) — exact, precise, in detail; (adv.) — just, exactly, precisely; quite

genehmigen (v.t.) — to approve, to grant, authorize

geneigt (adj.) — inclined; willing

* **genial** (adj.) — gifted; brilliant

genießen, genoß, hat genossen (v.t.) — to enjoy

****genug** (adv.) — enough

****gerade** (adj.) — straight, direct, sincere; (adv.) — just, exactly, precisely

geradeaus (adv.) — straight ahead

geradezu (adv.) — immediately; virtually; frankly

das **Gerät (-es, -e)** — implement

geraten, geriet, ist geraten (v.i.) — to get, fall, land

gerecht (adj.) — just, fair

die **Gerechtigkeit — justice

das **Gericht (-es, -e)** — court of justice; law-court, judgement

gering (adj.) — small, petty

****gern** (adv.) — with pleasure; **gern haben** — to like to

das **Gerücht (-es, -e)** — rumor

gesamt (adj.) — whole, entire

* der **Gesang (-s, ̈e)** — song

das **Geschäft (-es, -e)** — business, trade, transaction; duty

die **Geschäftigkeit** — activity, industriousness

****geschehen, geschah, ist geschehen** (v.i.) — to take place, happen, to occur

das **Geschenk (-s, -e)** — gift

die **Geschichte (-en) — history, story

geschickt (adj.) — skillful

das **Geschlecht (-es, -er)** — sex, species, race, generation

geschlossen (adj.) — closed, united; unified

der **Geschmack (-es, ̈er)** — taste

das **Geschöpf (-s, -e)** — creature

das **Geschrei (-s)** — cry, scream

das **Geschwätz (-es)** — chatter

* **geschweige (denn)** — not to mention

gesegnet — blessed

gesellen (v.t.) — to join, ally

** die **Gesellschaft (-en)** — society, community

das **Gesetz (-es, -e)** — law, act, decree, principle

* **gesetzt** (adj.) — fixed, established (conj.) — granted, supposing

das **Gesicht (-s, -er)** — face, countenance, appearance

der **Gesichtspunkt (-en)** — viewpoint

die **Gesinnung (-en)** — disposition

gespannt (adj.) — strained; tense; **gespannt sein** — to be in suspense

das **Gespenst (-es, -er)** — ghost

das **Gespräch (-es, -e)** — conversation, discourse; discussion

die **Gestalt (-en)** — form, shape, figure; manner; character

das **Geständnis (-ses, -se)** — admission, confession

gestatten (v.t.) — to permit, allow

gestehen, gestand, hat gestanden (v.t.) — to confess

** **gestern** (adv.) — yesterday

gestohlen — stolen

gesund (adj.) — healthy

die **Gesundheit** — health

das **Getränk (-es, -e)** — drink

gewähren (v.t.) — to grant, give

die **Gewalt (-en)** — power, authority, control, violence; force

das **Gewerbe (-s, -)** — trade, profession

** **gewesen** — been (see **sein**)

das **Gewicht (-es, -e)** — weight; gravity, importance

gewinnen, gewann, hat gewonnen (v.t.) — to win, gain, get

** **gewiß** (adj.) — sure, certain; (adv.) — certainly, to be sure

das **Gewissen (-s, -)** — conscience

gewissermaßen (adv.) — to some extent

** **gewöhnen** (v.t.) — to accustom; (v.r.) — to become accustomed **(an)** to

die **Gewohnheit (-en)** — habit, custom

gewöhnlich - usual (adj.); usually (adv.)

das **Gift (-es, -e)** — poison, toxin

glänzen (v.t.) — to glisten, shine, to excel, to be outstanding

gläsern — glass

glatt (adj.) — smooth, even, flat; plain, clear; (adv.) — quite

** der **Glaube (-ns, -n)** — faith, belief

** **glauben** (t. & i.) — to believe

** **gleich** (adj.) — same, like, equal; (adv.) — just; immediately, at once

gleichen (v.i.) — to resemble, equal

das **Gleichgewicht (-s, -e)** — balance

gleichgültig — indifferent

das **Gleichnis (-ses, -se)** — image, simile, allegory, parable, metaphor

gleichviel (adv.) — nonetheless

gleichwohl (adv.) — nevertheless, yet

gleichzeitig (adj.) — simultaneous

die **Glocke (-n)** — bell, chime

****das Glück (-es)** — happiness, fortune, luck

glücken (v.i., aux.s.) — to succeed

glücklich — happy, lucky

die **Gnade** — grace, mercy

gönnen (v.t.) — to grant

die **Gotik** — Gothic

****der Gott (-es, ⸚er)** — God, god

das **Götterbild (-s, -er)** — idol

die **Gottheit** — divinity; godhead

göttlich (adj.) — divine

gottlos — godless

der **Götze (-n, -n)** — idol

das **Grab (-es, ⸚er)** — grave, tomb; end

graben, grub, hat gegraben (v.t.) — to dig, excavate

der **Grad (-es, -e)** — degree; extent

der **Graf (-en, -en)** — count

grau — grey

grausam (adj.) — cruel; dreadful

greifbar (adj.) — ready, on hand; tangible, obvious

greifen, griff, hat gegriffen (v.t.) — to seize, grasp; (v.i.) — to touch; be effective

die **Grenze (-n)** — boundary, limit, border

der **Grieche (-n, -n)** — Greek

das **Griechentum (-s)** — Hellenism

griechisch — Greek

grob (adj.) — rough, crude, coarse

****groß** (adj.) — tall, high; large, great, immense; eminent

großartig (adj.) — great, grand, splendid

die **Größe** — height; stature

großenteils (adv.) — mainly, mostly

größtenteils (adv.) — mostly

der **Großvater (-s, ⸚)** — grandfather

die **Grünanlage (-n)** — green area

****der Grund (-es, ⸚e)** — foundation, basis; **im Grunde** — fundamentally; reason, cause; **aus diesem Grunde** — for this reason; ground, earth; land

der **Grundbegriff (-s, -e)** — fundamental concept

* **gründen** (v.t.) — to establish, set up; base; (v.r.) — rest, rely, be based on

die **Grundlage (-n)** — foundation

der **Grundsatz (-es, ⸚e)** — principle

der **Grundzug (-s, ⸚e)** — essential feature or characteristic

die **Gruppe (-n)** — group, category

der **Gruß (-es, ⸚e)** — greeting

grüßen — to greet

gültig (adj.) — valid, effective

der **Gummi (-s)** — rubber

die **Gunst** — favor; advantage

****gut** (adj. — good; (adv.) — well

das **Gut (-es, ⸚er)** — property, possession, estate; good thing

die **Güte** — kindness, goodness

das **Gute** — good (thing or part)

die **Gutheißung** — approval

gutherzig — good-natured

H

das **Haar (-s, -e)** — hair

die **Habe** — property, goods

**haben, hatte, hat gehabt (v.t.) —
to have

der **Hafen** (-s, ⸚) — harbor;
haven

* **-haft** (suff.) — designates a type
or quality; **wesenhaft** — essential

der **Hahn** (-s, ⸚e) — rooster

halb (adj.) — half; (adv.) — by
halves

-halber (suff.) — on account of

halbstark — rowdy

die **Hälfte** — half

der **Hals** (-es, ⸚e) — neck,
throat

**halten, hielt, hat gehalten (v.t.)
— to hold, keep, retain; to think,
deem, consider; (v.i.) — to stop,
hold out; (v.r.) — to hold out,
last; behave; follow; adhere to

die **Haltung** — bearing, attitude;
behavior; position

das **Hammelfleisch** — mutton

die **Hand** (⸚e) — hand; handwriting; side; source; **mit der
Hand** — by hand

der **Handel** (-s, ⸚) — trade,
transaction; deal; action

**handeln (v.i.) — to act; to bargain
(um) for; (v.r.) — **es handelt
sich um** — it is a question or
matter of

die **Handlung** — action, deed;
plot

hängen — to hang; caught

hart (adj.) — hard, difficult,
troublesome; (adv.) — hard **(an)**
— close by

die **Härte** — harshness, severity

hartnäckig — stubborn; persis-
tent

der **Haß** (-sses) — hatred

häßlich (adj.) — ugly, hideous,
repulsive; nasty

der **Hase** (-n, -n) — rabbit

hassen — to hate

die **Hast** — haste, hurry

der **Hauch** (-es, -e) — breath;
tinge, trace; aura

häufig (adj.) — frequent; (adv.)
— frequently, often

**das Haupt (-es, ⸚er) — head,
leader, chief, principal

die **Hauptabsicht** (-en) — main
object

die **Hauptfigur** (-en) — main or
central figure

die **Hauptsache** (-en) — main
point or issue

die **Hauptstadt** (⸚e) — capital

das **Haus** (-es, ⸚er) — house

häuslich (adj.) — domestic

die **Hausmacht** (⸚e) — power
base

die **Haut** — skin

heben, hob, hat gehoben (v.t.) —
to lift; accentuate; (v.r.) — to
improve

der **Hebräer** — Hebrew

das **Heer** (-es, -e) — army

* das **Heft** (-es, -e) — paperback
book, pamphlet, brochure;
handle

heftig (adj.) — violent, severe

heil (adj.) — whole, uninjured

das **Heil** — well-being, welfare,
salvation

heilen — to heal

heilig (adj.) — holy, sacred

heim — home

die **Heimat** (-en) — home, native
country

heimlich (adj.) — secret, hid-den

heim-suchen (v.t.) — to afflict

der **Heimweg (-s, -e)** — way home

die **Heirat (-en)** — marriage

****heiß** (adj.) — hot, ardent

****heißen, hieß, hat geheißen** (v.t.) — to name, call; to command; (v.i.) — to be called; **es heißt, daß** — it is said that

heiter (adj.) — cheerful, clear

heizen (v.t.) — to heat

das **Heizöl** — heating oil

der **Held (-en, -en)** — hero

die **Heldendichtung** — heroic or epic poetry

****helfen, half, hat geholfen** (v.i.) — to help, aid, support

****hell** (adj.) — clear, bright; light

hellicht — **hellichter Tag** — broad daylight

henken — to hang

****her** (adv.) — here, this way; **hin und her** — to and fro; **von weit her** — from afar; (time) — since, ago; **wie lange ist es her** — how long ago is it

herab (pref.) — movement downwards

herab-fallen (i., aux.s.) — to fall down

herab-schreien — to call down

herab-setzen (v.t.) — to lower, to reduce

herab-steigen (i., aux.s.) — to climb down, dismount

heran (adv. and pref.) — movement into the proximity of the speaker; near

heran-kommen (v.i.) — to draw or come near

* **heran-ziehen** (v.t.) — to draw near; to procure; to quote; to enlist; to attract; to raise, bring up; (v.i.) to approach, draw near

heraus (adv. and pref.) — movement from inside a place as seen by the person outside; out; forth

heraus-finden (v.t.) — to find out, to discover; (v.r.) — to extricate oneself

die **Herausforderung** — challenge, provocation

der **Herausgeber (-)** — editor

heraus-holen (v.t.) — to get or take or draw out, to extract; to elicit; to gain

heraus-nehmen (v.t.) — to take out, to remove; (v.r.) — to presume

heraus-stellen (v.t.) — to expose, to set forth; (v.r.) — to appear, to turn out

herbei (adv., sep. pref.) — indicates a movement from a remoter place to a nearer one; near, here

herbei-führen (v.t.) — to bring about or produce

der **Herbst (-es, -e)** — autumn

die **Herde (-n)** — flock, herd; crowd

herein (adv. and pref.) — indicates movement into a place as seen by a person inside; in, in here

her-kommen (irr. v.i., aux.s.) — to come here, to approach

das **Herkommen (-s)** — origin, extraction

die **Herkunft (-̈e)** — origin or descent; derivation (of a word)

der **Herr (-n, -en) — master, lord, God, ruler, gentleman, Mr.

der **Herrenhund (-s, -e)** — aristocrat's dog

herrlich (adj.) — magnificent

* die **Herrschaft (-en)** — dominion, power; command, domination; manor; master and mistress

herrschen (v. & i.) — to rule, reign, prevail, be in vogue; dominate

der **Herrscher (-s, -)** — ruler, governor

her-stellen (v.t.) — to set up, establish, create; place here

herum (adv. and pref.) — indicates a movement around, or an approximate time or amount

herum-gehen (i., aux.s.) — to go around, associate

herunter-kommen (irr. v.i., aux.s.) — to deteriorate, decay; to come down(stairs); to get over

hervor-bringen (irr. v.t.) — to bring forth, produce; utter

hervorragend (adj.) — prominent, protruding, outstanding

hervor-treten (irr. v.i., aux.s.) — to come forward; stand out; to become evident; emerge from

** das **Herz (-ens, -en)** — heart, feeling, soul

das **Herzeleid** — suffering

herzlich (adj.) — hearty, cordial

der **Herzog (-es, -e or -̈e)** — duke

die **Heuchelei (-en)** — hypocrisy

** **heute** (adv.) — today; **heute abend** — this evening; **heute früh** — this morning

hier (adv.) — here, present; on this occasion; now

hierher — to this place; **bis hierher** — up to now, so far

** der **Himmel (-s, -)** — heaven, heavens, sky

das **Himmelreich** — kingdom of heaven

** **hin** (adv.) — expresses motion away from the speaker; expresses duration of time into the future; **hin und her** — to and fro; **hin und wieder** — now and then

hinab (adv. and pref.) — down

hinab-fallen (i., aux.s.) — to fall off

hinan-steigen (i., aux.s.) — to climb (up)

hinauf (adv. and pref.) — up

hinaus (adv. and pref.) — outside, forth

* **hinaus-gehen** (irr. v.i., aux.s.) — to surpass; to go out; **hinaus-gehen auf** — to aim at

hinaus-kommen (irr. v.i., aux.s.) — to come out; to go beyond; **hinauskommen auf** (acc.) — to come or amount to

hindern — to hinder

hinein (adv. and pref.) — into

hinein-passen (i.) — to fit in

hin-geben (irr. v.t.) — to give up, surrender, sacrifice

hin-gehen (irr. v.i., aux.s.) — to go to that place; to elapse, to pass

hinken (i.) — to limp

hinsichtlich (prep.) — with regard to, concerning

hinten (adv.) — behind

** **hinter** (prep. and pref.) with dat. or acc. — behind; after

hintereinander (adv.) — one after the other, in succession

der **Hintergrund (-s, -̈e)** — background; (pl.) hidden difficulties

hinterlassen (irr. v.t.) — to leave, to leave behind, to bequeath

hinüber (adv., pref.) — over there, across, beyond

hinüber-laufen (i., aux.s.) — to walk past

hinweg (adv., pref.) — away, off

hin-weisen (irr. v.i.) — to point to, indicate; point out, allude to

hinzu (adv., pref.) — to, towards, besides, in addition

hinzu-fügen (v.t.) — to add, append; to enclose

der **Historiker** (-s, -) — historian

die **Hitze** (-n) — heat, ardor

hoch (adj.) — high, tall, lofty, sublime; **hoher Genuß — great enjoyment; (adv.) — highly

die **Hochachtung** — high esteem, admiration; deep respect

hochachtungsvoll — respectfully

hochgestellt (adj.) — high-ranking

der **Hochmut** — pride, arrogance

höchst (sup. adj.) — highest, utmost; (adv.) — extremely

die **Hochzeit** (-en) — wedding

hoffen (v.i.) — to hope (**auf**) for

die **Hoffnung** (-en) — hope, anticipation

höflich (adj.) — polite

die **Höhe** — height, loftiness, summit, level or price or volume, musical pitch

der **Höhepunkt** (-s, -e) — highest or culminating point, peak, climax

holen (v.t.) — to get, fetch; **holen lassen** — to send for

die **Hölle** — hell

das **Holz** (-es, ¨er) — wood

der **Holzapfel** (-s, ¨) — crab apple

horchen (v.i.) — to listen (**auf**) to

hören (v.t., v.i.) — to hear, to listen; **hören auf — to listen to, heed, obey

das **Hörensagen** — hearsay

das **Horn** (-s, ¨er) — horn

das **Hosenbein** (-s, -e) — pant leg

das **Hufeisen** (-s, -e) — horse shoe

das **Huhn** (-s, ¨er) — hen, fowl

huldigen (v.i.) — to do homage

* **human** (adj.) — humane

der **Humanismus** — humanism

der **Hund** (-es, -e) — dog

hundertjährig (adj.) — centenary

hundertprozentig (adj. and adv.) — hundred per cent; completely

der **Hunger** — hunger

das **Husten** (-s, -) — coughing

der **Hut** (-es, ¨e) — hat, cover, lid

die **Hut** — protection, shelter; **auf der Hut sein** — to be on guard

hüten (v.t.) — to guard, take care of; (v.r.) — to watch out (**vor**) for

die **Hütte** (-n) — hut, cottage

die **Hypothese** (-n) — hypothesis

I

ich — I; **Ich — self, ego

die **Idee** (-n) — idea, notion; **fixe Idee** — obsession

die **Iden** — Ides

der **Ideologe** (-n, -n) — ideologist

**ihr — you, to her, her, their

immer (adv.) — always, constantly; **noch immer — even now; **immer wieder** — again and again; immer & comparative is an intensifier — **immer mehr** — more and more; **immer höher** — higher and higher;

(part.) in any case, after all; **er ist doch immerhin dein Bruder** — after all, he is your brother

imponieren (v.i.) — to be impressive or imposing

imstande (pred. adj.) — capable of

**in (prep.) — with dat. or acc. — in, into

der **Inbegriff** — perfect example

**indem (conj.) — as, while; by

der **Inder (-s, -)** — Hindu, Indian

das **Indien** — India

infolge (prep.) with gen. — as a result of; owing to

* der **Inhalt (-s, -e)** — contents, capacity, volume; subject, substance, gist

das **Inhaltsverzeichnis** — index

das **Inland (-s)** — inland; native country

inne (adv. pref.) — within

innehalten (irr. v.i.) — to pause; to stop

innen (within) — within

inner (adj.) — inner, interior, domestic, spiritual

innerhalb (adv., prep.) — within

innerlich (adj.) — mental, spiritual

innig (adj.) — hearty

der **Insasse (-n, -n)** — inmate

insbesondere (adv.) — in particular

die **Insel (-n)** — island

insofern (adv. and conj.) — **(in)** so far as; if

* die **Instanz (-en)** — authority

das **Interesse (-s, -n)** — interest

interessieren (v.t.) — to interest **(für)** — in; (v.r.) — to be interested

intim (adj.) — intimate

inzwischen (adv.) — meanwhile

der **Ire (-n, -n)** — Irishman

* **irgend** (adv.) — any, some; **irgendein** — someone, anyone; **irgendwann** — at some point; **irgendwo** — somewhere or another

ironisch — ironic

irr(e) (adj.) — in error; crazy

irre-gehen (i., aux.s.) — to go astray

irren (v.i.) — to go astray, to err, (v.r.) — to be mistaken

der **Irrtum (-s, ⁻er)** — error

das **Italien** — Italy

J

**ja (adv., part.) — yes; indeed, certainly, of course, after all

ja sagen — to affirm, say yes

jagen (v.t.) — to hunt, chase, pursue

das Jahr (-es, -e) — year; **nach Jahren — after many years; **seit Jahren** — for years; **vor einem Jahr** — a year ago

der **Jahrgang** — age-group, year of publication

das **Jahrhundert (-es, -e)** — century

der **Jammer (-s)** — misery

je (adv., conj.) — ever, at any time; **je nach — according to; **je . . . desto** — the . . . the

jede (adj.) — each, every; (pron.) each, everyone

jedenfalls (adv.) — in any case

jedesmal (adv.) — each or every time

jedoch (adv.) — however, still

**jemand (pron.) — someone

jene (adj.) — that, those; (pron.)
that one, those people
* **jener** — that, that one, the former
jenseits (prep.) with gen. — on
the other side of
** **jetzt** (adv.) — now, at present; **für
jetzt** — for the present
jeweilig (adj.) — at the moment,
respective; or **jeweils** (adv.) —
at times, from time to time
der **Jude** (-n, -n) — Jew
die **Jugend** — youth, young people
** **jung** (adj.) — young, new, recent
der **Junge** (-n, -n) — boy, youth
der **Jünger** (-s, -) — disciple,
follower
die **Jungfrau** (-en) — virgin,
maiden
* **jüngst** (sup. adj.) — youngest,
latest, (adv.) — recently, lately
Jura (pl.) — law

K

kahl (adj.) — bald; bare, naked,
empty; bleak
der **Kaiser** (-s, -) — emperor
kaiserlich (adj.) — imperial
das **Kalb** (-es, ¨er) — calf
der **Kalender** (-s, -) — calender
* **kalt** — cold
das **Kamel** (-s, -e) — camel
der **Kamerad** (-en, -en) — companion, colleague, comrade
der **Kamin** (-s, -e) — fireplace
der **Kampf** (-es, ¨e) — battle,
fight, struggle, contest
kämpfen (t. & i.) — to fight
die **Kanone** (-n) — cannon
die **Kanzlei** (-en) — chancellery
die **Kapelle** (-n) — chapel

das **Kapitel** (-s, -) — chapter;
topic; period
die **Kappe** (-n) — cap
karg (adj.) — scanty, stingy,
sparse
die **Karikatur** (-en) — caricature
Karl der Große — Charlemagne
die **Karriere** (-n) — career
die **Karte** (-n) — card, map, chart,
ticket
die **Kartoffel** (-n) — potato
der **Kasten** (-s, ¨) — box, chest
die **Kathedrale** (-n) — cathedral
die **Katze** (-n) — cat
der **Kauf** (-s, ¨e) — purchase
kaufen (v.t.) — to buy, purchase
kaum (adv.) — hardly, scarcely
* **kehren** (v.t.) — to turn (over);
(v.r.) — to heed; (v.i.) — **in sich
kehren** — to be lost in thought,
meditate
der **Keim** (-es, -e) — germ, seed,
origin
** **kein** (adj.) — no, not a; (pron.) —
keiner — no one
keinesfalls, keineswegs (adv.) —
by no means; under no circumstances
keinmal — no time
der **Kellner** (-s, -) — waiter
** **kennen, kannte, hat gekannt**
(v.t.) — to know, be acquainted
with, to understand
kennen-lernen (v.t.) — to become
acquainted with
die **Kenntnis** (-se) — knowledge,
cognizance, awareness
das **Kennzeichen** (-s) — distin-
guishing marks or features
der **Kern** (-es, -e) — kernel, core
die **Kernforschung** — nuclear
science
die **Kernfrage** — central issue

die **Kette (-n)** — chain, series
der **Ketzer (-s, -)** — heretic
der **Kieselstein (-s, -e)** — pebble
das **Kind (-es, -er)** — child
kindisch (adj.) — childish
kindlich (adj.) — child-like
die **Kirche (-n)** — church
die **Kirchenglocke (-n)** — church bell
die **Kirchenlehre (-n)** — church doctrine
die **Kirchenmaus (-̈e)** — church mouse
der **Kirchhof (-̈e)** — churchyard
kirchlich (adj.) — ecclesiastical, religious
die **Klage (-n)** — complaint, lament; action, suit
klagen — to complain
der **Klang (-es, -̈e)** — sound
klar (adj.) — clear, plain; **an sich klar — self-evident
die **Klassenlage** — class position
die **Klassik** — classical period
die **Klaue (-n)** — claw
das **Kleid (-es, -er)** — dress
klein (adj.) — little, small, tiny, short (size), insignificant, petty; exact; **die kleinen Leute — the lower middle-class, the common people; (adv.) **klein denken** — to have narrow views; **im Kleinen** — on a small scale, in detail
der **Kleriker** — cleric, priest, clergyman
klingeln (i.) — to ring, chime
die **Klinke (-n)** — latch
die **Kluft (-̈e)** — crevice, crack, chasm
klug (adj.) — clever, intelligent
der **Knabe (-n, -n)** — lad, boy

knapp (adj.) — narrow; scant(y), scarce; accurate; (adv.) — barely, only just
knirschen (i.) — gnash
der **Koch (-es, -̈e)** — cook
kochen — to cook
der **Kohl** — cabbage
* die **Kombination** — surmise, inference; combination; scheme
komisch — funny
****kommen, kam, ist gekommen** (v.i.) — to come, arrive, approach, occur, happen, arise; **mir kam der Gedanke** — it occured to me; **hinter die Wahrheit kommen** — to discover the truth; **kommen über** (acc.) — to fall upon, to befall; **zu sich kommen** — to recover one's senses
die **Komödie** — comedy
komponieren (v.t.) — to compose
der **König (-s, -e)** — king
das **Königreich** — kingdom
* die **Konjunktur (-en)** — economy
* der **Konkurrent (-en, -en)** — competitor, rival
* **konkurrieren** (v.i.) — to compete
****können** (modal) — to be able to; to be allowed to; **er kann nichts dafür** — he can't help it
* **konsequent** (adj.) — consistent
konstatieren (v.t.) — to see, notice
konstruieren (v.t.) — to construct, design; **der konstruierte Fall** — hypothetical case
* der **Konvent (-es, -e)** — gathering, convention
* das **Konzept (-es, -e)** — draft; (pl.) notes

der **Kopf (-es, ⸚e) — head; top; heading; ability, sense

das **Kopfweh** (-s) — headache

der **Körper** (-s, -) — body; bulk; substance

kosten (v.t.) — to taste, enjoy; (v.i.) — to cost; require

köstlich (adj.) — exquisite, wonderful; priceless

die **Kraft (⸚e) — strength, power, force; energy, validity; **außer Kraft setzen** — to annul; **in Kraft treten** — to become effective

kraft (prep.) with gen. — by virtue of, on the strength of

die **Krähe** (-n) — crow

der **Krämer** (-s, -) — merchant

krank (adj.) — ill, sick, ailing

kränken (v.t.) — to offend

der **Kreis** (-es, -e) — circle, district, sphere

das **Kreuz** (-es, -e) — cross, crucifix, burden

der **Krieg (-es, -e) — war, warfare

die **Krankheit** (-en) — illness

der **Kranz** (-es, -e) — wreath

die **Krise** (-n) — crisis, turning-point

die **Kritik** (-en) — criticism, review, critique

der **Kritiker** (-s, -) — critic

die **Krone** (-n) — crown

die **Krücke** (-n) — crutch

der **Krug** (-es, ⸚e) — jug

krumm (adj.) — crooked

die **Küche** (-n) — kitchen

die **Kuh** (⸚e) — cow

kühl — cool

kühn (adj.) — bold, brave, daring

die **Kultur** (-en) — culture, civilization

der **Kulturfilm** — documentary

kulturgeschichtlich (adj.) — referring to the history of civilization

kümmern (v.t.) — trouble; concern, worry; (v.r.) — to mind, to take care of, to worry (**um**) about

* die **Kunde** (-n) — information, news

* der **Kunde** (-n, -n) — customer, client

kundig (adj.) — versed, skilled, expert

künftig (adj.) — future, next

die **Kunst (⸚e) — art, skill; **die schönen Künste** — the fine arts

künstlerisch (adj.) — artistic

künstlich — artificial, synthetic

der **Kurs** (-es, -e) — course; exchange rate

kurz (adj., adv.) — short, brief, curt; **kurz und bündig** — briefly, concisely; **in kurzem** — soon, shortly; **seit kurzem** — lately, of late

kürzen (v.t.) — to shorten, condense

die **Kurzgeschichte** (-n) — short story

kürzlich (adv.) — lately, recently

küssen — to kiss

die **Küste** (-n) — coast, seashore

L

lächeln (v.i.) — to smile (**über**) at

lachen (v.i.) — to laugh (**über**) at

lächerlich (adj.) — laughable, ridiculous, absurd

laden, lud, hat geladen (v.t.) — to load; to invite

* die **Lage (-n)** — situation, position, site; outlook, circumstances; covering

der **Laie (-n, -n)** — layman, novice

das **Land (-es, ⁻er) — land, country, region, territory

die **Landschaft (-en)** — landscape, scenery, countryside

****lang** (adj.) — long, tall, high; (adv.) — for, during; **vier Jahre lang** — for 4 years; **sein Leben lang** — all his life

****lange** (adv.) — for a long time

die **Länge** — length; size; height

langen (v.i.) — to be sufficient; **langen nach** — to reach for

die **Langeweile** — boredom

****langsam** (adj.) — slow

längst (adv.) — long ago; **längst nichts** — not by a long way

der **Lärm (-s)** — noise, din, uproar

****lassen, ließ, hat gelassen** (v.t.) — to leave; let go; let (do), allow, permit; make (do), cause (to do), have (done); **sich lassen** — can be; **das läßt sich sagen** — that can be said

die **Last (-en)** — load, burden

das **Latein** — Latin

lauern (i.) — to lurk

* der **Lauf (-es, ⁻e)** — run, circulation; course

laufen, lief, ist gelaufen (v.i.) — to run, walk, work, extend, elapse; be in progress

laufend (adj.) — current, running, steady, consecutive

die **Laune** — mood; whim

die **Laus (⁻e)** — louse

laut (adj.) — loud; (adv.) — aloud; **laut werden** — to become public

* **laut** (prep.) — with gen. or dat. — according to

lauten (v.i.) — to sound; to be; to read; to go

* **lauter** (adj.) — clear, pure; (adv.) — nothing but

****leben** (v.t.) — to live, exist, dwell, stay

das **Leben (-s, -)** — life, existence

lebendig (adj.) — living, animate, alive, lively

die **Lebensaufgabe (-n)** — life's task

der **Lebenslauf** — career, vitae

das **Lebensmittel** — food

lebhaft — lively, vivacious; vivid

leer (adj.) — empty, vacant

****legen** (v.t.) — to lay, put, place; (v.r.) — to lie down, cease, die

legitim (adj.) — legitimate

die **Lehre (-n)** — doctrine, teaching

* **lehren** — to teach

der **Lehrer (-s, -)** — teacher

der **Lehrsatz (-es, ⁻e)** — thesis, doctrine

der **Leib (-es, -er)** — body

****leicht** (adj.) — easy, effortless; light; insignificant; (adv.) — easily; lightly

leichtfertig (adj.) — careless, irresponsible

leid — **es tut mir leid** — I am sorry

das **Leid (-es)** — suffering

leiden, litt, hat gelitten (v.t.) — to suffer, bear, tolerate; to allow, admit; **ich kann sie nicht leiden** — I can't stand her; (v.i.) —

leiden (unter) — to be afflicted (with)

die **Leidenschaft (-en)** — passion

****leider** (adv.) — unfortunately

****leise** (adj.) — low, soft, gentle

* **leisten** (v.t.) — to do; accomplish

die **Leistung (-en)** — achievement

leiten (v.t.) — to lead

der **Leiter (-s, -)** — leader, conductor

lenken (v.t.) — to turn, guide, direct

****lernen** (v.t.) — to learn, study

****lesen, las, hat gelesen** (v.t. & v.i.) — to read; to lecture

****letzt** (adj.) — last, final, extreme

letztens (adv.) — recently

leuchten (v.i.) — to shine, illuminate

die **Leute (pl.) — people, folk, public

das **Licht (-es, -er)** — light; genius

lieb (adj.) — dear; (when used as a pred.) — agreeable; **es ist ihr lieb** — she is glad . . . ; **der liebe Gott** — God (Almighty)

die **Liebe (-n) — love, fondness

lieben — to love

****lieber** (adv. comp. of gern) — rather, preferably; sooner; better

liebevoll — affectionate

die **Lieblingsmeinung (-en)** — favorite opinion

das **Lied (-es, -er)** — song, poem, tune

* **liefern** (v.t.) — to deliver; to supply; to yield

****liegen, lag, hat gelegen** (v.i.) — to lie, be located, to be; **liegen (an)** — to be due to, to depend on

liieren (v.t.) — to bring together

lind — gentle

lindern (v.t.) — to mitigate, soften

die **Linie (-n)** — line; **in erster Linie** — in the first place

links (adv.) — to the left; **linksgerichtet** (adj.) — leftist

* die **List (-en)** — cunning, craft

* die **Liste (-n)** — list, catalogue

die **Literatur (-en)** — literature, bibliography

das **Lob (-es)** — praise

loben (v.t.) — to praise

das **Loch (-es, ⁻er)** — hole, gap

locken (v.t.) — to entice

der **Logiker (-s, -)** — logician

lohnen (v.t. & v.i.) — to reward, to be worth

los (pred. adj., adv.) — loose, free, disengaged; **was ist los** — what's the matter?

los- (pref.) — separation; commencement, violence

-los (suff.) — less; **hilflos** — helpless

löschen — to extinguish

lösen (v.t.) — to release; to solve, answer; to loosen; to cancel

los-lassen (irr. v.t.) — to set free

* die **Lösung (-en)** — solution; denouement; cancellation

der **Löwe (-n, -n)** — lion

die **Lücke (-n)** — gap

die **Luft (⁻e)** — air, breeze

die **Lüge (-n)** — lie, fib

lügen, log, hat gelogen (v.i.) — to lie, to fib

der **Lügner (-s, -)** — liar

lukullisch (adj.) — epicurean

die **Lust (⁻e)** — pleasure, desire

die **Lyrik** — lyric poetry

M

machen (v.t.) — to make, do; produce, form; cause; **das macht nichts — that's all right; (v.r.) — to come about, happen; **es läßt sich nichts machen** — it cannot be done; **sich auf den Weg machen** — to set out

die **Macht** (-̈e) — might, authority

mächtig — powerful

die **Machtpolitik** — power politics

das **Mädchen** (-s, -) — girl

Magen (-s, -̈, or -) — stomach

mager — thin, lean

der **Magistrat** (-es, -e) — town or city or municipal council

das **Mahl** (-s, -̈er) — meal

mahnen (v.t.) — to remind, warn, admonish, urge

das Mal (-es, -e) — time, occasion; **zum ersten Mal — for the first time

* -mal (suf.) — **einmal** — once; **dreimal** — three times; **manchmal** — sometimes

malen (v.t.) — to paint, portray

**man (pron., always nom.) — one, someone

manch (adj.) — many a; **manche — some

**manchmal (adv.) — sometimes

der **Mangel** (-s, -̈) — lack, need

mangeln (v.t.) — to want, to be deficient

**der Mann (-es, -̈er) — man, husband

mannigfach or **mannigfaltig** (adj.) — diverse, manifold

der **Mantel** (-s, -̈) — coat

die **Mappe** (-n) — briefcase, file

der **Markt** (-s, -̈e) — market

März — March

das **Maß** (-es, -e) — measure, extent; **in hohem Maße** — in a high degree

die **Masse** (-n) — mass, heap; the masses, the people; substance

die **Massenbeeinflussung** — propaganda

maßgebend (adj.) — decisive, authoritative

mäßig (adj.) — moderate; mediocre

* -mäßig (suff.) — like (having the quality of); -wise

die **Maßnahme** (-n) — measure, action

der **Maßstab** (-̈e) — standard; measure; scale

der **Mast** (-es, -e & -en) — mast

matt (adj.) — faint, weak, dull

die **Mauer** (-n) — wall

die **Maus** (-̈e) — mouse

die **Medien** — media

die **Medizin** (-en) — medicine

**das Meer (-es, -e) — ocean

mehr (adv.) — more; **nicht mehr — no longer; **nichts mehr** — nothing more

**mehrere (adj., pron.) — several

mehrfach (adj.) — multiple, numerous

meiden — to avoid

**mein — my

meinen (v.i.) — to believe, think

**die Meinung (-en) — opinion, view

meist (sup. adj.) — most; **die meisten the majority of them; **meistens** (adv.) — mostly, generally

der **Meister** (-s, -) — master

das **Meisterstück** (-es, -e) — masterpiece

melden (v.t., v.i.) — to announce; to recount, to tell; (v.r.) — to announce oneself, to register

die **Menge** (-n) — quantity, multitude, crowd

der **Mensch (-en, -en) — person, human being; (pl.) — people, mankind

das **Menschenalter** — generation

der **Menschenfreund** — philanthropist

die **Menschenkunde** — anthropology

die **Menschenmenge** — crowd

die **Menschheit** — humanity

menschlich (adj.) — human, humane

merken (v.t.) — to observe, realize, feel, perceive; (v.i.) — **merken (auf)** — to pay attention (to)

das **Merkmal** (-s, -e) — sign, characteristic; indication

merkwürdig (adj.) — odd, curious

messen, maß, hat gemessen (v.t.) — to measure

die **Miene** — countenance, expression

das **Messer** (-s, -) — knife

mildern (v.t.) — to soften, ease

minder (adj. & adv.) — less

mindern (v.t. & v.r.) — to diminish

mindest (adj. & adv.) — least; **mindestens** — at least (adv.)

mischen (v.t., v.r.) — to mix, mingle

die **Mischung** — mixture

die **Misere** (-n) — plight, misery

miß- (pref.) — mis, dis, bad

der **Mißbrauch** (-s, ̈-e) — misuse; abuse

der **Mißerfolg** (-s, -e) — failure

mißglücken (v.i.) — to fail

das **Mißverständnis** (-ses, -se) — discrepancy

mißlungen — unsuccessful

mißverständlich — misleading

mißverstehen (i.) — to misunderstand

****mit** (prep.) with dat. — with, along with, by means of; (adv.) — together with

mit- (pref.) — fellow, joint, co-

die **Mitarbeit** (-en) — collaboration

mit-bringen — to bring with one

miteinander — with one another

mit-gehen (irr. v.i., aux.s.) — to accompany

das **Mitglied** (-s, -er) — member

das **Mitleid** — pity, compassion

mit-nehmen (irr. v.t.) — to take along with; to affect; to wear out

der **Mittag** (-es, -e) — noon

die **Mitte — middle, center, midst

mit-teilen (v.t., v.r.) — to communicate

* das **Mittel** (-s, -) — means, measures; (pl.) — means, resources, funds

das **Mittelalter** — Middle Ages

mittels (prep.) with gen. — by means of

die **Mitternacht** — midnight

mit-wirken (v.i.) — to collaborate

die **Mode** — fashion, vogue

die **Moderne** — modern age

****mögen** (modal) — want, wish, be inclined; **das mag sein** — that may be

****möglich** (adj.) — possible

die **Möglichkeit (-en) — possibility

der **Monat** (-s, -e) — month

der **Mond** (-es, -e) — moon
der **Mondschein** — moonlight
das **Moos** — moss
die **Moral** — morals, morality, ethics
der **Mord** (-s, -e) — murder
der **Morgen** (-s, -) — morning; dawn
morgen (adv.) — tomorrow
das **Morgenland** (-s) — Orient
das **Motiv** (-s, -e) — motive; subject; motif
die **Möwe** (-n) — sea gull
die **Mücke** (-n) — gnat
müde (adj.) — weary, tired
die **Mühe** (-n) — trouble, effort, difficulty
der **Mund** (-es, -e or ⁻er) — mouth, opening
mündig — **mündig sein** — to be of age
die **Münze** (-n) — coin, coinage
mürbe (adj.) — mellow; weary
die **Musik** — music
der **Muskel** (-s, -n) — muscle
müssen (sie muß) — to have to, must; **mußte** — had to
müßig (adj.) — idle, vain
das **Muster** (-s, -) — model, ideal, example
der **Mut** (-s) — courage, spirit
mutig — courageous
mutmaßen (v.t. & v.i.) — to conjecture
die Mutter (⁻) — mother

N

nach (prep.) — with dat. — according to, after, following, towards; **nach wie vor** — as usual

nach-ahmen (v.t.) — to imitate
der **Nachbar** (-s, -n) — neighbor
nach-bilden (v.t.) — to reproduce, copy
* **nachdem** (conj.) — after, when; (adv.) — afterwards, subsequently
nach-denken (irr. v.i.) — to ponder
der **Nachdruck** (-s, -e) — emphasis; reprint
die **Nachfolge** (-n) — sequence; succession
nach-forschen (v.t.) — to investigate
nach-geben (irr. v.i.) — to yield
nachgelassen (adj.) — posthumous
nachher (adv.) — afterwards; later
der **Nachkomme** (-n, -n) — descendent
* **nach-kommen** (irr. v.i., aux.s.) — to come after; to comply with
der **Nachlaß** (-sses, ⁻sse) — legacy; posthumous works; rebate
nachlässig (adj.) — careless
der **Nachmittag** (-s, -e) — afternoon
nach-rennen (i., aux.s.) — to chase, pursue
nach-prüfen (v.t.) — to check, verify
die **Nachricht** (-en) — news, message
nach-sagen (v.i.) — to credit with
nach-schlagen (irr. v.t.) — to refer to, to look up
nach-schleichen (i., aux.s.) — to creep after
die **Nachschrift** — copy; postscript

* **nach-sehen** (irr. v.t.) — to examine, inspect; to overlook, pardon

nach-sinnen (irr. v.i.) — to reflect

nächst (adj.) — next, nearest; (prep.) — next to or after; aside from

nächstens (adv.) — very soon, shortly

die **Nacht (¨e) — night

der **Nachteil** (-s, -e) — disadvantage

die **Nachtigall** (-n) — nightingale

das **Nachtlied** (-es, -er) — night song

der **Nachtrag** (-es, ¨e) — supplement

der **Nachweis** (-es, -e) — proof

die **Nachwelt** — posterity

nach-wirken (v.i.) — to be felt afterwards

das **Nachwort** (-s, ¨er) — epilogue

nach-zählen — to check, count again

nach-ziehen (irr. v.i., aux.s.) — to follow

nackt (adj.) — naked

die **Nadel** (-n) — needle

der **Nagel** (-s, ¨) — nail

****nah** (adj.) — near, forthcoming, close on, impending

die **Nähe — nearness; vicinity

nahe-liegen (irr. v.i.) — to be obvious

nähern (v.r.) — to approach

nahezu (adv.) — nearly, almost, virtually

nähren (v.t.) — to feed, nourish

der **Name** (-ns, -n) — name

namenlos (adj.) — nameless; indescribable; unspeakable

namens (adv.) — called; (prep.) — on behalf of

* **namentlich** (adv.) — especially

* **nämlich** (adv.) — namely

der **Narr** (-en, -en) — fool

die **Narrheit** (-en) — foolishness

die **Nationalökonomie** — political economy

die **Natur** (-en) — nature; character, disposition; **von Natur aus** — by nature

naturgetreu (adj.) — true to nature

die **Naturlehre** — natural philosophy, (physical) science

natürlich (adj.) — natural, innate; (adv.) — of course, naturally

naturwidrig (adj.) — unnatural

der **Nebel** — fog; veil

****neben** (prep.) with dat. or acc. — beside, next to

die **Nebenabsicht** (-en) — secondary objective; die **Nebenbedeutung** — secondary meaning

nebeneinander (adv.) — side by side

nebeneinander-stellen (v.t.) — to compare

****nehmen, nahm, hat genommen** (v.i.) — to take (from); **auf sich nehmen** — to assume (a burden)

der **Neid** — envy, jealousy

neigen (v.i.) — to lean or incline (**zu**) to; (v.t.) to bend; (v.r.) — to slant, bow

* die **Neigung** — inclination; tendency; fondness

****nein** (adv.) — no

****nennen, nannte, hat genannt** (v.t.) — to name, mention die **Nessel (-n)** — nettle

nett (adj.) — nice, neat

neu (adj.) — new, recent, latest, novel; **neuere Sprachen — modern languages; **in neuerer Zeit** — in recent times

die **Neuerung** — innovation

die **Neufassung (-en)** — revised text

neugierig (adj.) — curious

neulich (adv.) — recently

nicht (adv.) — not; **nicht besser als — no better than; **nicht mehr** — no longer

das **Nichts** — nothingness

**nichts (pron.) — nothing

**nie (adv.) — never

nieder (adj.) — inferior; lower; (adv.) — down low

nieder-drücken (v.t.) — to depress; to press or weigh down

nieder-gehen (i., aux.s.) — to descend, set

die **Niederlage** — defeat; failure

nieder-legen — to lay down; to give up

der **Niederschlag (-s, -̈e)** — outcome, result

nieder-werfen — to throw down

niedrig (adj.) — low, inferior

niemals (adj.) — never

**niemand (pron.) — no one

nimmer (adv.) — never

nirgendwo (adv.) — nowhere

noch (adj.) — still, yet; in addition; **noch einer — one more; **noch einmal** — once again; **noch nicht** — not yet

die **Nonne (-n)** — nun

nördlich (adj.) — northern, northerly (adv.) — to the north

nordöstlich (adj.) — northeast(ern)

die **Not (-̈e)** — need; **aus Not** — from necessity; **not-** (pred. adj.) — necessary

nötig (adj.) — necessary

nötigen (v.t.) — to force

die **Notlage** — predicament

der **Notstand (-̈e)** — state of distress

notwendig (adj.) — necessary

die **Novelle (-n)** — short story, short novel

nüchtern (adj.) — sober; temperate

null (adj.) — nil, zero

die **Nummer (-n)** — number, issue (of a journal)

**nun (adv.) — now, at present; (part.) — now, well

nur (adv., part.) — only, alone; just; simply; **wenn nur — if only

nutzen or **nützen** (v.i.) — to be of use; **es nützt nichts** — it is no use

nützlich (adj.) — useful

O

**ob (conj.) — whether, if

**oben (adv.) — above, on the surface

oben-erwähnt or **-genannt** or **-gesagt** (adv.) — aforesaid

ober — upper

der **Oberbau** — superstructure

obere (adj.) — situated above, supreme

oberflächlich (adj.) — superficial

oberst (adj.) — uppermost; supreme

obgleich (conj.) — although

das **Obst (-es)** — fruit (mainly central-European fruit such as apples and plums, but not oranges and bananas)

obwohl — although

öde (adj.) — empty, desolate; dull

****oder** — or; **entweder . . . oder** — either . . . or

der **Ofen** (-s, -̈) — oven

offen (adj.) — open, frank, out-spoken

offenbar (adj.) — apparent, evident; obvious

offenbaren (v.t.) — to reveal

offenkundig (adj.) — clear, overt

offensichtlich (adj.) — obvious

öffentlich (adj.) — public

die **Öffentlichkeit** — public

öffnen (v.t. & v.r.) — to open

****oft** (adv.) — often

oftmals — often

****ohne** — without; **ohne . . . zu** — without . . . -ing

die **Ohnmacht** — impotence, faint

das **Ohr** (-s, -en) — ear

die **Ökonomie** (-s, -) — economy, economics

das **Öl** (-s, -e) — oil

der **Opferkrug** (-es, -̈e) — sacrificial vessel

opfern — to sacrifice

ordentlich (adj.) — orderly

ordnen (v.t.) — to arrange, classify

die **Ordnung** — the classification, order, arrangement; routine

der **Ort (-es, -e) — place, site

örtlich (adj.) — local, endemic

der **Osten (-s) — east; Orient; East Germany

das **Ostern** (-) — Easter, Passover

das **Österreich** — Austria

östlich (adj.) — eastern, easterly

die **Ostsee** — Baltic Sea

der **Ozean** (-s, -e) — ocean

P

* das **Paar** (-es, -e) — pair

****paar** (indecl. adj.) — couple; a few; some; **ein paar Blumen** — a few flowers

paaren (t. & r.) — to mate

* der **Pair** (-s, -s) — peer

der **Pakt** (-s, -e) — pact

das **Papier** (-s, -e) — paper, document

der **Papst** (-es, -̈e) — pope

das **Paradies** (-es, -e) — para-dise

der **Park** (-es, -̈e) — park

die **Partei** (-en) — faction, party; **Partei ergreifen** or **nehmen für** — to side with

* **parteiisch, parteilich** (adj.) — partial

passen (v.i.) — to be suited to; (v.r.) — to be proper

passieren (v.t.) — to pass; (v.i., aux.s.) — to happen

* **pathetisch** (adj.) — lofty, solemn, expressive, overemotional

das **Pech** (-es) — **Pech haben** — to have bad luck

die **Pein** — pain

peinlich (adj.) — painful, embarrassing; meticulous

der **Pelz** (-es, -e) — fur, pelt

der or das **Pendel** (-s, -) — pendulum

die **Perle** (-n) — pearl

* das **Personal** (-s) — personnel

persönlich (adj.) — personal

die **Personifizierung** — personification

* die **Pest** — plague

der **Pfarrer** (-s, -) — minister

die **Pfefferminze** — peppermint

das **Pferd (-es, -e)** — horse

das **Pfingsten** — Pentecost

die **Pflanze (-n)** — plant

die **Pflanzenkunde** — botany

* **pflegen** (v.i.) — to be in the habit of (v.t.) — to care for; cultivate

die **Pflicht (-en)** — duty, obligation

das **Pfund (-es, -e)** — pound, half a kilogram

die **Phantasie** — imagination

* der **Philosoph (-en, -en)** — philosopher

die **Philosophie** — philosophy

* der **Photograph (-en, -en)** — photographer

der **Pilger (-s, -)** — pilgrim

die **Pinie (-n)** — pine

die **Plage (-n)** — nuisance; plague

das **Plakat (-s, -e)** — sign, placard

der **Plan (-es, ⁻e)** — scheme, plan; chart, diagram

platt (adj.) — flat, dull, trite

der **Platz (-es, ⁻e)** — place, site, locality; **Platz nehmen** — to sit down

****plötzlich** (adv.) — suddenly

* **plump** (adj.) — clumsy, awkward

der **Pöbel (-s)** — mob, rabble

das **Polen** — Poland

die **Politik** — politics, policy

der **Posten (-s, -)** — post, position

prächtig (adj.) — magnificent, splendid

prägen (v.t.) — to stamp, emboss, impress; mold

* die **Prägnanz** — precision, terseness

prahlen (i.) — to brag

die **Praktik (-en)** — practice

predigen (v.t.) — to preach

die **Predigt (-en)** — sermon

der **Preis (-es, -e)** — price; prize

* **preis-geben** (irr. v.t.) — to surrender; to reveal; to expose; to abandon

der **Priester (-s, -)** — priest

der **Prinz (-en, -en)** — prince

das **Prinzip (-s, pl. -e** or **-pien)** — principle

die **Probe (-n)** — trial, test; sample

probieren (v.t.) — to test; to try

der **Prophet (-en, -en)** — prophet

die **Prosa** — prose

das **Prozent (-s, -e)** — per cent

der **Prozeß (-sses, -sse)** — legal proceedings, procedure, process

die **Prozession (-en)** — procession

prüfen (v.t.) — to examine, investigate, scrutinize; consider

das **Publikum (-s, no pl.)** — public

der **Pudel (-s, -)** — poodle

das **Pult (-es, -e)** — desk, lectern

der **Punkt (-es, -e)** — point, place, item, subject

pünktlich (adj.) — punctual

* **punktuell** (adj.) — selective

Q

die **Qual (-en)** — torment

quälen (v.t.) — to torture, torment; (v.r.) — to toil, struggle

das **Quartal (-s, -e)** — quarter of a year or of a day

* die **Quelle (-n)** — source; origin; **aus guter Quelle** — from a reliable source

quer (adj.) — diagonal; (adv.) — crosswise

der **Querschnitt** (-s, -e) — cross-section; profile

die **Quittung** — receipt

R

rächen (v.t.) — avenge; (v.r.) — to take revenge

* der **Rahmen** (-s, -) — background, setting, framework, scope

* die **Rakete** (-n) — rocket, missile

der **Rand** (-es, ̈-er) — edge, border

* der **Rang** (-es, ̈-e) — rank, degree, quality; **ersten Ranges** — first-class

* der **Rapport** (-s, -e) — report

rar (adj.) — rare

rasch (adj.) — quick; fast

rasen (v.i.) — to rage

die **Rasse** (-n) — race

der **Rat** (-es, pl. **Ratschläge**) — advice

raten, riet, hat geraten (v.i. & v.t.) — to advise; to guess, to conjecture; to solve

das **Rätsel** (-s, -) — riddle, mystery, enigma

die **Ratte** (-n) — rat

rauben (v.t.) — to steal, rob

der **Räuber** (-s, -) — robber

der **Rauch** (-es) — smoke

rauh (adj.) — rough, uneven, coarse

der **Raum** (-es, ̈-e) — room, space; scope, sphere

räumen (v.t.) — to remove; to clean

der **Rausch** (-es, ̈-e) — intoxication, frenzy; ecstasy

der **Realismus** — Realism

rechnen (v.t. & v.i.) — to count, calculate; estimate; rank

****recht** (adj.) — right-(hand); right, proper, fitting; (adv.) — well, rightly, rather, quite, very

das **Recht (-es, -e) — right; law; privilege; justice; **mit Recht** — with good reason

rechtfertigen (v.t.) — to justify

rechts (adv. prep.) — on the right, to the right

rechtsradikal (adj.) — extreme rightwing

rechtzeitig (adj.) — timely

der **Redakteur** (-s, -e) — editor

die **Redaktion** — editing

die **Rede** (-n) — speech, conversation; **eine Rede halten** — to make a speech; **der in Rede stehende Gegenstand** — the subject under discussion

****reden** (v.t. & v.i.) — to speak, talk, converse

redlich (adj.) — honest

das **Referat** (-es, -e) — lecture, report, review

die **Regel (-n) — rule, principle; **in der Regel** — as a rule

regeln (v.t.) — to regulate, control

der **Regen** (-s, -) — rain

regieren (v.t. & i.) — to rule, govern

die **Regierung** (-en) — government

regnen (v.i.) — to rain

reich (adj.) — rich, abundant, copious

das **Reich** (-es, -e) — empire, realm, kingdom

reichen (v.t.) — to reach; give; (v.i.) — to reach, extend, suffice

der **Reichtum** — wealth

reif (adj.) — ripe, mature, ready

die **Reihe** — row; rank; series

rein (adj.) — pure, sheer, clean

die **Reise (-n)** — journey, trip

reißen, riß, hat gerissen (v.t.) — to rip, tear; snatch, seize

reiten, ritt, ist geritten — to ride

der **Reiter (-s, -)** — rider

der **Reiz (-s, -e)** — attraction, incentive, stimulous

* **reizen** (v.t.) — to stimulate; to charm, appeal to; to irritate

reizend — charming

rentieren (v.i. & r.) — to be worthwhile

* der **Rest (-es, -e)** — remains; rest

retten (v.t.) — to save; (v.r.) — to escape

die **Reue** — repentance, remorse

der **Revolutionär (-s, -e)** — revolutionary

richten (v.t.) — to set right; to prepare; to direct; (v.i.) — to judge; to execute; pass sentence on

der **Richter (-s, -)** — judge

****richtig** (adj.) — right, correct, real; (adv.) — duly, properly

die **Richtung (-en)** — direction

riesig (adj.) — gigantic, enormous

ringen, rang, hat gerungen (v.i.) — to struggle (for)

rings (adv.) — all around

* der **Riß (-sses, -sse)** — gap, split; plan, sketch, outline

der **Ritter (-s, -)** — knight

roh (adj.) — raw, unrefined, rough

die **Rolle (-n)** — role, roll, part

das **Rom** — Rome

der **Roman (-s, -e) — novel

die **Romantik** — Romanticism

römisch (adj.) — Roman

die **Rose (-n)** — rose

das **Roß (-sses, -sse)** — horse, steed

rot — red

der **Rowdy (-s, -s)** — scoundrel

die **Rubrik (-en)** — category; column, rubric

rücken (v.t.) — to move, shift; (v.i., aux.s.) — to move

die **Rückkehr** — return

die **Rücksicht (-en)** — respect, regard

der **Rücktritt (-s, -e)** — resignation, withdrawal, retirement

rückwärts (adv.) — backwards

der **Ruf (-es, -e)** — call; repute, reputation, name, renown

rufen, rief, hat gerufen (v.t.) — to call; to send for

die **Ruhe** — rest, peace, calm

ruhen (i.) — to rest, sleep

der **Ruhetag (-es, -e)** — day of rest

der **Ruhm** — fame, glory

rühmen (v.t.) — to praise; (v.r.) — to boast

rühren (v.i.) — to touch, to come into contact with; (v.t. & r.) — to stir, move; to touch, set in motion

rund (adj.) — round; circular; (adv.) **rund heraussagen** — to say straight out

der **Rundfunk (-s)** — radio, broadcasting

das **Rußland** — Russia

die **Rüstung** — armaments, equipment, preparations

rutschen (v.i., aux.s.) — to slide, to move

S

die **Saat (-en)** — seed

der **Sabbat** — Sabbath

die **Sache (-n)** — thing, matter, cause, subject; business

sachlich (adj.) — factual, objective

der **Sack (-es, -e)** — sack

**sagen — to say, tell

die **Saite (-n)** — lyre; string

sammeln (v.t.) — to gather, collect; (v.r.) — to assemble; to concentrate

der **Sammelname (-ns, -n)** — collective name

die **Sammlung (-en)** — collection; composure

samt (prep.) — with dat. — together with, including

sämtlich(e) Werke — complete works

die **Sanduhr** — hourglass

sanft (adj.) — gentle, soft

satt (adj.) — full, satiated

der **Sattel (-s, -)** — saddle

**der Satz (-es, ⁻e) — sentence, clause, proposition

die **Sau (⁻e)** — sow

sauber (adj.) — clean, honest

sauer (adj.) — acrid, tart

saufen — to drink; to drink to excess

die **Säule (-n)** — column, pillar

säuseln (v.i.) — to rustle, whisper

die **Schablone (-s)** — stencil; routine; cliche

schade (pred. adj.) — pity

schaden (v.i.) — to harm; damage

das **Schaf (-es, -e)** — sheep

schaffen, schuf, hat geschaffen (v.t. & i.) — to create, to procure; to do, accomplish, provide

die **Scham** — shame

schämen (v.r.) — to be ashamed of

schamlos — shameless

die **Schande** — disgrace

die **Schar (-en)** — crowd

**scharf (adj.) — sharp, biting, caustic, precise, exact

der **Schatten** — shadow, shade

der **Schatz (-es, ⁻e)** — treasure; love

schätzen (v.t.) — to value, assess

die **Schau (-en)** — sight, view, show

schauen (v.t.) — to see, perceive; (v.i.) — to look, gaze

das **Schauspiel (-s, -e)** — spectacle, drama

der **Schauspieler (-s, -)** — actor; die **Schauspielerin (-nen)** — actress

* scheiden, schied, ist geschieden (v.i.) — to separate, depart

der **Schein (-es, -e)** — appearance, shine, pretense

scheinbar (adj.) — apparent

**scheinen, schien, ist or hat geschienen (v.t. & i.) — to appear, to shine

scheitern (v.i., aux.s.) — to fail, break down

das **Schema (-s, -s or -ta)** — scheme, model, pattern, diagram

schenken (v.t.) — to give, present

die **Scherbe (-n)** — fragment

scherzen (i.) — to joke, kid

scheu (adj.) — shy

die **Scheu** — shyness; awe, dread

scheuen — to shun, avoid

die **Schicht (-en)** — layer; shift, division

* **schicken** (v.t.) — to send, dispatch; (v.r.) — to happen, to be fitting
** das **Schicksal (-s, -e)** — destiny, fate
schieben, schob, hat geschoben (v.t., r. & i.) to push, shove, delay
schief (adj.) — oblique; inappropriate; (adv.) — aslant, askew
schießen, schoß, hat geschossen (v.i.) — shoot; burst forth
das **Schiff (-es, -e)** — ship
der **Schild (-es, -e)** — shield, emblem
schildern (v.t.) — to portray, describe
schimpfen (v.t.) — to insult, scold
die **Schlacht (-en)** — battle
schlachten (v.t. & i.) — to slay
der **Schlaf (-es)** — sleep
schlafen, schlief, hat geschlafen (v.i.) — to sleep
der **Schlag (-es, ⁻e)** — blow, stroke
schlagen, schlug, hat geschlagen (v.t.) — to hit; (v.t. & i.) — to beat, strike
das **Schlagwort (-s, -e or ⁻er)** — slogan
* die **Schlange (-n)** — line; snake
schlank (adj.) — slim, slender
schlau (adj.) — sly, clever
** **schlecht** (adj. & adv.) — bad, wicked
schleichen, schlich, ist geschlichen — to creep
der **Schleier (-s, -)** — veil, haze
schlicht (adj.) — plain, simple
schlichten — to arrange, adjust
** **schließen, schloß, hat geschlossen** (v.t.) — to close, end; conclude; to strike a bargain
** **schließlich** (adj. & adv.) — final, finally; after all
das **Schloß (-sses, ⁻sser)** — lock; castle
der **Schluß (-sses, ⁻sse)** — end, conclusion; closing
der **Schlüssel (-s, -)** — key
schmachvoll — disgraceful
schmählich (adj.) — ignominious
* **schmal** (adj.) — narrow, slim
schmecken (v.i.) — to taste
schmeicheln (v.i.) — to flatter
der **Schmerz (-es, -en)** — pain
schmerzlich — painful
der **Schmutz (-es)** — dirt, filth
der **Schneeball** — snowball
schneiden, schnitt, hat geschnitten (v.t. & i.) — to cut
** **schnell** (adj. & adv.) — fast, quick
* der **Schnitt (-es, -e)** — cut, section; style; editing
** **schon** (adv.) — already; even; before; certainly; really; just
** **schön** (adj.) — beautiful; good (adv.) — beautifully, very
der **Schöpfer (-s, -)** — creator
die **Schöpfung** — creation
der **Schoß (-es, ⁻e)** — lap
schräg (adj.) — slanting; suspicious
schrecken — to frighten, scare
schrecklich (adj.) — frightful
der **Schrei (-es, -e)** — cry, shout
** **schreiben, schrieb, hat geschrieben** (v.t. & i.) — to write
schreien, schrie, hat geschrien (v.t. & i.) — to cry, shout
schreiten, schritt, ist geschritten — to stride, to proceed (**zu**) to; to march

* die **Schrift (-en)** — writing, script, publication; die **Heilige Schrift** — the Holy Scriptures

der **Schriftsteller (-s, -)** — author, writer

der **Schritt (-es, -e)** — step, pace; **den ersten Schritt tun** — to make the first move

schroff (adj.) — rough, abrupt; curt

schrumpfen (v.i., aux.s.) — to shrink, depreciate, decline

der **Schuh (-es, -e)** — shoe

die **Schularbeit (-en)** — school work

das **Schulbeispiel (-s, -e)** — classic example

die **Schuld (-en)** — debt, obligation; guilt, sin; blame, responsibility

schulden (v.t.) — to owe, be indebted to

schuldig — guilty

die **Schule (-n)** — school, college, school of thought

der **Schüler (-s, -)** — schoolboy; disciple, follower

* der **Schuß (-sses, -̈sse)** — shot; **in Schuß kommen** — to get going; **im Schuß sein** — to be in full swing

der **Schuster (-s, -)** — cobbler

der **Schutz (-es, no pl.)** — shelter, refuge; **in Schutz nehmen** — to defend

schützen (v.t.) — to protect **(vor)** — from, against

schwach (adj.) — weak, poor, sparse

die **Schwäche (-n)** — weakness, shortcoming

schwanken (v.t.) — to sway, waver; oscillate; hesitate

der **Schwärmer (-s, -)** — dreamer, visionary; fanatic, zealot

schwarz (adj.) — black, gloomy; illicit; der **schwarze Markt** — the black market

schweben (v.i.) — to soar; hang (in the air); be pending

der **Schwede (-n, -n)** — Swede

schweigen, schwieg, hat geschwiegen (v.i.) — to be silent

das **Schwein (-s, -e)** — swine

die **Schweiz** — Switzerland

die **Schwelle (-n)** — threshold; brink

schwellen, schwoll, ist geschwollen (v.i.) — to swell, expand

****schwer** (adj.) — heavy, serious; difficult; severe

schwerlich (adj.) — hardly

die **Schwermut** — melancholy

der **Schwerpunkt (-s, -e)** — center of gravity; main focus

die **Schwester (-n)** — sister

schwierig (adj.) — difficult; die **Schwierigkeit (-en)** — difficulty

schwimmen, schwamm, ist or **hat geschwommen** — to swim

der **Schwindel (-s)** — dizziness; fraud

schwinden, schwand, ist geschwunden (v.i.) — to shrink, dwindle; to disappear; fade

schwingen, schwang, hat geschwungen (v.t.) — to swing, wave; (v.r.) — to leap, soar; (v.i.) — to swing; linger

schwören, schwor, hat geschworen (v.t. & i.) — to swear

der **Schwung (-s, ¨e)** — verve, momentum

* **sechs** — six

* der **See (-s, -n)** — lake, pond

* die **See (-n)** — sea, ocean

die **Seele (-n)** — soul, spirit, heart; human being

seelisch (adj.) — spiritual, emotional, mental

der **Segen (-s, -)** — blessing; prosperity

****sehen, sah, hat gesehen** (v.t.) — to see, perceive, watch; **sehen lassen** — to show; **sich sehen lassen** — to appear; **sehen auf** (acc.) — to look over; to pay attention to

sehnen (v.r.) — to long, yearn **(nach)** — for

die **Sehnsucht (¨e)** — yearning

****sehr** (adv.) — very, most; very much

****sein** (adj.) — his, its

****sein, war, ist gewesen** (v.i.) — to be, exist, occur, be alive; **der Ansicht** or **der Meinung sein** — to be of the opinion; **es ist mir, als ob** — I feel as if, it seems to me

das **Sein** — being, existence

seinesgleichen (indecl. adj., pron.) — people like him

seinethalben, seinetwegen, seinetwillen (adv.) — on his account, for his sake

****seit** (prep.) with dat. — for; since

seitdem (conj. and adv.) — since

die **Seite (-n)** — side; page; feature

seither (adv.) — since (then)

****selber, selbst** (indecl. adj.) — self; **das versteht sich von**

selbst — that goes without saying; **selbst** (adv.) — even

selbständig (adj.) — self-reliant, independent

die **Selbsterkenntnis** — self-knowledge

selbstgefällig (adj.) — self-satisfied

selbstsicher (adj.) — self-assured

die **Selbstsucht** — egoism, selfishness

die **Selbstüberwindung** — self-conquest; will-power

selbstvergessen (adj.) — absent-minded

selbstverständlich (adj. & adv.) — obvious

****selten** (adj.) — rare, unusual; (adv.) — seldom

seltsam (adj. & adv.) — odd, peculiar

die **Semmel (-n)** — roll

die **Sendepause** — interval; deathly silence

senkrecht (adj.) — perpendicular

* **sensibel** (adj.) — sensitive

* **sensitiv** (adj.) — hypersensitive

****setzen** (v.t.) — to place, set; **den Fall setzen** — to suppose; **Grenzen setzen** — to set limits; **gesetzt, es wäre so** — supposing it were so; (v.r.) — to seat oneself; to settle

seufzen (v.i.) — to sigh

der **Seufzer (-s, -)** — sigh

****sich** (refl. pron.) — himself, herself, itself, themselves, yourself; **es fragt sich** — it is a question whether

sicher (adj.) — secure, safe; sure; certain, confident

sicherlich (adv.) — surely, certainly

sichern (v.t.) — to secure, make safe; (v.i.) — to be watchful

die **Sicht** — sight, view

sichtbar (adj.) — visible, evident

**sie — she, her, they, them

**Sie — you

der **Sieg (-es, -e)** — conquest, victory

sinken, sank, ist gesunken (v.i.) — to sink, subside; decline, decrease

* der **Sinn (-es, -e)** — sense, tendency; meaning, significance

das **Sinnbild (-es, -er)** — symbol

sinnen, sann, ist (or **hat**) **gesonnen** — to think, brood, muse

sinnlich (adj.) — sensual; sensuous, perceptible

sinnlos (adj.) — senseless; futile

die **Sitte (-n)** — custom, habit, tradition; practice

die **Sittenlehre** — ethics, moral philosophy

sittlich (adj.) — moral, ethical

der **Sitz (-es, -e)** — seat; residence

sitzen, saß, hat gesessen (v.i.) — to sit; to be, to be situated

die **Sitzung (-en)** — session, conference

so (adv.) — so, thus, in this or that way; **ein so — such a; **so etwas** — such a thing; **so sehr** — to such a degree; **so . . . wie** — as . . . as; (conj.) — therefore, consequently

sobald (conj.) — as soon as

sofern (conj.) — inasmuch as; provided that

sofort (adv.) — immediately

**sogar — even, in addition, besides

sogenannt (adj.) — so-called

sogleich — at once, immediately

der **Sohn (-es, ̈-e)** — son

solang(e) — as long as

**solch (adj.) — such

der **Soldat (-en, -en)** — soldier

sollen (modal) — to be obliged to; to be said to; should; **er soll es geschrieben haben — he is said to have written it; **man sollte meinen** — one would think; **Jahre sollten vergehen, bevor** — years were to pass before . . .

somit (adv.) — consequently

die **Sonderausgabe (-n)** — special edition

sonderbar (adj.) — singular, strange

* **sondern** (v.t.) — to separate; to distinguish

**sondern (conj.) — on the contrary

die **Sonne (-n)** — sun

der **Sonnenschein (-s)** — sunshine

sonst (adv.) — else, otherwise, moreover

die **Sorge (-n)** — concern, worry

sorgen (i.) — to take care, attend to

sorgfältig (adj.) — careful

souverän (adj.) — sovereign

soviel (conj.) — as far as; **soviel ich weiß** — as far as I know

sowieso (adv.) — anyway

der **Sowjet (-s, -s)** — Soviet

sowohl (conj.) **als** — both . . . and; as well as

der **Soziologe (-n, -n)** — sociologist

der **Spalt (-es, -en)** — cleft, fissure

spannend (adj.) — exciting, tense

die **Spannung (-en)** — stretching, strain; suspense, tension

sparen — to save, spare

spärlich (adj.) — scanty, sparse

sparsam (adj.) — economical

der **Spaß** (-es, -̈e) — fun; **es macht mir Spaß** — I enjoy (it)

****spät** (adj. & adv.) — late

spätestens (adv.) — at the latest

sperren (v.t.) — to barricade; to spread or stretch out; to ban

der **Spiegel** (-s, -) — mirror, reflector; das **Spiegelbild** (-es, -er) — reflection; **spiegeln** (v.t.) — to reflect; (v.r.) — to be reflected

das **Spiel** (-es, -e) — play, sport, game; **aufs Spiel setzen** — to risk

spielen — to play

der **Spielkamerad** (-en, -en) —

das **Spielkind** (-es, -er) — playmate

der **Spießbürger** (-s, -) — narrow-minded person, bourgeois

die **Spinne** (-n) — spider

der **Spion** (-s, -e) — spy

die **Spitze** (-n) — point, peak; summit; **auf die Spitze treiben** — to carry to extremes

* **splendid** (adj.) — generous; handsome

der **Spott** (-es) — mockery, scorn, sarcasm

die **Sprache** (-n) — language; speech

der **Sprachforscher** (-s, -) — linguist, philologist

sprachlos — speechless

****sprechen, sprach, hat gesprochen** (v.t & v.i.) — to speak, talk (**mit**) to or with; (**über, von**) — about

das **Sprichwort** (-es, -̈er) — proverb

springen, sprang, ist (or **hat**) **gesprungen** — to spring, leap; to gush, burst

der **Spruch** (-es, -̈e) — maxim; verdict

der **Sprung** (-es, -̈e) — jump, leap; **auf dem Sprung sein, etwas zu tun** — to be about to do something

spucken (t. & i.) — to spit

spüren (v.t.) — to feel, perceive, experience; (v.i.) **nach-spüren** — to track down, search for

der **Staat (-es, -en) — state, nation; die **Staatskunst** — politics; **Staatswissenschaft** — political science

der **Staatsstreich** (-s, -e) — coup d'état

der **Stabreim** (-s, -e) — alliteration

der **Stachel** (-s, -n) — thorn, quill

der **Stacheldraht** — barbed wire

die **Stadt (-̈e) — city, town

der **Stall** (-̈e) — stable

* der **Stamm** (-s, -̈e) — tribe, race, stem; core; regular customer

der **Stand** (-es, -̈e or **no pl.**) — foothold; situation, condition, state; **gut im Stand sein** — to be in good condition; **Leute von Stand** — people of rank

das **Standesbewußtsein** — class-consciousness

ständig (adj. & adv.) — fixed, constant, permanent

der **Standpunkt** (-es, -e) — viewpoint

****stark** (adj.) — strong, thick, heavy (adv.) — greatly, very much die **Stärke (-n)** — strength, power; magnitude; greatness

starr (adj.) — rigid, inflexible, stubborn

**statt (prep.) — with gen. — instead of; (conj.) — instead of

die **Statt (-)** — place, stead

die **Stätte (-n)** — place, abode

statt-finden (irr. v.i.) — to take place, happen

der **Staub (-es)** — dust

stechen, stach, hat gestochen (v.t. & i.) — to prick, pierce

stecken (v.t.) — to put, place, insert; (v.r.) — **sich hinter eine Sache stecken** — to get behind something; (v.i.) — to be, stay, remain; to lie hidden

stehen, stand, hat (ist) gestanden (v.i.) — to stand; to be situated; to be written; to stand still, to stop; **auf einem Zettel stehen — to appear on a note; **es steht bei ihnen** — it is in their power; **fest stehen** — to be firm

stehen-bleiben (irr. v.i., aux.s.) — to remain standing; to stand still; to stop

stehen-lassen (irr. v.t.) — to ignore; to forget; overlook

stehlen, stahl, hat gestohlen (v.i. & t.) — to steal

steif (adj.) — stiff, rigid **(vor)** with; clumsy, awkward

steigen, stieg, ist gestiegen (v.i.) — to climb; to increase; rise; to advance; to take place, be held

steigern (v.t.) — to raise, increase; to heighten; (v.r.) — to become greater or intensified

der **Stein (-es, -e)** — stone; **Stein des Anstoßes** — stumbling-block; **Stein der Weisen** — philosopher's stone

der **Stein(ab)druck** — lithograph

* die **Stelle (-n)** — position, site; passage (in a book); **auf der Stelle** — on the spot

stellen (v.t.) — to put, place, lay, set; impose (conditions on); **einen Antrag stellen — to make a motion; **Bedingungen stellen** — to impose conditions; **in Frage stellen** — to call into question; **zur Diskussion stellen** — to throw open to discussion; (v.r.) — to place or post or position oneself; to appear; to surrender; to pretend to be; **sich stellen gegen** — to oppose; **die Probleme, die sich allen Gelehrten stellen** — the problems confronting all scholars

die **Stellung** — position; attitude; post; situation; social position; supply

die **Stellungnahme (-n)** — point of view

**sterben, starb, ist gestorben (v.i.) — to die

sterblich (adj.) — mortal

der **Stern (-es, -e)** — star

das **Sternchen** — asterisk

sternenklar — starlit

**stets (adv.) — constantly, always

die **Steuer (-n)** — tax

steuern (v.t.) — to steer; to drive; to control; (v.i., aux.s.) — to put a stop to; to head

* der **Stich (-es, -e)** — stab, prick; tinge; hint; suggestion

der **Stichel** — style, graving tool

stichhaltig (adj.) — sound, valid, lasting; conclusive

das **Stichwort (-es, -e)** — key word, cue, party-cry (pol.)

der **Stier (-es, -e)** — steer

stiften (v.t.) — to found, establish, endow; cause

der **Stifter (-s, -)** — donator; founder

* der **Stil (-es, -e)** — style, manner

****still** (adj.) — silent, soft, still, calm; **Stiller Freitag** — Good Friday; **Stiller Ozean** — Pacific Ocean

die **Stille** — quiet, silence, stillness

* **stillos** (adj.) — without style

die **Stimme (-n)** — voice, vote, opinion

stimmen (v.i.) — to agree, be right

die **Stimmung** — mood, atmosphere; morale

stocken (v.i.) — to falter; to reach a deadlock; to break off

die **Stockung** — interruption, breakdown

der **Stoff (-es, -e)** — matter, material; subject

stolz (adj.) — proud, arrogant, conceited; majestic

stören (v.t.) — to interrupt, disturb, inconvenience; (v.i.) — to intrude

stoßen, stieß, hat gestoßen (v.t.) — to push, thrust, shove, strike; to drive out; (v.r.) **sich stoßen an** — to take offence at; (v.i.) to border, touch, adjoin; (aux., s.) — swoop down, encounter

die **Strafe (-n)** — punishment, penalty, retribution

straff (adj.) — stretched, taut; austere, stern

das **Strafrecht** — criminal law

strahlen (v.i.) — to radiate, shine; glow

die **Straße (-n) — street, road, highway, route; **auf der Straße liegen** — to be there all around us

sträuben (v.r.) — to struggle against

streben (v.i.) — to strive, to struggle, to aspire

strecken (v.t.) — to stretch, extend, elongate, spread out

der **Streich (-es, -e)** — stroke; prank

* **streichen, strich, hat gestrichen** (v.t.) — to stroke, touch; (v.i., aux.s.) — to extend, stretch, roam; (v.t.) to strike, cut, erase, cancel; to paint

streiten, stritt, hat gestritten (v.i.) — to quarrel, argue; **darüber läßt sich streiten** — that is a moot point

die **Streitschrift (-en)** — polemic

****streng(e)** (adj.) — severe, strict; (adv.) — **sich streng halten an** — to adhere strictly to

strenggläubig (adj.) — orthodox

der **Strich (-es, -e)** — stroke, line, dash; sketch; region

das **Stroh (-es)** — straw

der **Strom (-es, ̈e)** — stream, current, crowd

die **Strophe (-n)** — stanza, verse

das **Stück (-es, -e)** — piece, part; extract (from a book)

der **Student (en, -en)** — student

die **Studie (-n)** — sketch, study

studieren — to study

die **Stufe (-n)** — stage, phase; degree; nuance

stufenartig (adj.) — gradual

der **Stuhl (-es, ̈e)** — chair

stumm (adj.) — mute, silent, dumb

stumpf (adj.) — blunt, obtuse; dull, indifferent

****die Stunde (-n)** — hour; **zu guter Stunde** — in good time

stundenlang (adj. & adv.) — lasting for hours

der **Sturm (-es, ⁻e)** — storm; tumult; turmoil; **Sturm und Drang** — Storm and Stress; emotion

* **stürzen** (v.i., aux.s.) — to fall or tumble down, to plunge; (v.t.) — to throw down, overturn, upset

* **stützen** (v.t.) — to support; (v.r.) — to rest, lean on; to rely, depend, be based on

****suchen** (v.t. & i.) — to seek, desire, search **(nach)** for

die **Sucht (⁻e)** — passion; obsession

der **Süden (-s)** — South

südlich (adj.) — south, southern, southerly; **südöstlich** (adj.) — south-easterly; **südostwärts** (adv.) — south-easterly

südwestlich (adj.) — southwestern

die **Summa (pl. Summen)** — **in summa** — in short, to sum up

die **Summe (-n)** — sum; total

die **Sünde (-n)** — sin, transgression

der **Sündenbock (-s, ⁻e)** — scapegoat

die **Suppe (-n)** — soup

süß (adj.) — sweet, charming, dear

der **Symbolismus** — Symbolism (in art)

sympathisch (adj.) — congenial, likeable; pleasant

die **Szene (-n)** — scene; **in Szene setzen** — to stage

T

der **Tadel (-s, -)** — reprimand, reproach; criticism, censure

die **Tafel (-n)** — board, blackboard, tablet, table, chart, diagram

der **Tag (-es, -e) — day, daylight; **alle Tage** — every day; **an den Tag bringen** — to bring to light, to disclose; **dieser Tage** (past) — recently, (fut.) — one of these days; **in acht Tagen** — in a week; **der Jüngste Tag** — Doomsday

das **Tagebuch (-s, ⁻er)** — diary, journal

tagelang (adj. & adv.) — for days

tagen (v.i.) — to hold a meeting; **es tagt bei ihr** — it dawns on her

das **Tageslicht (-s)** — daylight; **ans Tageslicht kommen** — to become known

die **Tagesordnung** — agenda

täglich (adj.) — daily

* der **Takt (-es, -e)** — time (music), rhythm; tact

das **Tal (-es, ⁻er)** — valley

der **Tanz (-es, ⁻e) — dance, ball

tanzen (v.t. & v.i.) — to dance

das **Tapet** — **aufs Tapet bringen** — to introduce (a subject)

tapfer (adj.) — brave, heroic

tarnen (v.t.) — to camouflage; disguise, mask

die **Tastatur (-en)** — keyboard

tasten (v.i.) — to touch, feel

* die **Tat (-en)** — deed, act; **in der Tat** — in fact

tätig (adj.) — active, busy, engaged, effective

die **Tatsache** (-n) — fact

tatsächlich (adv.) — really; (adj.) — real

taub (adj.) — deaf; oblivious

der **Taube** — deaf one

die **Taube** (-n) — pigeon

tauchen — to immerse, dip

taugen (v.i.) — to be of use (zu) for; **zu nichts taugen** — to be worthless

* **tauschen** (v.t. & i.) — to exchange; to swap

* **täuschen** (v.t. & i.) — to deceive, betray; (v.r.) — to be mistaken

tausend (adj.) — thousand

die **Technik (-en) — technical or applied science, engineering; technology; technique

der **Teich** (-es, -e) — pond

der or das **Teil (-s, -e) — part, portion, share; **zum Teil** — to some extent, in part

teilen (v.t.) — to divide, separate, share; (v.r.) — to participate in

teil-haben (irr. v.i.) — participate

teil-nehmen (irr. v.i.) — to participate, collaborate

teils (adv.) — partly, part

der **Tempelraub** — sacrilege

der **Termin** (-s, -e) — appointed or fixed time or term of date or day; deadline

****teuer** (adj.) — dear, expensive, beloved

der **Teufel** (-s, -) — devil

der **Teufelskreis** — vicious circle

die **Textkritik** — textual criticism

das **Thema** (-s, pl. -ta or -men) — theme, subject; topic

der **Theologe** (-n, -n) — theologian

der **Theoretiker** (-s, -) — theorist

die **These** (-n) — thesis, postulate

der **Thron** (-es, -e) — throne; der **Thronräuber** — usurper

****tief** (adj.) — deep, profound, low, innermost, utmost, extreme; (adv.) — deep, deeply; profoundly; **tiefer begründen** — to substantiate more fully

die **Tiefe** (-n) — depth, profundity, abyss

die **Tiefenpsychologie** — depth psychology, psychoanalysis

tiefgreifend (adj.) — far-reaching, through-going, fundamental

der **Tiefsinn** — pensiveness; profundity

das **Tier** (-es, -e) — animal, beast

der **Tierkreis** — zodiac

die **Tierkunde** — zoology

tilgen (v.i.) — to extinguish, to obliterate, cancel; to pay off

der **Tisch** (-es, -e) — table

der **Titel** (-s, -) — title, heading, claim; section

die **Tochter** (-) — daughter

der **Tod (-es, most commonly with no pl.) — death, decease

die **Todesangst** — mortal terror

tödlich (adj.) — fatal, deadly, mortal

das **Tohuwabohu** (-s, -s) — hullabaloo, chaos

toll (adj.) — mad, wild, crazy (coll.) — terrific

der **Ton** (-es, -̈e) — sound; note (mus.); **den Ton angeben** — to give the note, to set the tone

das **Tonband** (-es, -̈er) — (recording) tape

die **Tondichtung** — musical composition; symphonic poem

tönen — to sound, to shade

tonlos (adj.) — soundless, voiceless, toneless

die **Tönung (-en)** — shade, tint, tone, shading

der **Topf (-es, ⏞e)** — pot

* der **Tor (-en, -en)** — fool

* das **Tor (-en, -e)** — gate, portal

töricht (adj.) — foolish

torkeln (i.) — to stagger

** **tot** (adj.) — dead, defunct, extinct; das **Tote Meer** — the Dead Sea

töten (v.t.) — to kill

totgeboren (adj.) — stillborn, abortive

trachten (v.i.) — to strive **(nach)** after or for

träge (adj.) — sluggish

** **tragen, trug, hat getragen** (v.t.) — to carry, bear, wear (clothes); to support, sustain, uphold, endure; (v.r.) — **sich tragen mit** — to have on one's mind

die **Tragik** — tragedy

die **Tragödie (-n)** — tragedy, calamity

die **Träne (-n)** — tear(drop)

die **Traube (-n)** — grape

trauen (v.i.) — to trust; (v.r.) — to venture, dare; (v.t.) — to marry

die **Trauer** — mourning, grief

der **Traum (-s, ⏞e)** — dream, vision

das **Traumbild (-es, -er)** — vision

träumen (t. & i.) — to dream

traurig (adj.) — sad, melancholy

** **treffen, traf, hat getroffen** (v.t.) — to hit, strike, affect, concern, encounter; **Maßnahmen treffen** — to take action; das **Unglück traf ihn** — he had the misfortune; (v.r.) — to meet; **es**

traf sich, daß . . . — it so happened that . . .; **treffen auf** (acc.) — to come upon

treffend (adj.) — appropriate

trefflich — excellent

* **treiben, trieb, hat getrieben** (v.t.) — to drive, set in motion, operate; impel, induce; pursue, cultivate; **eine Politik treiben** — to pursue a policy; **sich treiben lassen** — to take things as they come

trennen (v.t. & r.) — to separate, divide, sever

treten, trat, ist (or **hat**) **getreten** (v.i.) — to step, stride; **ans Licht treten** — to come to light, appear; **zur Seite treten** — to step aside; **zutage treten** — to appear, become evident

treu (adj.) — faithful, loyal

der **Trieb (-es, -e)** — impulse, urge, desire

trinken, trank, hat getrunken (v.t.) — to drink, absorb

das **Trinklied (-es, -er)** — drinking song

trocken (adj.) — dry, dull, uninteresting, tedious

der **Trost (-es, no pl.)** — comfort, consolation, solace

trotz (prep.) with gen. — in spite of; der **Trotz (-es)** — defiance

trotzdem (adv.) — nevertheless; (conj.) — even though, although

trübe (adj.) — muddy, cloudy; gloomy, melancholy; bleak

trüben — to pollute

trügen, trog, hat getrogen (v.t.) — to deceive, delude

tüchtig (adj.) — fit, able; (adv.) — well, thoroughly

die **Tugend (-en)** — virtue

****tun, tat, hat getan** (v.t.) — to do, perform, execute, make; **es tut nichts** — it does not matter; (v.i.) — to act, do; **er tut, als wäre er glücklich** — he acts as if he were happy; **das will getan sein** — that needs to be done; **das läßt sich tun** — that may or can be done

die **Tür (-en)** — door; **vor der Tür stehen** — to be forthcoming

der **Turm (-es, ⁻e)** — tower, spire

typisch — typical

U

übel (adj.) — evil, bad, wrong, ill

üben (v.t.) — to exercise, practice; **Geduld üben** — to have patience; **Nachsicht üben** — to show consideration; **geübtes Auge** — trained eye

****über** (prep.) — with dat. or acc. — over, above, about; (adv.) — over, above, too much

über- (pref. to nouns and adjs.) — over, super, hyper, etc.

über- (verb pref.) — in intransitive verbs, the prefix is usually inseparable; with most compound transitive verbs, the prefix may be both separable and inseparable; when the verb is separable, the meaning is usually literal (**übersetzen** — sep. — to set over); when the verb is inseparable, the meaning is usually figurative (**übersetzen** — insep. — to translate)

überall (adv.) — everywhere

der **Überbau (-es, -e)** — superstructure

der **Überblick (-es, -e)** — overview, survey, synopsis; perspective

überdies (adv.) — besides, moreover

überdrüssig — bored with

der **Überdruß (-sses)** — boredom, ennui

übereinander (adv.) — one upon the other, about each other

überein-kommen (irr. v.i.) & **überein-stimmen** (v.i.) — to agree, to reach an agreement

über-fallen — to come over

der **Überfluß (-sses)** — abundance, plenty, wealth, superfluity; **überflüssig** (adj.) — superfluous

überfragen (v.t. & i.) — to overwhelm with questions; **ich bin überfragt** — I don't know

der **Übergang (-s, ⁻e)** — transition, conversion; crossing

übergeben (irr. v.t. insep.) — to hand over; to entrust; to surrender

übergehen (irr. v.i., aux.s.) — to overflow, to merge; to change; (sep. v.t.) — to overlook

****überhaupt** (adv.) — on the whole, generally; **überhaupt nicht** — not at all

überhin (adv.) — superficially, sketchily

überholen (v.t.) — to overtake, to surpass; **überholt** — antiquated

über-kochen (i.) — to boil over

überlassen (irr. v.t., insep.) — to relinquish, abandon

überlaufen (irr. v.t. insep.) — to overrun, to seize; (sep., i., aux.s.) — to overflow

überleben (v.t., insep.) — to survive, outlive

* **überlegen** (v.t. & i.) — to reflect on; think, consider

* **überlegen** (adj.) — superior to

überliefern (v.t. insep.) — to deliver, hand over, hand down; die **Überlieferung** — tradition

übermäßig (adj.) — excessive

der **Übermut (-s)** — high spirits; arrogance

übernehmen (irr. v.t., insep.) — to accept, receive, to take charge of; (v.r., insep.) — to overexert, take on too much

überparteilich (adj.) — nonpartisan

überraschen (v.t.) — to surprise

überreden (v.t. insep.) — to persuade; **sich überreden lassen** — to let oneself be persuaded

überschätzen (v.t.) — to overestimate (insep.)

der **Überschlag (-s, ¨-e)** — (rough) estimate

über-schreiten — to cross over

* **übersehen** (irr. v.t.) — to survey, glance over; to overlook, fail to notice

übersetzen (v.t.) — to translate

die **Übersicht** — survey, review, outline, synopsis

überstehen (irr. v.t., insep.) & **übersteigen** (irr. v.t., insep.) — to transcend; get through; survive

* die **Übertragung** — transference; translation; communication; broadcast

übertreiben (irr. v.t., insep.) — to exaggerate

der **Übertritt (-es, -e)** — conversion

übervoll — overflowing

überwältigen (v.t., insep.) — to defeat; overcome; overwhelm

überwinden (irr. v.t., insep.) — to overcome, prevail over; die **Überwindung** — overcoming, self-control

überzeugen (v.t.) — to convince, persuade; **der Überzeugung sein** — to be convinced

die **Überzeugung (-en)** — conviction

üblich (adj.) — usual, customary

übrig (adj.) — left over, remaining

** **übrigens** (adv.) — by the way, moreover

die **Übung (-en)** — exercise, practice

das **Ufer (-s, -)** — shore

** die **Uhr (-en)** — clock, watch, o'clock, hour; **um fünf Uhr** — at five o'clock

das **Uhrwerk (-es, -e)** — clockwork

** **um** (prep.) with acc. — at (with time), around (with place); **um . . . willen** (prep.) with gen. — for the sake of; **um . . . zu** — in order to (conj.); **die Zeit ist um** — the time is up

die **Umarbeitung** — adaptation

umarmen — to embrace

um-bringen (irr. v.t.) — to kill

um-deuten (v.t.) — to give a new meaning or interpretation to

um-drehen (v.t.) — to turn, rotate

um-fallen (i., aux.s.) — to fall down

der **Umfang (-es, ̈e)** — circumference, extent, range, volume

* **um-fassen** (v.t.) — to enclose, to surround; to include; **umfassend** — complete, comprehensive

die **Umfrage** — survey

der **Umgang** — contact; acquaintances

die **Umgebung** — surroundings, environment, background

* **um-gehen** (irr. v.i., aux.s.) — to circulate; **umgehen (mit)** — to deal with, associate with; **mit etwas umgehen** — to be occupied with; (v.t., insep.) — to evade, avoid

umgekehrt (adj.) — opposite, reverse; (adv.) — on the contrary

um-gestalten (v.t.) — to alter, transform; to reform; to reorganize

umher (adv.) — about, around; all around

um-hüllen (v.t., insep.) — to envelop, cover; to veil

um-kehren (v.i., aux.s.) — to turn around, to reform; (v.t.) — to overturn

um-kommen (irr. v.i., aux.s.) — to perish

der **Umriß (-sses, -sse)** — sketch, outline

* **um-schließen** (irr. v.t.) — to enclose, surround; include

um-setzen (v.t.) — to shift, transfer; translate ideas into action, convert

die **Umsicht** — caution, prudence

umsonst (adj.) — for nothing; in vain

* der **Umstand (-es, ̈e)** — circumstance; situation; (pl.) — particúlars, details; **unter Umständen** — in certain cases; **Umstände machen** — to cause trouble

umständlich (adj.) — circumstantial; complicated, intricate

umwälzend (adj.) — involved; radical

der **Umweg (-es, -e)** — roundabout way; **auf Umwegen** — indirectly

die **Umwelt** — environment

um-werfen — to knock over

um-werten (v.t.) — to revalue, reassess

un- (neg. pref.) — un-, in-, non-

unabänderlich (adj.) — unalterable

unabhängig (adj.) — independent **(von)** — of, or irrespective of

unablässig (adj.) — incessant

unbedacht (adj.) — inconsiderate, careless, indiscrete

unbedingt (adj.) — unconditional, absolute; (adv.) — in any case, by all means

das **Unbehagen (-s)** — discomfort, malaise

unbeholfen (adj.) — clumsy

unbekannt — unfamiliar

unbesehen — indiscriminately

** **und** (conj.) — and; **und zwar** — that is; **und so weiter (usw.)** — and so on (etc.)

unendlich (adj.) — infinite

unersättlich — insatiable

der **Unfall (-es, ̈e)** — accident

unfreiwillig — involuntarily

der **Unfug (-es)** — nonsense

ungeachtet (prep.) with gen. — despite, notwithstanding

**ungefähr (adj.) — approximate, casual; (adv.) — about

ungeheuer (adj.) — huge, immense, monstrous; outrageous

ungelenk (adj.) — awkward

ungemein (adj.) — immense

ungern (adv.) — reluctantly

unglaubwürdig (adj.) — implausible

ungleichmäßig — irregular

das **Unglück (-es, -e)** — misfortune, unhappiness

unheimlich (adj.) — frightening, eerie, sinister

**die Universität (-en) — university

* unmittelbar (adj.) — immediate; (adv.) — directly

unnütz (adj.) — useless, superfluous

**unmöglich — impossible

unruhig — restless

**uns — us

unsäglich — unspeakable

die **Unschuld** — innocence

**unser — our

**unten (adv.) — below, underneath

unter (prep.) with acc. or dat. — under, among; **unter anderem — among other things; **unter diesem Gesetz stehen** — to be subject to the law; **unter diesem Gesichtspunkt** — from this point of view; **unter vier Augen** — face-to-face

unter- (noun and verb pref.) — usually, when the verb has a literal meaning, it is separable, and when it has a figurative meaning, it is inseparable

unterbrechen (irr. v.t.) — to interrupt

unter-bringen (irr. v.t.) — to shelter

unterdrücken (v.t.) — to oppress; suppress; repress

untereinander (adv.) — between or with each other

* der Untergang (-s, ̈-e) — setting, sinking; ruin, decline, end

* unterhalten (irr. v.t.) — to support; (v.r.) — to converse

die **Unterlage (-n)** — support; proof, evidence, voucher; document

unterlassen (irr. v.t.) — to discontinue, refrain, neglect (to do something)

unternehmen (irr. v.t.) — to undertake

der **Unterricht (-s, -e)** — instruction

unterscheiden (irr. v.t.) — to distinguish, differentiate

der **Unterschied (-s, -e)** — difference

die **Unterschrift (-en)** — signature, caption

die **Untersuchung** — examination, investigation; scrutiny

unterwegs (adv.) — on the way, en route

die **Unterwelt** — underworld

unterziehen (irr. v.t.) — to submit; (v.r.) — to submit, undergo

unumgänglich (adj.) — essential

unverhofft (adj.) — unexpected

unverkennbar — undeniable

unvollkommen (adj.) — incomplete

unzählig — countless

**die Unze (-n) — ounce

üppig (adj.) — abundant; opulent; lush

* ur- (pref.) — indicates origin or source or being primitive

uralt (adj.) — very old

die **Urkunde** — deed, document

der **Urlaub** (**-es, -e**) — leave of absence

die **Ursache** (**-n**) — cause, reason, origin, motive

die **Ursächlichkeit** — causality

der **Ursprung** (**-s, ⁻e**) — source, origin, beginning, cause

das **Urteil** (**-s, -e**) — judgement, decision, opinion, view, sentence, verdict

urweltlich (adj.) — primeval

V

die **Variante** — variant reading

der **Vater** (**-s, ⁻**) — father

das **Vaterland** — native country

das **Venedig** — Venice

ver- (insep. pref. to some verbs, and pref. to some nouns) — removal, loss; reversal; expenditure; alteration; intensification; changing nouns or adj. into verbs

verabreden (v.t.) — to agree upon, arrange; (v.r.) — to make an appointment

verabschieden (v.t.) — to dismiss

verachten (v.t.) — to despise

veralten (v.i., aux.s.) — to go out of date, become obsolete

veranlassen (v.t.) — to cause, bring about, give rise to

**verändern — to change

die **Verantwortung** — responsibility

verärgern (v.t.) — to anger, vex

der **Verband** (**-es, ⁻e**) — association

verbergen, verbirgt, verbarg, hat verborgen — to conceal

**verbessern — to improve

verbieten, verbot, hat verboten — to forbid

verbinden (irr. v.t.) — to unite, combine, connect

verbindlich (adj.) — binding

verblüffen (v.t.) — to amaze

verblühen (i., aux.s.) — to wither

* verborgen (v.t.) — to lend out; **verborgen** (adj.) — hidden, concealed

der **Verbrauch** (**-s**) — consumption, expenditure

verbrechen (irr. v.t.) — to commit (a crime or an offence)

verbreiten (v.t. & r.) — to spread, circulate, propagate; (v.r.) — to hold forth

verbrennen — to burn

die **Verbundenheit** — solidarity

der **Verdacht** (**-s**) — suspicion, distrust

verderben, verdarb, hat verdorben (v.t.) — to spoil, corrupt, demoralize; (v.i., aux.s.) — to spoil, deteriorate, perish

verdichten (v.t.) — to condense; concentrate; (v.r.) — to take shape (in one's mind)

verdienen (v.t.) — to earn, gain, deserve

verdrängen (v.t.) — to drive out

der **Verdruß** (**-sses, -sse**) — displeasure, frustration

verdunkeln (v.t.) — to darken, to obscure; to grow dim

verehren (v.t.) — to admire, to honor

der **Verein** (**-s, -e**) — organization, society; union, club

vereinbaren (v.t.) — to agree upon

vereinigen (v.t.) — to unite, combine; die **Vereinigten Staaten** — the United States; **sich vereinigen lassen** — to be compatible

vereinsamen (i., aux.s.) — to become isolated

verewigen (v.t.) — to immortalize

* **verfahren** (irr. v.i.) — to act, behave, proceed; (v.t.) — to spend; (v.r.) — to lose one's way

der **Verfall (-es)** — decay, decline

* **verfallen** (irr. v.i., aux.s.) — to deteriorate; to expire; to come into the power or possession of

die **Verfassung (-en)** — state or frame of mind; constitution

verfechten (irr. v.t.) — to defend

verfeinern (v.t.) — to refine, improve

verfluchen — to curse

verfolgen (v.t.) — to follow, persecute

* die **Verfügung** — disposal; decree; arrangement; **ihr zur Verfügung stehen** — to be at her disposal

verführen (v.t.) — to lead astray; to seduce; to prevail upon

vergangen (adj.) — past, gone

** die **Vergangenheit** — past

* **vergeben** (irr. v.t.) — to award; to give away; to forgive

vergebens (adv.) — in vain

vergehen (irr. v.i., aux.s) — to pass or fade away; to die off; (v.r.) — to err, offend, transgress

vergelten — to repay, reward

** **vergessen, vergaß, hat vergessen** (v.t.) — to forget; **in**

Vergessenheit geraten — to fall into oblivion

vergleichen, verglich, hat verglichen (v.t.) — to compare; (v.r.) — to reach a settlement; der **Vergleich** — comparison

vergnügen (v.t.) — to amuse, delight; (v.r.) — to enjoy oneself

vergönnen (v.t.) — to permit, allow, grant

vergöttern (v.t.) — to deify, idolize

vergrößern (v.t.) — to enlarge, magnify; to exaggerate; (v.r.) — to grow larger, increase

verhaften (v.t.) — to arrest; **verhaftet** — closely bound to, dependent on

verhalten (irr. v.r.) — to behave, to conduct oneself

das **Verhältnis (-sses, -sse)** — relation, proportion; situation, financial state; circumstances; condition

verhältnismäßig (adj.) — relative

verhandeln (v.t.) — to negotiate; (v.i.) — to discuss, debate

verhängen (v.t.) — to impose, cover

verharren (v.i., aux.s. & h.) — to continue; remain; persist

verheiraten (v.r.) — to marry

verheißen (irr. v.t.) — to promise; **Land der Verheißung** — Promised Land

verhetzen (v.t.) — to stir up

das **Verhör (-es, -e)** — interrogation

verhungern (v.i.) — to starve

verirren (v.r.) — to lose one's way

verjagen — to chase away

* **verkaufen** — to sell
  der **Verkehr** — traffic; communication; sexual or social intercourse; trade
  verkehrt (adj.) — wrong
  verkennen (irr. v.t.) — to misjudge
  verkörpern (v.t.) — to embody, typify, represent
  verkünd(ig)en (v.t.) — to announce, publish, proclaim; to preach
  der **Verlag** (-s, -e) — publishing house
  verlangen (v.t.) — to demand, claim, call for
  verlängern — to lengthen
** **verlassen** (irr. v.t.) — to leave, quit, abandon; (v.r.) — to rely upon, depend on
  der **Verlauf** (-s, ⁻e) — course; end; issue
* **verlegen** (v.t.) — to transfer; to misplace; to delay; (adj.) — embarrassed
  der **Verleger** (-s, -) — publisher
  verleiten (v.t.) — to lead astray
  verletzen (v.t.) — to hurt, injure
  verleugnen (v.t.) — to deny, disown, (v.r.) — **sich nicht verleugnen** — to become clear
** **verlieren, verlor, hat verloren** (v.t. & i.) — to lose
  verlöschen (v.t.) — to extinguish
  der **Verlust** (-es, -e) — loss
  vermehren (v.t.) — to increase
  vermeiden, vermied, hat vermieden (v.t.) — to avoid, shun, escape from
  vermitteln (v.i.) — to mediate; (v.t.) — to adjust, arrange, settle; to impart

das **Vermögen** (-s, -) — ability; fortune; property
** **vermögen** (irr. v.t.) — to be able to; **er vermag** — he is able to
  vermutlich (adj. & adv.) — presumably, probably
  vernachlässigen (v.t.) — to neglect
  vernehmlich (adj.) — perceptible
  vernichten (v.t.) — to annihilate, eradicate; to destroy
* die **Vernunft** — reason, understanding; common-sense;
  vernünftig — reasonable, sensible
  veröffentlichen (v.t.) — to publish
  die **Verpflichtung** — obligation
  verraten (irr. v.i.) — to betray, divulge
  verrichten — to execute, to do
  verrückt (adj.) — mad, crazy
  verrufen (adj.) — disreputable
  der **Vers** (-es, e) — verse, poetry, line
  versagen (v.t.) — to deny; (v.i.) — to fail
  versammeln (v.t.) — to assemble, to gather, collect; die **Versammlung** — assembly, collection
  versäumen (v.t.) — to miss, omit; das **Versäumnis** (-ses, -se) — failing, omission
  verschärfen (v.t.) — to heighten, to intensify
  verschieben (irr. v.t.) — to move, change (v.r.) — to shift
** **verschieden** (adj.) — different
  verschließen — to close; lock up
  verschlingen (irr. v.t.) — to entwine; devour
  verschmähen (v.t.) — to disdain, to reject

verschüttet — buried, submerged

verschwinden (irr. v.i., aux.s.) — to vanish, disappear

* **versehen** (irr. v.t.) — to provide; (v.r.) — to make a mistake

versetzen (v.t.) — to transfer, displace; to put, place; die **Versetzung** — mixing, transfer

die **Versicherung** — insurance, assurance; affirmation

versöhnen (v.t.) — to reconcile

verspäten (v.r.) — to be delayed

versprechen (irr. v.t.) — to promise

****der Verstand (-s)** — mind, intellect; understanding, reason

****verstehen** (irr. v.t.) — to understand, comprehend, grasp; (v.r.) — to be in agreement with; **das versteht sich von selbst** — that goes without saying

verstellen (v.t.) — to adjust; to disguise, to block

verstopfen — to plug

* **verstricken** (v.t.) — to involve

****versuchen** (v.t.) — to attempt, try

die **Versuchung (-en)** — temptation

versunken — lost; sunk

die **Versunkenheit** — engrossment

verteidigen (v.t. & r.) — to justify, to defend

vertiefen — to deepen; **sich vertiefen in** — to become absorbed in

* der **Vertrag (-es, ⸚e)** — treaty, contract, covenant

vertragen (irr. v.t.) — to endure, tolerate (v.r.) — to get on well

* **vertraut** (adj.) — familiar

vertreiben (irr. v.t.) — to drive away; disperse, scatter; banish

vertreten (irr. v.t.) — to replace, represent; to support

der **Vertreter (-s, -)** — adherent, representative

verurteilen (v.t.) — to condemn

die **Verwaltung** — administration

die **Verwandlung** — change, transformation; metamorphosis

* **verwandt** (adj.) — related; allied

verweigern (v.t.) — to refuse

verwenden (v.t.) — to use, employ

verwirren (v.t.) — to confuse

verzehren (v.t.) — to consume; (v.r.) — to languish

* das **Verzeichnis (-ses, -se)** — list, table, schedule, catalogue

verzeihen (irr. v.t. & i.) — to forgive

verzerren (v.t.) — to distort

verzichten (v.i.) **(auf)** — to renounce, abandon

verzögern (v.t.) — to defer, delay

der **Verzug (-es)** — delay, postponement

verzweifeln (v.i., aux.s.) — to despair

****viel** (adj., adv.) — much, a great deal; **viele** (pl.) — many

****vgl. (vergleiche)** — cf. (compare)

vielfach (adj.) — multiple repeated; (adv.) — often

vielfältig (adj.) — varied

****vielleicht** (adv.) — perhaps, maybe, possibly; really

* **vielmehr** (adv.) — rather

das **Viertel (-s, -)** — quarter

der **Vogel (-s, ⸚)** — bird

****das Volk (-es, ⸚er)** — people, nation; masses

die **Völkerkunde** — ethnology

* **Volks-** (in compounds) — popular, national; public

voll (adj.) — sometimes with gen. or with **von** — full, filled, complete, whole

voll- (pref.) — signifying completion, accomplishment

vollbringen (irr. v.t.) — to accomplish, achieve

vollenden (v.t.) — to complete

völlig (adj.) — full, complete

vollkommen (adj.) — perfect, complete

die **Vollmacht (-en)** — (legal) power of authority

vollziehen (irr. v.t.) — to carry out; accomplish, execute

von (prep.) with dat. — of; from; by

vor (prep.) with dat. or acc. — before, in front of, in the presence of; ago; in preference to; **vor allem** — above all; **vor Angst** — with fear; **vor Freude** — with joy; **Achtung vor dem Gesetz** — respect for the law; **vor drei Jahren** — three years ago; **vor Hunger sterben** — to die of hunger; **vor Zeiten** — formerly

der **Vorabend (-s, -e)** — evening before; eve

vor-arbeiten (v.t.) — to prepare; (v.i.) — to pave the way

voraus (adv.) — in advance

voraus-berechnen — to calculate in advance

die **Voraussage (-n)** — prediction

voraus-setzen (v.i.) — to presuppose, to suppose, assume; die **Voraussetzung** — the presupposition; prerequisite

vorbei (adv.) — along, by, past, gone

vor-bereiten (v.t.) — to prepare

der **Vorbericht (-s, -e)** — introduction, preface

das **Vorbild (-s, -er)** — model, example

vorder (adj.) — fore, forward

der **Vordergrund (-s, ⸚e)** — foreground

vorderhand (adv.) — for the present

voreingenommen (adj.) — prejudiced

* **vor-fallen** (irr. v.i., aux.s.) — to occur, happen

der **Vorgang (-s, ⸚e)** — proceedings

vor-gehen (irr. v.i., aux.s.) — to take precedence; to take action; to happen, occur

vorgenannt (adj.) — aforementioned

die **Vorgeschichte** — prehistory, past or previous history

vor-haben (irr. v.t.) — to have in mind; to be engaged in; to intend

vorhanden (adj.) — at hand; available

vorher (adv.) — previously, before

vorig (adj.) — former, previous

vor-kommen (irr. v.i., aux.s.) — to occur; to seem, appear

die **Vorlage** — model, pattern, copy

vorläufig (adj.) — preliminary; (adv.) — temporarily

die **Vorlesung** — lecture, course

vorn (adv.) — in the front

vornehm (adj.) — distinguished; noble

vor-nehmen (v.r.) — to resolve

der **Vorrang (-s)** — preeminence, precedence

der **Vorschein** — **zum Vorschein kommen** — to appear, to turn up

der **Vorschlag** (**-s, ⁻e**) — proposition, proposal, suggestion

vor-schlagen — to suggest

die **Vorschrift** (**-en**) — regulation

vor-sehen (irr. v.t.) — to provide for; (v.r.) — to be careful

die **Vorsicht** — caution, care, prudence

vorsichtig — careful, cautious

vor-singen (i.) — to sing to

der **Vorstand** (**-es, ⁻e**) — committee

vor-stecken — to poke out or forward

****vor-stellen** (v.r.) — to introduce; to imagine, to suppose

die **Vorstellung** — representation; notion, conception

vor-täuschen — to feign

der **Vorteil** (**-es, -e**) — advantage

der **Vortrag** (**-es, ⁻e**) — lecture

vorüber (adv.) — along, by, past

das **Vorurteil** (**-s, -e**) — prejudice

vorwärts (adv.) — forward

vor-weisen (irr. v.t.) — to show, display; possess

vorwitzig — impertinent

das **Vorwort** (**-s, ⁻er**) — preface, introduction

der **Vorwurf** (**-s, ⁻e**) — reproach, rebuke

vorwurfsvoll — reproachful

die **Vorzeit** — antiquity, past ages

vor-ziehen (irr. v.t.) — to prefer

der **Vorzug** (**-es, ⁻e**) — preference

W

die **Waage** (**-n**) — scales, balance

wachen (i.) — to be awake

wachsam (adj.) — vigilant

****wachsen, wuchs, ist gewachsen** (v.i.) — to grow, expand

der **Wächter** (**-s, -**) — guard

wacker (adj.) — valiant; honest

die **Waffe** (**-n**) — weapon

wagen (v.t.) — to venture, risk

wählen (v.i.) — to choose, elect

der **Wahn** — illusion, madness, mania

wahnsinnig (adj.) — crazy, mad

****wahr** (adj.) — true, genuine, real

die **Wahrheit (**-en**) — truth

****während** (prep.) with gen. — in the course of, during; (conj.) — while

wahrlich (adj.) — truly; certainly

wahr-nehmen (irr. v.t.) — to notice, perceive; distinguish

der **Wahrsager** (**-s, -**) — prophet

****wahrscheinlich** (adj. & adv.) — probable; probably

der **Wald** (**-es, ⁻er**) — woods

der **Wall** (**-es, ⁻e**) — rampart, wall

walten (v.i.) — to rule, govern; to carry out; prevail

walzen — to roll

die **Wand** (**⁻e**) — wall

wandeln (v.t. or r.) — to change

wanken (v.i., aux.s. or h.) — to rock, sway, vacillate

****wann** (adv. & conj. & interr.) — when

wärmen — to warm

die **Warnung** (**-en**) — warning

die **Warte** — viewpoint

warten (v.i.) — to wait (**auf**) — for; (v.t.) — to attend to

****warum** — why

****was** (inter. pron.) — what, whatever; (rel. pron.) — what, that, which; **alles** (everything), **etwas** (something) and **nichts** (nothing), **was** — that

waschen, wäscht, wusch, hat gewaschen (t. & r.) — to wash

das **Wasser (-s, -)** — water

die **Wasserscheu** — hydrophobia

der **Wechsel (-s, -)** — change, alteration, variation

wechseln — to change

****weder ... noch** (conj.) — neither ... nor

der **Weg (-es, -e)** — way, road, path, course; **den Weg bereiten** — to pave the way; **ihr im Wege stehen** — to be or stand in her way

****weg** (adv.) — away, gone; **weg-** (pref.) — away, etc.

weg-bleiben (i., aux.s.) — to stay away

****wegen** (prep.) with gen. — because of

weg-werfen — to throw away

weh — alas!; **ihnen weh tun** — to hurt them, to grieve or wound or offend them

wehren (v.r.) — to defend oneself

das **Weib (-es, -er)** — wife, woman

weiblich (adj.) — female; feminine

weich (adj.) — soft, mild, yielding

weichen, wich, ist gewichen (v.i.) — to move; to retreat

weigern (v.r.) — to refuse, decline

weihen (v.t.) — to consecrate, inaugurate

die **Weihnachten** (literally: holy nights) — Christmas

****weil** (conj.) — because, since

die **Weile (-n)** — while

der **Wein (-s, -e)** — wine

weinen (v.i.) — to cry

der **Weintrinker (-s, -)** — wine drinker

weise (adj.) — wise

die **Weise (-n)** — manner, custom, way

-weise (adj. & n. & suff.) — denotes manner

weisen, wies, hat gewiesen (v.t.) — to show, point out, indicate; to refer to

****die Weisheit** — wisdom

****weiß** (adj.) — white, clean, blank

****weiß** (v.) — **er, sie,** or **es weiß** — see **wissen** — to know

****weit** (adj.) — wide, broad; (adv.) — far off, widely, by far; **bei weitem** — by far, much

****weiter** (comp. adj. and sep. pref.) — farther, further; (adv.) — farther; furthermore

weiter-gehen (v.i., aux.s., irr.) — to go on, continue

weiterhin (adv.) — furthermore, moreover

weitgehend (adj.) — far-reaching, extensive; (adv.) — largely

****welch** (indecl. pron.) — **welch eine Frau** — what a woman!; (inter. adj.) — which (inter. pron.) — which, who; (rel. pron.) — which, what, who, whom; (rel. adj.) — which, whichever; whatever

****die Welt (-en)** — world

die **Weltanschauung (-en)** — philosophy of life, view; outlook, ideology

der **Weltkrieg (-s, -e)** — world war

* **Weltraum-** (in compounds) — space

die **Wende** — change, turn

wenden, wandte, hat gewandt
(r.) — to turn

der **Wendepunkt (-s, -e)** — turning point

wenig (adj. & adv.) — little; **ein wenig — a little; with pl. — few; **die wenigen Male, daß** — the few times that

wenigstens (adv.) — at least

wenn (conj.) — when, whenever; if; wenn with subjunctive is always if; **wenn auch — even if

wer (pron.) — who, which; **wen — whom; **wem** — whom, to whom; **wessen** — whose

**werden, wurde, ist geworden
(irr. v., aux.s.) — to become, to grow, to turn, to get; **es wird dunkel** — it is getting dark; **es wurde dunkel** — it grew dark; **es ist dunkel geworden** — it has become dark; werden & an infinitive denotes the future — **sie wird hier sein** — she will be here; **sie werden das tun können** — they will be able to do that; werden & a participle is the passive — **es wird oft gesagt** — it is often said; **es wurde oft getan** — it was often done

werfen, warf, hat geworfen (v.t. & i.) — to throw, cast, fling; to overthrow, upset

das **Werk (-es, -e)** — act, deed; undertaking; publication, book, work

der **Werktag (-s, -e)** — workday

wert (adj.) — valued, useful; with gen. — worth; **nicht der Mühe wert — not worth the effort

der **Wert (-es, -e)** — value, worth, price; **die Werte** (usually) — the values

das **Wesen (-s, -e)** — essence; nature, entity, being, creature; state, condition, nature, character; conduct

wesenhaft (adj.) — real; intrinsic; essential

wesentlich (adj.) — essential, substantial, fundamental, intrinsic

weshalb (inter pron.) — why; (conj.) — on account of which; which is why

**wessen — whose

der **Westen (-s)** — the west, the occident

weswegen — on what account

die **Wette (-n)** — wager

das **Wetter** — weather; bad weather

**wichtig (adj.) — important, serious

wickeln (v.t.) — to wind; to wrap

wider (prep.) with acc. — against, in opposition to

**wider- (sep. and insep. verb pref., & noun pref.) — counter-, contra-, anti-, re-, with-

widerlegen (v.t.) — to refute

widerlich (adj.) — loathsome, repugnant

widerrufen (irr. v.t.) — to revoke

widersprechen (irr. v.i.) — to contradict

der **Widerstand (-s, ⸚e)** — opposition, resistance

widerwärtig (adj.) — disagreeable, hateful, offensive

widmen (v.t.) — to dedicate; (v.r.) — to devote oneself

wie (adv.) — how?, to what extent?; however; **wie dem auch sei — however that may be; (conj.) — as, like, such as; **wie**

gesagt — as has been stated;
wie oben — as above; how; **ich
weiß nicht, wie ich das tun
kann** — I don't know how I can
do that
**wieder (adv.) — again, once
more; **immer wieder** — again &
again
wieder- (noun and verb pref.,
usually sep.) — re-, back-
(again), in return (for)
wieder-aufbereiten (v.t.) — to
recycle
die **Wiederauferstehung** —
resurrection
* **wieder-geben** (irr. v.t.) — to
return; (art) — to reproduce;
to interpret; to quote (from a
text)
wiederholen (v.t.) — to repeat;
(v.r.) — to be repeated, to recur
die **Wiederholung (-en)** — repetition
die **Wiederkehr** — the return,
recurrence
wieder-kehren (i., aux.s.) — to
return
wieder-kommen (i., aux.s.) — to
return
wiegen, wog, hat gewogen (v.t.)
— to weigh; to carry weight
wieviel — how much
der **Wille (-ns, no pl.) — will,
volition; intent, wish; **mit
Willen** — on purpose;
willen (prep.) — with gen. —
um ... willen — for the sake
of; **um seinetwillen** — for his
sake
willkürlich (adj.) — arbitrary,
despotic
der **Wind (-es, -e)** — wind
die **Windmühle (-n)** — windmill

der **Wink (-es, -e)** — sign, wink,
hint, suggestion; **winken** (v.i.)
— to signal, wave; wink
der **Winter (-s)** — winter
winzig (adj.) — tiny, minute
****wir** — we
****wirken** (v.t.) — to cause, to work;
(v.i.) — to work, operate; have
an effect; to appear
wirklich (adj.) — actual, real
die **Wirklichkeit — reality
wirksam (adj.) — effective
die **Wirkung (-en)** — result,
effect, consequence, impact
die **Wirtschaft (-en) — economic
system, economy; state of
affairs; **freie Wirtschaft** — free
enterprise; inn
wirtschaftlich — economic
der **Wirtschaftsplan (-s, ¨-e)** —
budget
****wissen, wußte, hat gewußt** (v.t.)
— to know, be acquainted with,
understand; **er will davon
nichts wissen** — he'll have
nothing to do with it; (v.i.) — to
know **(um)** of or about; **ich weiß
nicht recht** — I don't really
know
das **Wissen** — knowledge; learning, education; **meines Wissens**
— as far as I know
die **Wissenschaft (-en) — science; knowledge
der **Wissenschaftler (-s, -)** — sci-
entist, scholar
wissenschaftlich — scientific
wittern (v.t.) — to smell; to sense
der **Witz (-es, -e)** — joke
****wo** (inter.) — where; (rel.) —
where, in which; (conj.) —
where, when; **es gab Zeiten, wo**
— there were times when ...

wobei (rel. adv.) — through which, whereby, in the course of which

**die Woche (-n) — week

woher (rel. and inter. adv.) — from where; from what or which place

wohin (rel. and inter. adv.) — where to; (indef. adv.) — somewhere

wohl (pred. adj. & adv.) — well; indeed; possibly; presumably; **das ist wohl möglich — I suppose that is possible

wohlbedacht (adj.) — deliberate, well-considered

wohnen (v.i.) — to live, dwell

die Wohnung (-en) — apartment

der Wolf (-es, ⸗e) — wolf

die Wolke (-n) — cloud

die Wolle (-n) — wool

wollen (modal) — to be willing; to wish, want, desire; to be about to do; to claim, require, demand; **ich wollte, ich wäre — I wish I were

das Wort (-es, ⸗er or -e) (⸗er with unconnected words, in all other cases, the pl. is **-e) — word, term, expression; **mit anderen Worten** — in other words

das Wörterbuch (-es, ⸗er) — dictionary

wörtlich (adj.) — literal

das Wortspiel (-s, -e) — pun

die Wortstammkunde — etymology

die Wunde (-n) — wound

wundern (v.r.) — to be surprised by

der Wunsch (-es, ⸗e) — wish, desire

**wünschen (t. & i.) — to wish

wünschenswert — desirable

die Würde — dignity, propriety; **akademische Würde** — academic degree; **unter meiner Würde** — beneath my dignity

würdigen — to value

der Wurm (-es, ⸗er) — worm

die Wurzel (-n) — root

wüst (adj.) — desolate, wild

die Wüste (-n) — desert

die Wut — rage, fury

wütend — enraged

X

x-mal (adv.) — any number of times

Z

* z.B. — zum Beispiel — for example

zaghaft — timid

zäh(e) — tough, tenacious, stubborn

die Zahl (-en) — number, figure

zahlen (v.t. & i.) — to pay for

zählen (v.t. & i.) — to count, reckon

zahm (adj.) — tame, docile, cultivated

zähmen — to tame

der Zahn (-es, ⸗e) — tooth

der Zank (-es, no pl.) — quarrel

zänkisch — quarrelsome, cranky

der Zar (-en, -en) — tsar, czar

zart (adj.) — delicate, soft, gentle

der Zauber (-s, -) — spell, charm, magic

**zehn — ten

zehren (v.i.) — to live or exist; to draw on; to wear something out

das **Zeichen (-s, -)** — sign, symbol; mark, reference

zeichnen (v.t. & i.) — to draw, sketch, portray; depict

der **Zeichner (-s, -)** — designer portrayer

****zeigen** (v.t.) — to show, display, indicate; (v.r.) — to show oneself, to appear; **es zeigt sich, daß** — it appears that

der **Zeiger (-s, -)** — hand of a clock

die **Zeit (-en) — time, epoch, age, era, period, season; **es ist an der Zeit** — it is time; **in früherer Zeit** — formerly; **in jüngster or neuester Zeit** — quite recently; **in letzter Zeit** — recently; **mit der Zeit** — in the course of time; **vor der Zeit** — premature; **zur Zeit** — at present

der **Zeitabschnitt (-s, -e)** — period, epoch

das **Zeitalter (-s, -)** — age, era; generation

der **Zeitgeist** — spirit of the times

der **Zeitgenosse (-n, -n)** — contemporary

die **Zeitgeschichte** — contemporary history

zeitig (adj.) — early; (adv.) — early, on time

zeitlich (adj.) — temporal, transitory

der **Zeitraum (-s, -̈e)** — interval; period, space of time

die **Zeitschrift (-en)** — journal, magazine, periodical

die **Zeitung (-en) — newspaper

zerbrechen (irr. v.i., aux.s.) — to break into pieces; to be destroyed, to collapse

die **Zeremonie** — ceremony

der **Zerfall** — ruin, decay, disintegration

zerreißen — to rip into pieces

zerschmettern — to smash

zerschneiden — to cut into pieces

die **Zersetzungsliteratur** — seditious or subversive literature

zerstören (v.t.) — to destroy

* **zerstreuen** (v.t.) — to disperse, dissipate, scatter, dispel; (v.r.) — to amuse oneself; **sich zerstreuen lassen** — to allow one's attention to wander

zertreten — to crush, trample under foot

der **Zettel (-s, -)** — note, slip of paper

das **Zeug (-es, -e)** — stuff

zeugen (v.i.) — to bear witness, to testify; (v.t.) — to procreate, beget; to create

das **Zeugnis (-ses, -se)** — evidence

die **Ziege (-n)** — goat

****ziehen, zog, hat gezogen** (v.t.) — to draw, pull; to cultivate, grow; to describe; **an sich ziehen** — to attract; (v.i.) — to prove attractive; (v.i., aux.s.) — to march, advance; (v.r.) — to stretch, extend; to distort

das **Ziel (-es, -e)** — goal, aim; objective, destination

* **ziemlich** (adj.) — considerable; (adv.) — rather, quite

die **Zierde (-n)** — decoration

zieren (v.t.) — to adorn; (v.r.) — to be affected; to make a fuss

die **Ziffer (-n)** — figure; clause; item

zirka (adv.) — approximately

das **Zitat (-es, -e)** — quotation

zittern (v.i.) — to tremble, shake **(vor)** with

* **zivil** (adj.) — civilian

die **Zivilisation** — civilization (especially in its technological aspects)

zögern (v.i.) — to hesitate; to delay; to defer

der **Zoo** (-s, -s) — zoo

der **Zorn** (-es, no pl.) — wrath, anger

** **zu** (prep.) with dat. — towards, up to; **zur Folge haben** — to have as a result; at, on, in: **zu Bonn** — in Bonn; **zur Hand** — at hand; **zu Hause** — at home; **zum ersten** — in the first place; **zur Nacht** — at or by night

* **zu** (adv.) — too; closed

* **zu** (part.) — **um ... zu** — in order to; **ohne zu** — without-ing; **anstatt zu** — instead of

** **zu** (inf. used passively after sein) — **ihm ist zu trauen** — he is to be (or can be) trusted; **es ist zu sehen** — it is to be seen

zu- (sep. pref.) — towards, closed

die **Zucht** (-en) — education, training, discipline, decency, propriety, manners

der **Zucker** (-s) — sugar

zuckern — to sugar; to put sugar in

zudem (adv.) — besides, moreover

zudringlich (adj.) — intrusive

zu-eignen (v.t.) — to dedicate

zuerst (adv.) — first; at first; first of all, especially

der **Zufall** (-es, ⁻e) — chance, accident

* **zu-fallen** (irr. v.i., aux.s.) — to fall to (one's) lot; to close

zufällig (adj.) — accidental; chance

zufolge (prep.) — preceded by dat. or followed by gen. — as a result of

zufrieden (adj.) — contented, satisfied

die **Zufriedenheit** — satisfaction

** der **Zug** (-es, ⁻e) — train; course; **Zug der Ereignisse** — course of events; outline; characteristic; trait

der **Zugang** (-es, ⁻e) — admittance, entry, access

zu-geben (irr. v.t.) — to grant, concede, admit, confess; to add

* **zu-gehen** (irr. v.i., aux.s.) — to happen, come to pass; to go, move towards; to close; to reach

zu-gestehen (irr. v.t.) — to concede, acknowledge; admit

zugleich (adv.) — at the same time

* **zugrunde** (adv.) — **zugrunde gehen** — to perish, be ruined; **zugrunde liegen** — to take as a basis

zu-hören (i.) — to listen to

** die **Zukunft** — future

* **zu-lassen** (irr. v.t.) — to grant, permit; to leave closed

zuletzt (adv.) — finally, ultimately, at last

** **zu-machen** — to close

zumal (adv.) — above all, especially, especially since

zu-muten (v.t.) — to expect, demand, ask

zunächst (adv.) — first of all; for the present

zu-nehmen (irr. v.i.) — to
   increase; to thrive, prosper
die **Zunge** (-n)— tongue
zupfen (i.) — to tug
zurecht-finden (r.) — to find
   one's way
zu-reden (v.i.) — to encourage
zu-richten (v.t.) — to prepare
**zurück (adv. and prep.) — back,
   backwards, behind
zurück-bringen — to bring back
* **zurück-führen** (v.t.) — to lead
   back; to trace back; to attribute
   to, to explain by
zurück-gehen (irr. v.i., aux.s.) —
   to return; to diminish, decline, to
   be cancelled; to go back
zurück-kehren (i., aux.s.) — to
   return, come back
* **zurück-kommen** (i., aux.s.) —
   to return, come back
zurück-stellen (v.t.) — to replace;
   to postpone; to defer
die **Zurückweisung** — refusal,
   rejection, repudiation
**zusammen (adv. and sep. pref.)
   — together
zusammen-fassen — to combine;
   to summarize
der **Zusammenhang** (-̈e) —
   connection, context
die **Zusammenkunft** (-̈e) —
   meeting
zusammen-setzen (v.t.) — to
   compose
zusammen-stellen (v.t.) — to
   group, classify, compile
zusammen-ziehen (irr. v.t.) —
   to draw together; to condense
der **Zusatz** (-es, -̈e) — additional remark

der **Zuschauer** (-s, -) — spectator
   (pl.) — audience
zu-sehen (i.) — to watch
der **Zustand** (-es, -̈e) — state,
   condition
zustande (adv.) — **zustande
   bringen** — to accomplish,
   achieve; **zustande kommen** —
   to happen
zuständig (adj.) — proper,
   appropriate; responsible
zu-teilen — to allot; grant
zu-tragen — to carry, to report;
   (r.) — to happen
zuverlässig (adj.) — reliable
die **Zuversicht** — confidence
zuvor (adv.) — before, previously
zuwider (prep.) with dat. —
   opposed to; (adv.) — repugnant
der **Zwang** (-es, -̈e) — force,
   coercion
zwangsläufig (adj.) — inevitable;
   (adv.) — necessarily
**zwar (adv.) — indeed, certainly
der **Zweck** (-es, -e) — aim, goal
**zwei — two
zweierlei (indecl. adj.) — two
   sorts of; **zweierlei ist zu
   beachten** — two things *are* to
   be noticed
der **Zweifel** (-s, -) — doubt,
   uncertainty, misgivings; **in
   Zweifel stellen or ziehen** — to
   call into doubt
der **Zweig** (-es, -e) — branch
zweimal — twice
zweitens (adv.) — secondly, in
   the second place
der **Zwerg** (-es, -e) — dwarf
der **Zwiespalt** (-s, -̈e) — dissension, discord, schism, dis-
   crepency

zwingen, zwang, hat gezwungen
(v.t.) — to force, compel; to
finish; (v.r.) — to force oneself
**zwischen (prep.) with acc. or dat.
— between (with reference to
two things); among (with reference to three or more things)

das **Zwischenspiel (-s, -e)** —
intermezzo, interlude; incident
die **Zwischenstunde** — interval,
intermission
der **Zwist (-es, -e)** — dissension,
discord, dispute
der **Zyniker (-s, -)** — cynic

Abbreviations

A

* **Abk. Abkürzung** — abbreviation
* **Abs. Absatz** — paragraph
allg. allgemein — general
allj. alljährlich — annual
allm. allmählich — gradual
* **Anh. Anhang** — appendix
Anm. Anmerkung — note
A. T. Altes Testament — Old
Testament

B

* **b. bei** — at, with, in care of
* **bes. besonders** — especially
betr. betreffend — concerning
* **bez. bezüglich** — with reference
to
bisw. bisweilen — sometimes
bzgl. bezüglich — with reference
to
* **bzw. beziehungsweise** — respec-
tively

C

* **ca. circa** — approximately

D

* **d.h. das heißt** — that is; i.e.
dt.(sch) deutsch — German

E

Ed. Edition, Ausgabe — edition
eig. eigtl. eigentlich — actually
einschl. einschließlich — inclu-
sively

F

fig. figürlich — figurative

G

* **geb. geboren** — born
* **ges. gesamt** — total

H

haupts. hauptsächlich — mainly
hpts. hauptsächlich — mainly
hrsg. herausgegeben — edited

I

i.b. im besonderen — in particular
id. identisch — identical
i.g. im ganzen — on the whole
inbegr. inbegriffen — included
insb. insbesondere — in particular
insg. insgesamt — altogether

i.S. im Sinne — in the meaning of
& in Sachen — re, in the matter of
i.w.S. im weiteren Sinne — in a broad sense

J

* **Jh. Jahrhundert** — century

K

* **Kap. Kapitel** — chapter
kg. Kilogramm — kilogram
kompl. komplett — complete

L

lfd. laufend — current, running
lt. laut — according to

M

m.A.n. meiner Ansicht nach — in my opinion
m.a.W. mit anderen Worten — in other words
* **m.E. meines Erachtens** — in my opinion
mind. mindestens — at least

N

n.J. nächsten Jahres — of next year
n.M. nächsten Monats — of next month
Nr. Nummer — number
N.T. Neues Testament — New Testament

O

* **o. oben** — above
* **o.ä. oder ähnlich** — or the like

P

Prof. Professor — professor

R

* **rd. rund** — roughly
Red. Redakteur — editor; **Redaktion** — editorial staff, editor's office

S

* **S. Seite** — page
* **s. siehe** — see
* **s.a. siehe auch** — see also
selbst. selbständig — independent
* **s.o. siehe oben** — see above
* **sog. sogenannt** — so-called
* **s.u. siehe unten** — see below
svw. soviel wie — as much as
s.Z. seinerzeit — at that time

T

Tit. Titel — title

U

* **u. und** — and
* **u.a. und anderes** — and others; **unter anderem** — among other things, inter alia

* **u.ä. und ähnliches** — and the like
  übl. üblich — usual
* **usf. und so fort** — and so forth
* **usw. und so weiter** — and so forth, etc.

V

* **v. von, vom** — of, from; by
* **vgl. vergleiche** — compare, cf.
  v.J. vorigen Jahres — of last year
  v.M. vorigen Monats — of last month
  v.u. von unten — from below

W

* **w.o. wie oben** — as abovementioned

Z

* **z. zu, zur, zum** — to at
* **z.B. zum Beispiel** — for example
  zgl. zugleich — at the same time
  z.T. zum Teil — partly
* **zuf. zufolge** — as a result of
  zus. zusammen — together
  zw. zwischen — between, among

Appendix I

German Proper Names

Adenauer, Konrad (1876-1967)—first chancellor of the German Federal
    Republic
Adler, Alfred (1870-1937)—Austrian psychologist
Ägyptian—Egypt
Albertus Magnus (c. 1200-1280)—German philosopher
Antillen—Antilles
Aristoteles—Aristotle
Ärmelkanal—English Channel
Asien—Asia
Barlach, Ernst (1870-1938)—German sculptor
Barth, Karl (1886-1968)—Swiss theologian
Bayern—Bavaria
Beckmann, Max (1884-1950)—German painter
Belgien—Belgium
Berg, Alban (1885-1935)—Austrian composer
Bismarck, Otto von (1815-1898)—German statesman
Bodensee—Lake of Constance
Böhme, Jakob (1575-1624)—German mystic
Böhmen—Bohemia
Böll, Heinrich (1917-85)—German author
Brandt, Willi (1913-92)—German politician
Braunschweig—Brunswick
Brecht, Bertolt (1898-1956)—German dramatist
Bruckner, Anton (1824-96)—Austrian composer
Brüning, Heinrich (1885-1970)—Chancellor of the Weimar Republic
Brüssel—Brussels
Buber, Martin (1878-1965)—German philosopher
Büchner, Georg (1813-37)—German dramatist
Bukarest—Bucharest
Bulgarien—Bulgaria
Bundesrepublik—Federal Republic
Calais—Straits of Dover
Celan, Paul (1920-)—German poet
Deutschland—Germany

Deutsche Demokratische Republik—German Democratic Republic—former East Germany

Diesel, Rudolf (1858-1913)—- German inventor

Donau—Danube

Dostojewskij—Doestoevsky

Dreißigjähriger Krieg (1618-1648)—Thirty years war

Dürer, Albrecht (1471-1538)—German painter

Dürrenmatt, Friedrich (1921-)—Swiss dramatist

Ebert, Friedrich (1871-1925)—first president of the Weimar Republic

Eckhart, Meister (c.1260-1327)—founder of German mysticism

Eichendorff, Joseph (1788-1857)—German poet

Eismeer—Arctic Ocean

Elbe—German river

Elsaß—Alsace

Engels, Friedrich (1820-95)—German philosopher

Erhard, Ludwig (1897-1977)—second chancellor of the Federal Republic of Germany

Ernst, Max (1891-1976)—German painter

Faust—drama written by Goethe

Feuerbach, Ludwig (1804-72)—German theologian

Fichte, Johann (1762-1814)—German philosopher

Florenz—Florence

Fontane, Theodor (1819-98)—German author

Frankreich—France

Frauenkirche—Church of Our Lady

Freud, Sigmund (1856-1939)—Austrian psychiatrist, founder of psychoanalysis

Friedrich der Große (1712-86)—Fredrick the Great

Frisch, Max (1911-91) —Swiss author

Genf—Geneva

Glück, Christoph (1714-87)—German composer

Goethe, Johann Wolfgang (1749-1832)—German poet

Grass, Günter (1927-)—German author

Griechenland—Greece

Grimm, Jakob (1765-1863) & Wilhelm (1786-1859) —German philologists

Grimmelshausen, Hans (1625-76)—German novelist

Grönland—Greenland

Großbritannien—Great Britain

Grünewald, Mathais (c.1475-1528)—German painter

Hahn, Otto (1879-1968)—German chemist

Hauptmann, Gerhart (1862-1946)—German dramatist

Hegel, Georg Willhelm Friedrich (1770-1831)—German philosopher

Heidegger, Martin (1889-1976)—German philosopher

Heine, Heinrich (1797-1856)—German poet
Herder, Johann (1744-1803) —German philosopher
Hesse, Hermann (1877-1962)—German poet
Hessen—Hesse (land of the German Federal Republic)
Hiob—Job
Hofmannsthal, Hugo (1874-1929)—German poet
Hohenzollern—German dynasty, beginning in the 12th century
Hölderlin, Johann (1770-1843)—German poet
Horaz—Horace
Humboldt, Alexander (1769-1859)—German naturalist
Indien—India
Irland—Ireland
Island—Iceland
Italien—Italy
Jaspers, Karl (1883-1969) —German philosopher
Johannas—John
Jung, Carl (1875-1961)—Swiss psychiatrist
Kafka, Franz (1883-1924)—Czech author
Kant, Immanuel (1724-1804)—German philosopher
Karl der Große (c. 742-814)—Charlemagne
Keller, Gottfried (1819-90)—Swiss author
Klee, Paul (1879-1940)—Swiss born painter
Kleist, Heinrich (1777-1811)—German poet
Kohl, Helmut (1930-)—German Chancellor
Köln—Cologne
Konstantin—Constantine
Konstanz—Constance
Leibniz, Gottfried (1646-1716)—German philosopher
Lessing, Gotthold (1729-81)—German poet
Lothringen—Lorraine
Ludwig—Louis
Lukas—Luke
Luther, Martin (1483-1546)—German Reformation leader
Luzern—Lucerne
Mahler, Gustav (1860-1911)—Austrian composer
Mailand—Milan
Main—German river
Mann, Thomas (1875-1955)—German author
Marc, Franz (1880-1916)—German painter
Markus—Mark
Marokko—Morocco
Matthäus—Matthew
Metternich, Clemens (1773-1859)—Austrian statesman

Minnesang (12th century)—German courtly love poetry
Mittelmeer—Mediterranean Sea
Mörike, Eduard (1804-75)—German poet
Mosel—Moselle
Moskau—Moscow
München—Munich
Neapel—Naples
Nibelungenlied—German epic (c.1200)
Niederlande—Netherlands
Nietzsche, Friedrich (1844-1900)—German philosopher
Nil—Nile
Nordsee—North Sea
Norwegen—Norway
Oder—German river
Ostasian—Eastern Asia
Österreich—Austria
Ostsee—Baltic
Palästina—Palastine
Parzival—Percival
Paulus—Paul
Pfalz—Palatinate
Platon—Plato
Polen—Poland
Pommern—Pommerania
Prag—Prague
Preußen—Prussia
Regensburg—Ratisbon
Rhein—Rhine river
Rilke, Ranier Maria (1875-1926)—Austrian poet
Rom—Rome
Röntgen, Wilhelm (1845-1923)—German physicist, discoverer of X-rays
Ruhr—German river
Rußland—Russia
Saale—German river
Sachsen—Saxony
Schiller, Johann Christian Friedrich (1759-1805)—German poet
Schlegel, Friedrich (1772-1829)—German poet
Schlesien—Silesia
Schliemann, Heinrich (1822-90) —discoverer of Troy
Schnitzler, Arthur (1862-1931)—Austrian dramatist and novelist
Schönberg, Arnold (1874-1951)—German composer
Schopenhauer, Arthur (1788-1860)—German philosopher
Schottland—Scotland

Schwaben—Swabia
Schwarzwald—Black Forest
Schweden—Sweden
Schweitzer, Albert (1875-1965)—German theologian
Schweiz—Switzerland
Siberien—Siberia
Singapur—Singapore
Sizilien—Sicily
Sowjetunion—Soviet Union
Spanien—Spain
Spengler, Oswald (1880-1936)—German philosopher
Spinoza, Baruch (1632-77)—German philosopher
Stifter, Adelbert (1805-68)—Austrian author
Strauss, Richard (1864-1949)—German composer
Themse—Thames
Thüringen—Thuringia
Tolstoj—Tolstoi
Trakl, Georg (1887-1914)—Austrian poet
Tschechoslowakei—Czechoslovakia
Türkei—Turkey
Ungarn—Hungary
Vatikan—Vatican
Venedig—Venice
Vereinigte Staaten—United States
Wagner, Richard (1813-83)—German composer
Walther von der Vogelweide—(c.1170-1230) German poet
Warschau—Warsaw
Weiß, Peter (1916-82)—German dramatist
Werfel, Franz (1890-1945)—Austrian author
Weser—German river
Wien—Vienna
Wittgenstein, Ludwig (1889-1951)—German philosopher
Wolfram von Eschenbach (c.1170-1220) —German poet
Zweig , Stefan (1881-1942)—Austrian author
Zwingli, Ulrich (1484-1531)—Swiss Reformation leader
Zypern—Cyprus

Index